DUNS SCOTUS
LOURDES CO
SYLVANIA, C

WITHDRAWN

The

Pocket

a-z

of **Criminal Justice**

Bryan Gibson

Putting justice into words...

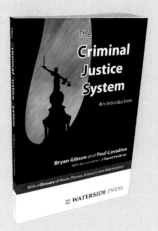

Have **you** visited
WatersidePress.co.uk lately?

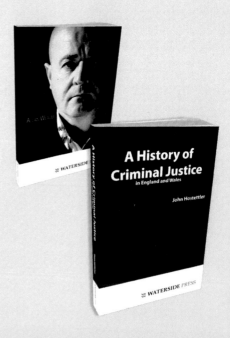

The
Pocket

a-z

of **Criminal Justice**

Bryan Gibson

WATERSIDE PRESS

Pocket A-Z of Criminal Justice

Bryan Gibson

Published 2009 by
Waterside Press
Sherfield Gables
Sherfield on Loddon
Hook
Hampshire
United Kingdom RG27 0JG

Telephone +44(0)1256 882250 Low cost UK landline calls 0845 2300 733
E-mail enquiries@watersidepress.co.uk
Online catalogue www.WatersidePress.co.uk

ISBN 9781904380 504 (Paperback)

Copyright © 2009 This work is the copyright of Bryan Gibson. All intellectual property and associated rights are hereby asserted and reserved by the author in full compliance with UK, European and international law. No part of this book may be copied, reproduced, stored in a retrieval system or transmitted in any form or by any means, including in hard copy or via the internet, without the prior written permission of the publishers to whom all such rights have been assigned.

Cataloguing-In-Publication Data A catalogue record for this pocketbook can be obtained from the British Library.

Cover design © 2009 Waterside Press.

North American distributor International Specialised Book Services (ISBS), 920 NE 58th Ave, Suite 300, Portland, Oregon, 97213-3786, USA
Tel: 1 800 944 6190 Fax 1 503 280 8832 orders@isbs.com www.isbs.com

Printed by the MPG Books Group in the UK

e-book *The Pocket A-Z of Criminal Justice* is available as an e-book and also for subscribers at myilibrary.com - ISBN 9781906534 769 (e-book)

Contents

Making best use of the A-Z

The entries in this pocketbook appear in alphabetical order in the location determined by everyday use of the words, etc. concerned, except in the section on *Key Dates and Events* which is naturally in chronological order.

Thus **criminal justice unit** and **trial unit** appear under **C** (for **criminal**) and **T** (for **trial**), not under **U** (for **unit**); **drug action team** and **youth justice team** under **D** and **Y** not as as species of **action, justice** or **team**. Where a topic is substantial enough in its own right it has its own separate entry: **imprisonment, community sentence** and **fine** are examples. They appear as *Main Entries* under **I, C** and **F** rather than within the more general entry for **sentence/sentencing**. Various items of more general interest such as **adversarial system, cold case, Stockwell shooting, Tyburn** and **zero-tolerance** appear alphabetically in *Touchstones and Curiosities*.

Cross-references (in italics) point to connections, contrasts, comparisons or the correct location of a word, etc. However, words such as **court, crime, offender** and **trial** are so much a part of the fabric and everyday language of criminal justice that they are not routinely cross-referenced. These and other frequently recurring terms are listed in the next section, *Understanding the basics*.

Again, for clarity, entries appear in the location dictated by their full form, name or title, e.g. under **Association of Chief Police Officers** rather than **ACPO**. Acronyms and abbreviations are noted after the full form of words as with **Police and Criminal Evidence Act 1984 (PACE)**. Many also appear later in the book in a list of *Acronyms and Abbreviations*. Occasionally, where the short form has transcended the long in everyday use, the former is given precedence, e.g, **CCTV, DNA** and **GCHQ**. A small number of very common abbreviations are used within the ordinary text, such as **CJS** for **Criminal Justice System** and **MOJ** for **Ministry of Justice**.

With regard to opposites, the most common CJS usage has been given precedence, e.g. **justice** covers **injustice, acceptable** takes in **unacceptable** and **respect** also contains a note on **disrespect**. But **disadvantage, disability** and certain other 'reverse' concepts feature in their own right as that is how they chiefly impact upon matters of criminal justice. Note also the idiosyncratic use of **no, non** and **not** in terms such as **non-conviction** and **no case to answer**. These are dealt with in the entries to which they relate. However, see generally *no/non/not* in *Main Entries*.

The aim was not to present an in-depth account but to concentrate on the language of criminal justice and the larger picture: to show how a diverse and multi-layered topic operates as a whole. The *A-Z* thus focuses on:

- **basic terminology** (see also *Understanding the basics*);
- **key matters** and a **representative selection** of words, etc;
- brief **definitions, explanations** and **alternative meanings**;
- **connections** (see *Making connections*);
- **nuances** (see *Spotting shades of meaning*);
- **oddities of language** and **striking words and phrases**; and
- **starting points** for further exploration.

1 abscond/absconding

Words used in various CJS contexts to signify quitting, leaving or disappearing, e.g. when wanted by the police; failing to stop after a *road traffic* 4 ident; fleeing from a *crime scene* (aka 'making a getaway'). Note also especially: **absconding from prison**: see *prisoner*; **absconding when on bail**: see *bail*. 4

3 absolute discharge See *sentence/sentencing* 4

Main section key

1 Main entries

2 Key terms within an entry

3 Subject locators

4 *Cross-references* to *Main Entries* unless indicated otherwise (e.g. see *Touchstones*)

Touchstones key

1 Touchstones

2 Key terms within an entry

3 *Cross-references* to *Main Entries* (purple section), unless indicated that they are in *Touchstones* (green section) using '*above*' or '*below*'.

1 Centre for Crime and Justice Studies (CCJS) An independent charity based at King's College London (KCL) that informs and educates re all aspects of crime and the CJS: 'Our vision is of a society in which everyone benefits from justice, safety, economic and social security. Our mission is to promote just and effective *responses* to crime and related harms by informing and educating through critical analysis, research and public debate'. The CCJS publishes a journal, *Criminal Justice Matters* **3**, makes an ann **2 Una Padel Award** in memory of a former director. See crimeandjustice.org.uk

Understanding the basics

Familiarity with certain **core entries** will assist from the outset. The following appear as *Main Entries* but are not routinely cross-referenced.

accused/accusation (taking in **allegation**)
acquittal
Act of Parliament (aka **statute**)
adult
advice
agency/service (and **multi-agency**, etc.)
charge
child/children
Common Law
conviction
court
crime/crime reduction/crime prevention
criminal/criminal justice/Criminal Justice System (CJS), etc.
Crown Court
Crown Prosecution Service (CPS)
Department for Children, Schools and Families (DCFS)
Home Office (HO)
human rights
judge/juror/jury
juvenile
law/legal/legislation
magistrate (aka **justice of the peace** (JP): But see **magistrate**)
Ministry of Justice (MOJ)
offender
party/parties
plea (including of **guilty** and **not guilty**)
police/policing
prison/prisoner (and **HM Prison Service**)
probation (which covers the **National Probation Service**)
prosecution/prosecutor
Rule of Law
sentence/sentencing
statute/statutory
suspect
young offender
young person
trial
verdict
victim

Decoding criminal justice

Criminal justice occupies a distinct niche. It stands apart from other public affairs and justice in general. It has its own language. Ever since Fyodor Dostoyevsky wrote his novel *Crime and Punishment,* these words have touched the popular imagination. But within the field of criminal justice ('forensically' as it is sometimes put) they take on special and more precise resonances. Indeed, behind many **CJS** words, etc. there lies a wealth of meaning depending on the context and the intentions of the speaker or author (see also *Weighing up the context,* below).

Mystique and ingenuity

'All is not as it appears,' as Lewis Carroll's Alice in Wonderland was informed at her trial. Despite modern developments, education, mass media and representations of the CJS in novels, drama or on screen, the language of criminal justice can seem rather foreign at times. It can be intimidating to outsiders (and even to insiders if they have not picked up on the latest developments). In the section headed *Touchstones and Curiosities* there is an entry for **policespeak**. Some of the items noted there come from a police primer. It contains few 'real' words. So also in the courtroom where mystique can reach an even higher watermark. Equally intriguing are prison, underworld or drug-related slang with their often ingenious contributions.

The changing world of communication

In modern times, there have been various steps to challenge language that citizens might not understand, or which is inappropriate or exclusive. More generally in relation to public affairs these include:

- **Plain English** campaigns against complex terminology;
- initiatives to prevent the use of **exclusionary language**;
- 21st century **drafting** and **presentational** techniques as used by Parliament or government in relation to legislation, reports, White Papers, Green Papers and other publications;
- **user friendly** forms, literature, guidance and instructions;
- **democratisation** and **engagement** in general;
- **less condescending attitudes** among professionals and officials due to **awareness** training and the acquisition of **listening skills**;
- **political correctness (PC)** which despite a backlash as to its merits and a counter-PC movement can make many people feel less marginalised or excluded.

Some such developments are directly CJS-related such as:

- Article 6 of the European Convention On Human Rights (ECHR) which demands a **fair trial** - a side-effect being that steps must be taken to ensure that people under suspicion, standing trial or whose liberty may be affected by court or other decisions, understand what is happening;
- the emergence of victim, witness and other support schemes to try and ensure that people coming into contact with the CJS are better equipped for the occasion, less anxious and more informed;
- increasing duties to give **reasons** and **explanations** for formal actions and decisions - often demanding the use of **ordinary language**; and
- **interpreting facilities** for people who do not understand English.

Some of these developments have been more successful than others in de-mystifying CJS processes. But there remains a need for decoding in relation to many professional, forensic or 'in-house' interchanges. The *Pocket A-Z*:

- provides **snapshots** and **basic explanations**;
- places **key aspects** of a topic in **context** (see also *Weighing up the context*);
- draws attention to **interesting** or **unusual** items; and
- lays a foundation for **better understanding**.

Hopefully, it will also encourage readers to develop an ear for the special language of criminal justice. It was designed with beginners in mind, but I hope that it will also be of interest to seasoned practitioners, criminologists and general readers.

Trying to deal with matters across the whole spectrum of criminal justice means that I have needed to trespass on specialist fields. Experts or frontline practitioners are likely to be more up to speed than is possible for someone piecing together information from diverse sources. The building blocks of criminal justice have been significantly remoulded in modern times. If I have missed or misinterpreted anything then corrections will be gratefully received (atoz@watersidepress.co.uk).

Some of the words, etc. in the book will be well-known. These items are included not just for completeness but because other CJS-related matters would be largely incomprehensible without them - and in my experience it is frequently the simplest or 'most obvious' of things which are the hardest to put into words.

Weighing up the context

The context for a word, etc. is important for various reasons, e.g:

- it **may not mean the same forensically** as it does in everyday speech; and
- its meaning will often depend on **the precise criminal justice context** in which it is being used.

Take the word **caution**. In CJS terms it signifies a warning, admonition or rebuke. But in order to learn which it is necessary to know more. Taking events chronologically in terms of CJS processes, it may signify:

- a **caution** given by a police officer, etc. **at the time of an arrest** concerning the suspect's various rights; or
- a formal warning by a police officer to an offender to avoid misbehaving in future under the **scheme for cautions** and **conditional cautions** that exists as an alternative to prosecution; or
- a **caution given in court** by a court legal adviser about an offender's rights concerning trial by a jury in the Crown Court and related matters.

Other, looser uses of the word caution are also possible. Many examples of 'multiple meaning' can be found in the pages which follow. It is perhaps a matter of developing a second sense for such things.

Watchwords

Certain 'watchwords' occur repeatedly but are not topics with hard and fast boundaries. They are of a more fundamental nature as compared with the (sometimes rapidly) changing content of criminal justice in its technical sense. They appear as *Main Entries* or are touched upon at appropriate points in the book.

abuse (including abuse of authority or abuse of power)
accountability (of Ministers, officials, practitioners, etc.)
balance (in decision-making and perspective)
best practice
communication and **liaison**
confidence (in the CJS and its parts)
consent (in an individual or democratic sense)
consistency (of decision-making, approach, etc.)
control (personal, official and social)
discretion
due process
duty
enforcement
equality of arms, opportunity and treatment, etc.
ethics
fairness
freedom(s)
good practice
guidance/guideline
independence/interdependence (as explained in the text)
justice
legitimacy
the **merits** of an individual case
miscarriage of justice
openness and **visibility**
planning, policy and **strategy**
proportionality
protection (of **citizens**, the **State**, etc.)
reasonableness
respect (for the law, other people, etc.)
rights (and responsibilities as noted in that entry)
risk (and its various connotations)
safety (public and personal)
security
seriousness
standards (personal, professional and above all in **public** life)
transparency
values (such as decency, humanity, integrity)

Spotting shades of meaning

The way in which things are described conveys a lot. Much of course depends on how well and accurately they are referred to, but there is also a great deal to be understood from 'reading between the lines', or interpreting the true message. A word, etc. may be underpinned by well-rehearsed **views** or **opinions**, the outcome of discussion, liaison or research. Protocols may exist about what to call something. Or, in some instances, someone may have gone off on what lawyers call 'a frolic of his or her own', when the words he or she uses may be categorised as **idiosyncratic, innovative, misplaced, reactionary** or **wrong**.

Criminologists, especially, routinely state the terms by which their assertions or conclusions are to be understood. This may indicate that they belong to a particular school of thought or are introducing concepts of their own. There are commentators who use **prison** not **prisons**: the absent 's' indicating that they mean **incarceration** not multiple prison **establishments** (incarceration is a graphic description that some people insist on rather than **custody** or **imprisonment**; establishment is used within **HM Prison Service (HMPS)** to describe prison-related premises). Such nuances occur in many areas, e.g. campaign or support groups may use the term **survivor** rather than **victim**; or prefer **misuse** of drugs, alcohol, etc., to **abuse**.

Some people avoid certain usages to prevent **labelling** or **stereotyping**. Even the word **criminal** is contentious. Penal reformers may dislike it for its potentially lasting effects and vagueness (does it mean a serial killer or a transient TV licence evader?). They may prefer to say **offender** or describe him or her as **someone in trouble**. Conversely, those of a more punitive bent emphasise that offenders, especially, e.g. terrorists, traffickers, paedophiles, activists or those involved in organized crime are indeed criminals. Yet stronger epithets may be used by politicians or the media: **thug, yob, wicked** and **evil**. Practitioners of restorative justice may reject punitive terminology altogether, some refusing even to condone use of the word **punishment** despite its almost universal role in this field. Whatever the great debate re these more forward-looking ideas, care is needed with terms such as **black or minority ethnic (BME), disability, (im)migrant, mental impairment** or **physical impairment**.

Using a different kind of nuance, some professionals tend to express **opinions** as if asserting **facts**, or may ask a rhetorical **question** (one suggesting the answer). In either case this should be taken as an invitation to accept, reject or disagree.

Misdescriptions and misnomers

Because the possibilities are considerable and diverse it is not easy to do other than advise readers to look out in relation to everyday events for **misdescriptions, misnomers** and **commonly misused** words and not to be confused or misled by them, whether the failing is one of mispronunciation or lack of precision.

As an example, an **informant** is not an **informer** or vice-versa. The first of these is any citizen who provides information to the police, e.g. about a neighbour who is acting suspiciously or causing trouble. An informer provides intelligence covertly, e.g. as a grass, supergrass or infiltrator of organized crime.

The language of criminal justice also embraces **euphemisms** (sometimes to 'disguise' unpalatable events), as do (sometimes telling) slang, colloquial or 'in-house' terms. Examples are noted at various points in the book and there are a number of dedicated entries in the section headed *Touchstones and Curiosities*.

Making connections

Some years ago, I suggested to a researcher that understanding criminal justice involves making connections: between law, practice, procedure, developments, events, information, history and evidence of what has gone before or the effectiveness of outcomes, methods and approaches. Her answer: 'Many people don't'.

This pocketbook is built around connections as much as it is around descriptions and explanations. The former act as bridges between aspects of the **CJS**, different processes, duties, tasks, responsibilities and the like. They point up its networks, partnerships and the ways in which CJS practitioners act in an interdependent way in order to deliver services and outcomes. Making connections is perhaps nowadays more routine, what with the internet and familiarity with clicking from one topic to another. But it also involves a certain kind of mind-set: and a desire to build on information.

Almost any CJS topic can be linked to an historical timeline. We no longer have a **hue and cry** but we do have **hot pursuit** and there may be a **manhunt** for a suspect who is **wanted** and on-the-run. The most severe sentence that a court can pass, **life imprisonment**, began as an **alternative** to **capital punishment**. The word alternative also signifies **diversion** from prosecution or custody. The **search for alternatives** is not new: it is how criminal justice has always developed, i.e. by governments, practitioners and reformers seeking out (usually) less draconian and more effective methods of providing - or what some people call 'delivering' or 'doing' - justice.

Other connections show how the work of the **police** dovetails with that of the **Crown Prosecution Service (CPS)**; that of **HM Prison Service (HMPS)** with the **National Probation Service (NPS)**; or the way in which agencies and services are brought together in **partnerships** and **working relationships.** Understanding the import of terms such as **crime prevention/crime reduction** or **risk-assessment** may be aided by a knowledge of the different ways and contexts in which such things happen. Everything 'connects up' to the whole by one route or another.

There are also connections when 'what goes around, comes around', e.g. resort to recurring ideas: that offenders, particularly juveniles, should be given a **short sharp shock**; **nipping offending in the bud**; or the notion of a **revolving door** with regard to habitual offenders. Other aspects of criminal justice can be traced to Britain's **radical heritage** which links to **freedom of speech, protest, demonstration** and **uprising** across the centuries and forward to modern-day **civil liberties** or **terrorism**.

Connections breathe life into what can sometimes be a somewhat technical or 'anti-septic' subject. They also make for better overall understanding, easier recall and show how CJS matters function through networks of agencies, services, departments, practitioners, organizations, groups or individuals given to the pursuit of a particular objective, theory, mission or ideal.

Acknowledgements

Finally, I could not have compiled this pocketbook but for having worked alongside a diverse range of practitioners, authors and experts over many years. I cannot mention them all, but I am grateful in particular to:

David Faulkner (government, citizenship and matters of State), John Hostettler (legal history and biography), Angela Devlin (women's imprisonment, links between education and offending, and prison slang), Bob Turney ('going straight', alcoholism, drugs, dyslexia and the Underworld), Deborah Cheney, Tim Newell, Ursula Smartt, Martin Narey, Nick Flynn and Mark Leech (prisons, their various regimes and very much more), Andrew Rutherford (criminology, prisons and juveniles), John Harding (probation and parole), John Alderson, Peter Villiers, Robert Adlam and Seumus Miller (policing, leadership, human rights and police ethics), Anver Jeevanjee (diversity), Leonard Jason-Lloyd, Penny Green, Carol Martin, Elaine Player, Margaret Malloch and Anita Kalunta-Crumpton (drugs), David Wilson (criminology, prison education, serial killers and the impact on the CJS of popular culture), David Moxon and Gordon Barclay (evidence-based research), Roderick Munday (evidence), Elizabeth Burney (social exclusion), Roger Ede and Anthony Edwards (defence matters), Mike Nellis, Julian Broadhead and Laura Kerr (prison writing), Paul Cavadino, Stephen Shaw, Juliet Lyon, Frances Crook, Vivienne Stern, David Ramsbotham and Frank Longford (penal reform), Rod Morgan (probation, youth justice and fines), David Stott and Dick Whitfield (probation, community sentences and electronic monitoring), Andrew Ashworth and David Thomas QC (criminal law and sentencing), Susan Stewart (conflict resolution), Brian Harris QC, Winston Gordon, Mike Watkins, Neil McKittrick, Tony Heath, Kevin McCormack, Nick Stevens, David Simpson, Gaynor Houghton-Jones, David Brewer, John Griffin, Jonathan Black, Kerry Barker, Andy Wesson, Laurie Cramp, George Tranter, Andrew Mimmack, Robin Haynes, Martin Hamilton, Peter Lydiate, David Chandler, Stephen Peckham and Eileen M Boult (magistrates' courts, youth courts, sentencing, evidence, criminal procedure, diversity, road traffic and much more), Roger Billingsley (covert policing), Anthony Stokes (Oscar Wilde), Brian P Block (capital punishment and 'boot camps'), Chris Bazell and Elaine Laken (family law and domestic violence), Helen Simpson and Wendy Crompton (miscarriages of justice), Allan Weaver and Bobby Cummines (violence and 'going straight'), Jonathan Burnside and Nicola Baker (relational justice), Martin Wright and David J Cornwell (victims and restorative justice), John Pugh (capital punishment), Audrey and Paul Edwards (deaths in custody and the tendency of CJS institutions to be 'in denial'), Lynne Ravenscroft (radical reform), Clark Baim, Sally Brookes and Alan Mounford (the use of drama to change lives), Thomas Mathiesen (criminology, prison and silencing of dissent), Tom Murtagh (resettlement and the fragility of our Parliamentary processes), His Honour John Baker (the Crown Court), His Honour John Wroath (women's rights), Sarah Curtis and Richard Powell (juveniles), Russell Pond and Mick Ryan (criminology and radical criminology), Joan Colin and Ruth Morris (interpreters and the CJS) and Ruth Chigwada-Bailey (women, black people and class).

My thinking has been informed by all of the people mentioned above as it has by contact with organizations and networks across the CJS. I am also grateful for the considerable support of Alex Gibson, Nikki Kenny and Jane Green at Waterside Press.

Bryan Gibson April 2009

Putting justice into words...

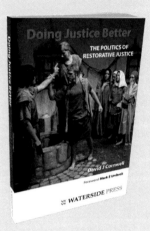

Have **you** visited
WatersidePress.co.uk lately?

The author

Bryan Gibson is a barrister, former co-editor of *Justice of the Peace* and a regular contributor to specialist journals. He has also written for *The Times, Guardian, Sunday Express,* BBC TV and *The Stage*. He founded Waterside Press in 1989 where as director and editor-in-chief he has for 20 years been engaged in 'putting justice into words' through a range of books about the courts, sentencing, prisons, policing, human rights, diversity, restorative justice, legal history and penal reform.

He was for 25 years a justices' clerk and during much of that time an elected member of the Council of the Justices' Clerks' Society (and chair of its influential Criminal Law Committee and founder of its National Criminal Law Network) when he also served as legal adviser to the Magistrates' Association's Sentencing of Offenders Committee.

In the 1990s he worked on a blueprint for Unit Fines which spread through local initiatives and reached the Statute Book (briefly since it was abolished 18 months later!). Whilst working in Basingstoke, Hampshire he helped to develop the country's first 'Custody-free Zone' for juvenile offenders which was sustained for over three years.

He is the author of *The Criminal Justice System* (3rd edition 2008) (with Paul Cavadino); *The New Ministry of Justice* and *The New Home Office* (both 2007; 2nd editions 2008); *Law, Justice and Mediation: The Legend of St Yves* (2008) which introduced the patron saint of lawyers to an English audience; *The Magistrates' Court* (5th edition 2009) and *The Waterside Press A-Z of Criminal Justice* (forthcoming) on which the selection of abridged entries here is based.

Main Entries

The Language of Criminal Justice

abscond/absconding
Words used in various CJS contexts to signify quitting, leaving or disappearing, e.g. when wanted by the police; failing to stop after a *road traffic* accident; fleeing from a *crime scene* (aka 'making a getaway'). Note also especially: **absconding from prison**: see *prisoner*; **absconding when on bail**: see *bail*.

absolute discharge See *sentence/sentencing*

acceptable behaviour/unacceptable behaviour
The term **acceptable behaviour** connotes a minimum standard of behaviour that is appropriate in given circumstances, e.g. in the *assessment* of a *police officer, probation officer, youth justice worker* or *court* according to the situation under consideration - as contrasted with **unacceptable behaviour** which falls below that standard and may be questionable, *nuisance*-type or *low-level* misbehaviour or 'minor misdeeds' (not necessarily criminal offences). Hence **acceptable behaviour contracts (ABCs)** between *supervisors, referral* agencies and offenders or people at-*risk* of offending when support/access to a programme, *sentence plan* or resource may be available only if the person agrees to an ABC. See *'going straight'* and compare *anti-social behaviour.*

access to justice
Access to the courts, avenues of *appeal*, legal *advice*, redress, mechanisms for settling disputes and regulation of the *legal profession*. Since 2008, there has been an **Access to Justice Director General** at the MOJ to deal with 'justice issues' (see generally *justice*) and 'bring together' a range of related matters. The **Access to Justice Act 1999** is the key statute: 'An Act to establish the *Legal Services Commission*, the *Community Legal Service* and the *Criminal Defence Service* ... make further provision about legal services ... *appeals*, courts, judges and court proceedings ... '. Controversy has arisen re whether the rhetoric concerning ease of access to legal services in particular matches the actual provision (see *legal aid*).

accomplice See *assisting crime*

accountability
The principle that people exercising power or authority re *citizens* should be held to account for their actions, decisions, etc, via scrutiny, *inspection; monitoring; review*; duties to *report* and/or give *reasons; management* systems, avenues of *complaint* and *judicial* processes such as *appeal*. Similarly, departments, agencies/services, etc. should operate thus and in a context of *openness* and *transparency*. Hence also **Ministerial accountability**: see *Minister of State; democracy.*

accusation/accused
Accusation is synonymous with 'allegation', i.e. of a criminal offence (rather than, e.g. of a *civil* wrong or (un)*acceptable behaviour*). Used as a noun, **accused** is shorthand for **accused person**, i.e. someone facing a charge or *indictment* rather than mere rumour, *suspicion* or an *investigation*. Such words belong to the terminology of the *adversarial system*: see *Touchstones*. They emphasise the *presumption of innocence*; and that the case in question must be at the pre-trial and/or pre-conviction stage.

acquittal

A finding of not guilty by a jury or magistrates following a trial (as opposed, e.g. to the matter being otherwise *cleared up* following an *investigation*). Acquittal leads to the discharge of the accused person and his or her *release* (unless being held in *custody* re some other matter). Normally, he or she will also be awarded the *costs* of his or her *defence* from *public funds* (except if covered by *legal aid*). **Autrefois acquit/autrefois convict**: historic principles of the Common Law whereby no-one can be tried twice for the self-same matter, whether previously acquitted (*autrefois acquit*) or convicted (*autrefois convict*). For inroads into the principle, see *double jeopardy*. It is possible for certain *civil behaviour orders* (CBOs) to be made following an acquittal.

Act of Parliament (often shortened to Act)

The primary form of *legislation* passed by Parliament following the introduction of a Bill into either House of Parliament; assuming completion of all Parliamentary stages and then royal assent (see generally *Crown*). Acts are aka **statutes**: but see *statute/statutory* for other uses of such terms. Acts appear in writing soon after being passed and are placed in volumes, e.g. Vol. 1 of 2010 (or they may be identified by the year of the reign, especially historically). Newer Acts can be accessed at the Office of Public Sector Information (OPSI): see opsi.gov.uk/acts (and older ones incrementally).

action

(1) The events surrounding an allegation. (2) A dynamic approach to an aim or objective: as, e.g. with **Action On Youth Crime**: see *youth*; or an **action plan** to tackle *offending behaviour*, a *threat* or *risk* (as might be devised by the police, or a *youth offending team* (YOT) re a juvenile). (3) A pro-active approach such as that of a **drug action team (DAT)**: see *drugs*. (4) An **action group** that *campaigns* in a given field, such as **Action for Prisoners Families and Friends**: see *prisoner*. (5) A word used to emphasise that proceedings are *civil* in nature, i.e. what is termed a **civil action**.

actus reus (or sometimes just 'actus')

The act or event prohibited by the criminal law: one of the two basic *ingredients* of an offence, i.e. its physical aspects (but sometimes extending to omissions, failures, etc.) as opposed to any mental element required (see *mens rea*). Some offences require only an *actus reus*: for 'absolute liability' and 'strict liability' see works on criminal law.

adjournment

Putting the hearing of a case back to a later time, whether on a fresh date or later in the same day; either a **simple adjournment** or *remand* and adjournment. **Adjournment sine die** means one 'without limit of time'. This would only be likely to occur in quite unusual circumstances re criminal proceedings.

administration/administrative

(1) Matters of *management* or organization such as the running of the courts and CJS agencies/services as opposed to *judicial* or professional functions. Such terms may also be used to signify functions of a *policy*-making or *strategic* nature. An analogous distinction occurs as between frontline and backroom tasks such as the preparation of *case files* by **the administration** (aka 'the office'). (2) Contrast **The Administration** which denotes the Government of the day. (3) Note also, e.g. **administrative fine**: see *fine*; and (4) **administrator** for senior manager: see also especially *Crown Court*.

(5) The term **administration of justice** may be used in a broader sense to point to all CJS functions including an amalgam of administrative and judicial ones; and hence also the formula 'people involved in the administration of justice'.

admission
(1) An **informal admission** of an offence (or some aspect of it: often referred to as a **partial admission**) made to someone 'not in authority'; that may later be given in *evidence* against the person making it. **(2)** A **formal admission** of an item of evidence under statutory or other *procedures*. **(1)** and **(2)** should be contrasted with a *confession*. **(3)** More loosely, 'admission' may be used instead of a guilty plea, especially re *cautions, TICs* or juveniles (re whom, historically, 'plea' was not used).

adult
Someone of or above the age of majority i.e. at least 18 years old; which is also the age threshold for the **adult court** (the routine shorthand for **adult magistrates' court**) as opposed to the *youth court*. But note informal use of **'full adult'** or **'adult for all purposes'** to distinguish people aged 21 or over from *young offenders*. References to adults in this work are to **adults over 18** unless otherwise stated. An **appropriate adult (AA)** is someone aged 18 or over such as a relative or *social worker* who is (sometimes must be) called upon to *safeguard* the interests of a *child* or *vulnerable* person in their dealings with the police, etc. in situations affecting their *rights, welfare*, etc, in particular when in police *detention* under the *Police and Criminal Evidence Act 1984* (PACE); when investigators must take reasonable steps to involve an AA at the earliest stage unless counter to the *interests of justice*. An AA can offer *advice* and support but not meddle or interfere. Note also the **Adult Court Benchbook**: see *Judicial Studies Board*. See further *age*.

advance disclosure See *disclosure*

advice
The giving (aka 'proffering' or 'tendering') of advice occurs across the criminal justice *process*. Hence, e.g. **advice and guidance**: see *guidance/guideline;* **advice and support**: see *help and support*. The **Citizens Advice Bureau (CAB)** is a charitable, *voluntary sector* service helping people nationwide to resolve *legal, money* and other problems via free **information and advice** at over 3,200 locations. This extends to basic advice re criminal cases: some *barristers* or *solicitors* work with or alongside CABs. The CAB also seeks to influence related *policy* (see citizensadvice.org.uk). For **legal advice** and **police advice** see *legal; police/policing* respectively. Advice is also used as a synonym for *opinion* (as, e.g. per **counsel's advice**: see *barrister*) and see generally *expert; referral*. For **Advisory Committee**, see *magistrate*.

advocate
(1) Generic term for lawyers in a courtroom (or elsewhere, e.g. at an inquiry) who speak for clients: see generally *barrister; solicitor*. **(2)** A word also used to describe non-lawyers making *representations* in other spheres, e.g. re a *campaign* or dispute, or for *children, vulnerable people,* etc. **(3) Lord Advocate** (aka *Her Majesty's* Advocate) is the title of the chief *law officer* of the Scottish devolved Government and the *Crown* in Scotland re criminal and *civil* matters; and the chief *public prosecutor* (see also *Crown Prosecution Service*/'Crown Office'). **(4)** Other public roles may be styled 'advocate', such as the **Independent Mental Capacity Advocate (IMCA)**: see dh.gov.uk and generally *health; mental impairment*. **(5)** A **special advocate** is one vetted re national

security, e.g. for functions related to the National Security Appeals Panel (NSAP) or Special Immigration Appeals Commission (see generally *immigration*). For this specialist area, see 'A Guide to the Role of Special Advocates and the Special Advocates Support Office (SASO)' at attorneygeneral.gov.uk

affirmation

As an alternative to swearing a religious *oath* (see generally that entry), a *witness* is entitled to affirm, by stating: 'I do solemnly and sincerely declare and affirm that the *evidence* I shall give will be the *truth*, the whole truth and nothing but the truth'.

age

The age of a *suspect*, accused person, etc. may affect *jurisdiction*, *powers* or *rights*. Different considerations often apply to *adults, juveniles* (see also *child; young person*) and *young offenders*, e.g. as to *safeguards*, sentencing, *practice* and *procedure*. The **age of criminal responsibility** is ten in England and Wales (but the younger the child the more likely *diversion* or *intervention* will occur rather than formal CJS processes, based on *welfare* considerations and/or more generally in the *public interest*). Similarly, re other *vulnerable people* or due to *old age* (see also *grey crime* in *Touchstones*). Certain offences involve statutory **age-limits**, e.g. those re the sale or supply of *alcohol* or other *substances* to minors. There are sometimes **'non-standard'** age limits, e.g. re *bail*/'young offenders'; *sentence/sentencing*/'attendance centre'.

agency/service

Words used more or less interchangeably to describe bodies working within or alongside the CJS (or in other spheres), e.g. the police, CPS, HM *Court Service. Judicial* entities are not usually so described, but the broader-based term **justice services** may be heard which can, in certain contexts, include courts, judges and magistrates. For **multi-agency**, **service delivery** and **law enforcement agency** see those entries. For examples of **executive agencies**, see HM *Prison Service; Identity and Passport Service.*

aggravate/aggravation

(**1**) Certain offences exist in a basic and **aggravated form**, the latter intrinsically more *serious*: see, e.g. *hate crime; race/racism; religion, sexual orientation,* and, generally, *sentence/sentencing*. (**2**) **Aggravating factors** (aka plus factors) make any offence more serious, e.g. hostility, malice, spite, cruelty or greed (contrast 'mitigating factors': see *mitigation*). (**3**) **Aggravation** is an informal description for provocation, etc. or similar conduct leading, e.g. to a breach of the peace (see *keeping the peace*). Hence informal expressions such as **giving aggravation** by taunts; *harassment*, etc.

alcohol

Alcohol use (and correspondingly **alcohol misuse**: a term that seems to be generally preferred rather than **alcohol abuse**) and its links to offending have been long debated and are a subject of special study; as has whether *drunkenness* should rank as an *excuse*, or conversely an aggravating factor (see previous entry). For a range of *information* and *data* about alcohol and crime, see homeoffice.gov.uk under the heading 'Alcohol-related crime'. Many offences are directly referable to alcohol, such as being drunk and disorderly, excess alcohol (and other alcohol related *road traffic* offences: see that entry). An **alcohol education course** may form part of a *community sentence* or *imprisonment*. For **alcohol testing**, see *prisoner*. Apocryphal tales abound concerning the prison still or the ease with which alcohol can be obtained in prison, it being banned there and subject to various strategies to detect its use. **Alcoholics Anonymous (AA)** is a fellowship of men and women who 'share their experience, strength and hope to solve their common problem and desire to stop drinking [and] stay sober and help other alcoholics to achieve sobriety': see alcoholics-anonymous. org.uk For a useful overall survey of connections between alcohol and offending, see cjp.org.uk/news/offender-management

allegation See *accusation/accused*; **allegiance** See *Crown*.

alibi

A specific *defence* whereby the accused claims he or she was or could not have been at a *crime scene* at the time of the offence. Since the 1960s (before wider duties of defence *disclosure* existed) someone wanting to raise an **alibi defence** has been obliged to give notice to the *Crown Court*. This avoids a **last minute alibi** being sprung on a *jury*; and allows the alibi to be verified as a **true alibi** or challenged by the police, etc. The scope for a **false alibi** has declined with advances in *science* and *technology* (e.g. *CCTV, DNA*, global satellite positioning (GSP)). For a famous *murder* case where the accused person's life turned on this defence, see *Hanratty, James* in *Touchstones*.

allocation

A mechanism for making choices between options, categories, locations, etc. **(1) Allocation and sending (A&S)** is the embryonic *procedure* (set to replace **mode of trial**) whereby magistrates make decisions re *either way offences*; by hearing an outline of the *accusation* to see whether their powers would be sufficient (see *sentence/sentencing/*'maximum powers') or whether the case should be sent to the *Crown Court* for trial. The defendant also has a free-standing *right* to chose trial by jury (aka an 'election for trial'), i.e. by not giving *consent* to summary trial. This is explained by the court legal adviser along with a *warning* that he or she may be committed to the Crown Court for sentence if this later turns out to be appropriate (aka a *caution*) (and so long as this power subsists). Note also 'plea before venue' (see generally *plea*) whereby before the A&S decision is made the accused person can indicate his or her wish to plead guilty and the magistrates can indicate their likely sentence. **(2) Prisoner allocation**: *see prisoner*. **(3)** The **sharing-out of tasks or responsibilities** between practitioners, agencies/services, departments, etc, especially re *partnership*.

alternative

Criminal justice has often developed via a search for alternative approaches, methods outcomes, etc. Hence, specifically, the terms **alternative to custody** and **alternative to prosecution**: forms of *diversion* from such processes via alternative routes. The alternative to *custody* movement was at its height in the 1980s beginning with strategies re younger offenders and later extending to many *adults* facing lesser charges (for a closely observed account re juveniles, see *Growing Out of Crime: The New Era* (3rd. edn. 2002), Rutherford A, Waterside Press. Well-established **alternative mechanisms** for avoiding court proceedings if appropriate include police *cautions, warnings and reprimands, referral* schemes and tests applied by the *Crown Prosecution Service* (CPS): see those entries. Note also **alternative verdict**: see *verdict*.

ancillary order See *sentence*; **Anglo-Saxon** See *Touchstones*; **antecedents** See *character and antecedents*.

anger

Anger may be a *motive* for and/or *cause* of crime, particularly re offences of *violence*, those motivated by revenge or involving loss of self-*control*. Hence **anger manage-ment**: a key *offending behaviour programme* in *prison* or with regard to *community sentences*, including, e.g. re *domestic violence*. Note also the **anger experienced by victims** which initiatives such as those of *Victim Support* seek to counter.

animals

The laws relating to the breeding, rearing, keeping, movement and slaughter of ani-mals (including from time-to-time *emergency* provisions) are extensive and specialist, re which dedicated works should be consulted. Similarly re offences, e.g. of **animal cruelty** or **abandoning an animal**. Other areas of particular interest are the links between keeping animals and *nuisance* or *anti-social behaviour*; offences by **animal activists** (often categorised as 'animal terrorism': see *terrorism/terrorist*) and others concerned with **animal rights**; *restrictions* re **dangerous animals** (and **danger-ous dogs**: see also the note under *weapon*); **disqualification from keeping an animal** (see generally *disqualification*); and the phenomenon of (spates) of **attacks on animals** such as horses or cats (sometimes viewed with hindsight as a prelude to attacks on humans). Note also the work of the Home Office **Animals Scientific Procedures Division** (part of its Science and Research Group) comprising an Ani-mals in Scientific Procedures Licencing and Policy Team and Animals in Scientific Procedures Inspectorate: see scienceandresearch.homeoffice.gov.uk The work of the **Royal Society for the Prevention of Cruelty to Animals (RSPCA)** (a *charity*) ex-tends to using 'all lawful means [to] prevent cruelty, promote kindness to and allevi-ate suffering of animals'. It also has a *prosecution* function: see rspca.org.uk Analogous dedicated provisions and organizations relate to other forms of livestock and, e.g. the *protection* of wild birds, often with CJS-related implications.

anti-social behaviour (ASB)

A modern dimension in terms of crime prevention/crime reduction and/or social *control* is the development of the **anti-social behaviour order (ASBO)** (and other *civil behaviour orders* (CBOs): see further that entry). ASBOs began in the *Crime and Disorder Act 1998* to deal with minor misdeeds (not necessarily criminal in kind and originally described by Government as *nuisance*-type behaviour). An application to a court for an ASBO is a *civil* matter following *liaison* between the police and *local authority*. If an ASBO is not complied with (see generally *enforcement*) that becomes a *criminal* offence punishable with up to five years' *imprisonment* (two years' *custody* re older juveniles). The Police Reform Act 2002 allowed on the spot *fines* for a range of (here criminal) behaviour **loosely categorised as anti-social**. Tackling ASB was a central tenet of the Government's *Respect Agenda* (2000 onwards); and such strategies have become central to CJS work despite some criticisms. ASBOs can also be made in the county court. A **criminal anti-social behaviour order (CRASBO)** (similar in effect to a civil one) can be made following conviction for any offence. Note also the **'gangster asbo'** (whose official name is the Serious Crime Prevention Order (SCPO)), introduced by the Serious Crime Act 2007. This is again initially a civil order. It can be used, e.g. to impose *conditions* restricting where an individual can live and limiting their work and/or travel arrangements. SCPOs can last for up to five years and breaching them can result in imprisonment for up to five years. An ASB-related **'premises closure order'** was introduced by the Criminal Justice and Immigration Act 2008: see specialist works. **ASBO Concern** is an amalgam of interest groups which views the *criminalisation* (see *Touchstones*) of low-level behaviours, especially via civil methods and when *safeguards* may be lacking, as a questionable trend; as it does an increase in **ASBO-related methods**: see asboconcern.org.uk

appeal

A plea to a *higher court* challenging a decision of a lower one; or a comparable procedure re the cancelling-out and/or substitution of a decision by a public authority, e.g. to refuse a licence, permission, etc. The workings of the *Rule of Law*, the legitimacy of the CJS and the extent of *access to justice* can be tested by asking whether there are adequate avenues of appeal. The main ones are noted below.

Anyone convicted at the *Crown Court* can **appeal to the Court of Appeal (CA)** on questions of *law.* If the case turns on the facts (i.e. the verdict of a jury) that person may only appeal after obtaining a certificate from the *Crown Court* judge that the case is **fit for appeal** or, more usually, **leave to appeal** from the CA itself. The CA must allow an appeal against conviction on the (sole) ground that it is unsafe. There is also a *right* of appeal to the CA against a sentence imposed by the Crown Court, with the leave of the latter court. The CA may quash the sentence and substitute any which the Crown Court could have made if, taking the case as a whole, the **appellant** (a term routinely used in the context of appeals to describe the party making the appeal) is not dealt with more severely. **Appeal by way of case stated** to the *High Court* (aka simply **case stated**) is the avenue for taking a point of *law* from (usually) a magistrates' court to the *High Court* (although it can be from the Crown Court re an appeal to that court from a magistrates' court). The appeal is heard by a Divisional Court (DC) of the Queen's Bench Division (QBD). The magistrates set out in writing the facts which they found to exist and say what legal principles they observed. The DC either upholds their *interpretation* or makes some other decision, e.g. to *quash* the conviction or to order a re-hearing. Magistrates can refuse a frivolous application to state a case or ask the applicant to identify the matter of law concerned. An **appeal to the Crown Court** against the decision of a magistrates' court may be made: against conviction within 21 days (or any extension of time allowed by the *Crown Court:* known as **leave to appeal out of time**); or against sentence (when the offender risks an increase in his or her sentence though bidding for a decrease). Note also the existence of an **appeal to the magistrates' court** re *fixed penalties.* For **appeal to the European Court of Human Rights (ECHR)**, see *human rights*; **appeal to the House of Lords**, see *House of Lords*; **appeal to the Supreme Court**, see *Supreme Court.* Note also the **Attorney General's reference** re an unduly lenient sentence or certain tariffs (see *Attorney General*); and the role of the *Criminal Cases Review Commission* (CCRC). The CA can refer points to the *House of Lords* as necessary. Similar to an appeal is a High Court **declaration** which can be applied for by either party. Public authorities (e.g. courts, the police, the CPS and *Criminal Defence Service*) will act upon the law as so declared. Re primary *legislation*, the *higher courts* can make a **declaration of incompatibility** with *human rights* law. They cannot strike it down or alter it. They can adapt UK secondary legislation. The *Criminal Justice Act 2003* introduced **in-trial appeals** against evidentiary and other rulings by a *trial judge* (usually expedited to avoid *delay* re the trial itself); but not, e.g. extending to a ruling that a jury be discharged; or if an appeal can be made to the CA in the ordinary way. **Judicial review (JR)** is a process via which *participants* who are 'aggrieved' by a decision of a magistrates' court may, within six months (usually), ask the High Court to consider whether the magistrates acted judicially (see *judicial/judicially*). If they did not, the High Court can *quash* their decision, order a re-hearing and/or make orders to prevent the error recurring: see specialist works. Judicial review can also be sought against other public entities or public officials, including, e.g. *Ministers of State*. See also *rectification*.

appropriate adult (AA) See *adult*; **Archbold** See *Touchstones*

area

CJS services may be categorised as national, regional, area or local according to their geographical reach, *jurisdiction* and *remit*. Examples (of many) are the **Area Judicial Forum (AJF)** (see *judicial/judicially*) and **HM Prison Service Areas** (see generally *HM Prison Service*). Note also **local area** as in **local justice area (LJA)**: see *local*.

argument

(1) Inherent in the *adversarial system* of justice (see *Touchstones*) lies the fact that events, *law* or *practice* are ultimately a contested matter involving *assessments* (including weighing the *evidence*), *interpretations* and *opinion*; causing lawyers to **argue cases**, propositions, etc. Similarly, commentators, *criminologists* or penal *reformers* **argue the merits or demerits** of a theory, approach, method, outcome, etc. (in effect debate it from differing perspectives). **(2)** Many offences stem from or begin as arguments, which have simmered and/or escalated, e.g. via forms of *anti-social behaviour* into *harassment, hate, violence,* etc. Hence, e.g. the importance of arrangements for *access to justice, advice, help and support* and those for 'conflict resolution'.

arraign/arraignment

Whereas an accused person is *charged* in the magistrates' court he or she is **arraigned** in the *Crown Court*, i.e. by the clerk of that court calling on him or her by name, reading out the formal *indictment* and asking: 'Do you plead guilty or not guilty?'

arrest

(1) Arrest by assuming *control* over the physical movements of a person. *Arrest, bail, detention* and *charge* are inter-related processes at the *front end* of the CJS; governed by, among other provisions, the *Police and Criminal Evidence Act 1984* (PACE) and PACE Codes. Hence **arrest on suspicion** of committing an offence when the person concerned may be held in police detention and interviewed in accordance with PACE. He or she can be released (usually on police *bail*) to return to the police station later for that interview to continue. Some arrests occur at or close to the *crime scene*, others during an *investigation*. Once charged, the accused person may be released on *bail* to appear in court. Special provisions exist re juveniles, including re the need for an appropriate adult to be present: see *adult*. The police have wide **powers of arrest** (and *search*) under the general *law* or re specific offences; and since 2003 can arrest people for any offence, not simply an **arrestable offence** (broadly one attracting at least five years' imprisonment). Certain procedures depend on the offence being a **serious arrestable offence** (as listed in PACE), e.g. a superintendent (or above) may authorise delay in an accused contacting people beyond the police station if that might lead to *interference* with or *harm* to *evidence* or *witnesses*, *assault*, the alerting of other suspects, or hinder recovery of property. The *Police National Computer* (PNC) records arrest and prosecution *data*. For **citizen's arrest**, see *citizen*. Other commonplace arrest-related scenarios include: **arrest for failure to surrender to bail** and **arrest for breach of bail**: see *bail*; **arrest for non-payment of a fine**: see, generally, *fine enforcement*; **arrest for breach of a community sentence**: see *community sentence*; **arrest for being unlawfully at large**, i.e. following an escape: see *prisoner*; **arrest for (a person's own) protection**: see *protection*; **arrest under a warrant**: see *warrant*. A *witness*, juror or others can be placed under **arrest for contempt of court**. In the UK **house arrest** is an informal term for detention under a control order (see *detention*), or possibly a similar outcome secured by using intensive *bail conditions*. In some foreign *jurisdictions* it is a form of arrest/detention in its own right. For **arrest referral scheme**, see *referral*. **(2)** Arrest is also used in the sense of keeping something in check, such as an *addiction*: see generally *Touchstones*.

arson

Criminal damage by fire. Under the Criminal Damage Act 1971, this offence must be charged as 'arson' and records so marked; **arsonists** being *dangerous offenders*, fire quick to spread and hard to *control*. **Arson with intent to endanger life** or reckless in that regard is an *aggravated* form of arson triable only in the Crown Court.

assault

There are various **Common Law assaults**, including **assault and battery** and **common assault** (virtually any non-consensual touching, but nonetheless *violence*: see generally that entry). Assaults usually lead to prosecution under the *Offences Against the Person Act 1861* (OAPA, or just OAP); a statute overdue for modernisation. OAPA assaults include: **assault occasioning actual bodily harm** (ABH) (section 47); **assault intending to cause grievous bodily harm** (GBH) (section 18); and **malicious wounding** (section 20). The OAPA *targets* other activities prejudicial to the physical integrity of a person, e.g. administering a noxious substance (a *drug* and/or *poison*). **Sexual assaults** are provided for separately: see *sexual offence* and for further details re either type of assault see works on *criminal law*.

assessment

(1) A considered conclusion based on facts, *information* and/or *intelligence* according to the situation made at any point of the CJS whether by a court, an agency/service or practitioner. Hence, e.g. an **assessment in a pre-sentence report**: see *sentence/ sentencing*; the **Offender Assessment System (OASys)**: see *offender*; a **medical assessment**: see *medical aspects*; **risk-assessment**: see *risk*; or **threat-assessment**: see *threat*. **(2)** More loosely any considered determination or decision.

asset/assets

(1) Gains from crime may involve **assets obtained by fraud** or bought with stolen *money*: generally called *proceeds of crime*; hence **asset recovery** which is one function of the *Serious Organized Crime Agency* (SOCA). **(2)** Asset may also be used to signify **'value store'**, as per the **assets of an agency/service or practitioner** (including knowledge, facilities or resources); or an undercover police officer might describe an *informer* as 'his or her asset'. This use of the word has also been variously applied, e.g. to *sentencing guidelines* and even the European Convention On Human Rights (see *human rights*). See also *payback* in *Touchstones*. **(3)** **ASSET** is an name used by the *Youth Justice Board* in relation to *assessment* tools: see *youth offending team* (YOT).

assisting crime

Secondary participation in crime can occur in various ways, via **aiding and abetting** and/or **counselling and procuring** it. Such an offender is aka an **accessory**

(hence the original **Accessories and Abettors Act 1861;** and analogous provisions re *magistrates' courts*). Following two *Law Commission* reports on participation in crime (see lawcom.gov.uk), the *Serious Crime Act* 2007 (SCA) introduced modern, replacement offences of **incitement** and **encouragement** (see further the entry for *incitement*). This type of crime is also sometimes called **inchoate crime** (as are *attempts*); and hence also terms such as **co-accused** or **co-defendant.** It is possible to participate jointly in crime via a *conspiracy* (see that entry). In general, an aider and abettor risks the same *punishment* as the **principal offender** he assists; but may be able to put forward *mitigation* according to the extent of his or her involvement. See also *informer* for public interest immunity (PII). For the doctrine of **joint enterprise** and other connected matters, consult specialist works.

Assizes and Quarter Sessions See *Touchstones*

association

(1) Various CJS membership or collaborative bodies style themselves as associations such as the: **Association of Chief Executives and Chief Officers of Probation (ACECOP):** see *probation*; **Association of Chief Police Officers (ACPO)** and **Association of Police Authorities**: see *police/policing*; and **Magistrates' Association**: see *magistrate*. **(2) Association between prisoners**: see *prisoner*. **(3)** A **link or connection**, e.g. between *evidence* and the accused person and/or as per a chain of evidence. **(4)** The process of association when *Making connections*: see the start of this work. **(5)** Interaction between **criminal associates** via personal or other **dubious associations** which offenders, ex-*prisoners* and people at-*risk* of offending are discouraged from; which may also, e.g. lead to a **non-association condition** re *bail*.

asylum

A concept with historic overtones in free nations whereby someone may be allowed and/or assisted to remove himself or herself from a hostile environment in their country of origin, aka **political asylum** where they are under *threat* from a foreign *State* (or in former times from sovereign or internal domestic powers). Political asylum connotes that the individual is a refugee or 'displaced person' (the latter category of people may also be allowed to remain in the UK depending on *border* strategies and may become an **asylum seekers** individually). Only after the need of an asylum seeker to be given British *protection* will he or she enjoy refugee status and be given *leave* to remain in the UK; bringing with it certain *rights* and obligations. Pending this, he or she may be held in an immigration *detention* centre. In 2009, the **asylum system** as a whole was seeking to clear a backlog estimated at around 335,000 cases (including **asylum legacy cases** dating back up to ten years); the National Audit Office reporting that a **New Asylum Model** (2006) under which a single immigration manager managed an asylum application throughout had led to 'more claims being settled more quickly'. The **Asylum and Immigration Tribunal (AIT)** forms part of the Tribunals Service, an executive agency of the MOJ (which superseded the former Immigration Appellant Authority (IAA) in 2005). It decides on *appeals* against the *Home Office* re asylum, immigration and nationality. See further ait.gov.uk

attempt

An attempt to commit a crime occurs once the accused person takes steps which go beyond mere preparation and he or she begins actively to carry out the offence;

something which will always be a question of fact and degree. But note also now that certain preparatory acts (including those re *terrorism/terrorists*) are an offence in their own right. Consult specialist works on *criminal law,* including for **attempting the impossible**, the classic conundrum re whether someone who, e.g. stabs a corpse believing it to be a live person can be convicted of attempted *murder* or *assault*.

attendance centre order See *sentence.*

attorney

Short for **attorney-at-law**: a generic term for lawyers with a general practice as opposed, e.g. to *advocates*, and for *solicitors* as rather than *barristers*. A term more common in everyday use in the USA, except re specific UK responsibilities, titles or functions. Hence the **Attorney General (AG)**, the government's chief *law officer* and chief legal adviser, appointed by the Prime Minister (PM) and accountable to Parliament (see *accountability*) for the CPS; Serious Fraud Office (see *fraud*); HM Treasury Solicitor's Department; Department of the Director of Public Prosecutions for Northern Ireland; CPS Inspectorate; and HM *Revenue & Customs* Prosecution Office. He or she may appear personally (or via his or her staff) in a *high profile* or sensitive case, or one involving national *security*. Certain prosecutions require the AG's consent (aka **Attorney General's fiat**). There are other responsibilities, e.g. to *appeal* to the *Court of Appeal* where he or she considers that there has been an *unduly lenient sentence* (a power which has been extended to an increasing number of situations); or against certain sentencing *tariffs*. He or she also acts as 'the guardian of the *public interest*', including by intervening in criminal (and other) *cases*. The role dates back five centuries. It has attracted controversy, notably re advice given to the PM re the legality of the Iraq War (see also, e.g. *freedom/* 'Information Tribunal') and re the *BAE Systems* case (see *Touchstones*). The Green Paper, *The Governance of Britain* (2007) (justice.gov.uk) stated that public *confidence* should be restored. In 2007, Baroness Scotland became the first woman AG. **Office of the Attorney General** is the name of his or her department: see further attorneygeneral.gov.uk

audience

An **audience with a court** (usually but it can, e.g imply one with a committee, commission, or more loosely the head of an agency/service, etc.) i.e. to address the court, speak to it: sometimes described as **obtaining the ear of the court**. The parties and their *lawyers* have **rights of audience** before a court unless forfeited due to misconduct, etc. (see further below). *Victims* do not have such *rights* (but see *victim impact statement*). Automatic *rights* of address in courts are confined to *barristers* and *solicitors* (in the *Crown Court* only those solicitors licensed to practise there). Lawyer employees of the Crown Prosecution Service (CPS) do not represent the CPS in the Crown Court and CPS cases are handed over to a practising barrister once they reach that level. A move which would have given *Crown prosecutors* such *rights* foundered in 1995. The **Courts and Legal Services Act 1990** enabled a wider range of people to acquire rights of audience whilst European obligations may impact on the structure of the *legal profession* and consequently such rights as a whole: see specialist works. Courts have inherent *discretion* to 'hear' who they see fit. Following the 'stringent requirements' of the 1990 Act, they should only do so in rare circumstances, especially re individuals who apply habitually (per Lord Woolf a former *Lord Chief Justice*). See also similar comments under *McKenzie friend.* That Act also allows courts to refuse to hear someone who has rights of audience, e.g. due to *contempt* or other misconduct.

Auld Report See *Touchstones*; **automatic conditional release** See *release*; **autrefois acquit/autrefois convict** See *acquittal*.

baby farm See *Touchstones*; **back end (of the CJS)** See *front end of the CJS*; **BAE Systems** See *Touchstones*.

bail

The **Bail Act 1976** gives a *right* to bail to people charged with offences, i.e. a right not to be held in *custody* unless an exception to that right exists in *law* and on the facts as judged by the court or police (as applicable). If a court finds that an exception exists, the accused person can be *remanded* in custody, usually for not more than eight clear days at a time before conviction. Longer remands in custody are possible, up to 28 days, or after the case reaches the *Crown Court*. After conviction and pending sentence, the limit is normally 21 days. Key aspects of bail are set out below.

Absconding when on bail, i.e. **(1)** failure to surrender to bail: see, further, below; or **(2)** disappearing after being required to remain in a given area or place. People refused bail by *magistrates* can *appeal* to a judge of the *Crown Court* or a *High Court judge;* and *prosecutors* can appeal against the granting of bail (sometimes shortened to **'a grant'**) in certain instances. **Bail hostel**: the National Probation Service (NPS) formerly provided such *hostels* and may still help to arrange such accommodation; but hostels are now used mostly for high-*risk* offenders (see also *Touchstones*/'heavy end') under *supervision*, either as part of a *community sentence* or where offenders are on *licence* after their *release*. Bail hostels may still be provided by the *voluntary sector*. **Bail information, bail support, etc.** are services for people facing a *remand* hearing; and are provided under various schemes including those operated by the NPS and/ or HM Prison Service (HMPS) and *youth offending teams* (YOTS). **Bail information schemes (BIS)** provide information relevant to a bail decision to the CPS and *defence*. Matters not yet considered are looked into, e.g. a fixed address, the possibility of temporary accommodation, or of a surety or security (below). The results are put to the court at the next hearing; and may be linked to *referral schemes*. **Conditional bail** means bail with **bail conditions** attached to it, e.g. to live at a given address; report to the police; not to associate with the victim or *witnesses* or other named people (aka a **non-association condition**); or to stay away from a given location. *Reasons* must be given for conditions. A defendant can be *arrested*, with or without a *warrant*, for breach of a bail condition. Unlike failure to surrender to bail (below) it is not an offence. **Court bail**: that granted by a court rather than the police (below).

Failure to surrender to bail is a criminal offence in its own right. An absconder risks being arrested and the failure will also be a ground for refusing further bail (below). Bail can normally only be refused if a court is satisfied that a statutory **exception to the general right to bail** exists. Exceptions are known as **grounds** and the explanation as a **reason**. Magistrates must announce their **grounds and reasons for refusing bail** in *open court*. A copy of the decision must be given to the accused at his or her request. Bail can be refused before conviction re any offence that carries *imprisonment* if there are substantial grounds to believe that if set free the accused would: fail to surrender (above); commit an offence; or interfere with *witnesses*. The scope for refusing bail is greater after conviction; less if the offence does not carry possible *imprisonment*. Defendants can always be held in *custody* for their own *protection*; or if there has been a previous **breach of bail** by absconding and the court believes that the accused would abscond again. An offender need not be granted bail if the offence is *indictable only* or an *either way offence* if already on bail for an offence when another was (allegedly) committed. Jurors are *disqualified* if on bail: see generally *juror/jury.* **Offending on bail**, i.e. committing a criminal offence is not in itself an offence but may be a reason for refusing bail, cancelling it or treating the underlying offence more seriously when sentencing. **Reasons for granting bail** must be given in the case of *murder* and re prescribed offences; whilst **bail cannot be granted at all** re *murder*, attempted murder, rape, attempted rape or manslaughter if the accused already has a conviction for such an offence. Bail can be granted by the police during an *investigation* or after someone is charged: aka **police bail.** Since 2003, the police can grant most types of *conditional bail* (above) and **street bail**, literally 'on the street' at the *discretion* of the arresting officer rather than the officer taking the person back to a police station to be dealt with by a custody sergeant. **Repeat applications for bail** are inhibited by law to counter 'never-ending' applications. The court may allow a **security** to be deposited with the court by an accused person or third party, i.e. a valuable item as a guarantee that the accused will attend court for his or her next scheduled appearance; failing which the security can be forfeited by a court. (English bail arrangements do not mirror those in the USA where 'bail bonds', possibly purchased from the *private sector* are commonplace). A requirement that the accused 'find a **surety**' is a frequent bail condition, i.e. a responsible individual who will, in effect, vouch for the accused's re-appearance. The surety enters into a *recognizance*: see further that entry. For **warrant 'backed' for bail**, see *warrant.* A **written bail record** to be made where a court or police officer grants or withholds bail. Re **young people and bail** those aged 17 to 20 refused bail are held in a *remand centre* (RC) or *prison*. Below the age of 17, a refusal of bail operates as a remand to local authority accommodation unless, exceptionally, strict criteria for more secure *custody* are met.

banishment

A *punishment* of former times involving exile, outlawry or transportation (see, e.g. outlaw, *Six Acts* and *transportation* in *Touchstones*); which also resonates in relation to modern-day forms of *social exclusion*: see, e.g. *Crime and Banishment: Nuisance and Exclusion in Social Housing* (1999), Burney, E, Waterside Press.

barrister (aka 'counsel')

A member of the Bar of England and Wales, i.e. a lawyer who has qualified as a barrister under the rules of the Bar Council. Barristers may be: **practising barristers** who have apart from passing their **bar examinations** completed 'pupillage' with an experienced barrister and obtained a seat in chambers (the name for a barrister's office); or **non-practising barristers** (the latter usually in a full-time legal position, e.g. within the CJS or other spheres of public life). He or she must belong to one of the four Inns of Court, i.e. Gray's Inn, Lincoln's Inn, Inner Temple and Middle Temple (all situated in the same area of London as the *Royal Courts of Justice*). Under professional *codes*, he or she can normally only be approached via a *solicitor* (aka instructing solicitor). Members of the *judiciary* were until modern times appointed virtually exclusively from the ranks of practising barristers, but this has changed so that solicitors can be appointed (though prior to the *Judicial Appointments Commission* few were: see further that entry). Every barrister is *independent* and his or her advice should be beyond the *influence* of extraneous, non-*legal* considerations. Barristers are aka **counsel** and those retained by the *Crown* are known as **Treasury Counsel**. Hence also **Queen's Counsel (QC)** aka 'a silk', 'leader' or 'senior' (hence also 'junior' for all other barristers): the upper rank of barrister who wears a black silk gown rather than one made of stuff (a kind of cloth). QCs have enhanced rights of *audience* and must normally be accompanied by a junior to carry out routine tasks whilst they focus on being an **advocate** (putting forward *representations* in a courtroom or elsewhere) or writing legal *opinions* (tasks which all practising barristers perform to varying degrees).

Basic Command Unit See *police/policing*; **Beeching Report** See *Touchstones*.

bench

A term that is used flexibly to signify: (**1**) the *judiciary* as a whole; (**2**) the judge, judges or magistrates sitting in court on a particular day; (**3**) the entire body of magistrates in a *local justice area;* or (**4**) the raised dias or platform in a courtroom where judges or magistrates sit to dispense justice. Other common derivatives include: **bench warrant**: see *warrant;* **bench chair**: see *magistrate;* **bench office**, i.e. at the police station dealing with court-related matters; often nowadays more commonly known as a *Criminal Justice Unit;* and **benchmark** re *guidelines*, starting points, etc.

best practice (or sometimes Best Practice)

The finest way of dealing with a given matter, *process*, task, etc. as, e.g. determined by senior *management* within an agency/service or by *experts* and promulgated to managers, frontline practitioners, etc. The term connotes that competing practices have been considered in order to arrive at a paramount method; often after *multi-agency* consultation. The term is also sometimes used in relation to *judicial* matters.

bias/lack of bias See *fair/fairness*

bill/Bill

A formal document whose nature and status depends on the context. Hence, e.g. **bill of cost**: see *taxation;* **Parliamentary Bill**: see *Act of Parliament; legislation;* **voluntary bill of indictment**: see *Crown Court; indictable/indictment*.

binding over to keep the peace

The historic power of *magistrates* dating from the *Justices of the Peace Act 1361*, allowing them to bind over individuals to be of good behaviour and keep the peace. Those being bound over must enter into a *recognizance* (a promise to pay a sum of money in the event that the order is breached). The power is *civil* in nature but with *sanctions* equating with *punishment*, such that it faced challenges under *human rights* law. It has been displaced to an extent by the more modern *anti-social behaviour order* (ASBO).

black economy see *Touchstones*

blackmail

The offence of **blackmail** under section 21 *Theft Act 1998* occurs when someone 'with a view to gain for himself [or herself] or another or with intent to cause loss to another ... makes **any unwarranted demand with menaces**': for further legal implications, especially re the parameters of the offence and when a demand is 'unwarranted' as opposed to justifiable and lawful, see specialist texts on *criminal law*. Typically, blackmail involves or is associated with extortion, intimidation, *threats* (especially of *violence*), revelation of compromising details, or kidnapping (i.e. when the unwarranted demand is in the nature of a ransom demand). Blackmail may thus frequently occur alongside other offences committed by either the perpetrator or the victim (placing the latter in dilemma as to whether or not to *report* the matter to the police). Historically, it was also strongly associated with sexual infidelity (sometimes involving a 'honeytrap') or homosexuality (especially before *decriminalisation*). For two notorious cases involving blackmail, see *Black Panther* and *Hosein Brothers* (both in *Touchstones*). Note also (extra-*legal*) forms of **emotional blackmail** as may be present in the backdrop, e.g. to *abuse*, *controlling behaviour* or *domestic violence*.

black or minority ethnic See *discrimination; ethnicity; race/racism*.

blind/blindness
(1) The maxim **justice is blind** exerts a strong influence with regard to even-handed treatment and notions of *equality; fair/fairness*. It is symbolised by the blindfold worn by the statue of Justicia atop the *Old Bailey* (see *Touchstones*). The idea of **turning a blind eye** or 'looking the other way' is embedded in *popular culture* (see generally *Touchstones*). It takes on a special resonance re CJS matters. Ignoring relevant facts, circumstances or events may be *evidence* of an everyday criminal offence or of *corruption* or misconduct in public office; even if there may be circumstances in which 'not asking too many questions' is legitimised, e.g. re an *amnesty* (see *Touchstones*), an *informer*, or national *security*. More generally, **willful blindness** may amount to *mens rea* or possibly *perjury* especially re offences based on knowledge of certain facts; or it may undermine the *defence* of someone who claims not to have been aware of material facts. (2) **Blindness**, i.e. lack of sight, is a disability which may affect anyone at any time from a variety of causes, re which allowance is made by the CJS. Increasingly, **blind magistrates** have been appointed (heirs to pioneers such as John Fielding: see *Fielding, Henry* in *Touchstones*). David Blunkett MP was the first and only **blind Home Secretary**. Famously, the father of *barrister*, novelist and playwright John Mortimer (1923-2009), was a **blind barrister** and Queen's Counsel as portrayed in Mortimer's autobiographical play 'A Voyage Around My Father' (1963 onwards). (3) Note also the **blindness to events** associated with *denial*: see *Touchstones*.

border
Border control is the modern term for the policing of State borders: in the interest of *safety* and *security*, including by keeping out undesirable aliens. It extends to *controls* on foreigners allowed into a country, e.g. as visitors, students, temporary workers, on a visa, or under **open border** arrangements as per the European Union. Such matters are a high *priority* due to international *terrorism/terrorists* and *organized crime*, including re illegal *immigration*, smuggling and *trafficking*. The **UK Border Agency (BA)** (aka **UK Border Force** or **UK Borders**) was launched by the Home Office in 2008. Staff wear uniforms and there have been moves 'to strengthen the powers and surveillance capabilities of those working to stop terrorists and other would-be illegal entrants'. The BA integrated the former Borders and Immigration Agency (BIA), those parts of HM *Revenue & Customs* covering ports and airports and UK Visas (which considers applications to enter the UK). It enforces immigration and customs *regulations* as well as considering applications to enter/stay in the UK (the latter aka '*leave* to remain': hence also 'overstayer' for someone who exceeds that leave), for

citizenship or (political) *asylum*. For details, see *The New Home Office: An Introduction* (2nd. edn. 2008), Gibson B, Waterside Press; and www.bia.homeoffice.gov.uk

Bow Street See *Touchstones*; **bringing offenders to justice** See *justice.*

British Crime Survey (BCS)

A key source of *research* data re public perceptions of and attitudes to crime. BCS findings help to inform criminal *policy*-making. Its annual and other surveys measure crime in England and Wales (originally Scotland also: that country and Northern Ireland now have their own surveys) by asking individual members of the general public about any crimes they have experienced during a given timeframe. The BCS, a Home Office venture, includes crimes not reported to the police (see *report*). It collates information, e.g. re: victims of crime; the circumstances in which crime incidents occur; aspects of *offending behaviour*, *anti-social behaviour* and *fear* of crime. It also focuses on whether there is *confidence* in the CJS, *effectiveness and efficiency* and the need for crime prevention/crime reduction measures. See homeoffice.gov.uk/rds See also the figures reproduced within the entry for *crime*/'crime rate'.

britishness See *Touchstones* and also *citizen; democracy*

British Transport Police (BTP)

A non-geographic police force which provides a policing function and services to rail operators, their staff and passengers throughout England, Scotland and Wales. 'Every day, we police the journeys of over six million passengers and 400,000 tonnes of freight over 10,000 miles of track. We believe travelling is about more than just getting there. It's about ensuring *safety* and *security* all the way'. BTP's history can be traced to the early 1800s, alongside developments in policing and public transport generally. There is an independent **British Transport Police Authority (BTPA)** (see *police authority*) which is responsible for ensuring *effectiveness and efficiency* re the policing of the entire rail network. For details see btp.police.uk

'Building Communities, Beating Crime' and **Bulger case** See *Touchstones* for both; **burden of proof** See *evidence.*

bullying

A word with varying definitions: in broad terms intimidation, *harassment, threats* and/or coercion, often repeated and involving offences. It may be physical (as with *assault),* verbal, written or psychological (see generally *psychiatry/psychology* including in modern times by email. It remains a concern of the CJS: **(1)** within agencies/services, e.g. by staff upon staff; staff on 'clients' and vice versa; **(2)** including in prison where HM Prison Service has introduced anti-bullying initiatives (see, e.g. hmprisonservice. gov.uk under 'Violence and Bullying'); **(3)** of suspects and/or *witnesses* by the police, by *legal representatives* (including during cross-examination: see generally *evidence*); **(4)** between *gangs*, re *organized crime* (e.g. in the sex industry) and *domestic violence*; and **(5)** in *schools*. Hence over some years Childline (see *child/children*) has been contacted by over 20,000 children re bullying. In 2003, the government introduced a 'Don't Suffer in Silence' *campaign*, in which disruptive children as young as five were *targeted* in 3,500 primary schools using classroom activities to **stamp out bullying** and associated *anti-social behaviour* (ASB) using consultants and sometimes *zero-tol-*

erance approaches (see *Touchstones*). National and local **Anti-bullying Charters** have been used and there is an **Anti-bullying Alliance** (see anti-bullyingalliance.org.uk) Other useful sources include bullying.co.uk; childline.org.uk; parentscentre.gov.uk

burglary

Burglary is an offence under section 9 *Theft Act 1998*, in its basic form of entering a building as a trespasser with the intention of committing *theft*, grievous bodily harm (see also *assault*), *criminal damage* or rape (see *sexual offence*), or, having entered a building as a trespasser committing any of those offences. It also exists in various *aggravated* forms according to the intention of the accused person and, e.g. whether a *weapon* was used: see section 10 of the 1968 Act and specialist works on *criminal law*. Note also in particular the distinction drawn between **burglary in a dwelling** and **burglary of commercial premises** (especially re sentencing); re both of which schemes such as *Neighbourhood Watch* and Business Watch are active. Historic terms for burglary such as **breaking and entering** or **housebreaking** are still often heard albeit that no 'breaking' is nowadays required by *law*. Burglary is often seen as a barometer of *crime rates*. According to the Home Office, 'burglary rates have been dropping for some time thanks to a wide-ranging approach to tackling the problem: ... domestic burglaries fell by 11 per cent between 2006/7 and 2007/8 (along with other household thefts which fell by 12 per cent; and 'reports of criminal damage' by 13 per cent'. For such trends, see homeoffice.gov.uk under the link for 'Burglary'.

C

Cabinet/Cabinet Office

The highest form of governmental committee headed by the Prime Minister (PM), comprising senior *Ministers of State*, and the office (or government department) which serves the **Cabinet**. In a criminal justice context, the **Cabinet Office** is concerned, with cross-departmental *liaison, partnership,* matters affecting *social exclusion* and a range of associated items including bravery awards. From the early-2000s onwards it has played an increasingly active role vis-a-vis CJS matters. A **Cabinet Committee on Crime and the Criminal Justice System (CCCCJS)** was established in 2007 and is chaired by the PM. The *Justice Secretary, Home Secretary* and *Attorney General* are all members. The resulting 'special relationship' is balanced by competing individual duties and understandings, e.g. concerning constitutional sensitivities (see *constitution/constitutional*), especially with regard to *safeguards* in relation to the *judiciary*.

camera See *CCTV; media/press; open court/*'in camera'; *photography; road traffic/*'speed camera'; *surveillance; technology; video/*'amateur cameraman'.

campaign

A word commonly used to describe a range of situations, activities or events, especially: (**1**) a **campaign of offences**, often of a similar kind, highly *targeted* or conducted as per a **military campaign**, such as a **bombing campaign** or when offences are committed in support of a given objective, such as damage to the environment (aka **'direct action'**); (**2**) a **crime reduction/prevention campaign**, blitz or crackdown or, e.g. a **road safety campaign**; or (**3**) a **campaign for reform**: see *reform* including for or against a particular *law*, method, *practice*, etc. Hence also (**4**) a **Par-**

liamentary campaign to similar ends; **(5)** that of a movement or pressure group, especially one styling itself so, e.g. **Campaign for Nuclear Disarmament (CND)**; **(6)** a *moral* crusade as conducted by Mary Whitehouse (1910-2001) and the Festival of Light against public representations of *violence,* pornography and 'bad language'; and **(7)** a **media/press campaign** as per, e.g. re the *Bulger case* in *Touchstones.*

case

The key focus of criminal justice is the individual **case to hand** (aka the **present case**) and its he facts and merits. Hence, e.g. **bringing a case to court**: see *commencement; Crown Prosecution Service;* **case conference**: usually a *multi-agency* meeting to consider aspects of a case, e.g. *reports,* progress, problems. The **case file** (or 'bundle' of papers) relevant to a given case (increasingly an **e-case file**). For **case law** see *Common Law; precedent.* **Case management** occurs within agencies/services, including in the courts via a **Criminal Cases Management Framework (CCMF)** and Simple, Speedy Summary Justice (CJSSS) (see *summary*). For **case stated** see *appeal;* **case to answer** *no case to answer;* **defence case** *defence.* For **prima facie case** see that entry; **prosecution case** see *prosecutor/prosecution; trial.*

cash

Cash has always been a *target* of criminal activity, including *burglary, robbery* and *theft.* It is doubly attractive due to its liquidity, relative untraceability and the fact that it represents funding. It remains central to the *black economy:* see *Touchstones.* **'Brown envelope'** is a metaphor for hidden payments from one person to another (or to or from an organization, business, etc.); which in a modern context may involve *money laundering* (see also *proceeds of crime*), tax evasion (see *taxation*) or other illicit activity. **Cashpoints** have been: **(1)** a *target* for thieves, extending to wholesale removal using, e.g. JCB diggers; **(2)** the focus of a rapidly abandoned suggestion by Prime Minister Tony Blair that offenders guilty of *anti-social behaviour* or *low-level* offences be taken to the nearest cashpoint and required to withdraw funds to pay an on the spot fine (see *fine*); and **(3)** a *target* of offenders cloning debit cards from photographs taken by *surveillance* cameras hidden in the hood of a cashpoint, i.e. of pin numbers (PIN) (a leading *security* device) entered by cardholders. For **'cash for honours'** see *Touchstones.* Note also the **cash-in-transit industry** which is a major aspect of *private sector* activities; and a frequent *target* of robberies; leading also to the development of protective *technology* and specially equipped vehicles to counter such attacks.

categorisation/category

It is impossible to understand the CJS processes without some knowledge of the **three categories of offence**: *summary offences; either way offences* and *indictable only offences*: see those entries. Note also in particular **prison(er) category**: see *prisoner.* A similar term is 'classification' to signify, e.g classes (or 'categories' of *drugs*) or types of *evidence, information, intelligence* or *offence* (such as 'acquisitive crimes': see *theft*).

causes of crime

Causes of crime are many, various and much debated. Among the more commonly cited candidates are poverty, *social exclusion, disadvantage,* lack of *education* and/or *employment, mental impairment,* lack of *control,* stability, relationships or of a stake in society. See also, e.g. *broken windows* in *Touchstones.* From another perspective are greed, jealousy, revenge or disaffection, although many people would class these primarily as *motives* rather than underlying triggers. Other explanations look to specific causes, such as *drugs* or *alcohol*. **Tackling the causes of crime** has been an aim of Governments of all hues; it can involve seeking to eradicate *social exclusion,* regenerate run-down areas, provide *education*, ensure employment and eradicate lack of *equality* and opportunity. This, however, could be to misunderstand the overall nature of crime, which is committed by people of all types, including at a more sophisticated level than connoted by such matters: see, e.g. *organized crime* (and also *black economy* and *white collar crime* in *Touchstones*). Some crimes defy 'cause-based' explanations, but may be large in scale, such as *road traffic* offences or those against petty regulations. Causes of crime are generally envisaged as relating to a narrow range of crimes committed by marginal groups (not the behaviour of 'respectable 'people which might be prosecuted if *priorities* or *concerns* were different). For much useful information see crimereduction.homeoffice.gov.uk Other valuable sources include *Exploring Delinquency: Causes and Control* (1996), Rojek D G and Jensen G F (eds.), Oxford University Press; and *Mass Imprisonment: Social Causes and Consequences* (2001), Garland D W, Sage Publications (about the USA but of wider import). See also *tough/ toughness* in *Touchstones* for the **'tough on crime, tough on the causes of crime'.** Many crimes have no single discernible cause or or 'tidy' explanation; whilst others can be individually baffling: see, e.g. *Shipman, Harold* in *Touchstones.*

caution

(1) Even when an offence is discovered and a suspect identified, the police are not obliged to start criminal proceedings. They have an inherent *discretion* whether or not to do so or refer the matter to the CPS with a view to a *caution.* That decision is made by the CPS and the Code for Crown Prosecutors contains related *guidance.* When an offender admits his or her *guilt* and there is enough evidence for a conviction, the offender *consents,* and the *public interest* does not demand prosecution, a police caution, i.e. a formal *warning* about future behaviour may be authorised. This is administered by a senior police officer, usually in uniform and at a police station. Police *advice* may also be given. Comparatively few people who are cautioned re-offend, especially those committing minor offences for the first time. In its early days, cautioning lost credibility from over-use; nowadays seemingly corrected. Cautions are cited in court if the offender commits a further offence and may affect the sentence for the new offence. Since 2003, *requirements* can be added to a **conditional caution** and the offender brought to court if these are not complied with (aka 'breach'); or cautioning may be postponed to see whether it is appropriate, aka a **deferred caution** (possibly being superseded). Re juveniles there is a system of *warnings and reprimand.* Other uses of 'caution' include: **(2)** that by a **court legal adviser** re the accused person's *rights* concerning *allocation and sending*; and **(3)** a **police caution on arrest** (or before each interview) re the 'right to silence' and its implications: see under *silence.*

CCTV

Closed circuit television: **(1)** a primary means of *surveillance*, crime prevention/crime reduction and *evidence* gathering; many CCTV systems being installed by local authorities, *Crime and Disorder Reduction Partnerships* (CDRPs), or the *private sector*, the latter, e.g. in shopping malls, car parks and other privately owned or managed public spaces; **(2)** a secure means of visual and audio communication between courts, prisons and other CJA related-locations, sometimes referred to as *video links.*

Central Criminal Court See *Old Bailey in Touchstones*

centralisation

The movement of power and direction away from local areas towards the centre of governance, tending to the *national* rather than the *local*, under: (1) a nationwide organization/headquarters; or (2) government itself. Either may be accompanied by assurances that what is happening is, e.g. the centre is simply 'lending weight' to powers which are in fact exercised in individual regions, areas or localities. Whatever the reality, elements of *discretion* or 'original authority' (see, e.g. *police/policing*) remain with individual CJS practitioners within any greater or supervisory framework created.

Centre for Crime and Justice Studies (CCJS) and **centre stage** See *Touchstones*; **CENTREX** (former) See *Touchstones*/'Bramshill'.

chambers

(1) **In chambers** (or **in the judge's chambers**) signifies that matters are taking place in private rather than in a courtroom, e.g. a *criminal directions hearing*, or that aspects of a case are being heard in camera (see *open court*). (2) **Barristers' chambers** is the name for their 'offices', normally grouped together in **a set of chambers**.

character and antecedents

Once someone stands convicted of an offence, the court will, as part of the sentencing process, receive details from the prosecutor of his or her character and antecedents, i.e. any relevant information about the offender held on police records. This may include but is wider than a list of previous *convictions*. Care is taken to avoid prejudicial material being included and such information can be challenged/corrected.

charge

A word used in several contexts where a defendant is confronted with an accusation, e.g. by a police officer (hence **arrest and charge**: see the general description at *arrest*), a prosecutor, or in court when the charge is put to the accused person. Words may be used such as, '**You are charged** that on [a certain date] at [a certain time] you [did such and such], contrary to [a given legal provision]'. This may be accompanied by a *warning* (aka *caution*). Charge also serves to distinguish events in the magistrates' court from those in the Crown Court, when, re the latter, the terminology is that of *indictment* and *arraignment*. **Charge and requisition** is the modern way of *commencing criminal proceedings* as introduced by the *Criminal Justice Act 2003*; replacing former procedures: see also *information and summons*. Under the new arrangements (when operative). A public prosecutor (see *prosecution/prosecutor*) can normally only institute criminal proceedings by way of a **written charge** alleging the offence and **written requisition**, i.e. requiring the accused person to attend at a magistrates' court. A **holding charge** is a nominal charge for the purposes of ensuring that a suspect is kept in *custody* or *detention*; and which may later be replaced by a **substantive charge** (or the person concerned must be released as soon as it becomes clear that the holding charge cannot be 'firmed up' or otherwise proceeded with).

charitable/charity

Various CJS activities are promoted or supported by charitable trusts and organizations usually as part of the *voluntary sector*. They are diverse and often highly specialised. A number of these are noted at appropriate points in this work.

child/children

According to the context, words referable to: (**1**) minors, i.e. people below the age of 18, in contrast to *adults* (normally meaning 18 and over: see that entry); (**2**) in a *youth justice* context: (**a**) juveniles of whatever age as opposed to adults or young offenders; or (**b**) **children** aged 10-13 in contrast to **young persons** (14-17), children being subject to lesser sentences or a greater impetus towards *diversion*, early *intervention, welfare* considerations and so on; or (**3**) people below a prescribed minimum age for a given purpose, e.g. employment; sale or supply of certain items. For some key connections, see *abuse; age of criminal responsibility; bullying; welfare; Youth Justice System*. There are wide-ranging **child protection** measures to avoid children becoming victims; including child-related aspects of **Multi-agency Public Protection Arrangements (MAPPAS)**: see that entry; since 2005 the **Child Exploitation and Online Protection Centre (CEOP)** which operates in the UK and internationally; and **ContactPoint** an embryonic *database* of all UK children. CEOP also provides internet *safety advice* for parents and carers and a 'virtual police station' which is contactable by email: see ceop.gov.uk It grew out of initiatives such as Operation Ore that from 2002 *targeted* 7,000 or more suspects re downloading child pornography. CEOP is is affiliated to the *Serious and Organized Crime Agency* (SOCA) with links to a *Virtual Global Taskforce* (VGT). Its main powers stem from the *Serious Organised Crime and Police Act 2005* (SOCPA). Based in Pimlico, central London, it uses *outreach* networks at home and abroad. **Children and Young Persons Act (CYPA** or **C&YPA)** is the description used to describe *legislation* re children of all ages, key Acts being those of 1933, 1963 and 1969. There are also diverse family law protections: see specialist works. The **Department For Children, Schools and Families (DCSF)** has emerged as the lead agency/service (with the MOJ) re *youth justice* with a mission: 'to make England the best place in the world for children and young people to grow up ... [to] make [them] happy and healthy; keep them safe and sound; give them a top class education; and help them stay on track'. For its **Children's Plan** and approaches to youth crime and unacceptable behaviour (see *acceptable behaviour*) see dcsf.gov.uk

circuit

Description at one time given to areas of England and Wales for the purposes of *management* by what is now HM *Court Service* and also still the geographical working divisions of *barristers*, e.g. **the Wales and Chester Circuit; Western Circuit;** there being eight in all, traceable to the times when judges went out from London on **Assize Circuits**, lodging and dining (aka 'messing': a term also used by the *military*) with *barristers*. A **circuit judge** is a judge of the *Crown Court*: see *judge*.

citizen (UK citizen)

Anyone resident in the UK and entitled to stay there permanently due to his or her British nationality, i.e. where he or she has always been or has become a **British citizen**. Hence the idea that citizens, including *children*, might be expected to demonstrate their allegiance to the *Crown* or *State*; and associated (controversial) developments re **citizenship ceremonies** and **citizenship tests** for people adopting British nationality (since 2007). Citizens might be expected to be pro-active in matters of *law and order*, whether by avoiding offending (see generally *desistence*), re crime prevention/crime reduction or by reporting wrong-doers or assisting the police. For a short note on the wider debate re *Britishness* see *Touchstones*. When individual *rights* are mentioned, this usually means **UK citizens' rights**; but the term **citizen of Europe** has begun to be heard, e.g. re *freedom* to travel or work within the European

Union (EU). Under a **citizen's arrest** an offender can be apprehended by a private citizen under historic Common Law powers. Citizens enjoy less leeway in this regard re their *judgement* than do police officers; and the suspect must be handed over to the police, etc. at the earliest opportunity. Official exhortations have veered between *warnings* not to take on offenders and urging citizens to 'have a go' (*Justice Secretary,* Jack Straw having famously made such an arrest). For a survey of CJS-related matters see *Crime, State and Citizen: A Field Full of Folk* (2nd. edn. 2006), Faulkner D, Waterside Press. For **Citizens Advice Bureau**: see *advice*.

civil

Appertaining to personal or private matters and *rights*, i.e. as between individuals and/or bodies (including sometimes the *State* in this capacity) as opposed to *criminal* matters which are the prerogative of the *Crown*. Hence, e.g. **civil courts** and **civil proceedings** (as opposed to criminal courts/criminal proceedings). **Civil claims** involve such matters as negligence, *nuisance* and what are called torts (i.e. civil wrongs). **Civil disobedience** is a form of 'direct action' (or inaction), usually undertaken by *citizens* on the basis of their own conscience, belief and/or a perception of (sometimes gross) injustice (see *human rights*; and *radical heritage* in *Touchstones* and also consult specialist works). The **civil standard of proof** is 'on a preponderance of probabilities': for the criminal standard, see *evidence*; and *Woolmington v Director of Public Prosecutions* in *Touchstones*. 'Civil' is also used, e.g. to distinguish everyday matters from *military* matters, as with the **civil police** as opposed to the *military police* (or historically a militia: see, e.g. *Peterloo Massacre* in *Touchstones*); just as the word **civilian** may be used in various context to indicate non-*military*, non-police service or other non-professional personnel; especially those working behind the scenes, e.g. in the *administration/administrative* roles, or from the *private sector*. **Civil behaviour order (CBO)** is a generic term covering a range of orders based initially on *civil* powers but that are backed by criminal *sanctions* if breached. The Crown Court or a magistrates' court can, after complying with the Criminal Procedure Rules 2005 (as amended in 2008) make CBOs under various powers (sometimes even following an *acquittal*), e.g. under the Domestic Violence, Crimes and Victims Act 2004 (see *domestic violence*); Football Spectators Act 1989 (see *football*/'football banning order'); Protection from Harassment Act 1997 (see *harassment*); *Crime and Disorder Act 1998*; Sexual Offences Act 2003 (see *sexual offence*); *Serious Crime Act 2007*; or re *mental impairment*. **Civil liberties** are fundamental *rights* as now contained, e.g. in *human rights* law and/or as espoused by **civil liberties organizations** such as *Liberty* (see *Touchstones*). Hence also expressions such as **civil rights and liberties**. References to the **Civil Rights Movement** may be, e.g. to that: **(1)** in the USA from the 1960s; **(2)** Northern Ireland vis-a-vis *The Troubles* (see *Touchstones*); **(3)** various former Eastern Bloc countries; or to **(4)** the combined efforts of civil libertarians generally.

CJS See *Criminal Justice System;* **classification** See within *categorisation/category.*

clear up/clear up rate

Terms referable to the closing of *case files* once a case has been dealt with/is no longer 'live'; as when the accused has been charged; someone *cautioned* for an offence; there is an *admission* whereby it could be *TICd*; or *no further action* is taken; provided there is *evidence* to establish who the culprit was. Similarly, where the offender is below the *age of criminal responsibility*, or suffering from *mental impairment*, or the victim or key *witnesses* are unavailable. But note also *'cold case'* in *Touchstones*.

Clinks (Community Links) See *Touchstones*

code

(**1**) Official, statutory or formal instructions or *guidance* within a coherent framework; such as the **Codes of Practice** under the *Police and Criminal Evidence Act 1984* (PACE) or the **Code for Crown Prosecutors**, see *Crown Prosecution Service*. (**2**) An internal code within an agency/service, etc. setting out the basis on which certain aspects of its responsibilities will or should be discharged. (**3**) A statutory code of practice as provided for in *legislation* or a statutory responsibility to create and issue a code. For **criminal code** see that entry; and for **highway code** see *road traffic*. (**4**) A **code number** such as a pin number may be used to protect premises, computers or *cash* machines from improper access. (**5**) One used to encrypt information.

cold case See *Touchstones*

commencing criminal proceedings

Virtually all criminal cases begin in the magistrates' court and are dealt with there to their conclusion. Re *either way offences*, the accused may be sent to the *Crown Court* for trial: see especially *allocation and sending* and note that *indictable only* matters are sent straight away to the Crown Court by magistrates subject to formalities. The *Criminal Justice Act 2003* introduced a new method of starting proceedings for public prosecutors: see *charge*/'charge and requisition'. See also *information and summons*.

commission/commissioner

Words associated appointments by the *sovereign,* Government or other authorities to act in a public capacity, whether as an individual or a member of a group, aka **'being commissioned'**. Hence the **commission of the peace**: see *magistrate*. See also *Independent Police Complaints Commission; Criminal Cases Review Commission; Law Commission* and Royal Commission on Criminal Justice (see under *Crown*). Note also **commissioner** for people who serve on commissions, as with the **Commissioners of Revenue & Customs**: see *Revenue & Customs;* or who like the **Metropolitan Police Service Commissioner** are employees: see *Metropolitan Police Service*. (**3**) For **commissioning services**, see *private sector*, and *Carter Report* in *Touchstones*.

commitment

A word used to signify: (**1**) engagement or involvement, a will to achieve a particular end, especially, e.g. with regard to mission statements or *partnerships* (to which the various parties 'sign up'); (**2**) action or the *paperwork* relating to a 'committal' (as described in that entry and sometimes used as a misnomer).

committal

(**1**) The sending of someone to a place, venue, etc. by lawful order, such as **committal for sentence**: see under *sentence/sentencing*; **committal for trial**: see *allocation and sending*; or **committal to prison**: see *imprisonment*. (**2**) The *paperwork* (aka 'process') involved, such **committal papers** or a **committal warrant** (see *warrant*).

Common Law

That part of the *law* which stems from the legal *rulings* and *interpretations* of the judges in the *higher courts* (aka the **law of precedent**: see *precedent*); in contrast to *legislation* in its various guises (see that entry). Certain principles of the Common Law are regarded as fundamental, such as the *presumption of innocence* (which is reinforced by *human rights*) and the rules relating to the burden and standard of proof (see *evidence*). Hence **Common Law country** for one that has adopted this legal tradition; and **Common law offence** of which *murder* is the most striking example.

communications

(1) Those between or within agencies/services, good communications being fundamental to an *effective* CJS and, e.g. as between *communities* and the police (see, e.g. criticism re the *Brixton Riots* in *Touchstones*). **(2)** Communications between suspects which may in some instances justify the **interception of communications (IOC)**: see that entry. **(3)** For **Judicial Communications Office (JCO)**: see under *judicial*.

community

A key CJS term and concept signifying events, etc. occurring in the everyday (or 'outside') community (as opposed to 'inside' a prison); or at the behest of a given community rather than government or officialdom. Since 2003, **community sentence** means **generic community sentence**: a broad-based form of order containing requirements selected by the court: *supervision*; unpaid work; activities; programmes; prohibited activities; a curfew; exclusion requirements; those re *residence, mental impairment, drugs* (including in substitution for the *Drug Treatment and Testing Order* (DTTO) introduced in 1998) or *alcohol* treatment; or to attend an attendance centre (for people up to the age of 25). These may, or in some instances must, be reinforced by *electronic monitoring* (EM). The origins of such sentences lie in the probation order (1907 onwards) and the **community service order** (1974): see specialist works. **Enforcement of a community sentence** follows if there is a breach of the order, i.e. a failure to abide by its terms, or further offending; when a court takes into account the extent to which the order has run, the level of compliance by the offender and his or her *response* to the sentence before deciding what action to take: see specialist works. The **Community Legal Service (CLS)** is a network to provide mainly *civil* legal advice: see legalservices.gov.uk **Community Legal Advice** (formerly known as Community Legal Service Direct) is a telephone helpline and online facility paid for by *legal aid*: see communitylegaladvice.org.uk **Community provision** is a generic term for a range of services or facilities provided in a community setting. **Community justice** is an innovation in *local justice* pioneered in the UK by the North Liverpool Community Justice Centre, established in 2005, and similar schemes in other parts of England and Wales from 2007. Based on the Red Hook Centre, New York, USA, it is a **community resource** providing a court function and crime prevention measures linked to *social services*. A judge is in charge (holding a joint appointment as district judge and circuit judge: see *judge*). Much of the work focuses on *low-level* offending, *anti-social behaviour* (ASB) and the *enforcement* of court orders. The judge can try more serious criminal cases when appropriate. Co-ordination of CJS services and the involvement of the local *community* in providing, e.g. *help and support* are key features. For **community prisons**: see *prison*. The term **community programme** is sometimes used to refer to *local* efforts to promote, e.g. the use of community sentences, *employment* of offenders re unpaid work benefitting local communities, and the involvement in this of the *voluntary sector*, as well as in providing services to offenders, victims and their families; or sometimes to signify more general initiatives/strategies. For **police community support officer (PCSO)**, see *police*.

compensation

Financial recompense to a *victim* for *injury*, loss or damage, which must come before *punishment* by way of a *fine*; and is an automatic consideration by courts in other cases. It may be additional to any other method of dealing with an offender, i.e. an ancillary order (see *sentence/sentencing*) or a stand alone sentence, aka **compensation in its own right**. *Reasons* for not awarding compensation must be given by a court which does not make such an award if it could have done so. The **Criminal Injuries Compensation Authority (CICA)** operates a scale of payments that it can make to victims of *violence* where adequate court-based compensation is not obtained; known as the **Criminal Injuries Compensation Scheme (CCCS)**: see further cica.gov.uk

complaint

(1) Arrangements exist across the CJS for **complaints by dissatisfied citizens**, including re the non-*judicial* activities of judges or magistrates via an **Office for Judicial Complaints (OJC)** (with *magistrates* initially via their Advisory Committee). Court decisions as such must be challenged by way of an *appeal*. **(2) Reports of offences** to the police, etc. are often styled 'complaints', especially re a*ssaults, violence* and *sexual offences;* and the victim may be referred to as **the complainant. (3)** Complaint may also used to mean **'application'**, especially re some *civil* cases.

complex/complexity

Special arrangements exist re matters of complexity, e.g. there is a **Complex Crime Unit**: see *Crown Prosecution Service*. Re **complex fraud**, see *fraud*. Magistrates may commit a case to the *Crown Court* for trial if it involves particularly **complex issues** even though it is otherwise well within their *jurisdiction*: see *allocation and sending*.

computers For the main computer related entries, see *hacking, global/international dimensions, internet* (all in *Main Entries*) and also *cybercrime* in *Touchstones*.

Concordat (The Concordat)

An understanding between the *Lord Chief Justice* and *Justice Secretary* enabling matters of common concern as between the MOJ and *judiciary* to be discussed outside of the political arena, consistent with *judicial independence*. See, also, *Judicial Office*.

condition/conditional

Words signifying a contingency re given events. Hence, e.g. **conditional bail**: see *bail*; **conditional discharge**: see *sentence/sentencing*; **condition** of a **community sentence** (better now described as 'a requirement') or **condition of a release licence** (again really a 'requirement'). *Sanctions* may follow if conditions are breached.

confession

An 'admission' of guilt made to someone in authority, which is subject to special rules of *evidence* and *procedure*. A **false confession** is one obtained, e.g. under duress or oppression or in breach of the *Police and Criminal Evidence Act 1984* (PACE); re which (both before and since 1984) there have been various *miscarriage of justice*. For an example of a key pre-PACE case, see *Birmingham Six* in *Touchstones*.

confidence

(1) A key aim of the mechanisms for *law and order* and the *administration of justice* is to inspire confidence in the CJS or its parts. **(2)** Confidence in the CJS is also a statutory purpose of sentencing: see *sentence/sentencing*. **(3)** Other uses of 'confidence' include **con** or **con trick** and **con man** (someone who plays such a trick): see *fraud*.

confiscation order See *proceeds of crime; sentence/sentencing/*'ancillary order'

consent

(1) The consent of a court, officer or the accused person is required in a wide range of situations, see in particular: *allocation and sending; Attorney General; caution*; *Director of Public Prosecutions*. Note, also, the use of consent: **(2)** as part of a *contract* (see the various meanings given in that entry); and **(3) policing by consent**: see *police/policing*. **(3)** Consent may be a *defence* to certain crimes, such as *assault* or *sexual offences* provided that this is genuine, the person concerned has the capacity to consent and the events do not go beyond what it is permissible under the law: see specialist works. Note also that **belief in consent** may sometimes be a *defence*, in particular in relation to offences under the *Theft Act 1968* or 'mistake': again see specialist works.

conspiracy

A former Common Law offence whose principal ingredient consists of an agreement between two or more people to carry out an offence, i.e. beyond the conspiracy itself, such as **conspiracy to rob** or **conspiracy to defraud**, essentially what is popularly called **a plot**. There is nothing to prevent a single individual being convicted, provided that the existence of such an agreement is clear from the *evidence*. It is the unlawful agreement itself which constitutes the offence, not any action or conduct designed to put it into effect (contrast an attempt: see *crime*) (although acting on a conspiracy may be sound evidence of that agreement: as well as being a substantive offence in its own right). The old law of conspiracy attracted criticism, e.g. **conspiracy to corrupt public morals** was not previously an offence 'known to the law' when it was identified as a crime by the House of lords: see *moral aspects* in *Touchstones*. Most forms of conspiracy became a **statutory conspiracy** under the **Criminal Law Act 1977** (based on the Law Commission report 'Criminal Law: Report on Conspiracy and Criminal Law Reform' (1976), HC 176). Under the 1977 Act a **criminal conspiracy** occurs if someone 'agrees with another person or persons that a course of conduct shall be pursued' which, if the agreement were to be carried out would either necessarily amount to or involve the commission of an offence or offences by one or more of the parties to the agreement, or would do so but for the existence of facts which render the commission of the offence or any of the offences impossible (as amended by the Criminal Attempts Act 1981). Some special statutory forms of conspiracy are of an extra territorial nature (see *jurisdiction*), such as those re *terrorism* or computer *hacking*. For exceptional situations and rules re the parties to a conspiracy, see specialist works on *criminal law*. A consultation paper was published in 2007: see lawcom. gov.uk A conspiracy charge can be used 'as a *political* tool' to enhance *seriousness*, or more legitimately where planning is tenuous or contingent in order to disrupt the progress of a plan. A **conspiracy theory** is an explanation that seeks to discover a hidden *motive*, undercurrent or place a gloss on events to show that they are not what the appear to be; often aimed at *corruption* and/or a cover-up.

constitution/constitutional

Criminal law, criminal justice and **constitutional matters** frequently inter-relate, due, e.g. to the Rule of Law and other fundamental principles which form the backdrop to the work of the courts, CJS and its agencies/services. Note also in particular the *separation of powers*. All such matters fall to the MOJ which since 2008 has a **Democracy, Constitution and Law Director** whose remit includes '[bringing] together work on ... **constitutional reform**, including a possible new British Bill of Rights and Responsibilities ... democratic engagement, devolution and information *management*'. Since the Glorious Revolution (1689) there is a **constitutional monarchy**, i.e. *judges, juries* and *magistrates* not the sovereign, decide cases and the judges the scope of *legislation* passed by Parliament and 'assented to' by the *Crown*. For modern-day implications see *The Governance of Britain* (2007; Cm. 7170) and associated publications re **constitutional renewal**; where the absence of a **written constitution** for the UK is discussed. The **Constitutional Reform Act 2005** switched functions of a *judicial* nature from the Lord Chancellor (see *Justice Secretary*) to the Lord Chief Justice and various independent bodies; created a *Supreme Court*; and led to a **Constitutional Renewal Bill** (2008). The **Department for Constitutional Affairs (DCA)** (2002-2007) was the forerunner of the MOJ.

consumer protection See *Trading Standards*

contempt of court

All courts, including the *Crown Court* and *magistrates' court* have powers to punish for contempt, a key provision being the **Contempt of Court Act 1981** under which anyone who wilfully insults the court, judge, magistrates, jurors, officers of the court, lawyers or witnesses (in court or when going to or returning from court) commits an offence. Similarly, if someone interrupts court proceedings or misbehaves in the courtroom. Offenders can be detained until the end of the proceedings and, if the court sees fit, committed to *custody* and/or fined. Such a *committal* can be revoked, e.g. where the offender apologises: known as **purging contempt**.

contract

A *civil* rather than a criminal construct: **contracts proper** normally involve an exchange of *value* or 'consideration' as between the parties; but in the CJS context the word 'contract' (or sometimes 'compact') may signify various consensual arrangements: **(1)** an ordinary commercial contract between the *public sector* and *private sector,* e.g. to provide services or resources, as per privately managed *prisons*; **(2)** comparable arrangements between different public services (as with HM Prison Service and the National Health Service); sometimes called **Public Service Agreements (PSAs)**; **(3)** between the public sector and *voluntary sector* or, e.g. a university *research* department; or **(4)** consensual (i.e. not strictly contractual) arrangements to facilitate work with offenders, e.g: **(a)** as between a *probation officer* or member of a *youth offending team* (YOT) and an offender whereby requirements of a *community sentence* or *action plan* are implemented; **(b)** an **acceptable behaviour contract**: see *acceptable behaviour*; or **(c)** going straight contract: see '*going straight*'. The term also features re **(5)** the modern-day **contractual fine**: see *fine*.

control

CJS functions are sometimes described in the context of **social control**, or the work of the police, etc. as involving **crime control**; a concept with wider implications and that can be seen as self-perpetuating, see e.g. *The Culture of Control: Crime and Social Order in Contemporary Society* (2002), Garland D W, University of Chicago Press;

Crime Control as Industry (2000), Christie Nils, Routledge. Other allusions include **crowd control** when police seek to ensure public *safety* at events; **control centre**: see *police/policing*; **drugs control**: see *drug*; **control and restraint (C&R)** and **security and control** re both of which see *HM Prison Service*; *prison*; and **possession by having custody and control**: see *possession*. Note also 'out of control' for someone who knows no constraint*s* (and may be on an 'offending spree'); and **self-control** re *anger management*. Many other CJS departures are designed to **control behaviour**, especially re *violence* and/or crime prevention/crime reduction generally. For **border control**, see *border*. For **control order**, see *detention without charge*.

conviction

A word signifying that: **(1)** magistrates or a jury have found someone guilty of a criminal offence following a trial; or **(2)** that he or she has entered a guilty plea to a *charge/indictment*. Hence, also the word **convict** to describe a convicted *prisoner* (and hence **convict prison**, i.e. one where prisoners serve their sentences rather than wait for their trials on *remand,* although use of that term is mainly historical). For **appeal against conviction**, see *appeal*. 'Non-conviction' is a term sometimes applied (particularly in police circles) to a *fixed penalty* or other method of dealing with an offence that does not involve recording it as a crime: and see *no, non, not*. A **previous conviction** is one incurred on an earlier occasion, i.e. before the present conviction or the date when some new offence was committed, depending on the context. A **list of previous convictions** (if any) is produced to the court by the prosecutor after conviction and before sentence is passed. The rule that previous convictions were not admissible in *evidence* pre-conviction, i.e. to prove the present offence was relaxed by the *Criminal Justice Act 2003*; which also requires a court to **take previous convictions into account** when sentencing. They may also show, e.g. that an offender is in breach of an earlier sentence. An **unsafe conviction** will be quashed by the *Court of Appeal:* see *appeal*. See also *character and antecedents; Criminal Records Bureau.*

correction/corrections

(1) Correcting mistakes See *appeal; miscarriage of justice; rectification.* **(2)** Correctional Policy Framework: that within which sentencing *policy* is set by government. **(3) Correctional Services Accreditation Board/Panel**: descriptions applied to bodies charged with the *accreditation/*oversight of programmes, *courses* and *standards* in relation to generic *community sentences;* and similarly where these are delivered inside *prisons* (see, generally, those entries). In the context of **(2)** and **(3)** 'corrections' is an Americanism imported into the UK in modern times. It signifies 'correcting behaviour' through *punishment, treatment* and/or other CJS-related outcomes.

corruption

Under the **Prevention of Corruption Act 1906** (and later *legislation*), a gift to a public officer is deemed to have been corruptly given unless the contrary is proved by him or her (an example of when the burden of proof lies, unusually, with the accused person: see *evidence*). Across the past 30 years in particular there have been major corruption inquiries within certain police forces or prisons involving, e.g. *abuse of power*, bribery, *drugs* or perverting the course of *justice;* when individual officers have been prosecuted and in some instances convicted and sentenced to *imprisonment*; sometimes despite 'obstructive tactics' based, e.g. around the idea that certain illicit gains were simply 'perks'. Commissioners of the Metropolitan Police Service (MPS) who sought to tackle such matters were at times vilified for their efforts: see also *Touchstones*/'bent copper' (including for **noble cause corruption**). The offence of **misconduct in public office** applies across public services: see cps.gov.uk/legal and specialist works. From a different perspective there have been concerns about **corruption of the system**, e.g. when profits from *law enforcement* (e.g. speed cameras: see *road traffic*) have funded new resources; or *private sector* interests have urged *crime control* measures to enhance their investments. See also *Touchstones* under *basket justice; 'cash for honours'; Poulson, John* for diverse forms of **corruption in public life**. See also *miscarriage of justice* (*Main Entries*) and its links to CJS *denial* (*Touchstones*).

cost/costs

(**1**) The **costs of a criminal case** can be ordered to be paid by either party according to the outcome and circumstances of a case, known as **an award of costs** (or simply 'an award'). If a defendant secures an *acquittal,* or a case is *discontinued*, he or she is normally entitled to **costs from public funds;** or they can be ordered against the CPS (or other) prosecutor. Conversely, after conviction, the accused might expect to have to pay all or part of the **prosecution costs**, including of civilian *witnesses*. Courts can order *legal representatives* to pay **wasted costs.** For **bill of costs** and **taxation of costs**, see *bill/Bill; taxation*. (**2**) Contrast the concept of **costs and criminal justice**: the CJS as a consumer of public funds must like other public services be **cost-effective**: see *effectiveness and efficiency; financial aspects; value*.

counterfeiting (and forgery)

Historically, counterfeiting was a term associated with making false coins, banknotes, documents and other fakes, etc. i.e. the process via which these were made, and that in a modern context extends to other unlawful copying of such things as credit cards (sometimes called **cloning**); pirate CDs or DVDs (see also generally *piracy* and note a similarly 'romantic' backdrop to some varieties of counterfeiting); passports (see also *identity*/'identity theft'). Hence the term **coining** for the making of false coins or sometimes (when coins were made of gold or silver) paring metal from their edges. **Forgery** signifies the making or altering of documents, papers etc. with the intention to pass them off genuine (aka **'passing-off'**) and so as to defraud or deceive; aka making a **false instrument**, a term commonly used when the false item is a cheque, certificate or guarantee. Hence also 'uttering' a **false instrument**. Common forms of forgery include imitating someone's signature and the printing of counterfeit bank- notes. Such was the *fear* of forgers that, again under the Bank Act 1697, forgery attracted *capital punishment* (see generally *Touchstones*) (and over 600 people were executed under that statute in the early part of the 18th century); and at one stage it was punishable by mutilation (often involving having the ears severed and nostrils slit), plus *forfeiture* of estates and/or perpetual *imprisonment*. Early such offences included the counterfeiting of official seals (deemed to be *treason* by the Assize of Northampton (1176): see generally *Touchstones*), especially if 'directly against the King or a Lord'. Under Charles I, benefit of clergy (see *Touchstones*) was denied as a *defence* to forgery. After the first handwritten banknotes were issued by the Bank of England (1664) a forgery (of a £100 note) appeared within a fortnight, following which four men were each fined and ordered to stand in the *pillory* (see *Touchstones*) for 'cheating'; eventually leading to the 1697 Act above. In a unique CJS event, a Dr. Caleb Charles White was sentenced to imprisonment for two months and fined £50 in 1880 for forging a letter to stop an execution, that of a Charles Shurety. Notoriously, during the Second World War the German Nazi Government printed forged

English banknotes to the *value* of some £140 million to try and undermine British credit abroad (Operation Bernhard). There are various accounts of people who could, in former times, produce first-class forged notes by hand using pen and ink; whereas modern-day operations tend to be typified by their sophistication and level of quasi-commercial investment. **Art forgery** is a niche all of its own: art world *experts* having been frequently taken in by (sometimes) primitive reproductions and exhibitions displaying forged art as craft. Modern anti-forgery **legislation** began with the **Forgery Act 1913**. Other key developments include the **Forgery and Counterfeiting Act 1981**. Information abounds concerning a wide range of fakery and associated *frauds,* and the specialist methods and techniques employed in the *detection,* suppression and prevention of forgery, and can readily be found by searching the internet.

court

A **court proper** should be contrasted with other forms of tribunal charged with making decisions re *citizens,* i.e. in terms of the intrinsic nature of a **court of law**, its duty to observe particularly exacting *standards*, its powers and *jurisdiction*, and the status of those sitting in *judgement* (i.e. judges, juries and magistrates). For key references in this work, see *appeal; Crown Court; Court of Appeal; High Court; House of Lords; magistrates' court; Queen's Bench Division; Supreme Court.* **HM Court Service** (**HMCS**) is an executive agency of the MOJ whose remit is to 'deliver *justice*' with *effectiveness and efficiency.* Its role encompasses *administration* of the *magistrates' court, Crown Court,* and (together with a *Royal Courts of Justice* group) the *High Court* and *Court of Appeal:* see further hmcourts-service.gov.uk The Courts Act 2003 established area **Courts Boards** to work in *partnership* with HMCS. Their role is to give advice and make constructive recommendations to foster administrative improvements. They cannot question *judicial* decisions or the work of the judiciary: see Courts Boards Guidance (2005)(Cm. 6461). See also **Courts Martial**: under *military*. Court-related Acts include the **Courts Act 1971**; **Courts Act 2003**; **Courts and Legal Services Act 1990**; **Constitutional Reform Act 2005**; and various **Magistrates' Courts Acts** (all of which are referred to within appropriate entries).

The **Court of Appeal (CA)** (aka 'Appeal Court') deals only with appeals. It consists of two divisions, *criminal* and *civil* and is housed in the *Royal Courts of Justice* (but may sit elsewhere). Decisions are by a majority of the three judges of which it is usually composed (sometimes two). It may *refer* points of *law* to the *House of Lords* (from 2009 the *Supreme Court*). The **Court of Appeal (Criminal Division)** hears appeals from the *Crown Court* against conviction and/or sentence. A main significance of the CA is its *rulings* on matters of law and on appeals against sentence; the latter now needing to be understood in the light of the work of the *Sentencing Guidelines Council* (SGC); which in turn looks to the CA to provide *advice* through its *judgements*. Various CA judges have been tasked with providing advice to the SGC on aspects of sentencing. Key CA rulings are known as 'guideline *judgements*'; and most of its judgements appear in specialist *law reports*. CA Judges are styled *Lord Justice*.

cracked trial See *trial*; **credit for a guilty plea** See *sentence/sentencing.*

crime

A word which according to the context can mean **a specific criminal offence**, a **particular type of crime** or **crime in general**. Essentially, all crimes consist of actions, behaviour or events prohibited by the *criminal law* as opposed to lesser forms of wrongful, inappropriate or unacceptable behaviour (see *acceptable behaviour*). Classic texts point to the difficulties of further or abstract definition; even if it is relatively easy to identify the nature and ingredients of individual crimes such as *assault, criminal damage, theft, manslaughter, murder, road traffic offences* and *sexual offences*. A unifying feature is that an allegation of crime attracts the kind of procedures, processes, sentences and safeguards noted throughout this work (although a purist might point out that this is somewhat circular unless it is clear what a crime is to begin with). Among very many uses of 'crime', the following are particularly worthy of note.

An **attempt to commit a crime**, i.e. going beyond 'thinking about it' to put it into effect is equally an offence; as are certain preparatory acts, e.g. re *terrorism/terrorists*: see specialist works. The **Crime and Disorder Act 1998** is an example of crime-related *legislation*, aka a *Criminal Justice Act* (below). It introduced **Crime and Disorder Reduction Partnerships (CDRPs)** between the police, *local authorities* and other *partners* with a view to **crime prevention/crime reduction**: which is the umbrella under which such initiatives are usually discussed ('prevention' signifying, e.g. pre-emptive moves such as burglar alarms, *CCTV*, 'designing-out' crime through better town and rural planning, good street lighting and forms of *deterrence*; and 'reduction' not just such methods but broader strategies to confront *social exclusion,* improve *education* and regenerate run down areas (see also *Touchstones*/'broken windows')). The **Crime Reduction Programme (CRP)** is the general head under which such events occur. **Crime concern** is: (**1**) a preoccupation of *citizens* and government: see crimereduction.homeoffice.gov.uk; and (**2**) a reference to **Rainer Crime Concern**: see *Touchstones*. **Crime rates** measure the number/level of crimes over time: a basic indicator of the *performance* of the CJS or an agency/service; as published, e.g. in *Criminal Statistics* (CS) and the *British Crime Survey* (BCS). Thus, e.g. the first quarterly figures released in 2009 showed that whilst the number of *recorded crimes* was stable, possibly on a downward trend of three per cent and 'bottoming out' (contrast the rising *prison(er) population*) there were significant variations: *violence* down six per cent (CS); gun crime down 29 per cent (see generally *weapon*), car *theft* down ten per cent, *criminal damage* down eight per cent (all BCS); with rises of four per cent for domestic *burglary*, 16 per cent for *fraud* and forgery (see *counterfeiting and forgery*), 18 per cent for 'street *robbery*' and nine per cent for *drug* offences (CS). The BCS showed that the risk of becoming a victim of crime remains at a historically low level, despite *citizen's* concerns about *public order* and *drunkenness*. Some 46 per cent of people felt that *anti-social behaviour* was 'being tackled'. See further at homeoffice.gov.uk; and for *data* compiled for the MOJ re cases in court, justice.gov.uk **Crimestoppers** is an independent *charity* 'working to fight crime' (see crimestoppers-uk.org). **Crimewatch** a long-running BBC1 TV programme which *appeals* for help with unsolved crimes, including via a 'Most Wanted' feature. It also operates online where it is possible to view requests for help and respond: see bbc.co.uk/crimewatch. See also *Dando, Jill* in *Touchstones*. 'Crime' is a pre-fix for many other things, such as a **crime scene**, the standard description for the place (or 'venue') where an offence took place. In serious cases it may need to be secured and guarded (see *police/policing*/'cordon') to ensure its integrity and be *searched* by *scenes of crime officers* (SOCOs)

criminal

(**1**) Appertaining to *crime* in the sense described under that entry above and thus attracting the panoply of provisions, rules, laws, etc, that apply to such matters rather than lesser forms of conduct, etc. (**2**) Description of someone who has committed one or more **criminal offences**; but see the note on the use of this term in the entry for *offender*. A number of key contexts are noted below.

The **Criminal Cases Review Commission (CCRC)** has power to examine a suspected *miscarriage of justice* and to refer the case to the *Court of Appeal* (or other appropriate court). Until the 1990s, this was a function of the *Home Secretary* (acting under the royal prerogative: *see Crown*). Following the Royal Commission on Criminal Justice of 1993 and its examination of various high profile alleged miscarriages of justice, this was superseded by the creation of the CCRC (originally 'Authority'). The CCRC is an independent public body. It normally has 13 members who are appointed by the Queen (see generally *Crown*) on the recommendation of the Prime Minister; one of whom is designated as its chair. It has a chief executive and 90 or so staff. It can now consider cases heard in *magistrates' courts* or the *Crown Court,* and refer matters if it considers that there is a real possibility that a conviction would not be upheld. It does 'not consider innocence or guilt, but whether there is new *evidence* or *argument* that may cast doubt on the *safety* of an original decision'. It also investigates and reports on any matter referred to it by the Court of Appeal itself and assists the *Justice Secretary* re the prerogative of *mercy*. Its purposes include promoting public understanding of its role; and enhancing public *confidence* in the CJS: see further ccrc.gov.uk.

Criminal code refers to: **(1)** A codified body of law within which offences, procedures and associated provisions are set out, as per the Indian Penal Code (drafted under British rule). Aspirations for such a code for England and Wales have a long history but have never been fulfilled. Some work in that direction by the Law Commission resulted in drafts re various areas of the criminal law; whilst statutes such as the *Theft Act 1968* and *Criminal Damage Act 1971* are in codified form. The idea of a comprehensive criminal code resurfaces from time-to-time. Historically, it is associated with the judge and jurist Sir James Fitzjames Stephen (1829-1894) and his ultimately abortive efforts in this regard. **(2)** In a lesser sense, the entire body of criminal law, etc. that does exist. **Criminal damage (CD)** is the offence of intentionally or recklessly causing damage to property as prohibited by the **Criminal Damage Act 1971**. It exists in an *aggravated* form re *arson:* see that entry; or where life is endangered. Criminal damage charges attract special *allocation and sending* procedures based on the *value* of the damage (see specialist works). The **Criminal Defence Service (CDS)** provides *legal* assistance and *advice* to people in police *detention* or accused of crimes through a mix of contracts with private and salaried defenders so as to ensure *access to justice*. It operates under the auspices of the *Legal Services Commission* and uses *solicitors* with a franchise from the LSC or who work for the CDS to provide *legal aid*. For **Criminal Division**: see *Court of Appeal*; **criminal evidence**: see *evidence*; **criminal injuries compensation**: see *compensation*; **Criminal Investigations Department (CID)**: see *police/policing*. For **criminalisation**, see *Touchstones* and see *decriminalisation* (in *Main Entries*). For **criminal justice**, see the separate entry, below. The **criminal law** is contained principally in those *Acts* of Parliament which prohibit and define offences. There are also some Common Law offences, the most striking being *murder*. It also encompasses the **general principles of criminal liability**. These include the nature of an *actus reus* and *mens rea* and forms of *assisting crime, conspiracy, incitement* etc; as well as general or special *defences*. **Criminal policy** and **criminal policy framework** are terms associated with the overall direction and aims of the CJS: see generally *policy*. **Criminal procedure** is a topic in its own right covering the many arrangements for *commencing criminal proceedings,* processing or dealing with them and, e.g. *time limits*. It is normally contained in rules or regulations, i.e. delegated *legislation*. *Practice Directions* (PD) may also be issued from time-to-time by the *Lord Chief Justice* who heads a **Criminal Procedure Rules Committee (CPRC)**. A central provision is the **Criminal Procedure Rules 2005**; present initiatives being in the direction of a single *code* of procedure for all criminal courts leading to *effectiveness and efficiency* re criminal trials and *case management*. The **Criminal Procedure and Investigations Act 1996** deals with aspects of procedure as they relate to *investigations*. **Criminal record** means the record of an offender detailing his or her offences (aka 'previous convictions' or 'previous record': see *conviction; character and antecedents*). Hence the **Criminal Records Bureau (CRB)**, an Executive Agency of the Home Office, providing authorised access to *data* via its *disclosure* service (see that entry and crb.gov.uk). **Criminal statistics** record data such as the number, frequency and nature of offences within a given time frame. Some are published as official *Criminal Statistics* and are available at www.homeoffice.gov.uk; others by various CJS-related bodies, *research* departments and interest groups.

criminal justice

A term used in several contexts, but chiefly **(1)** to encompass the chain of events, activities, tasks or functions that make up the official *response* to offending and problems of *law and order*, including, e.g. crime prevention/crime reduction; the *arrest* and *prosecution* of suspects; the hearing of cases by the courts; sentencing and the *administration* and *enforcement* of court orders; *parole* and other forms of *release* licence. Other common nuances are: **(2) a dedicated form of justice that applies in relation to criminal cases** as opposed to *civil* or *administrative* ones: with its own laws, principles, procedures, codes, practices and thinking; **(3)** any of the outcomes flowing from decisions during the **criminal justice process**, e.g. whether to *interview* or *arrest* someone, *charge* them with an offence, grant *bail*, find them guilty, what sentence to pass, or - at the back end of that process (see *front end*) - whether to grant *parole,* etc. **Criminal Justice Act** (aka 'Crime Act') describes an Act of Parliament designated by that title, e.g. Criminal Justice Act 1948, 1991 or 2003; or more loosely any Act dealing with aspects of criminal justice (of which there have been around 65 since 1997). Examples noted elsewhere in this work include the **Criminal Justice Act 1948; Criminal Justice Act 1991; Criminal Justice and Public Order Act 1994; Crime and Disorder Act 1998; Criminal Justice and Court Services Act 2000; Criminal Justice Act 2003; Criminal Justice and Immigration Act 2008. Criminal Justice Board** is short for either the **National Criminal Justice Board (NCJB)** or one of 42 **Local Criminal Justice Boards (LCJBs)** nationwide), all *multi-agency* forums to coordinate CJS work: see further lcjb.cjsonline.gov.uk **Criminal justice process** is how some commentators preferred to describe the CJS in its less 'systematic' days, especially pre-MOJ. Thus, e.g. in 2002 the *Auld Report* (see *Touchstones*) stated: 'The word "system" ... is misleading. There is no "system" worthy of the name, only a criminal justice process to which a number of different Government departments and agencies and others make separate and sometimes conflicting contributions' (see *Chapter 8* of that report at criminal-courts-review.org.uk).

Criminal Justice System (CJS) is the description normally applied to the totality of the arrangements for criminal justice. Hence **CJS Online** a government web-site (address as above) where it is stated that the purpose of the CJS is 'to deliver justice for all, by convicting and punishing the guilty and helping them to stop offending, while protecting the innocent'. CJS Online also notes that the key goals of the CJS are: to improve *effectiveness and efficiency* in bringing offences to justice; to increase public *confidence* in the *fairness* and effectiveness of the CJS; to increase *victim satisfaction* and *witness satisfaction*; to consistently collect, analyse and use good quality ethnicity *data* to identify and address race disproportionality in the CJS (see *race/racicm*); and to increase the recovery of criminal *assets*. Under the heading 'Working Together to Cut Crime and Deliver Justice' CJS Online refers to the **Criminal Justice Strategic Plan** 2008-2011 against which all such developments now takes place and which sets out how the CJS agencies 'will work together to deliver a justice system which: is effective in bringing offences to justice, especially serious offences; engages the public and inspires *confidence*; puts the needs of victims at its heart; and has simple and efficient processes'. **Criminal Justice Unit (CJU)** is the name often given to a local working arrangement (usually) jointly staffed by the CPS/police that concentrates mainly on preparing cases for the magistrates' court (compare *Trial Unit*).

criminology

Criminology is the science or study of *crime* and *punishment* focusing principally on *causes of crime* and the *effectiveness* of approaches to it (exact definitions are likely to vary): all extensive topics in their own right, which overlap with aspects of *criminal justice* itself. It is the specialism of **criminologists** who will often have concentrated on a defined subject or area; ranging from fundamental or philosophical matters to practical, quite specific or applied forms of the discipline, frequently linked to *data* gathering, statistical analysis, *research* and evaluation. See also *evidence*/'evidence based practice': which bridges such investigation and everyday matters of *policy, strategy* and *best practice*. Some of the key themes of criminology are touched on in other entries in this work. For an overview of what is a diverse and multi-faceted subject, see the *Oxford Handbook of Criminology* (2007)(3rd. edn.), Macguire M, Morgan R and and Reiner R (eds.), Oxford University Press; *Sage Dictionary of Criminology* (2005)(2nd. edn), McLoughlin E and Muncie, J (eds.), Sage Publications.

cross-agency See *multi-agency*; **cross-examination** See *evidence*.

Crown

Under the UK constitution, prosecutions are brought and criminal justice administered in the name of the sovereign; who in turn enjoys *immunity* from prosecution: see generally *constitution/constitutional*; *Rule of Law*. Hence the use of R (for Rex or Regina), the prefix *Her Majesty's* (HM) and names such as **Crown Court** and **Crown Prosecution Service (CPS)**: see the separate entry below. Some CJS practitioners swear an **oath (or affirmation) of allegiance to the Crown**, e.g. judges, magistrates; as since 2007 do new British *citizens* (see that entry and also *affirmation; oath*); whilst police officers 'attest' to serve the Crown in a similar way. Many activities continue **in the name of the Crown** (which also exercises influence in various quarters); albeit the convention has long been for these to be nominal and discharged in practice by the Executive (apart possibly from decisions to wage war or touching directly on royal status); as with the **Queen's Speech**: see *Touchstones*; **royal assent** to *Acts of Parliament* before they become *law*; and the **royal prerogative** (including the **prerogative of mercy**: see *mercy*; *Privy Council*). In effect, 'royal' signifies the high status of certain actions and/or rank, the latter as with **royal commissioner** or **royal judge** (especially historically: to distinguish senior judges from *local* ones). Hence also **Royal Commissions** including the **Royal Commission on Criminal Justice** of 1991-93 chaired by Viscount Runciman of Droxford (and thus aka Runciman

Commission): 'To examine the *effectiveness* of the CJS in ... securing the conviction of those guilty of criminal offences and the acquittal of those who are innocent . . .'; which was required to look into (among other things) the conduct of *investigations*, the roles of prosecutors and *experts* and *defence* arrangements; the extent to which the courts might draw *inferences* from *silence*; and the powers of the courts to give *directions*. It also looked at the role of the *Court of Appeal* and the way in which alleged *miscarriages of justice* were investigated (by the Home Office at that time and see now that entry). It made 352 recommendations including for (what is now) an independent *Criminal Cases Review Commission* (CCRC). The **Royal Courts of Justice** are home to the *High Court* and *Court of Appeal* in The Strand, London (hence aka 'The Strand'). The **Royal Society for the Prevention of Cruelty to Animals (RSPCA)** and **Royal Society for the Protection of Birds (RSPB)** are examples of bodies with the royal imprimatur and *investigation* and *prosecution* functions. The Magistrates' Association (see *magistrate*) was granted a **Royal Charter** in 1962.

Crown Court

The Crown Court deals with *cases* at some 90 locations in England and Wales (aka **Crown Court Centres**). It replaced *Assizes and Quarter Sessions* in 1972 following the *Beeching Report* and Courts Act 1971: see *Touchstones*). The **administration of the Crown Court** is a function of HM *Court Service* (HMCS) (under the MOJ). **Crown Court circuit** is a description given to its regional groupings for *administrative/administration* purposes (originally based on historic Assize Court or Bar circuits). Each circuit is headed by a **Crown Court administrator** (aka **'circuit administrator'**); and each Crown Court Centre, of which there are 77 (2009), by a **Crown Court manager** (formerly known as a 'chief clerk'). The latter is responsible among other things for the running of his or her centre, including the listing of cases (see *list/listing*) and *witness care* (subject re *judicial* matters to the *direction* of a judge). A member of HMCS staff acts as a court clerk, calling on *cases*, swearing in *jurors* and *witnesses*, reading out the *indictment* and dealing with routine matters in court; and does not have to be a lawyer (though some are), nor does he or she give legal *advice* or carry out *judicial* functions (contrast *justices' clerk*). Some functions of court managers are quasi-judicial, but one of these, the *taxation of costs* (see that entry) has now been passed to a dedicated agency/service. For *allocation and sending* to the Crown Court, see that entry; **appeal to and appeal from the Crown Court**: see *appeal*; **Crown Court judge**: see *judge*/'circuit judge'; **role of the judge and jury**: see *judge*. Re its *jurisdiction* the Crown Court deals with relatively *serious offences*, the two to three per cent of *either way offences* that filter beyond the magistrates' court (including matters where the accused has chosen jury trial). It also deals with purely *indictable offences* such as *murder, manslaughter,* rape or *robbery*. These are sent straightaway to the Crown Court after the accused person is charged with the offence in the magistrates' court and initial matters of *bail* and *legal aid* have been settled. Certain *summary* matters can be dealt with by the Crown Court. It also deals with allegations of *grave crimes* re **juveniles**; and *committals for sentence* by magistrates (whilst this procedure subsists); and hears *appeals* from magistrates' courts (before a judge who may be aided by magistrates, i.e. but without a *jury*). For maximum Crown Court sentences, see *sentence/sentencing*. **Trial Unit (TU)** is a description frequently given to that part of the CPS which processes trial papers and matters, etc. Compare *Criminal Justice Unit* (CJU). The ancient **voluntary bill of indictment** remains a way of *commencing criminal proceedings* in the Crown Court following application direct to a *High Court judge*: see specialist works. See also *HM Inspectorate of Court Administration*.

Crown Prosecution Service (CPS)

The CPS is responsible for most public prosecutions in England and Wales and may take over any *private prosecution* or other *public prosecution*, but not where that would require *authorisation* by the *Attorney General*. It has a duty to consider prosecuting cases following police *investigations* ('police' here widely defined by statute). The governing provision is the **Prosecution of Offences Act 1985** under which the CPS was established and which places duties on the Director of Public Prosecutions (DPP) (the head of the CPS: below). **Specialist prosecutors** deal with certain types of offences, e.g. rape, *domestic violence, hate crime* or those involving juveniles; and there is a **Complex Crime Unit**. The **Code for Crown Prosecutors** explains day-to-day CPS functions, processes of decision-making and the CPS's relationship to the CJS (see generally *independence/interdependence*). There is a short form of the code and a more detailed version for internal use and which, due to sensitivity, is not generally available to the public. Otherwise, the code is widely used by the police, *lawyers* and certain other CJS practitioners. **Code tests** are applied when considering whether or not to prosecute (evidential; full code; public interest; and threshold tests: see cps. gov.uk). All prosecutors are styled **Crown prosecutor** whatever their rank (although senior Crown prosecutors also occupy management roles, including at headquarters). A **designated case worker** is a CPS employee qualified and authorised to deal with given matters in court. The **Director of Public Prosecutions** is the head of the CPS. He or she reports to the *Attorney General*, whose authority is needed re certain prosecutions (or the AG may prosecute himself or herself: see that entry). Inevitably, where decisions have had a political or similar import, the role has been *high profile* and decisions have needed to be made in the glare of the *media/press* spotlight; when a level of robustness has been called for. In Scotland, prosecutions on *indictment* are conducted in the name of the Lord Advocate (see *advocate*) by the *Crown Office*.

curfew See *bail; home detention curfew; generic community sentence*

custodial/custody

Umbrella terms used to signify situations whereby someone is held in a secure setting, whether in prison, police cells or elsewhere; the exact nature of which depends on, e.g. the person concerned, the stage of the proceedings and nature of the powers relied upon. Custody should be distinguished from *detention* in particular, albeit both involve *restriction of liberty* and the use of **custodial provision** in a broad sense. A **custodial sentence** must be distinguished from a **remand in custody** (see *remand*), including due to the different *prison/* regimes' used. Special arrangements exist re the custody of juveniles re which the *Youth Justice Board* makes the arrangements. For **custody minus, intermittent custody** and **custody plus** see the notes under *sentence/sentencing*. For **custody officer** see *police/policing* (but note this term may be used re *civilians* in that role). A **custody time limit** is a statutory limit on the time for which someone can be held pending their trial; to encourage the expeditious processing of cases by police and prosecutors. If the accused person is in custody, *either way cases* tried by magistrates must begin within 70 days (in some cases 56 days). Where such a case is sent to the Crown Court for trial, 112 days are allowed between the date when magistrates send the defendant to the Crown Court and *arraignment*. If a time limit expires, the defendant cannot be remanded in custody any longer for the offence concerned. He or she can still be prosecuted, but must be released, usually on *bail*, pending further stages (assuming the case is not *discontinued*). Time limits can be extended by a court for good reason. Practices exist to prevent a former *abuse* whereby if a time limit expired the accused might be 're-arrested' on a fresh 'holding charge'. Note also the term 'custody and control': see *possession*.

custom/customs

(1) **Custom and practice** are part and parcel of criminal justice in the same way that they are re other aspects of public life; filling gaps in formal or official mechanisms; in much the same way that inherent *discretion* operates: see that entry. **Customary law** was observed in primitive times as a predecessor of the Common Law, which emerged out of customary local practices. (2) For **customs duty**, see *Revenue & Customs*.

cybercrime See *Touchstones*

D

Dando, Jill See *Touchstones*

danger/dangerous

Various *legal* provisions and CJS arrangements seek to ensure public *safety* and *protection* from **dangerous offenders**: see those entries and, e.g. *Multi-agency Public Protection Arrangements* (MAPPAs); *indeterminate sentence for public protection* (ISPP); *life imprisonment*; *tariff*. Such offenders include psychopaths and people suffering from schizophrenia, insanity and other forms of *mental impairment* who may need *treatment* and/or to be detained in a special hospital rather than in *prison*: see also *medical aspects*; *psychiatry/psychology*. Other varieties of danger are *targeted*, e.g. by crowd control (see *control*); *health and safety* laws; *road traffic* laws (including re **dangerous driving**, etc.) and legislation re *borders* and *terrorism/terrorists*.

data

Recorded and stored *information*, especially as retained in an electronic **database**. In common with other aspects of daily life, the CJS has come to rely on (or is developing) databases; subject to **data protection laws** and the work of the *Information Commissioner* or **data protection officers** (as to which see ico.gov.uk); in some instances controversially, e.g. re *civil liberties*, issues of privacy, *surveillance*, etc., the sharing of information and the risk of confidential records entering the public domain, being damaged, proving inaccurate or being accessed by hackers (see, generally, *hacker/hacking*). Government plans for a **'superdatabase'** tracking all telephone and internet *communications* have brought mixed reactions: some commentators arguing that this would increase *safeguards* re crime prevention/crime reduction, others that it would allow the *State* to act intrusively on the pretext, e.g. of the *national interest* or by diluting *protections* as time goes by (see generally *function creep* in *Touchstones*); raising issues of *legitimacy* and proportionality. There has also been concern re the 'escape' of data (as in 2008, when prisoner records were lost by a *private sector* contractor). The Serious Crime Act 2007 allows **data sharing** between government agencies/services with the aim, e.g. of tackling *fraud*, *money laundering* and *serious crime*. The number of public *prosecutors* or *law enforcement* bodies who might be empowered to access such a database runs to several hundred. **Data matching** may include comparisons being made between, e.g. public, official or sometimes legitimately accessed *private sector* records. For some key databases, see *children*/'ContactPoint'; *Criminal Records*

Bureau; DNA; Driver and Vehicle Licensing Centre; identification/identity; Police National Computer (PNC). See also *Holmes* in *Touchstones*.

deception

An underlying ingredient or basis for various offences, including, especially, **obtaining property by deception** (section 15 *Theft Act 1968*) and **obtaining a pecuniary advantage by deception** (section 16: and subsequent similar provisions). But note that deception may also be integral, e.g. to a *fraud* or *conspiracy*; or to specific offences such as benefit fraud. The term **'police deception'** is sometimes used to describe the subterfuge that is essential to uncovering *evidence* of an offence, especially, e.g. re undercover policing, national *security* and/or *informers*.

declaration

A term used to describe: **(1)** a formal pronouncement or ruling, including one affecting the status of the law, i.e. a **High Court declaration** (see *appeal*); **(2)** a **declaration of incompatibility**: see *human right*; **(3)** a **statutory declaration**, i.e. a 'solemn declaration' by an accused person that he or she never knew of the proceedings against him or her before magistrates, which has the effect that the case is restarted.

decriminalisation

The situation which arises when behaviour, actions, omissions or events amounting to *ciminal offences* become no longer so. Just as offences can be created by *Act of Parliament* they can be abolished by that same process. Significant shifts of this kind over time include the decriminalisation of abortion (on medical grounds), gross indecency, i.e. homosexual activity between consenting male adults (1967) (a subsequent move to reduce that age to 16 being defeated in the *House of Lords* in 2000) and heresy. There is a significant lobby in favour of 'legalising' cannabis and other 'soft' *drugs* (something partially achieved via day to day policing or prosecution decision-making against taking action). See also the note on 'mercy killing' under *suicide*. Contrast **depenalisation**, i.e. downgrading or removing certain kinds of *punishment* but where the conduct, etc. remains an offence but at a lesser level (as when cannabis was downgraded to a Class C drug in 2005: before 're-upgraded' to a Class B drug in 2009). Compare also processes of *criminalisation* as outlined in *Touchstones*.

defence

(1) The answer by an accused person when *charged* or brought to *trial*, aka the **case for the defence**; either its general nature or exact content. The arrangements for **putting forward a defence** in court mirror those re the prosecution case (see under *trial*); but the defence normally has the last word, which **defence lawyers** regard as a valuable *right*. An accused person is not obliged to give *evidence* or call *witnesses* but since 1995 inferences can be drawn from *silence* (see that entry); and for duties of **defence disclosure** see *disclosure*. If there clearly is a **complete defence**, the CPS (or other prosecutor) should acknowledge this and *discontinue* the case. There are various **general defences** such as *mistake, consent* or lack of *mens rea* (including where applicable lack of knowledge); more specific ones such as **self-defence** when the accused claims he or she made a reasonable and proportionate *response* (see generally *reasonableness*) to some *threat*, or broad answers such as 'I didn't do it', 'It wasn't me' or 'I challenge you to prove it' (note also the nature of the *adversarial system* in *Touchstones*). **Special defences** may exist in given situations, such as *alibi*, diminished responsibility (see *mental impairment*) or provocation re a charge of *murder*, and dedicated **statutory defences** as contained in the Act creating the offence in question (usually), setting out situations in which conduct, etc. does not amount to that offence. These are often called 'exceptions': hence **'pleading the exception'**. See specialist works on *criminal law* for further information and examples of other defences. **(2)** The words **'the defence'** is often used to refer to the accused person's *legal* team and, e.g. any defence *experts*. See also *Criminal Defence Service*.

deferment of sentence See *sentence;* **deferred caution** See *caution.*

delay
The maxim is **'justice delayed is justice denied'** (see generally *justice*), hence initiatives to prevent delay at various stages of the criminal justice process, including, e.g. *case management*; the work of the *Criminal Procedure Rule Committee* (CPRC).

democracy
The CJS is both a consequence of and key component of an **open democracy** (sometimes called **western-style democracy** or a **liberal democracy**); under the Rule of Law and in which there is *accountability, openness, freedom of information, transparency* and an opportunity for *citizens* to influence the *State* via their political representatives; sometimes called **democratic engagement**. The *House of Lords* (as a whole: see that entry) has been criticised as **undemocratic**, i.e. because it is not **democratically elected**; albeit a proportion of its members are now appointed (by the Prime Minister of the day) rather than being hereditary peers; with further *reform* pending. Longer term aims for the **'democratisation'** of the UK are linked to notions of *Britishness* (see *Touchstones*); and in CJS-related terms, e.g. a broader-based *judiciary*, countering *social exclusion* and improved consultation before *rights* are altered. For the jury as a **democratic institution**, see *The Criminal Jury Old and New: Jury Power From Early Times to the Present Day* (2004), Hostettler J, Waterside Press.

demonisation See *Touchstones*

department/departmental
Either: **(1)** a **government department**, e.g. in a core CJS context the MOJ, Home Office, Office of the *Attorney General* and **Department For Children, Schools and Families (DCSF)**; or **(2)** a unit of an agency/service, etc. that styles itself thus, e.g. a **Criminal Investigations Department (CID)**: see *police*; Home Office department.

deportation
The removal from the UK by the UK authorities of an alien: **(1)** at the end of his or her sentence; **(2)** due to *border controls* at a port or airport if he or she is not entitled or free to enter the UK; **(3)** whose *leave* to remain in the UK has expired (when he or she is known as an 'overstayer'); **(4)** whose application for *asylum* has expired; or **(5)** at the behest of the *Home Secretary* as someone whose presence in the UK is 'not conducive to the public good': see further that entry. Contrast *extradition* which involves sending someone to another country at the behest of another *State*.

designation
The formal nomination or appointment of an individual, group or place, etc. for the

purposes of some task or purpose, as with a **designated case worker**: see *Crown Prosecution Service*; **designated police station**: see *police;* or a geographical area that has been designated for the purposes of an *exclusion order.*

desistence

Refraining from crime, avoiding becoming involved in offending; a term which usually connotes 'giving up' a former lifestyle. Hence, e.g. various theories concerning what has sometimes been styled 'life-course transition', pointing to the significance of life events in relation to offending, such as access to stable *employment*, relationships and opportunities (contrast, e.g. *social exclusion*). Similarly desistence from specific forms of behaviour, e.g. re consumption of *alcohol*; taking *drugs*. See, e.g. *Desistance from Crime and Deviance as a Turning Point in the Life Course* (2003), Mortimer J T and Shanahan M J, Springer (USA). Desistence is sometimes spoken of as *'going straight'*, around which a whole field of interest has developed: see further that entry.

destruction order See *sentence*/'ancillary order'

detection/detective

Detection is used in two contexts: **(1) detection of crime**, i.e. its discovery; and **(2)** solving crime through the **detection of suspects** (but see also *harvesting* in *Touchstones* when both processes occur simultaneously; as they also do if someone is caught 'red-handed'). Both forms are the focus of **detective work**, usually by **detectives** from a *police*/'Criminal Investigation Department (CID)', the *Serious Organized Crime Agency* (SOCA) or other specialist *law enforcement agencies*. Crimes are detected in various ways, e.g. due to a *report* by a victim or concerned *citizen*; *admissions*; *confessions*; the result of *forensic* tests (especially re *DNA*) and/or circumstantial *evidence*; *informers*; by *surveillance*; speed cameras (see generally *road traffic*); or following a *'cold case'* review. Much of this work is now *intelligence*-led, i.e. based on verified information/leads using and (also collated in) *databases* and recording systems (see, e.g. *Holmes* in *Touchstones* and *Police National Computer* (PNC)). **'Defective'** is *Underworld* and *prison slang* for detective (see *Touchstones* for both).

detention

(1) Police detention (or that of other authorised *law enforcement agencies*) of suspects as per the *Police and Criminal Evidence Act 1984* (PACE); aka **detention without charge**. Contrast **detention without trial** where a *citizen* is held without being brought to trial which can only occur in the form of a *remand* in *custody* (as opposed to detention as such) and which is subject to custody *time limits*. When someone is arrested (other than on a court *warrant*) and taken to a police station the custody officer (see *police/policing*) must *release* him or her unless there is enough *evidence* to support holding that individual for questioning. Release may be on (police) *bail* for that person to return to a police station later, See also *bail*/'street bail' which has the same effect. If on a compulsory periodic **review of detention** it becomes clear that detention is no longer justified the suspect must be released. But **further detention** can be authorised by a court up to a maximum of 96 hours in all by way of a **warrant of further detention** (see generally the *Police and Criminal Evidence Act 1984* (PACE) for intervening processes and time limits). Police powers have been greatly increased re *terrorism/terrorists* so that those involved can be held for up to 28 days (a move to increase this to 48 days being defeated in the *House of Lords* in 2008). Related to this, the **control order** re *terrorism/terrorists* as introduced by the Prevention of Terrorism Act 2005 allows the *Home Secretary* to make an order for detention based on *intelligence* (in effect when there is insufficient *evidence* for a prosecution) whereby the person concerned is made subject to stringent requirements going well beyond those normally associated with, e.g. *bail*. The order, which was introduced after a former system of **indefinite detention** of foreign/international terror suspects was held to be discriminatory (see generally *discrimination*) and disproportionate, has proved controversial. It is subject to *judicial* oversight under the auspices of the Special Immigration Appeals Commission (SIAC) (see generally *immigration*). (**2**) **Detention at Her Majesty's pleasure** (aka **detention for life**) can (or in some cases must) be ordered by the *Crown Court* instead of a sentence of *life imprisonment*); or re a *young offender* or someone who is unfit to plead or insane (see *fitness to plead; mental impairment*). (**3**) For **detention in a young offender institution**, see *young offender institution* (YOI). (**4**) For **detention in a special hospital** (or other hospital), see *mental impairment*. (**5**) For the **detention of foreign nationals** on account of their lack of visa or other permission to enter the UK in an **immigration detention centre** (aka 'holding centre'), see *asylum; immigration*. (**6**) For **home detention curfew**, see *home*. (**7**) For **detention for life** of juveniles, see under *grave crime*. The **detention centre order** was, until 1991, a form of custody for juveniles designed to provide a 'short, sharp, shock': see historical works.

deterrence

Discouraging people from crime, or 'putting them off crime', primarily by *punishment*. Some commentators point out that this can only 'work' if certain preconditions exist, principally re the offender's understanding of events and whether *fear* of punishment as opposed to the chances of *detection* affected his or her calculations. They also point to high re-offending rates, *displacement* theories and the failure of even *capital punishment* (see *Touchstones* for both of these) to deter people. Proponents of deterrent sentencing take a more pragmatic view and are as unconcerned with such niceties as they are with arguments against *zero-tolerance* (see *Touchstones*). Whatever the truth, a distinction must be drawn between **general deterrence** (things that may deter people in general, reinforced, e.g. by other crime prevention/crime reduction measures) and **individual deterrence** (e.g. whether an earlier sentence or the prospect of a heavier one due to *previous convictions* deterred someone). Anecdotal accounts regularly feature people who, having 'tasted imprisonment', vowed not to *risk* it again. Deterrence is a **statutory purpose of sentencing** (see *sentence/sentencing*). See, e.g. *Criminal Deterrence and Sentence Severity* (1999), von Hirsch A *et al*, Hart Publishing. Deterrence also occurs via those everyday precautions which discourage the commission of offences, e.g. *burglar* alarms and *CCTV*.

diminished responsibility See *mental impairment*

direction/director

The word **direction** is used to describe: (**1**) a form of instruction which may also amount to a formal and enforceable order of a court or other public authority and thus has the force of *law*, e.g. one given at a **criminal directions hearing (CDH)** or other *preliminary hearing* by a judge or magistrate requiring the parties to do certain things; (**2**) a **Practice Direction**, see that entry; or (**3**) the overall guiding of an agency/service or organization, including its **strategic direction**: see *strategy*. For **company director** see *disqualification*. **Director** or **Director General** is a description applied to various CJS positions, e.g. **Director General for Criminal Justice** and **Offender Management Strategy** as announced in 2008 with a remit 'to set the strategic direction (above) for *offender management* and regulate an increasingly diverse range of service providers and work with the *judiciary* on the proposals for a *Sentencing Commission*'. There is also a **Director General of Criminal Justice Information Technology**: see generally *technology*. For **Director of Public Prosecutions (DPP)** see *Crown Prosecution Service*; **Director of Probation** see *probation*; and **Director of the Serious Fraud Office** see *fraud*. Note also the term **directing mind** of an organization or *gang* which may be a basis of criminal liability or enhanced liability; and note also in this regard *manslaughter*/'corporate manslaughter'.

disadvantage

A generic term used to describe various negative features of the human condition, ranging across disability, deprivation, lack of opportunity, poverty, *mental impairment* and *social exclusion*. See also *marginal* in *Touchstones*. Various CJS and wider initiatives seek to counter such matters, including via the work of the *Cabinet Office*.

discharge

(1) A **discharge following acquittal**: see *acquittal*; *trial*. (2) A **discharge as a sentence**: see *sentence/sentencing*. (3) The act of **discharging a firearm, etc**: see *weapon*. (4) **Release from a prison** or other *custodial* institution: see *release*.

discipline

A term for: (1) various arrangements for *supervision*, disciplinary offences, *sanctions* and **punishments** beyond the courts of law, especially those relating to the work of an agency/service, profession (such as *barristers, solicitors* or the medical profession, including the General Medical Council (GMC)), trade or other self-regulating body; some examples of which appear within other entries. (2) The system of **prison discipline**: see *prison*. (3) Purported solutions to certain kinds of *offending behaviour*, particularly re the young, as with **parental discipline** (see *parent*); **school discipline** (see *school*). Note also **concerted indiscipline** to describe *civil disobedience*.

disclosure

(1) Revealing information, documents, reports etc. concerning aspects of a prosecution or *defence* case. Hence, e.g. **advance disclosure of the prosecution case** by the CPS to the defence before a decision is made concerning *allocation and sending*. The Criminal Justice Act 2003 amended the Criminal Procedure and Investigations Act 1996 which contained certain pre-trial disclosure provisions relating to both sides; notably re **disclosure of the defence case** so that this now extends to the making and updating of a 'defence statement' re the nature of the defence, any specific defence on which the accused relies, re points of *law*, including re the admissibility of *evidence* or *abuse of process,* and listing defence *witnesses* (including *experts*). The *Justice Secretary* can prescribe further matters. A court may draw *inferences* from shortcomings in defence disclosure; but cannot convict solely on that basis. Some commentators have expressed concerned that *civil liberties* are being eroded by such mechanisms. (2) **Disclosure of a pre-sentence report**: see *sentence/sentencing*. (3) **Disclosure of unused material.** Historically there were complaints that police or prosecutors withheld **unused material** which had it been disclosed may have assisted the defence. This featured in a number of *miscarriage of justice* cases. Since 2003 the prosecutor must disclose 'any prosecution material ... not previously ...

disclosed to the accused person and which might reasonably be considered capable of undermining the case for the prosecution … or of assisting the case for the accused'. Associated provisions place a continuing duty on the prosecutor to disclose such material and to keep the situation under *review*. Certain pre-existing disclosure requirements have also been replicated, including those re an *alibi* (see that entry). **(2)** Since 2002, following the Police Act 1997, the **Criminal Records Bureau (CRB)** provides authorised access and disclosure of information via its **disclosure service**; allowing organizations in the public, private and voluntary sectors to make safer recruitment decisions by identifying candidates who may be unsuitable for given work, especially that involving *children* or *vulnerable* adults. Organizations can ask successful job applicants to apply for one of two types of check depending upon the nature of the position, known as **standard disclosure** and **enhanced disclosure**: see crb.gov.uk **(3)** Note also **disclosure of information** under the *Freedom of Information Act 2000*.

discontinue/discontinuance

Terms referable to halting a prosecution, i.e. at the *discretion* of a Crown prosecutor (see *Crown Prosecution Service*) after a charge has been made and following a *review* of the *case file*. Discontinuance is not in itself a bar to further proceedings for the self-same matter (contrast *autrefois acquit/autrefois convict* noted under *acquittal*) nor does it bring into play the rules concerning *double jeopardy*. An accused person may in certain instances prefer that a prosecution continues so that he or she can secure an acquittal on the merits of the case and thereby 'clear his or her name'.

discount See *sentence/sentencing/*'credit for a guilty plea'.

discretion

A term central to various CJS processes, encapsulating the idea that people making decisions should do so according to their own *assessment* of the situation by taking all relevant matters into account. They should also discount irrelevant ones, act fairly (see *fair/fairness*) and so as to achieve , proportionality and *reasonableness*. Hence, e.g. **judicial discretion**: see that entry. As to **police discretion**, each individual police officer has what is known as 'original authority', i.e. he or she cannot be told to make an arrest but must use his or her own *judgement* and good sense; and **prosecution discretion**: see *Crown Prosecution Service*. Discretion should be actively exercised, and not evaded or ignored; unless constrained by *legal* and/or *mandatory* and/or *legitimate* supervisory *requirements*. For **inherent discretion**, see, e.g. *Home Secretary*; *judicial discretion*. For **discretionary conditional release**, see *release*.

discrimination

In a CJS context, unfair treatment of a person or group on the basis, e.g. of bias and prejudice (see generally *fair/fairness*); when it has often been associated, e.g. with the treatment of *black and minority ethnic* (BME) people, disability*, religion, gender, sexual-orientation, disadvantage, social exclusion* and *marginal* people (see *Touchstones*). Section 95 Criminal Justice Act 1991 requires the *Justice Secretary* to publish '. . . such information as he considers expedient for the purposes of . . . facilitating the *performance* by [persons engaged in the administration of criminal *justice*] of their duty to avoid discriminating against any person on the ground of race, sex or any other improper ground'. This applies to everyone in the CJS. Relevant materials have been published regularly since that date. The European Convention on Human Rights (see *human rights*) requires that all human rights are applied without discrimination.

displacement

The idea that *law enforcement* will not prevent crime as a whole, but shift some or all of it to another geographical area (aka **geographic displacement**: having more 'bobbies on the beat' may 'stop' offences but displace them elsewhere); or cause people to commit different types of offence that are less likely to be a *target* of the police, etc. (aka **target displacement**). For other forms of displacement including **tactical displacement** and **temporal displacement**, see www.crimereduction.homeoffice.gov.uk See also for a collection of related issues, *Theory for Practice in Situational Crime Prevention* (2004), Smith MJ and Cornish DB (eds.), Willan Publishing.

disqualification

(1) Various court powers exist to disqualify offenders, e.g. disqualification from acting as a **company director**; **driving disqualifications**: see *road traffic*; from **keeping an animal**. **(2)** Note also **disqualification of a judge or magistrate** on grounds of partiality or personal interest: see generally *fair/fairness;* or a **juror**: see *juror/jury*.

district judge See *judge*

diversion

Deflecting something from its ordinary course. Hence **diversion from prosecution**: see, e.g. *caution, warning and reprimand.* Various criminal justice approaches involve diverting offenders so that they are dealt with 'out of court', within less formal networks, including *referrals* which may also sometimes achieve that purpose. See also *road traffic*/'vehicle rectification scheme'. Some public bodies have the authority under particular Acts of Parliament to offer mitigated penalties (see *administrative fine*). Acceptance avoids the need for a prosecution and is a form of diversion. Note also **diversion from custody**. Both forms of diversion are also spoken of as *alternatives*.

diversity

The existence of difference in matters of everyday life, culture, etc; that has in modern times been associated with positive aspirations such as **encouraging diversity**; **respecting diversity** as well as negative ones of *discrimination*, inequality (see *equality; respect*) and unfair treatment (see *fair/fairness*). See also *Britishness* in *Touchstones*.

Divisional Court See *High Court*

DNA

Short for **deoxyribonucleic acid**: the genetic material of a living (or formerly living) cell which may be a unique form of *evidence* of *identification/identity*. DNA was discovered in the 1930s and brought into active use as a tool of investigation re the CJS from around 1984 onwards. The police may demand a DNA-sample from anyone who is *arrested* for a recordable offence (as well as taking their fingerprints: see *Touchstones*); whether the suspect agrees to this or not, by force if need be. Previously such events could only happen following charge or conviction respectively. The first of these changes together with other shifts in police powers has been partly responsible for generating a national **DNA-database** containing over four million **DNA profiles** (and hence also the term **DNA-profiling** to describe analysis of *samples*); albeit that in 2008 the European Court of Human Rights (see generally *human rights*) declared it to be a breach of Article 8 of the European Convention On Human Rights ('right to private and family life') for routine DNA-samples to be retained after *acquittal* or where no charge is brought; placing in jeopardy an estimated 850,000 of some four and a half million then held. **Low copy DNA** is obtained by scientifically enhancing microscopic or degraded DNA and **familial DNA** from a blood relative (see also *'cold case'* in *Touchstones*). DNA science and technology has revolutionised police work and is automatically relied on in practice whenever there is an arrest.

dock

The place in the *courtroom* - often a raised, timber-framed construction, sometimes incorporating (bullet proof) glass; where an accused person, especially a *prisoner,* sits/ stands during *criminal proceedings.* This is a matter of convention rather than law; some courtrooms having no dock even if **'in the dock'** may still be used metaphorically: as it is in non-CJS situations in which 'a finger is pointed'. **Dock brief** is the the name of the historic entitlement whereby a defendant in the dock can ask any available robed *barrister* in court to represent him or her for a modest fee (originally half a crown, 22.5 new pence), still extant but little used since the advent of *legal aid.* The inventive term **'dock asthma'** is sometimes used by *prisoners* to refer to mock gasps of surprise by an accused person at accusations made during a trial.

doctor See *medical aspects; mental impairment; psychiatry/psychology.*

document

Anything in written form; the contents of which may be admissible in *evidence.* This may be as: an exception to the *hearsay* rule; a *witness statement*; or *exhibit:* to prove its own existence, e.g. as a forgery (see *counterfeiting and forgery*) or *blackmail* demand.

doli incapax See *Touchstones*

domestic

A matter relating to: **(1)** a *State* as opposed, e.g. to the European Court or an international tribunal. Hence the term **domestic court** (sometimes called a 'national court'); or **(2)** certain family proceedings, especially in the magistrates' court, i.e. civil matters re partners or children. Hence also **(3) domestic violence**, i.e. *violence* within a family setting (aka *abuse*), usually re a child, partner, spouse, elder or relative; as per the **Domestic Violence, Crimes and Victims Act 2004** which contains a range of related provisions, including with regard to *harassment* and which makes breach of a civil non-molestation order a criminal offence: see, generally, *civil behaviour order.* Victims of domestic violence suffer on many levels, e.g. re their *health, home, education* or ability to continue with *employment.* Very many initiatives have taken place in this field, including the creation of **women's refuges** and *advice centres.* In announcing a **Domestic Violence Action Plan**, the Home Office describes such violence as 'any incident of threatening behaviour, violence or abuse between adults who are or have been in a relationship together, or between family members, regardless of gender or sexuality. [It] occurs across society, regardless of age, gender, race, sexuality, wealth and geography [but] the figures show, however, that it consists mainly of violence by men against women'. For further details and official **domestic violence helplines**, see homeoffice.gov.uk under 'Domestic Violence'. Note also connections between domestic violence and *mental impairment*: see that entry. Other useful resources can be accessed via Women's Aid at womensaid.org.uk

double jeopardy

(1) The historic Common Law rule preventing someone from being tried a second (or third, etc.) time for the self-same matter; essentially a rule against 'double *punishment*'. The classic terminology is: *autrefois convict* following an earlier conviction; and *autrefois acquit* following *acquittal*. In modern times, debate has been linked to events in the wake of the racist *murder* of Stephen Lawrence: see *Lawrence, Stephen* in *Touchstones*. The rule is grounded in the need for finality of proceedings and the idea that a prosecutor should not have 'two bites at the cherry', which could lead to lax standards and lack *fairness*. But with advances in *science* and *technology* and the potential for more reliable re-*investigation* than in the past, such pragmatic arguments have perhaps tended lose ground. Since *2003*, the rule does not, in any event, apply re certain more *serious offences* (which is seen as a key indictor of inroads into *civil liberties*). **(2)** The situation where a *foreigner* faces punishment in his or her home country as well as in the UK; as per a notorious 2004 Nigerian 'Decree 33' re *drug* couriers allowing them to be punished afresh on their return to that country.

drug

Many drugs are **controlled drugs** under *legislation* re the **misuse of drugs** (notably the **Misuse of Drugs Act 1981** and Medicines Act 1985). For an introduction to this wide-ranging topic, see *Misuse of Drugs: A Straightforward Guide to the Law* (2007), Jason-Lloyd, Waterside Press. They are available only on medical prescription, or in some cases not at all. Hence the terms **prohibited drug** or **proscribed drug** re which, e.g. possession, sale, supply or manufacture are normally offences (except, e.g. under licence; or when the police are lawfully seizing drugs). The intrinsic *seriousness* of a **drug offence** depends on the **classification** of the drug concerned: Class A (**hard drug**), B (sometimes styled 'hard') or C (**soft drug**). Classifications may change over time, sometimes causing controversy re 'downgrading' or 'upgrading': as per modern-day *arguments* about cannabis and ecstasy (always check specialist sources for the latest position). Note also **designer drug** for one newly invented to imitate an existing drug; which may be in vogue/lawful for a period then again replaced 'one step ahead of the law'; and **recreational drug** a *euphemism* that also encourages *normalisation*: see *Touchstones* for both. A **drug action team (DAT)** is a pro-active *multi-agency* team dealing with drug users and *referrals*. **Drug dealer** refers to a supplier (and hence also **drug deal** for the transaction concerned), usually meaning one at street level as opposed to a **drug baron**, someone behind or higher up in the **drug chain**. **Drug dependency** is a form of *addiction* (see generally *Touchstones*) (and hence also **Drug Dependency Unit (DDU)**). For **drugs squad**, see *police*; **mandatory drug-testing** and **voluntary drug-testing** of *prisoners*: see that entry. Nowadays, **drug testing** may occur under provisions giving police the power to test people who are in *detention* or *custody* for drugs or courts to order drug testing. Modern-day portable ('hand held') drug testing kits are routinely in use in some countries and under discussion for use in the UK (if not already in use in some locations). A **drug treatment** requirement can be included in a *community sentence;* replacing an earlier **drug testing and treatment order (DTTO)** introduced by the Crime and Disorder Act 1998 involving intensive *supervision*-cum-contact coupled with drug treatment, regular drug-testing and review. See also *prisoner*/'CARATS'.

The **drug culture** has given rise to many drug-related slang terms (often changing and 'secretive' in nature, or based around *euphemisms*: see generally *Touchstones*). **Drug-related issues** of criminal justice arise in many ways and from a range of perspectives. Among many other strands they include: **(1)** the vast range of further (or 'secondary') drug-related offences, including **drug trafficking**: re which, see, e.g. *Drugs Trafficking and Criminal Policy: The Scapegoat Strategy* (1998), Green P, Waterside Press; *Drugs, Victims and Race: The Politics of Drugs Control* (2006), Kalunta-Crumpton, Waterside Press; and more broadly *Drugs* (2008), Bean P, Willan Publishing; **(2)** whether *treatment* or *punishment* is appropriate for **drug users**, linked to questions of *rehabilitation* in particular; **(3)** the role of drugs as a *cause of crime* (i.e. other offences such as *theft, burglary* or involving *deception*), in part due to the present underground nature of the **drugs world** and/or the cost of drugs, effectively on the *black market* (see *Touchstones*); **(4)** links to *organized crime* and *money laundering* in particular together with a failure thus far to adequately *target* the head of the supply chain (but see now the work of the *Serious Organized Crime Agency* (SOCA)); **(5)** *defence* issues where the accused may have been under the influence of drugs at the time of the events in question, thus raising questions about culpability and/or *mens rea*; or re *mitigation* and *sentencing*; **(6)** the wider debate re such matters as geo-political influences beyond direct UK control; and **(7)** *decriminalisation*. **Release** (founded 1967) offers specialist services to professionals and the general public re drugs and the law. A *charity*/company limited by guarantee, it operates *helplines* and provides free, professional, non-judgemental, confidential advice to drug users, their families, friends, the CJS and other *public sector* agencies as well as the *voluntary sector,* so as 'to promote understanding of drug-related issues and to support an often marginalised section of society': see www.release.org.uk and also the entry for *marginal* in *Touchstones*. For a high profile drug-related case concerning **drug manufacture**, see *Julie (Operation Julie)* in *Touchstones*. See also *Touchstones*/'RAPt'.

due process

The principle of 'due process' has a lesser profile in England and Wales than it does, e.g. in the USA, where it rises to the status of a constitutional principle (see generally *constitution/constitutional*). But the term is increasingly used in the UK and English law does require that, e.g. *interviews, arrests* and court or other processes occur under the Rule of Law; and the *legitimacy* of many procedures can be tested by way of an *appeal* when a conviction may be invalidated. This is now reinforced by *human rights*. There have, however, been government-led suggestions that 'mere technicalities' should not be a basis for an *acquittal*. On what basis remains obscure.

duty solicitor See *Criminal Defence Service*

E

early release (from prison, etc) See *release*

education/education services

Lack of education is a key indicator in relation to the *risk* of offending and the provision of education, especially for those who are at-risk, an integral part of crime prevention/crime reduction, e.g. in *prison* (where the main provision is directed towards the acquisition of basic skills and 'cognitive skills': see specialist works) and re both prison and *community* programmes, e.g. *alcohol* or *drugs* education; it being recognised generally that **lack of education** is a form of *disadvantage,* which may well manifest itself in later life. For an interesting perspective, see *Criminal Classes: Offenders at School* (1995), Devlin A, Waterside Press. See also *prison(er)/*'education'. The **Department For Children, Schools and Families (DCSF)** (see generally that entry), **Department for Employment and Learning** and **local education authorities (LEAs)** are involved in aspects of the criminal justice process, including at a *local* level through *schools,* teachers, preparation of **school reports** and *youth offending teams* (YOTs). LEAs may also bring *prosecutions* against parents for **school non-attendance** (aka 'truancy'); provide *help and support* to prisoners/ex-prisoners or people on *community sentences*; as well as being involved in a range of *multi-agency* schemes and *partnerships.* See also the entry for *school.*

effectiveness and efficiency

Two key aims of the CJS (or its parts) and an aspect of *accountability.* Debates arise re what is effective/efficient in CJS terms, i.e. and whether, e.g. the measure should relate to outcomes, economics, social *control* or other factors. Key reference points are *crime rates* and *re-offending*; whilst closely associated fields include evidence-based *research, performance, value for money* (VFM) and *'what works'* (see *Touchstones*).

either way offence

One that can be tried in the magistrates' court or the *Crown Court,* depending on the outcome of a procedure now known as *allocation and sending* (aka historically 'mode of trial'). Either way offences include: *theft; handling stolen property*; various *deceptions* and *frauds; burglaries; criminal damage* where the *value* is high; *assault* occasioning actual bodily harm (ABH); and the possession or supply of certain prohibited *drugs.* See, also, *plea before venue; committal for trial* and *committal for sentence.*

election for trial by jury See *allocation and sending*

electronic monitoring (aka 'tagging' or EM)

(1) *Monitoring* (see generally that entry) that takes place from a remote control room via an electronic tag which is attached to the wrist or ankle (usually) of an offender or accused person as part of (or alongside) a generic *community sentence, home detention curfew* or a control order (see *detention*). **(2)** Similarly the tagging of animals or personal property including re crime prevention/crime reduction. See, also, *global satellite positioning* (GSP). See also generally the entries for *monitoring* and *surveillance.*

Ellis, Ruth See *Touchstones;* **employment** See *work*; *prisoner/*'work'; **endorsement of a driving licence** See *road traffic*; *sentence/*'ancillary order'; **end-to-end sentence** See *sentence/sentencing.*

emergency

A word with many CJS-connotations, many offences being themselves in the nature of an emergency and requiring the *intervention* of the police, etc. particularly re *violence,* many *sexual offences, threats* and *public order.* Other usages include: **(1)** a **defence of emergency** or 'necessity', i.e. to avoid a greater *evil* (see *Touchstones*): see generally *defence*; which if it fails as such may still be *mitigation*; **(2)** an **emergency call,** aka '999 call' (since the 1930s) or **non-emergency call,** i.e. 101 (modern times) (or as published locally); **(3)** a **state of emergency,** assumption of **emergency powers,** the passing of (temporary) **emergency legislation** and suspension of *habeus corpus* (see *Touchstones*); **(4) an emergency court** held outside usual hours (aka a 'special court'); **(5) an emergency protection order (EPO)** made in the family court (a *civil* order to protect a partner or children, including from *domestic violence*); or **(6)** the **emergency services**, including local fire services and ambulance services.

enforcement

The modern-day CJS has seen an emphasis on both **law enforcement**: the pursuit of offenders by the police and other **law enforcement agencies** and the **enforcement of court orders**; with a concerted effort across-the-board and including the courts, *probation* staff and other practitioners to make sure that action occurs re, e.g. *fine default* or breach of a *community sentence*. Similarly by the police, e.g. to ensure that recalcitrant offenders do not abscond (see *abscond/absconding*). For the **enforcement of sentences**, see *fine*/'enforcement'; *sentence*/'enforcement'.

equality

A word which is encountered repeatedly to signify longstanding *value*s of parity and egalitarianism, as per expressions/principles such as: **(1) equality of arms**: which requires that each party has a reasonable chance to present his or her case and without being placed at a disadvantage vis-à-vis an opponent (and which overlaps with ensuring a fair trial: see *fair/fairness*; and **(2) equality of treatment**, re allcomers, whether as individuals, agencies/services, groups, organizations, etc. The **Equality and Human Rights Commission (EHRC)** established under the **Equality Act 2006** (from October 2007) is a landmark along the route to ensuring a fairer society altogether. It works to eliminate *discrimination*, reduce **inequality**, protect *human rights*, build good relations and ensure that everyone has a fair chance of participating in society. Its work follows on from that of the **Equal Opportunities Commission (EOC)**, **Commission for Racial Equality (CRE)** (see *race/racism*) and the Disability Rights Commission (DRC). It also assumed a range of **equality responsibilities**, e.g. re *age, gender, sexual orientation, religion* or belief. It has various *law enforcement* powers and a remit to promote understanding of human rights. Various CJS-related agencies/services have **equality policies** and/or published **equality statements**. There is also an **Equal Treatment Benchbook**: see *Judicial Studies Board*.

equivocal plea See *plea*

ethnicity

Many CJS references touch on a person's ethnicity and the right to *respect* and *equality* of treatment in that and other regards; and also the self-explanatory term **black or minority ethnic (BME)** for people who belong to such groups. See generally *disadvantage, discrimination, social exclusion* and the entry for *marginal* in *Touchstones*.

European Convention On Human Rights; European Court of Human Rights
See *human rights* for both; **Europol** See *police/policing*.

evidence

(1) *Information, data*, statements or 'things' capable of supporting an inference of fact or *opinion* which are underwritten by *legal* procedures, usually involving *oath, affirmation, testimony* or certification, aka 'proof'. Hence the **law of evidence** which applies to this specialist field; re which texts on that subject should be consulted, e.g. *Cross and Tapper On Evidence* (11th edn. 2007), Tapper C (formerly Cross, R), Oxford University Press; *Archbold* (see *Touchstones*). Key aspects include the **burden of proof**: which rests on the prosecutor in a criminal case and must be discharged to the requisite **standard of proof**, i.e. beyond reasonable doubt (and see *Woolmington v. DPP* in *Touchstones*). Exceptionally, the law reverses this onus and the accused person must then establish something (e.g. that he or she had permission or re certain statutory *defences*); when the standard falls to the lesser *civil* standard ('on a balance of probabilities'). **Criminal evidence** is the term usually used to describe that part of the law of evidence which applies to criminal trials: when more stringent **rules of evidence** exist than re civil cases. Some longstanding rules have been changed or adapted, including by the *Criminal Justice Act 2003*, to allow greater leeway, e.g. re: **hearsay evidence**, i.e. evidence other than that given first-hand in the courtroom from memory by a *witness* who knows directly about the events in question; and **evidence of bad character**. An **exhibit** is a 'thing' such as a *weapon, drug, sample* or a letter containing a *threat*. Evidence may also take the form of an **exhibit**, i.e. a physical 'thing' (aka **real evidence**) which is **'produced in evidence'** by a witness (or under other *procedures*). Note also **hard evidence** to describe strong, possibly unassailable evidence (or sometimes a physical exhibit above). There is a revised *discretion* to disallow **prejudicial evidence**. For **confession evidence** see *confession*. Crown prosecutors apply an **evidential test** (among others): see *Crown Prosecution Service*. **Cross-examination** is the *forensic* technique whereby *barristers* or *solicitors* ask questions of a witness called by the opposing party after that witness has given his or her **evidence-in-chief** at the behest of the party calling him or her within the *adversarial system* (see *Touchstones*); a main purpose being to test, undermine or contradict what the witness has said or show that he or she is mistaken or unreliable. Cross-examination may be followed by **re-examination** by the original questioner to clarify matters arising from cross-examination. An **evidentiary ruling** is one by a judge or magistrates as to whether something is **admissible evidence** or **inadmissible evidence**, or concerning some other **point of evidence** (see also *appeal*). **Turning Queen's evidence** (or **'going Queen's'**) is a tag for a witness who might have been prosecuted but who gives evidence for the prosecution against a co-accused (usually), in the expectation of *leniency* or in an extreme situation *no further action*. **Video-recorded evidence**: that recorded, e.g. by CCTV or a video-recorder with a *witness* (as opposed to **live links**, i.e. usually a TV link from a prison or abroad to a courtroom; where such evidence is admissible: see specialist works). **(2)** The terms evidence and proof are also used re other processes, e.g. *research* as per **evidenced-based practice**. See *effectiveness and efficiency*; *'what works'* (in *Touchstones*)

evil See *Touchstones*; **examination** See *evidence*; *medical aspects*; **excess alcohol** See *road traffic*.

exclusion order

An order issued by the police or a court banning someone from a particular place or area at a given time or times. Hence, also, **exclusion zone**. See specialist works.

exhibit See *evidence*

expert

(1) An individual qualified in a particular field and thus able to proffer an *opinion* relating to his or her area of expertise. Experts of many kinds feature in criminal cases, such as doctors, psychiatrists, psychologists (see *medical aspects; psychiatry/psychology*), *forensic* experts, traffic examiners (see *road traffic*) and professionals including *lawyers* (i.e. **legal experts**) and others who routinely work within the CJS. The police, courts and others frequently rely on **expert reports** and/or **expert evidence**: see further *witness/*'expert witness'. (**2**) Note also **'criminal justice experts'**. Traditionally, considerable store was placed on the views of experienced practitioners and *criminologists* as advisers or innovators. This changed from the early-1990s as the notion arose that such people could be an impediment to 'progress'; coupled with a shift towards active decision-making by *Ministers of State* rather than civil servants. For an analysis see 'Better Government: More Justice, Success and Failure in Criminal Justice, 1992-1998', Faulkner D, Centre for Crime and Justice Studies (forthcoming 2009).

extended sentence for public protection (ESPP) See the note under *indeterminate sentence for public protection* (ISPP)

extradition

The process by which a foreign *State* requests that an individual be sent to it (or possibly a third country) for trial on a criminal charge. Issues have arisen in modern times re extradition to the USA especially, in that only minimal grounds and not necessarily reliable *evidence* are required for this purpose; in contrast to extradition from the USA to the UK. For a case in which such a request was resisted, see *hacking*.

F

fair/fairness

The CJS including the courts are guided by principles of fairness.. Historically these were grounded in the twin rules of **natural justice**, i.e. **no-one can be a judge in his or her own cause** (aka the rule against bias); and **hear both sides** (an aspect of 'even-handedness'). Fairness is now guided by *human rights*, especially the **right to a fair trial** in Article 6 of the European Convention On Human Rights. Anyone *charged* with an offence must be informed promptly, in a language that he or she understands, of the nature and cause of the accusation and given adequate time and facilities to prepare a defence (including via *legal* assistance and if appropriate *legal aid*). he or she must be allowed to examine and call *witnesses*; and to use an interpreter if necessary. Article 6 touches on all aspects of the criminal process, from *investigation*, to trial, sentence, *prison/*'discipline', *release* and *parole*. It states: 'In the determination of his civil *rights* and obligations or of any criminal charge against him, everyone is entitled to a fair and public hearing within a reasonable time by an independent and impartial tribunal established by law'. Article 6 also contains a *presumption of innocence*: see further that entry. Another effect is that a duty arises to give *reasons* and explanations. **Fair Trials Abroad** is a UK-based organization working internationally re those facing charges in a country other than their own. See fairtrials.net

fear

(**1**) Fear may be a basis for or ingredient of an offence, as where someone is placed in fear due, e.g. to threats or *blackmail*. (**2**) From one perspective, public *confidence* in or satisfaction with the CJS can be weighed by assessing general levels of **fear of crime**, whether *citizens* feel safe and believe (as opposed to necessarily know) that crime is increasing or decreasing. A key vehicle for this is the *British Crime Survey* which has regularly demonstrated that fear of crime tends to outstrip the actual *risk* of becoming a *victim*, especially re *serious crime*. **(3)** Playing on people's fears is a common *political* and/or *media/press* or Government ploy; and potentially an agent of social *control*.

Federal Bureau of Investigation (FBI)

The investigative branch of the USA Department of Justice, i.e. at federal rather than *State* level; established in 1908 by Attorney General Charles J. Bonaparte (1851-1921). Its original function was the *investigation* of 'violations' of federal law. It now also assists police forces and other *law enforcement agencies*, especially re *serious crime* and provides support to other States, including the UK; using state-of-the-art or what is sometimes called '*military grade* technology'. Hence also **FBI-style** to describe the *Serious Organized Crime Agency* (SOCA); and **FBI-tactics** re, e.g. *surveillance*.

financial aspects

The financial implications of CJS decision-making have been closely scrutinised in modern times in keeping with economic trends in financial *accountability* generally. CJS income, e.g. from *fines* or money realised by the seizure and sale of criminal *assets* occurs separately from decision-making; albeit concerns have arisen of vested interest, e.g. where income from speed cameras (see *road traffic*) is re-invested in CJS resources, or *agencies/services* need to compete with each other for resources. Under section 91 Criminal Justice Act 1991, the *Justice Secretary* has an obligation to keep people involved in the *administration of justice* informed re related financial implications.

fines and financial orders

Fines are monetary penalties imposed by a court (but the term can also be viewed as including *fixed penalties*: see that entry). **Financial orders** are matters such as *compensation*, *costs* or fees (rare now in criminal cases). Fines are unlimited in the *Crown Court* (but must be *reasonable* and proportionate). In the magistrates' court, maximum fine *values* occur on five levels, a **level five fine** (the highest) having a ceiling of £5,000 per offence (April 2009). The level re a given offence is set by the Act of Parliament creating the offence (usually). The court sets payment terms, e.g. forthwith, within a month, weekly/monthly (or, e.g. a substantial sum to be paid before *release* from a sentence of *imprisonment*, failing which time, sometimes years, will be added to it). The **collection of fines/other financial orders** occurs via the magistrates' court; as does **fine enforcement** (aka a **means inquiry**) when a defaulter is summonsed to court and given an opportunity to explain the non-payment. The main **enforcement methods** are: an attachment of earnings order (AEO), i.e. requiring an employer to make wage/salary deductions and send these to the court; distress *warrant* (sending in the bailiffs); money payment *supervision* order (MPSO) under the National Probation Service (NPS) (see generally *probation*); attachment of *State* benefits; or *committal* to prison for wilful refusal to pay, but only after a further *review* if committal is suspended on terms (e.g. 'seven days suspended on payment of £20 a week'). Maximum committal periods reflect the amount unpaid on a statutory scale. A defaulter can 'buy himself or herself out' of **imprisonment for default** by settling the balance due. Some 20,000 committals occur each year, often for short periods (and unnecessarily say bodies such as the *Prison Reform Trust*: see *Touchstones*). People such as *foreigners*, can be imprisoned straightaway if unlikely to remain in a place in the UK long enough for standard enforcement methods to be pursued; but there are now better

reciprocal enforcement arrangements as between some *States*. In other situations a vehicle can be seized (see generally *seizure*) and sold. Magistrates and certain officials can vary terms of payment and the former can in some circumstances order **remission of fines**, etc. (i.e. their cancellation or reduction: but not normally re compensation without consulting the victim). The court can compel *disclosure* of means by a **financial circumstances order**. An **administrative fine** is one levied by a body authorised to do so by law, such as HM *Revenue & Customs*; as an *alternative to prosecution*. In 2008, e.g. it was reported that some 60 *barristers* had agreed to pay such fines, back tax (see *taxation*) and surcharges totalling more than £500,000. Such fines are commonplace across a whole range of public bodies (see generally *administrative/administration*) including the Financial Services Authority (FSA) and *Health and Safety Executive* (if rarely reported in the *media/press*). **Contractual fine** is a misnomer for a *civil* contractual penalty within the burgeoning *security* industry, i.e. operated by the *private sector*; such as a penalty charge for 'overstaying' in a car park, wheel clamp release, based on contractual terms, e.g. that someone is deemed to have agreed to by entering a shopping complex. For **'on the spot fine'**, see *fixed penalty*.

fingerprint See *Touchstones*; **firearm** See *weapon*; **fitness to plead** See *mental impairment*.

fixed penalty

Minor misdeeds (aka *low-level* misbehaviour) and/or aspects of *anti-social behaviour* may be dealt with by way of (official) **fixed penalties** issued by the police, wardens or other authorised persons and notified to the offender in a **fixed penalty notice** (contrast administrative fines: see *fine*). These are styled 'non-convictions' in certain *records*, including on the Police National Computer (PNC). The person concerned can *appeal* to a magistrates' court when the notice is in effect replaced by prosecution, re which a conviction *will* rank as such (hence there is a built-in disincentive). Note also the **fixed penalty notice for disorder (FPND)** (aka simply **penalty notice for disorder (PND)**) of which just 1,000 were issued in 2006, but some 500,000 by 2008.

football

Usually in a CJS context a reference to soccer as opposed to rugby football. 'Foteballe' (along with 'hokkying') was banned in 1406 and again in 1586 when it became an offence and players were sentenced to *imprisonment*. In modern times, **football hooligan** (see also *Touchstones*/'hooligan') is a term that has been applied to 'supporters' involved in riots, *drunkenness, criminal damage, violence* and racism (see generally, *race/racism*), etc; re which English supporters abroad have an indifferent reputation. In the 1970s, events led to the Federation of International Football Associations (FIFA) banning English clubs from Europe for five years following the Heysel Stadium disaster (1976); when Liverpool FC were playing and 40 spectators were killed. Since the Football (Disorder) Act 2000 and subsequent *legislation* a court must make a (criminal) **football banning order** if the offender is convicted of a football-related offence re a 'regulated football match' (one at home or abroad involving a team from the Premier League, Championship, League One, League Two or the Blue Square Conference). In an early case, e.g. a fan who shouted 'Paki' at a Port Vale v. Oldham Athletic game was banned from grounds nationwide for three years; the *High Court* ruling that the term was intrinsically racially offensive even if the offender lacked malice. Alternatively, police can apply for a *civil* football banning order (FBO) (see generally *civil banning order* (CBO). *Ministers of State* have power to ban named supporters from travelling to matches abroad (as used on various occasions). From the early 2000s various **football gangs** were identified such as the Zulu Warriors (Birmingham City, known to have links with *organized crime*); the Head Hunters (Chelsea, linked to right-wing extremism); Soul Crew (Cardiff City, which also linked to organized crime) and City Firm (Leeds United, reputedly one of the largest). A *National Criminal Intelligence Service* (NCIS) report (2001) noted that two-thirds of football gangs were involved in *drug*-trafficking and a third in *counterfeiting* (including of match tickets). Since then, events have been better policed due in part to *self-regulation* by the clubs and Football Association (FA). In 2005, the CPS revised its policies re prosecution of players. Several have been convicted of offences committed during matches or training. FA initiatives include 'Kick Racism Out of Football' (2003 onwards) and an England Members Club, joining which is a prerequisite to buying tickets for England away games. Other common CJS-related aspects include obscene language (see *obscenity*) (including **football chants**: mass intonation, sometimes extending to **monkey chant** whereby primitive animal noises are directed at a black player; *public order* offences and *anti-social behaviour* (ASB)). In *popular culture* (see *Touchstones*) a **football bung** is a backhander (see *corruption*); re which there is a long history re managers and other personnel; of which the trial and *imprisonment* of three Sheffield Wednesday players (1956) is a notable example. In 2006, a BBC TV 'Panorama' programme alleged that 18 managers of Premiership sides had taken bungs re player transfers, leading to disciplinary hearings, several (unsuccessful) prosecutions and ongoing *investigations*. The **Safety at Sportsgrounds Act 1975** and subsequent *legislation* including the **Sporting Events (Control of Alcohol, etc) Act 1985** were already in place before the Hillsborough Disaster of 1989 (in which 96 spectators died) 56 people having already lost their lives in the Valley Parade (Bradford City) fire of 1985. Many modern-day policing or *security* procedures are a *response* to such incidents.

foreigner See *Touchstones*; **foreign prisoner** See *prisoner*; **foreign travel restriction order** See *restriction*.

forensic/forensics

Terms used to describe the application of knowledge to a problem, facts, *data*, etc., as where **forensic scientists** (see further below) specialise in the analysis of human or animal corpses, other remains or DNA as part of an *investigation*. Hence **forensic evidence**, that which has been subjected to **forensic analysis** (aka **forensic tests**), including by *sampling* and which may later be presented in court by an expert *witness* aka **forensic analyst**, **forensic examiner** (especially re equipment, materials, motor vehicles or *arson*) or **forensic scientist**. The **Forensic Science Service (FSS)** is a species of commercial undertaking known as a GovCo which carries out such work for UK police forces and others in competition with others from the *private sector*. For **forensic psychology**, see *psychiatry/psychology*. The term **forensic skills** is applied broadly to the work of professional people, such as those of a lawyer re *evidence*/ 'cross-examination'; or re any task involving specialist interpretation of minutiae.

forfeiture See *sentence*/'ancillary order'; **forgery** See *counterfeiting and forgery*; **formal admission** See *admission*.

fraud

Generic description for various forms of deception, dishonesty or trick re which a common denominator is that the victim is misled and suffers loss (including in some instances by *silence*). There is hardly any scenario out of which fraud, large or small, cannot be constructed. Common 'tricks' include **cons, scams, long firm frauds** (in which worthless companies aka 'bucket shops' accept pre-paid orders then 'evaporate') and **internet fraud** (see also *cybercrime* in *Touchstones*). Hence also **identity fraud**: see *identification/identity*; and a **judge-alone trial for fraud**: see *judge*. The **Serious Fraud Office (SFO)** is an independent government department with both *investigation* and *prosecution* functions. Key SFO acceptance criteria include whether the suspected fraud 'appears to be so *serious* or complex that its investigation should be carried out by those responsible for its [possible] prosecution'. The SFO focuses on major and complex fraud based on factors such as whether, e.g. the *value* exceeds £1 million, possible international dimensions, the need for knowledge of financial markets and whether there is a need to use the SFO's special powers (e.g. to order *disclosure* or demand answers: contrast *silence*/'right to silence'). The **Director of Serious Fraud** is appointed by and accountable to the *Attorney General*. SFO work has sometimes proved controversial, e.g. when resources have been spent on cases resulting in *acquittals* (although such prosecutions invite that *risk* and may turn on *legal* or accounting niceties); and the *BAE Systems* case (see *Touchstones*). See further sfo.gov. uk Other frauds are pursued by the CPS, including via its London **Fraud Prosecution Service** (FPS): see cps.gov.uk See also *carousel fraud* in *Touchstones*.

freedom

Individual and other *rights* and *liberties* are frequently spoken of as **freedoms** of which, e.g. **freedom of assembly, freedom of association, freedom of expression, freedom of thought, freedom of conscience** and **freedom of religion** (or belief) are perhaps the most vaunted, historical and well versed. For the **European Convention On Human Rights and Fundamental Freedoms**, see *human rights*. Freedoms are usually regarded as being balanced by responsibilities; but a Government move to bring in *legislation* to ensure such a balance appears to have been placed on hold. Under the **Freedom of Information Act 2000** (FOIA) *citizens* have access to a considerable amount of information that was previously classified as confidential or secret, It is the duty of the **Information Commissioner** to deal with applications for *disclosure* of public information and related matters; and an **Information Tribunal** (formerly known as the Data Protection Tribunal) hears *appeals* from notices issued by the commissioner under the 2000 Act, Data Protection Act 1998 (DPA) Privacy and Electronic Communications Regulation 2003 (PECR), and The Environmental Information Regulations 2004 (EIR). When a *Minister of State* certifies that something should not be made public on grounds of national *security*, a panel of the tribunal known as the National Security Appeals Panel (NSAP) (not open to the public), manages and hears *appeals*. In 2009, the tribunal ordered the Government to disclose Cabinet minutes for the very first time, re discussions of the legality of the invasion of Iraq in 2003, describing the need for this as 'exceptional' due to a powerful competing *public* interest, the commissioner having argued that the decision to go to war remained controversial as it was not based on 'self-defence' [see generally *defence*] or a united international *response* to aggression' (still pending).

front

A word that in CJS terms is often used to signify early or immediate processes or situations. Hence, e.g. **front end** to encapsulate those stages of criminal justice extending from *arrest* to trial and sentence in contrast to the work of the Parole Board or with offenders after their *release*, known as 'the back end' (and hence the expression '**back** end sentencing' to describe the *enforcement* of sentences, breach proceedings, *recall* to prison, etc.). The term **front line** is used to described those practitioners (such as police officers and police community support officers (PCSOs) who deal face-to-face with the general public, *crime scenes*, suspects, etc; although this may be extended e.g. to a probation officer who deals with someone who is under *supervision*, essentially directly. **Front man** is often used to describe the 'acceptable face' of *fraud*: someone of convincing appearance who approaches victims whilst less presentable individuals hide in the background. The **National Front** (NF) is a *political* organization whose members hold extreme right wing views; with a reputation for aggression. It is not a proscribed organization, see *terrorism/terrorist*: but, e.g. police officers and Church of England clergyman have been barred from membership by various mechanisms.

funding See *financial aspects*; **further detention** See *detention*.

G

Gambling

Gambling can be an *addiction* (see *Touchstones*); with the added risk of escalation, whatever a person's financial means. Losses can lead to further *risks* being taken, anxiety, increasing debts, and possibly acquisitive or other offences to obtain money to spend on betting. It also creates secondary victims (see *victim*). Hence **Gamblers Anonymous** (GA): a fellowship of men and women who join together to do something about their **gambling problems** and to *help and support* each other 'and all **compulsive gamblers**' to do the same. GA sees gambling as an illness, progressive in nature; that can be *arrested* but not cured. For information, see gamblersanonymous. org.uk Note also the reference to Fyodor Dostoyevsky in *Touchstones/'*redemption'. The **Gambling Commission** regulates gambling in the *public interest* 'by keeping crime out of gambling' (especially *organized crime*: gambling turnover is a convenient means of *money laundering*) and by ensuring that it is conducted fairly and openly, e.g. in casinos (where permitted: plans for a range of 'supercasinos' having been largely shelved due to a public outcry) and elsewhere and by protecting *children* and *vulnerable people* from being harmed (see generally *harm*) or exploited. The Commission also provides independent *advice* to the Government on gambling: see further for this and a range of connected items gamblingcommission.gov.uk

gang

A loose, often changing group of people who may, e.g. (**1**) 'hang out together' by way of social interaction (but may attract suspicion due to their 'different' or *marginal* ways: see *Touchstones*; (**2**) be involved in *petty offences* or *anti-social behaviour* (ASB); or (**3**) be part of the activities of the Mafia, Triads, Yardies, Hell's Angels or *organized crime*; especially when the terms **Gangland** (a mythical place geographically: whose features reflect those described in *Touchstones/'*Underworld') and **gangster** (or '**gangsta**') are used: with their further connotations of intimidation, *threats, violence, serious crime* and *weapons*. Note also now the *anti-social behaviour/'*gangster asbo'. See also *football gang*. Criminologists have tended to focus on **gang behaviour** whereby members act as part of a group in ways they would not alone; and **gang culture** with its secretive language, *codes,* hierarchies, rituals and self-*regulation*. For an insight, see *Gangland Britain: Inside Britain's Most Dangerous Gangs* (1995), Thompson, T, Hodder & Staughton. The term **gangmaster** has been widely used to describe someone employing numbers of vulnerable *people* such as *immigrants* without work permits, notoriously at Morecambe Bay, Lancashire (2004) where 21 Chinese cockle-pickers drowned, leading to *manslaughter* convictions (2006).

gaol/gaoler

Gaol is a synonym for *prison*; especially historically (and in the USA: though often spelled 'jail'); though some UK local prisons are known as gaols today which appears to be a matter simply of *local* custom and practice. **Gaoler** is: **(1)** usually a reference to **police gaoler** at a police station or courthouse (similar to a *police/*'custody officer'); or **(2)** historically (and sometimes today) a *prison governor* or *prison officer*.

GCHQ

Government Communications Headquarters (aka 'listening post'). An establishment for eavesdropping, *interception of communications* and working alongside the Security Services re foreign and internal threats. GCHQ is aka **Cheltenham** after its main base in Gloucestershire. It is now largely electronically-based: see gchq.gov.uk

gender

As with other forms of *discrimination*, **gender discrimination** has been to the fore and is equally unlawful, including under the **Sex Discrimination Act 1975** (and later provisions). *Gender, Crime and Criminal Justice* (2004) (2nd. edn), Walklate, Sandra, Willan Publishing identifies and considers different ways of theorising about gender and the relative impact of this on thinking about crime and victimisation (see generally *victim*) and contains *evidence* of 'gendered experiences' of crime victimisation. Hence the **Gender Agenda** of the *Equality Rights Commission* (ERC): see gender-agenda.co.uk See also generally, *domestic violence; hate crime.*

generic community sentence See *community sentence*

global/international dimensions

Increasingly and due to greater mobility and speed of *communications*, criminal justice has a global dimension; involving international agreements (especially re *law enforcement*), treaties, understandings and cross-border policing, especially re *serious offences* involving *drugs; money laundering; organized crime;* paedophiles; smuggling and *trafficking.* See also *border control* and for the roles of **Interpol** and **Europol**, see *police/policing.* There is also a **virtual global taskforce**: see also *cybercrime* in *Touchstones* (but considerable difficulty re the unregulated nature of the internet). There are also significant international dimensions to the work of the **European Court of Human Rights** (see *human rights*) and **International Criminal Court (ICC)**, founded in 2002 as an independent, permanent court to try people accused of the gravest crimes such as genocide, crimes against humanity and *war crimes.* Established by a 108 nation treaty, it is regulated by the Rome Statute of the International Criminal Court. It only hears cases not investigated or prosecuted by a national CJS (unless merely a 'show trial'). It began hearing its first case in 2009 (allegations against Congolese rebel leader Thomas Lubanga of recruiting children as soldiers in a civil war). Other proceedings are pending: see further icc-cpi.int The ICC stemmed from earlier **Special International Criminal Tribunals** established by the United Nations (UN) (e.g. re Rwanda; former Yugoslavia) to pursue atrocities during times of war, or genocide; but which are not a deterrent to leaders of a powerful or dominant nations such as the USA: see globalpolicy.org.intljustice. Other arrangements with which the ICC should not be confused are **International Military Tribunals (IMTs)** such as those at Nuremberg, post-Second World War and International Military Tribunal for the Far East (IMTFE)(1946); and **'national' proceedings with a global dimension**, as with the trial (under the Iraqi Interim Government) and execution of Saddam Hussein in Iraq in 2006, or, e.g. the trial by a **Scottish Court in The Netherlands** re the Lockerbie Bombing in 2002. Global and international events can impact on national policy. For two diverse examples, see *French Revolution* and *September 11* (both in *Touchstones*). The Treaty of Prüm framework allows EU sharing of *databases*.

'going straight'

A phrase regularly applied to the change of lifestyle, etc. that stems from an offender (an ex-*prisoner* in particular) giving up crime, aka *desistence* (see further that entry) so as to enhance self-esteem and lead a crime-free life. See, e.g. *Going Straight After Crime and Punishment* (1999), Devlin A and Turney B, Waterside Press which contains first-hand accounts by such people; and the work with reformed offenders of *Unlock* (see *Touchstones*). Hence also the **going straight contract**: see *contract*.

Governance of Britain, The See *Touchstones/*'Britishness'

grave crime

(1) Generally, the *youth court* deals with offences involving allegations against juveniles, however *serious* they may be. But some cases *must* be sent to the *Crown Court,* including when homicide (*murder, manslaughter,* etc.) is involved. Also, it must consider so committing re certain **grave crimes**, such as serious *assaults, arson* or when the juvenile is provisionally assessed as *dangerous* due to the charge involving a *sexual offence* or *violence.* Following the *Bulger case* (see *Touchstones*) the practices associated with these provisions attracted criticism from the European Court of Human Rights (see, generally, *human rights*) re the intimidating atmosphere of the Crown Court; which has since introduced a range of initiatives to offset this. Juveniles can be ordered to serve *detention* for life, *indeterminate sentences for public protection* (ISPPs) or extended sentences for public protection (ESPPs) (see the former re both), broadly speaking in analogous circumstances to an *adult.* **(2)** For use of the term **'the gravest crimes'**, see *global/international dimensions/*'International Criminal Court'.

Grendon Prison See *prison*; **grey crime** See *Touchstones.*

guardianship

Local authorities have responsibilities of a general nature re *children* and other *vulnerable people*, including to seek a *civil* **guardianship order** where this is essential for someone's *protection*; allowing compulsory steps re his or her *welfare, safety,* etc.

guidance/guideline

Words which have been applied to various forms of *advice* and *support* to and for practitioners and decision-makers, including, in particular, re **guideline judgements**: see *Court of Appeal;* **sentencing guidelines** and the work of the **Sentencing Guidelines Council** (SGC): see those entries. Note also Home Office guidelines, e.g. for use by the police or *border control*; MOJ guidelines; and those of other departments. The terms are also widely used re a range of *help and support*.

guilty plea See *plea;* **gun** See *weapon.*

H

habeus corpus See *Touchstones*

hacking
(**1**) The physical action of **'chopping'** at a person or property, e.g. with a *weapon* or blunt instrument, so as to cause an *assault* or *criminal damage;* in the extreme, **hacking to death**, i.e. meaning *murder* (usually). (**2**) Breaking into a computer hard disc and/or *database,* re which the **Computer Misuse Act 1990** and Police and Justice Act 2006 govern offences of 'unauthorised access', principally when the accused person acts with the intention (see generally *mens rea*) of committing or facilitating a further offence (e.g. *fraud*), or to make unauthorised modification, erase or alter content or cause malfunctions, e.g. by spreading a virus. The *jurisdiction* of UK courts is extra-territorial: it does not matter where, globally speaking, the *target* computer is located; whilst **hackers** may sometimes commit offences under UK law wherever they are (see specialist works). People accessing computers abroad from within the UK may commit offences under the national laws of those *States.* Hence a long-running (and continuing) attempt by USA *law enforcement* authorities, to *extradite* British *citizen* Garry McKinnon for allegedly hacking into USA defence and Nasa systems to leave a message 'Your *security* is crap'; halted in 2009 by the *High Court* pending judicial review (see *appeal*). It ruled that the *Home Secretary* had not given adequate consideration to his mental state (see generally *mental impairment*). As a sufferer from Asberger's syndrome he was said to be *vulnerable* to the effects of possible long-term incarceration abroad in breach of *human rights* (i.e. Article 3, 'inhuman or degrading treatment'); and the CPS was considering bringing a prosecution under UK law as noted in (2). (**3**) **Codebreaking** of encrypted data: see also generally *code.*

half-way house
One mid-way between *imprisonment* and life in the *community,* usually in the nature of a *hostel* that may be used during resettlement (see *reintegration and resettlement*) and/or following *release* from prison; on the way to 'independent living'.

Halliday Report See *Touchstones*

handler/handling
The term **handler** is used variously for: (**1**) someone convicted of the offence of **handling stolen property** under section 22 Theft Act 1968 (formerly known as 'receiving'): see texts on *criminal law;* (**2**) the **handler of an informer** or 'source' (see *informer*); (**3**) the **handling of an agent, source or spy** by the *security services;* (**4**) the **handling of a case**, i.e. *case management,* including by a judge or *lawyer.*

hanging See *Touchstones*

harassment
The **Protection From Harassment Act 1997** created the offence of harassment to make it easier to deal with, e.g. stalkers and other people involved in related forms

of pestering and annoyance; both a criminal **offence of harassment** and a parallel *civil* remedy; each based around the use of a **restraining order** to prevent continuation of a given course of conduct, i.e. there must be more than a one-off occurrence. Criminal offences of harassment are progressively more *serious* the longer the conduct continues or frequent it becomes. The restraining order was the first **civil behaviour order (CBO)** backed by criminal *sanctions*; a blueprint for other such laws.

harm

One key CJS focus is on the prevention of harm (see generally *crime prevention/crime reduction*), whether physical, emotional, economic or otherwise; and **repairing harm** whenever possible via *compensation*, restoration, restitution, etc. (see generally *sentence*/'ancillary order'). *Restorative justice* is directly concerned with this type of outcome: see that entry. Other terms regularly encountered include **serious harm** (a question of fact and degree); whilst certain offences or processes are designed to prevent **public harm** and ensure public *safety*. Use of the term **harm reduction** is a tacit acknowledgment that wholescale elimination of the **risk of harm** remains an ideal. **Self-harm** (aka 'cutting-up' or 'scratching') is the infliction of injuries by someone on their own body, mind or prospects, possibly associated with a range of personal problems (including what *prison officers* call 'anniversary syndrome' whereby a significant personal event 'on the outside' comes around; or e.g. a Dear John letter arrives: see *prison slang* in *Touchstones*); or may be linked to *mental impairment*. It can affect *vulnerable* offenders, especially, and lead to *suicide*: see specialist works.

'harvesting' See *Touchstones*

hate

Extreme dislike which may be accompanied by venom, spleen, etc. and be directed towards a particular individual, group or *community* (see generally e.g. *black and minority ethnic* (BME); *discrimination; gender; race/racism; religion; sexual orientation*). Hence the modern umbrella term **hate crime** to describe a range of **hate-related offences** and/or those with a **hateful motive** (see *motive*). These include a number of offences of **incitement to racial hatred** (and other forms of hate). CJS measures have *targeted* a growing range of such offences, via crackdowns by the police and, e.g. *priorities* of the CPS; whilst statutory provisions have created dedicated hate-related offences and/or require courts to treat such offences as intrinsically more *serious*; higher levels of *punishments* being reinforced by *sentencing guidelines*.

health

Health and the CJS interact at various points of the criminal process, ranging from **fitness to stand trial** or **fitness to plead** (see *plea; trial; mental impairment*); **medical reports** and **psychiatric reports** on victims or offenders (see *medical aspects; mental impairment; psychiatry/psychology*); and the work of the police, *Multi-agency Public Protection Arrangements* (MAPPAs), courts, HM Prison Service, National Probation Service and the *Parole Board*. The remit of the **Health and Safety Executive (HSE)** extends to the *enforcement* of safe systems of work and public spaces (and see generally *safety*). CJS agencies/services are themselves bound by such processes: see, e.g. *Stockwell shooting* in *Touchstones*. Local **health authorities** interface with the CJS re, e.g. *alcohol, drugs* and MAPPAs (above); whilst doctors may, e.g. be called as expert *witnesses* for either party. Various *referral* schemes exist touching on matters of health. The **National Health Service (NHS)** provides services to the CJS, e.g.

in relation to prisoners who need to be treated in an ordinary hospital rather than a prison **healthcare centre** (see *prison*) and *drug* treatment. It is also at the centre of events where there is a victim of *violence* through local Accident and Emergency Units (A&E); when doctors may become *witnesses* re the cause or severity of *injury*. Such units have been a focus of concerns re *assaults* on NHS staff (and other patients), *violence* generally and *anti-social behaviour*. There have been 'ethical dilemmas' in the face of demands for information concerning *suspicions* about offences. Whereas in the past these may have gone unreported by staff (see generally *report*) they are perhaps more likely to be so nowadays under crime prevention/crime reduction initiatives; as they are vis-à-vis general medical practitioners. Considerable concerns have been expressed concerning possible misuse of an emergent NHS-led patient *database*.

help

Arrangements for **help and support** exist across the CJS, often involving the *voluntary sector*, e.g. re victims and *witnesses*. Such **mechanisms** also include **bail support**: see *bail*; that for *prisoners*, their families and friends (in prison and on their *release*); those focusing on particular problems (see, e.g. *RAPt*; *Support After Murder and Manslaughter*: in *Touchstones*; *fair/fairness/*'Fair Trials Abroad' (in *Main entries*)). There is a long and proud tradition of support, *charity* and philanthropy re the development of criminal justice. For a key and particularly historic example, see *Rainer Crime Concern* in *Touchstones*. The police frequently **appeal for help** from the public to solve a crime, often accompanied by the assurance that information will be treated in confidence (which it may or not be, ultimately depending on such matters as court *rulings*, the granting of anonymity in court and public interest immunity (see *informer*)); as does 'Crimewatch' (see under *crime*). **'Helping the police with their inquiries'** is a more or less standard formulation for 'being questioned' by the police, often meaning in police *detention* (so that the expression may also be something of a *euphemism*: see generally *Touchstones*. But witnesses to a crime also help in this way). **Self-help** is regarded as a particularly worthy pursuit in that it demands *motivation* and *commitment*. **Self-help groups** include *Alcoholics Anonymous, Gamblers Anonymous, Narcotics Anonymous* and *Unlock* (see *Touchstones* for the last of these). Note also **helping someone to present their case**: see *McKenzie friend*; and the existence of a wide range of CJS-related **helplines**, such as Childline (see *children*) and those re *domestic violence, drugs* and *victims* of crime.

High Court /higher courts

The **High Court of Justice** is based at the Royal Courts of Justice in The Strand, central London (and hence may be referred to as 'The Strand'); and may sit at other venues across England and Wales. It deals mainly with more important and/or valuable *civil* disputes. There are three **divisions of the High Court**: Queen's Bench Division (QBD), Chancery Division and Family Division. Re the CJS, the **QBD** is the most significant; often presided over by the *Lord Chief Justice.* It deals with various kinds of *appeal* (see that entry) and has a general supervisory *jurisdiction* by way of judicial review and can make declarations (see *appeal*). Hence **High Court judge** to describe a *judge* of the High Court, known as Mr. Justice Smith, etc. The term **higher courts** is used to describe all courts above the *Crown Court*; none of which have what is termed 'first instance' *jurisdiction*, i.e. to hold a trial (except theoretically the *House of Lords*: but see the note at *trial by peers*); hence **lower courts** (plural) for the Crown Court and magistrates' courts (and comparable *civil* courts at that level). In the singular, **higher court** is used to refer to any court above the one it is being compared with, including, e.g. the Crown Court in relation to the magistrates' court; and hence **lower court** (again singular) or, in the converse situation, **'the court below'**.

HM Court Service (HMCS) See under *court*

HM Inspectorate of Constabulary (HMIC)

HMICs date back to the County and Borough Police Act 1856. They are appointed by the Crown on the recommendation of the *Home Secretary* and report to HM Chief Inspector of Constabulary (HMCIC), who is also the Home Secretary's principal professional policing adviser. But HMCIC is independent of both government and the police service (see *independence/interdependence*). HMIC functions include certifying police forces as efficient and thereby qualified to receive a grant. The role has been developed in the past 30 years to ensure greater *openness* and *transparency*; and to include not just *inspection* of individual forces but promoting *best practice*.

HM Inspectorate of Court Administration (HMICA)

HMICA was established by the Courts Act 2003 and came into being in 2005. Its remit includes: *inspections* and reports to the *Justice Secretary* on the (essentially administrative: see *administrative/administration*) support systems of the *Crown Court* and magistrates' courts (it also inspects the county court: the local *civil* court). Inspection excludes the work of people 'making *judicial* decisions or exercising any judicial discretion'. It acts independently (see generally *independence/interdependence*) to provide 'assurance to *Ministers of State* and the public about the safe and proper delivery of court services', contributes to their improvement and reports publicly. Key areas of inspection, include: *diversity* and its promotion/achievement; public governance and *accountability*, *transparency*, fairness (see *fair/fairness*), leadership and strategic *management* (see *strategy*); finance; buildings; information *technology*; equipment; administrative processes and their effect on *court users*; *enforcement* 'to ensure prompt and *effective* action re compliance with court orders'; and quality of service. Its work also covers *monitoring*, *targets*, *priorities*, *performance* and improvement action.

HM Inspectorate of Prisons (HMI Prisons)

Each prison is inspected periodically by HM Chief Inspector of Prisons (HMCI Prisons) or his or her team of full-time or specialist inspectors, the latter attached to HMI Prisons for particular purposes. HMCI Prisons publishes an annual *report* as well as a report of each *inspection*. It carries out general and thematic inspections (on dedicated aspects of the prison system). Essentially, it looks at the treatment of prisoners, regime quality, the morale of prisoners and staff, the quality of healthcare, the way in which an establishment is managed and the physical condition of prison premises (for most such topics, see *prison/prisoner*). HMCI Prisons reports to the *Home Secretary*. HM Prison Service must publish a considered reply. Reports have often been critical; and various HMCI Prisons have been *high profile* and frequently critical of conditions in *custodial* institutions and of prison regimes or purposes generally. See generally inspectorates.homeoffice.gov.uk/hmiprisons

HM Inspectorate of Probation (HMI Probation)

HMI Probation is an autonomous unit funded by the MOJ, charged with inspecting the work of the National Probation Service (NPS) and reporting to the *Justice Secre-*

tary. It also provides *Ministers of State* and officials with advice on probation matters and promotes the development of effective *management* and practice (see generally *effectiveness and efficiency; best practice*). Most inspectors come from within the ranks of the NPS; and generally have wide experience in the probation field. Statutory provision allows suitably qualified people from other disciplines to become inspectors. There are normally two kinds of *inspection*: **area inspections** (aka **quality and effectiveness inspections**); and **thematic inspections** (into a given aspect of probation-related work). Reports of thematic inspections may contain recommendations concerning the *performance* of other agencies within the CJS or government departments with an interest in criminal justice. Recommendations and commendations may be included. Reports are open to the public. See further inspectorates. homeoffice.gov.uk/hmiprobation (but note MOJ responsibility already mentioned).

HM Prison Service (HMPS)
HMPS (often just 'Prison Service') operates under the Prisons Act 1952 and Prison Rules 1999. There are comparable provisions re *young offenders*. It also uses an accumulation of internal **Prison Service Instructions** (PSIs), **Prison Service Orders** (PSOs) and **HMPS Manuals** covering all aspects of prison regimes (see generally *prison*). It is increasingly involved with other agencies/services, especially the National Probation Service, police, *Border Agency, Youth Justice Board* and *voluntary sector*. Since 2007, the National Offender Management Service (NOMS) (see *offender management*) comes under the MOJ and the former post of director general of HMPS was merged with that of chief executive of NOMS, then in 2008 a new post of **Director General for Criminal Justice and Offender Management Strategy** was created. HMPS is an executive agency of NOMS. It manages *public sector* prisons and contracts for the construction, development and *management* of *private sector* prisons. There are twelve **HMPS Areas** and headquarters in London. It publishes *Prison Service Journal* and *Prison Service News*. Other information can be accessed at hmprisonservice.gov.uk A Prisons Board acts as a senior *management* team which includes a number of non-executive directors from outside the service. HMPS aims are crystalised in the **HMPS mission statement** displayed in HMPS establishments, i.e. 'Her Majesty's Prison Service serves the public by keeping in *custody* those committed by the courts. Our duty is to look after them with humanity and help them lead law abiding and useful lives in custody and after release'. See also *imprisonment; prison*.

HM Revenue & Customs See *Revenue & Customs*

Holloway Prison
A *women's* prison and *young offender institution* (YOI) in North London, with an 'operational capacity' of just over 500; in single cell or dormitory-style accommodation. It takes 'all [women] *adult* and *young offenders* sent there by the courts', whether on *remand* or serving *imprisonment* (including *life imprisonment*); and thus caters for an unusually wide range of needs, across a large catchment area. Perhaps Britain's best known prison for women, it opened in 1851, originally for men and women, and was only later a prison exclusively for women (1903). A small unit for young women offenders was opened in 1998. It serves as a training prison and also, e.g. has a *bail* unit, mother and baby unit (MBU) (until the child is 18 months old) and facilities re *education, work, healthcare* and *mental impairment*. It has at times attracted criticism from HM Inspector of Prisons, including in 1995 when Sir David (now Lord) Ramsbotham and his *inspection* team 'walked out' due to the then poor conditions.

Most of its Victorian buildings were demolished and replaced between 1975 and 1985 (see generally *Victorian aspects* in *Touchstones*). It was a place of execution, including of Ruth *Ellis* (see *Touchstones*). In 2009 it was the subject of a three part ITV fly-on-the-wall documentary, 'Holloway'. For outline information re all prisons in England and Wales, see the 'Locate a Prison' facility at hmprisonservice.gov.uk

home

Having a regular home and 'place of abode' (i.e. somewhere to live rather than no fixed abode', being 'on the street' and/or without family or other ties) is a key factor in the lives of certain offenders and correspondingly an important aspect of crime prevention/crime reduction. Various charities are involved in such initiatives, including Shelter (see shelter.org.uk) and, especially re ex-offenders/ex-prisoners, *Nacro* (see *Touchstones*) and National Probation Service. The term **home alone** is one adopted in *popular culture* (see generally *Touchstones*) from television dramatisations to imply leaving children (or vulnerable people) unattended to fend for themselves; which has led to a significant number of convictions for *child abuse/child neglect* or even *manslaughter*. **Home detention curfew (HDC)** is the system whereby a prisoner can be *released* to serve a portion of his or her *imprisonment* 'at home' subject to a curfew and *electronic monitoring*; usually restricted to certain categories of prisoner/offender.

Home Office (HO) and Home Secretary

The **Home Office** is the historic office of *State* which dates from the late-1300s and (as a separate entity) 1782 (see further below) but which since key changes of 2007 focuses primarily on *law and order;* public *safety;* the *protection of the public;* policing (via independent local police forces and police authorities: see *police/policing*); crime prevention/crime reduction; *asylum* and *immigration* (via the UK *Border Agency*); *terrorism/terrorists* (including in conjunction with an Office for Security and Counter-Terrorism (OSCT) which gives advice to *Ministers of State*); and *emergency* powers. This amalgam of tasks is sometimes described as **homeland security** (an Americanism), i.e. matters referable to the internal *security* of the UK, external matters falling to the Foreign and Commonwealth Office (FCO). The HO is also responsible for *safeguarding* personal *identity*; and many CJS-related related developments in *science, technology* and *research*. It has links to *MI5* and *GCHQ*.

The responsible *Minister of State* is the **Home Secretary**; a position formalised and which became powerful under the Tudors. In 1782, the role which formerly covered internal and external matters was separated out into Home Secretary and Foreign Secretary. The Home Secretary participates in the *Cabinet Committee on Crime and the Criminal Justice System* (CCCCJS). Especially post-Human Rights Act 1998 (see *human rights*) Home Secretaries have found themselves in conflict with the *judiciary* on some occasions, e.g. re who should set *tariffs*; sentencing levels; *detention without trial* and control orders (see *detention*). A systemic failure to deport foreign prisoners led to the departure of Charles Clarke (Home Secretary 2004-2006). His successor, Dr. John Reid (2006-2007), famously declared that the then Home Office was 'unfit for purpose' (a comment Prime Minister Tony Blair had, on taking up office in 1997, made about the entire CJS); leading to the '**Home Office split'**, i.e. a splitting-off to the MOJ of excess responsibilities, including for *prisons* and *probation*. The Home Secretary has certain inherent powers (see generally *jurisdiction*), including to deport or exclude *foreigners* who are 'not conducive to the public good'; which has been used to exclude aliens in *war*-time or in modern times people involved in *organized crime*, such as hit-men, members of the Mafia, Chinese Triads, Jamaican Yardies, suspected al-Qaida terrorists and preachers of *hate*. Several Home Secretaries have gone on to become *Prime Minister* (for an interesting correlation, see *Sidney Street* in *Touchstones*), but the post has been 'a career graveyard' for others due to often fortuitous events. The first blind Home Secretary was David Blunkett (2001-2004)(see generally *blind/ blindness*); the first woman in that position, Jacqui Smith (2007). Lord Sidmouth is generally regarded as a benchmark for repression having been in charge of the Home Department at the time of the *Peterloo Massacre* and the *Six Acts*: see *Touchstones* for both. For an account of the department and its history, see *The New Home Office: An Introduction* (2008) (2nd. edn.), Gibson B, Waterside Press.

hospital order See *mental impairment*

hostel
A place where people can stay temporarily alongside others sharing accommodation, facilities and services according to the kind of hostel in question. Hence, in a CJS con-text: **bail hostel**: see *bail*; **half-way house**: see that entry: **probation hostel**: but see *probation*. Some prisons have hostels attached, for *reintegration and resettlement*.

House of Lords
The upper chamber of the Houses of Parliament and, in a CJS context (pending the *Supreme Court*), the highest court of *appeal* in the UK. The Appellate Committee of the House of Lords (ACHL) is presided over by a senior *Law Lord*. The ACHL consists of Law Lords (aka Lords of Appeal in Ordinary). It sits apart from the main business of the House in a committee room. Its rulings carry great *weight* (see *Touch-stones*). *Legal rules* may become known by the names of key HL rulings; which also tend to impact on future *legislation*. There have been instances when what the House decided altered the way in which courts applied the *criminal law,* to such an extent that it was accused of 'creating crimes' (as e.g. with conspiracy to corrupt public mor-als and marital rape: see specialist works). See also *trial by peers*. Members of the house convicted of serious criminal offences in modern times include Lord (Jeffrey) Archer (*perjury* 2001: see also that entry) and Lord (Conrad) Black (former proprietor of the Daily Telegraph, sentenced to *imprisonment* for six and a half years and fined $125,000 in the USA in 2007 for embezzlement. In 2009, Jack Straw, *Justice Secre-tary*, proposed changes to allow members to be expelled in such circumstances. For a striking example from history, see *Ferrers, Earl* in *Touchstones*. Details of the House and its general and judicial work can be accessed at parliament.uk

Howard League for Penal Reform and **hulk** See *Touchstones*

human rights (HR)
The fundamental, inviolable and entrenched rights of **human beings** individually or as a whole. It is impossible to understand modern-day criminal justice without refer-ence to such rights, which permeate every aspect of the CJS from *investigation* to *trial,* sentence and beyond. The correct application of **human rights law** can be tested in national courts (aka 'domestic courts'), via standard *appeal* processes and under a free-standing right of appeal to the **European Court of Human Rights** in Strasbourg. The **European Convention on Human Rights and Fundamental Freedoms** (ECHR) was a *response* to the denial of such rights in Nazi Germany especially and

the Holocaust in particular. A premise of its framers was that *abuse* can develop from small beginnings and escalate if left unchecked. The ECHR was signed in 1949 and incorporated into English law by the **Human Rights Act 1998**; since when European law takes precedence. It is regarded as a **living instrument** which adapts to times and circumstance (contrast the more static and intrinsically backwards-looking English doctrine of *precedent*). Key aspects of the ECHR are contained in the **Articles of the Convention** and jurisprudence (i.e. *rulings*) of the European Court. HR processes include the **declaration of incompatibility** which national courts (in practice *higher courts*) can make asserting that national primary *legislation* (i.e. an *Act of Parliament*) is incompatible with the Convention. This obliges the government (in practice in the UK the relevant *Minister of State*) to consider bringing a Bill before Parliament to bring national law into line with the ECHR; and possibly *fast-tracking* this. In the UK, new Acts are usually headed by a 'compliance statement', but this is not definitive; it being for courts, ultimately, to rule on what is or is not compatible.

For the central and all-pervading right to a **fair trial** in Article 6, see *fair/fairness*. The Convention mirrors various longstanding criminal justice concepts such as **'no punishment without law'** (i.e. there must be *transparency* in advance and certainty about what is an offence) and fundamental **freedoms** (see further and generally *freedom*). Human rights demand **proportionality** re the actions and *responses* of public institutions. There is an **absolute right** in Article 3 not to be subjected to *torture*, or inhuman or degrading treatment or punishment. Other rights are classed as **limited rights**, e.g. under Article 5, 'Everyone has the right to *liberty* and *security* of [the] person' and 'No-one shall be deprived of his liberty' except as described in that article, including by 'lawful detention . . . after conviction by a competent court' or forms of 'lawful arrest or detention'; or **qualified rights**, as in Article 8 which deals with **respect for private and family life**. This can be restricted by a *State*, e.g. to prevent disorder or crime. The ECHR does not contain a free-standing anti-*discrimination* right but Article 14 requires all human rights to be applied without discrimination. **Protocols** have been added for particular purposes (e.g. Protocols 6 and 13 banning *capital punishment* which the UK ratified in 2004). Any notion that extreme concepts such as torture or unlawful detention are things of the past has been dispelled, e.g. by allegations re the treatment of prisoners of war in Iraq and Afghanistan and UK complicity in USA 'rendition flights' whereby suspects are transported to countries whose human rights *protections* are less well developed. The UK has frequently breached the ECHR, including re *detention without trial*; raising questions re its commitment to a **positive obligation** to promote human rights demanded by European jurisprudence. Bodies whose remit includes **monitoring human rights** include *Liberty* (see *Touchstones*), Justice (see justice.org.uk), Statewatch (see statewatch.org) and Fair Trials Abroad (see *fair/fairness*). For the 1998 Act see *Human Rights and the Courts: Bringing Justice Home* (1999), Gibson B (ed.), Waterside Press.

I

identity/identification

Terms central to the work of the CJS, it being key to all its functions and processes that the correct people are identified, whether as accused people, suspects, *witnesses*, victims or practitioners (it not being unknown for false identities to be used, even re the latter); and similarly re, e.g. exhibits (see *evidence*) and *samples*. The **identification parade** or 'line up' (to which special rules apply: see specialist works) has long been part of police practice; now superseded in some instances by a 'video parade'. Passports are a central instrument of international travel, to which increasingly sophisticated mechanisms are being applied worldwide including by the **(UK) Identity and Passport Service (IPS)**; an executive agency of the Home Office (2006) building on the former UK Passport Service (UKPS). The **National Identity Scheme (NIS)** is an embryonic project in conjunction with **identity cards** that will, it is planned, lead to the recording on an electronic *database* of the details of everyone in the UK (and passing through its ports an airports: see also *children*/'ContactPoint'). The NIS and IPS are geared to the development of biometric passports and identity cards for internal UK purposes and *border control*. Associated developments included face-to-face interviews for applicants for new passports. **Identity fraud**, in essence passing oneself off as someone else for a range of criminal purposes (not necessarily *fraud* in a conventional sense), has become one of the fastest growing types of crime, spurred by the 'anonymity' of the internet: see also *cybercrime* in *Touchstones*. Despite longstanding use of identity cards abroad, attitudes in the UK tended to be equivocal (in some people's minds associated with repressive regimes and a propensity for *function creep* (see *Touchstones*) and *abuse of power*). Others claim that they are essential for policing in the modern era and that 'the innocent have nothing to fear'. Hence objectives such as **safeguarding identity**: see generally *Home Office; safeguard*.

ignorance

Ignorance may be an issue for *legal* reasons or those of fact. Hence, re the former, the maxim **'ignorance of the law is no excuse'**: everyone is presumed to know the law however complex or obscure it may be: see generally *presumption* (and the comments under *criminal law*). Ignorance through an honest and genuine **mistake of fact** can be a *defence*: see *mistake*. Hence also the idea that an offender is/was **'ignorant'** re his or her responsibilities; possibly connoting a more deep-seated problem.

immigration (sometimes styled 'migration')(hence (im)migrant)

Entry into a country by someone who is not a *citizen* of that country but who wishes remain there; hence *border controls*. The **UK Immigration Service (UKIS)** is since 2007 part of the UK *Border Agency*. Immigrants may suffer from the *disadvantages* of any *foreigner* in terms of misplaced *suspicion* or mistrust; albeit immigrants have been essential to the British economy for many years; in the modern era dating from the 1950s: 'The Windrush' being the first boat to arrive from the West Indies to mark the start such developments and also issues of *race/racism*. Slogans, placards and graffiti bearing the quasi-Colonial messages 'No Coloureds', 'Whites only' and 'Wogs go home' led to ghettos and *social exclusion*; and immigrants being offered menial work that British people avoided. It is possible to construct a line from 'The Windrush' via the *Notting Hill Carnival* (see *Touchstones*) (the first significant assertion of an alternative lifestyle), *discrimination* and repression, to the *Brixton Riots* (see *Touchstones*), multiculturalism and discussions of *Britishness* (see *Touchstones*). Where someone is in the UK unlawfully, he or she may be dubbed an **illegal immigrant**; a term in common use despite negative associations of involvement in illicit activities, including where the term is doubly misdirected towards legitimate *asylum seekers*. The **Criminal Justice and Immigration Act 2008** contains a range of measures to facilitate *deportation* of certain would-be immigrants including via a **special immigration status** for those who have committed *terrorism* or *serious offences*: see opsi.gov.uk

immunity

Under the Rule of Law no one should enjoy **immunity from prosecution** but there are various situations in which that does occur, i.e. **sovereign immunity**: see generally *Crown*; **diplomatic immunity** which stems from reciprocal arrangements and relations between *States* whereby the home *State* undertakes to deal with the matter under its own powers if one of its diplomats is not prosecuted in the country where the offence took place; but that has led to considerable tensions on occasion, beyond the scope of this work; and **public interest immunity (PII)**: see *informer*.

impartial/impartiality See *equality*; *fair/fairness*; *human rights*

imprisonment

Sending someone to prison by way of a sentence (contrast, e.g. a *remand* in custody which although involving temporary containment within a prison is of a different order). It can only be used where the offence **carries imprisonment,** i.e. where this is the maximum punishment (see generally *sentence/sentencing*); and except re **mandatory sentences of imprisonment** the length of such a sentence is at the *discretion* of the court. It is generally regarded as **a sentence of last resort**. The *Criminal Justice Act 2003* contains a **'so serious' threshold** test for imprisonment. Section 152(2) of that Act provides that a court must not pass a *custodial* sentence unless it is of the opinion that the offence, or the combination of the offence and one or more offences associated with it, was so serious that neither a *fine* alone nor a *community sentence* can be justified for the offence. An offender can also be imprisoned if he or she refuses consent to a requirement of a *community sentence* which requires consent (few now do) or in analogous circumstances on breach of a community sentence or an order for a pre-sentence *drug* test. It also introduced a new determinate sentence of 12 months or more where the *seriousness* of the offence requires this and unless the law allows and the court considers that a (sometimes *mandatory*) sentence is needed for *public protection,* i.e. either an **indeterminate sentence for public protection (ISPP)** re certain offences of *violence* or *sexual offences* or an **extended sentence**. Both of these are outlined and contrasted in the entry for the former. Normally, the question about the **length of a sentence of imprisonment** is a consideration separate from whether it should be used at all; which may be affected by *mitigation.* Discretionary sentences 'must be for the shortest term … that in the opinion of the court is commensurate with the *seriousness* of the offence, or the combination of the offence and one or more offences associated with it' and the court must give its *reasons* for using imprisonment. If the offender is not legally represented, *legal aid* will be offered and a pre-sentence report (PSR) obtained (see *sentence/sentencing*). Where there are several offences, separate terms of imprisonment can be made to run concurrently (simultaneously) or consecutively (one after the other). Offenders below 21 years of age cannot (currently) be sentenced to imprisonment but to detention in a *young offender institution* (YOI). A **suspended sentence of imprisonment** is one that is suspended, i.e. held in abeyance, for between one and two years. The court must first be satisfied that imprisonment is appropriate; then go on to decide that it is correct to suspend its operation. Until 2003 there had to be 'exceptional circumstances' to justify this, but that requirement has now gone. If it suspends the sentence, the court must also consider imposing a *fine* and *compensation*. If the offender commits an offence within the operational period of the suspended sentence, it then falls to be activated, i.e. put into effect. Normally it will, be unless there is some cogent reason against this; but there are other options: see specialist works. Conditions can be attached to a suspended sentence in the nature of *'requirements'* and breach can also lead to activation. Detention in a YOI cannot be suspended. See also *life imprisonment; tariff.*

incitement

The Serious Crime Act 2007 replaced the Common Law offence of incitement with new *statutory* offences of **encouraging or assisting a crime** (see further and generally *assisting crime* for a broader range of what are called 'inchoate offences'): intentionally encouraging or assisting an offence; encouraging or assisting an offence believing it will be committed; and encouraging or assisting offences believing one or more of them will be committed. The Act also introduces a statutory *defence* of 'acting reasonably' and it gives *protection* to victims in certain categories or circumstances. For further information consult specialist works and see the 2007 Act at opsi.gov.uk **Incitement to hatred** is a basis for various dedicated offences: see *hate*; as is **incitement to commit acts of terrorism**: see generally *terrorism/terrorist.*

incompatibility See *human rights;* **indecency/indecent assault** See *sexual offence*

independence/interdependence

A level of fragmentation of CJS responsibilities acts as a restraint on *abuse of power*, improper influence and overly-automated *responses*. Virtually all CJS *agencies/services* experience some degree of *strategic* direction but day-to-day decisions at operational or 'grass roots' level are taken free, e.g. of central control. But note re the *judiciary*, **judicial independence** (see *judicial*); and the special position of bodies such as *Independent Monitoring Boards* (IMBs), *Independent Police Complaints Commission* (IPCC), *HM Inspectorates*, the *Parole Board* and *Prisons and Probation Ombudsman*. More generally, one rationale is that each part of the CJS must operate separately but, of necessity, is partially reliant on other agencies/services in carrying out its own role. Hence **interdependence**, the idea that, e.g. the CPS can function only on sound information, etc. from the *police* (or other *law enforcement agencies*) whilst they need advice from the CPS concerning the *legal* status of given behaviour or events. Likewise, end-to-end sentencing (see *sentence/sentencing*) demands co-operation between HM Prison Service and the National Probation Service. A chain of inter-related *communications, risk-assessments* and actions may underpin the work, e.g. of *Multi-agency Public Protection Arrangements* (MAPPAs) or a *youth offending team* (YOT).

Independent Monitoring Board (IMB) A locally-based monitoring board is attached to each prison. As its name implies, it is independent of government, the MOJ, HM Prison Service or its staff (see generally *independence/interdependence*). Members have free access to 'their' prison and its prisoners (*security* and *control* permitting: see generally *prison*). IMBs consist of lay *volunteers*. They report to but are wholly independent of the *Justice Secretary*. They are appointed following an interview by two local IMB members and someone from another IMB; and act as unpaid 'watchdogs'. They must act fairly (see *fair/fairness)* and objectively but may consult with and advise the local *prison governor*. Their origins lie in the visiting committees established by the Prison Act 1877. They became Boards of Visitors and were once the main prison disciplinary authority (until 1992). There is a national IMB secretariat based in Westminster which provides information and training materials, co-ordinates applications to join IMBs, holds conferences and publishes reports and a journal, *The Independent Monitor* as well as publications such as a *Practical Guide to Monitoring Prisons* (2005). See, further, imb.gov.uk

Independent Police Complaints Commission (IPCC) Historically, the Police Complaints Authority (PCA) was the body that oversaw complaints against serving police officers in England and Wales. Additionally, voluntary (or 'non-complaint') referrals to the PCA were made by the police themselves and certain complaints or events had to be so referred, e.g. where death or serious *injury* occurred in police *custody* or stemmed from firearms (see generally *weapon*) being used by police or 'hot pursuit'. There was also a *discretion* to report other matters. So as to give reassurance and ensure *transparency* the IPCC (the emphasis being on 'independent') was established in 2004 under the Police Reform Act 2002 to investigate and oversee serious complaints against the police (those above the level suited to local processes). An aim was to give 'robustness' to the complaints system. Some people sue the police in the civil courts as an alternative to using IPCC procedures. See further ipcc.gov.uk

indeterminate sentence for public protection (ISPP)

Re what are in effect *dangerous offenders*, the *Criminal Justice Act 2003* introduced two new forms of sentence re offences committed from 4 April 2004. These are: **(1)** an **indeterminate sentence for public protection (ISPP)**; and **(2)** an **extended sentence for public protection (ESPP)**. *Dangerous offenders* are for these purposes defined as those convicted of *sexual* or *violent* offences (also listed in schedules to that Act). The **ISPP** is given to offenders convicted of such offences carrying a maximum penalty of ten years' imprisonment or more. The court sets a *tariff* for *punishment* and *retribution*, after which *release* is at the discretion of the *Parole Board*; following which the offender may remain on *licence* indefinitely but, unlike life licensees (see *life imprisonment*), offenders can apply to have their licences reviewed ten years after release. Parole Board *reviews* and *recalls* are managed by the *life imprisonment* section of the National Offender Management Service (NOMS)(see *offender management*). The **ESPP** is given to similar offenders convicted of offences which carry a maximum penalty of at least two but less than ten years' imprisonment. It consists of two parts: a *custodial* period of at least 12 months and an extended licence period of up to eight years. Release is again at the discretion of the Parole Board any time between the halfway point of the *custodial* period and the custodial end date. Parole Board *reviews* and *recalls* are managed by the early release and recall section of NOMS. The increase in the prison(er) population since 2004 has been partly attributed to such sentences. It is also the case that members of the judiciary have expressed their concern that their hands are often tied by the provisions, i.e. that their *discretion* is constrained. For an overview, see *Criminal Justice Act 2003: A Guide to the New Procedures and Sentencing* (2004), Gibson B, Waterside Press.

indictable/indictment

Terms chiefly referable to proceedings in the *Crown Court* and the procedural mechanism by which these are brought there (i.e. **by way of 'an indictment'**). Hence an **indictable only offence** is one which must and can only be tried in the Crown Court before a judge and jury. Such cases are now sent to the Crown Court from the outset once the accused person has appeared in the magistrates' court for *remand*, following *arrest* by the police and has first been charged before magistrates (normally). Such offences include: *murder*; rape; grievous bodily harm with intent (GBH) (see *assault*); *robbery*; aggravated *burglary*; *blackmail*; *conspiracy* by two or more people to commit an offence. Contrast *summary offence; either way offence* (and note that in some *legal* definitions the word **'indictable' encompasses 'either way'**).

informant/information
An **informant** is someone: (**1**) such as a conscientious *citizen* who provides information to the police; aka a 'complainant'; whether or not a victim (contrast *informer*); or (**2**) who 'lays an information' (below). **Information** may mean: (**a**) any facts, *data*, etc. communicated, e.g. to an agency/service or court (contrast *intelligence*); or (**b**) an **information to obtain a summons**: the longstanding method of *commencing criminal proceedings* in magistrates' courts (and the documents concerned); now being partly replaced by *charge and requisition* (see that entry); but which remains the method for private prosecutors or a public prosecutor seeking, e.g. a *warrant.* Hence an **'information on sight'**: one raised there and then in court, e.g. when a new or amended allegation is substituted. For details see works on *criminal procedure.*

informer
Someone who informs within a relationship defined by the Regulation of Investigatory Powers Act 2000 (RIPA) and who is now, in most cases, known by the technical term **covert human intelligence source** (CHIS) (sometimes shortened to **source**: but note that there may be other kinds of 'sources'). **Grass** is a slang term for informer and by extension **supergrass** (probably *media/press*-led), i.e. a *witness* who supplies *information* re substantial criminal activity and, e.g. as to his or her criminal partners/associates, often re *organized crime* or *terrorism/terrorists.* Informers should be contrasted with *informants.* The first publicly visible supergrasses were reported by the *media/press* from the 1960s. Hence nowadays a **supergrass system** with statutory and other rules, regulations and practices re the control, authorisation and *handling* of such arrangements (including under RIPA, above), *witness protection*, whether in prison (see *prison/*'Rule 45') or in the *community* and the prospect of public interest immunity (PII) being granted to an informer in certain instances where the potential *value* of the *evidence* that he or she may be able to give outweighs the justice-based consideration involved in his or her prosecution and/or *imprisonment.* Where an informer has assisted the police this is communicated to the court in confidence by way of what is called 'a text'. For an account, see *Covert Human Intelligence Sources: The 'Unlovely' Face of Police Work* (2009), Billingsley R (ed.), Waterside Press.

inherent jurisdiction/inherent power See *jurisdiction*

injury
Usually a reference to **physical injury** including **serious injury** or *harm* (both factual concepts although certain injuries are defined by name, e.g. actual bodily harm) as might stem from an *assault* and/or **psychological injury** such as shock or trauma (sometimes called 'psychological damage': see generally *psychiatry/psychology*); either of which may lead to an award of *compensation* to a victim including via a court or the **Criminal Injuries Compensation Board** (CICB). Hence also **non-accidental injury**: a *euphemism* (see *Touchstones*) for an injury with no identifiable cause but of a kind giving rise to *suspicion*; especially re *children* or *domestic violence.*

injustice See *justice* in *Main Entries* and *miscarriage of justice* in *Touchstones;* **innocence** See *presumption of innocence*; **insanity** See within *mental impairment*

inspection/inspector/inspectorate
For the main criminal justice inspectorates, see *HM Inspectorate of Constabulary* and the entries which follow there. In 2008 the House of Lords (i.e. in Parliament) re-

jected government proposals for a **Criminal Justice Inspectorate**, a single, unified cross-criminal justice entity, mainly because it would have undermined the independence of various CJS bodies and allowed pressure to be brought across agency/service boundaries. See generally *independence/interdependence*; *judicial independence*.

instruction

Clients (including accused people) give **instructions** to their lawyers; and the latter **'act on instructions'**. Lawyers may also need to **'take instructions'** as points arise during the course of a trial. Other professionals may take/act on analogous instructions. Note, also **Prison Service Instruction (PSI)** See *HM Prison Service*.

integrity See *value/values*

intelligence

Information or *data* that flows to a given point and that can be used in the process of an *investigation*, decision-making, etc. but that, essentially, has passed through processes and procedures whereby it has been checked and/or verified. Hence terms such as **intelligence-led policing** (and the routine if somewhat intriguing and uninformative expression **'acting on intelligence received'** (I did such and such)) and a police **National Intelligence Model** (NIM): see further under that heading at acpo. police.uk **Intelligence services** or **intelligence community** are terms which are sometimes used with a degree of imprecision, but which can be taken to encompass *MI5; MI6* and/or *GCHQ* (as well as **Defence Intelligence**, the Joint Terrorism Analysis Centre (JTAC) (see *terrorism/terrorist*) and related links to the *Cabinet Office* and **Joint Intelligence Committee (JIC)**). Section 59 Regulation of Investigatory Powers Act 2000 (RIPA) enables the *Prime Minister* to appoint an **Intelligence Services Commissioner (ISC)** who must be a person who holds or has held high *judicial* office within the meaning of the Appellate Jurisdiction Act 1876. He or she is appointed for three years (with the possibility of re-appointment) and has a responsibility to keep under review the issue of *warrants* by the *Home Secretary* (normally) authorising intrusive *surveillance* and interference with property, in order to ensure that this occurred on a proper basis; and who must report annually to the PM, the report then being laid before Parliament and published. Hence also **UK Intelligence Community Online** which 'reflects the Government's desire to be as open as possible about intelligence matters [see generally *open/openness*] while recognising the constraints imposed by national *security*'. For further explanation, see intelligence. gov.uk That website also refers to **Central Intelligence Machinery (CIM)** stating the Government's national *security* policies aim 'to: protect UK and British territories, and British nationals and property, from a range of *threats*, including from terrorism and espionage; protect and promote Britain's defence and foreign policy interests; protect and promote the UK's economic well-being; and support the prevention and *detection* of *serious crime*'. The USA has long had a **Central Intelligence Agency** (CIA) re which for current information see cia.gov

interception of communications (IOC)

The interception of communications in the course of their transmission, aka **'an intercept'**, whether postal communications or telecommunication (e.g. by telephone or the internet). The *law* allows intercepts by *law enforcement* and *intelligence services*: in the interests of national *security;* for the prevention of *serious* crime (see generally *crime prevention/crime reduction*) or its *detection*; or to *safeguard* the economic well-being of the UK. Subject to exceptions set out in the Regulation of Investigatory Powers Act 2000 (RIPA) (such as interception under *Prison Rules* or for business purposes under separate arrangements which provide for a *warning* that interception may occur) the police, etc. can use interception only if they have a warrant signed by the *Home Secretary*. They follow a statutory **Interception of Communications Code of Practice**. The **Interception of Communications Commissioner** independently scrutinises and reports annually on intercept activity: see official-documents.gov.uk Controversially, the *law* does not allow information obtained via intercepts to be used as *evidence* (except, e.g. re offences relating to the intercept itself; official secrets; and in proceedings, e.g. before the Special Immigration Appeals Commission (SIAC) (see *immigration*). Instead, they are used as *intelligence* to help with the disruption of *serious* crime and *terrorism/terrorists* and to enable the gathering of other admissible evidence. According to the Home Office, 'This policy is designed to protect the close and *effective* co-operation between *law enforcement* and intelligence agencies'. Some 2,000 intercept *warrants* are authorised per year. A two-year review of the use of such evidence ordered by the *Prime Minister* and completed in 2005 concluded that the risks of using intercepts evidentially outweigh the benefits of doing so (see the Chilcott Review: available at official-documents.gov.uk). See also *GCHQ*.

interests of justice

A criterion for decision-making and a basis for upholding the *law*, principle and *rights* of the *State* or *citizens*. Thus the interests of justice may be an over-riding or residual consideration according to the circumstances. For one statutory example, see *sentence/sentencing/*'deferment of sentence'. The concept has been criticised as being vague, flexible and not subject to any discernible *rules*. See generally *justice*.

intermediate treatment (IT)

A form of *supervision* for *juveniles* (see generally that entry and also *youth justice*) that was prevalent for more than a decade from the early 1980s. IT involved the construction of a *supervision* programme by youth justice workers to tackle the juvenile *offending behaviour*. It grew out of initiatives by local authority social services departments and in its operation was one of the earliest forms of *multi-agency* arrangements and *partnerships*. Strongly supported by central government it foreshadowed the work of *youth offending teams* (YOTs) and *'working together'* in general.

intermittent custody See *sentence*; **international aspects** See *global/international dimensions* and *police/policing/*'Europol'/'Interpol'.

internet

The internet has revolutionised the way in which some crimes can be committed; and also the way in which offences of many kinds are policed (see also generally *detection, investigation; science; technology*). There is a police-linked multi-agency **Internet Watch Foundation** co-sponsored by the European Union (EU) where illegal content on the internet can be reported, especially child sexual *abuse, obscenity* and (in the UK) *incitement* to racial hatred (see *hate; race/racism*)(see iwf.org.uk). The **UK Internet Crime Forum (ICF)** exists in order 'to promote, maintain and enhance an *effective* and proportionate working relationship between industry, government and *law enforcement* to tackle crime and foster *confidence* in the use of the internet'. The IWF draws certain distinctions re *computers* and offending: the use of computers to commit 'traditional crimes'; the emergence of new ways of committing 'old crimes'; crimes that are 'context specific' to, for example, the internet (see also *cybercrime* in *Touchstones*); and crimes 'where computers are the victim' not simply the medium via which offences occur (such as 'denial of service attacks' or other forms of *hacking*) (delineations which tend to shift like sands within a fast-moving environment). For some further information, see internetcrimeforum.org.uk

interpretation

(1) **Legal interpretation** describes the process whereby judges and lawyers by dint of their professional training and expertise determine the meaning to be given to the words of an *Act of Parliament*, other *legislation*, or earlier *rulings* under the law of *precedent*. There are established (if sometimes competing) **rules of interpretation** and an **Interpretation Act 1978** under which, e.g. England always includes Wales; the singular the plural. For this specialist area see works on *legal* interpretation. (2) Similarly, if less formalised, across the CJS re the meaning of the contents of a document, instruction, standard, protocol. (3) Increasingly, the need for **interpreters for foreign language speakers or deaf people** has been recognised across the CJ: for suspects during an *investigation*, for the accused person or *witnesses* at a trial, to serving *prisoners* and beyond (which may involve **remote interpreting** by telephone/a link). Considerations of *fairness* and *human rights* point to assistance being necessary if the accused person's first language is not English (including if it is Welsh) or where he or she is deaf so that 'signing' is required. In the courtroom, interpreters take an **interpreter's oath** (or make an *affirmation*) to truly interpret the *evidence*. Courts, police and other practitioners use lists of interpreters. For an overview, see *Interpreters and the Legal Process* (1996), Colin J and Morris R, Waterside Press.

intervention

Usually a reference to the formal and official processes whereby representatives of CJS agencies/services intrude into the lives of *citizens* in the interests of crime prevention/crime reduction and/or to support people, especially juveniles but also other people who are at *risk* of offending, sometimes linked to an *action plan, referrals*, etc. Intervention is a controversial topic, especially re **early intervention** which, of necessity, involves predictions as to who is likely to offend in the future and *labelling* effects (see *Touchstones*). There may be a dilemma: intervention could be a *mistake*, whilst a failure to act soon enough may allow *serious* offences to occur (as demonstrated by a number of *child protection* cases, of which one of the best known case of modern times is that of *Victoria Climbié*: see *Touchstones*. See also *youth justice*.

interview

This is usually a reference to an interview with a suspect or *witness* by or on behalf of the police or other *law enforcement agency* within the chain of events: *report, detection, investigation, detention, arrest* and *charge*. Hence various *safeguards*, including under the *Police and Criminal Evidence Act 1984* and its *Codes*: consult specialist texts. The word is used in other CJS contexts where one person asks questions of another.

investigation

An investigation into a criminal offence may involve interviewing many prospective witnesses and assembling other evidence such as exhibits, documents, and forensic or other *expert* reports (see also *witness; opinion*). Relevant information must only be

obtained within the law and special provisions come into play as soon as there is a suspect - breach of which may result in evidence later being ruled inadmissible by a court
(see *evidence*). Certain evidence may also be ruled out as prejudicial or under the fair
trials provisions of the European Convention On Human Rights: see *fair/fairness*.

J

joinder

A term that refers to **joining matters together** for the purposes of a *trial, charge* or
indictment, i.e. **(1)** **two or more offences**; or **(2)** **two or more accused people.**
Technical rules apply to (1) and (2) (and see *fair/fairness*). See also *assisting crime;
conspiracy* and texts on *criminal law* for what is known as the doctrine of **joint enterprise**. **(3)** For **joint working** by agencies/services see *partnership; working together*

judge

Generic description and 'job-title' of anyone appointed to make *judicial* decisions in
a court of law; without reference to the rank of judge. The term is also loosely applied
to magistrates (who **judge cases**); but a jury, who are also **judges of fact,** would not
be so described. Beneath the *higher judiciary* and special arrangements re the *military*
apart, the main judges in criminal cases are: **circuit judge** and **part-time circuit
judge** (the latter aka 'recorder' or 'assistant recorder') who sit in the *Crown Court*.
Suitably qualified people can apply to be assessed by the *Judicial Appointments Commission* (JAC) with a view to appointment. Each Crown Court centre has a **resident
judge** who acts as the link between all of its judges, *management* (see also *administra-
tion/administrative*), other court centres, CJS agencies/services and the *Judicial Office*.
Circuit judges are addressed as 'Your/His/Her Honour'. Around 100 **district judges
(magistrates' courts)** who are *barristers* or *solicitors* are full-time salaried magistrates
(contrast *magistrate/*'lay magistrate'). They sit on their own to hear cases and dispense
justice, including by holding trials and sentencing people. They operate mainly in
London, urban centres and larger counties; and may also sit as 'recorders' (above).
For **High Court judge**, see *High Court*; for **Lord Justice**, see that entry and *Court
of Appeal*; for **Law Lord** (i.e. a **judge of the House of Lords** (whilst this lasts)), see
Law Lord. A **Judges' Council** was originally set up by the Judicature Act 1873 and
chaired by the Lord Chancellor. All of the judges of the (old) *Supreme Court* were
members. It continued until 1981. Lord Lane, Lord Chief Justice (LCJ), set up a new
Judges' Council in 1988; chaired by the LCJ, with a smaller membership of senior
judges. In 2002, it adopted a written constitution and has since widened its membership to include representatives from all areas of the *judiciary*. In 2006 it was further
revised following the *Constitutional Reform Act 2005*.

Trial by a **judge and jury** is achieved by separating-out of the roles of each: the judge
has general charge of the trial and deals with matters of a *legal* nature (sometimes in
the absence of the jury). He or she rules on admissibility of *evidence, practice* and *procedure*; and decides questions of *mixed fact and law,* e.g. whether the jury should hear
of an alleged *confession* said by the *defence* to have been made under duress or oppression. He or she must withdraw the case from the jury if there is insufficient evidence
to support a conviction; and can direct the jury to bring in a verdict of not guilty.
The judge is responsible for giving *directions, preliminary hearings* and/or *case manage-*

ment. **Judge's ruling** is the term used to signify a ruling on a specific point which is at issue in a given case. Rulings on points of *evidence* are called evidentiary rulings: see also *appeal.* At the end of a trial, he or she sums up to the jury (aka the **judges' summing-up**), i.e. reminds them of the evidence and points out its potential *weight* (see *Touchstones*). When the jury has reached its *verdict*, he or she asks whether they find the accused guilty or not guilty. If the former, the judge passes sentence. A majority verdict can be accepted in certain circumstances: see *verdict*. A **judge-only trial** is one by a judge without a jury under the provisions of the *Criminal Justice Act 2003* after a prosecutor applies for this re certain *fraud* charges; if there is a *risk* of *jury tampering*; or a trial has collapsed and the jury has been discharged due to tampering.

judicial/judicially

Appertaining to the *judiciary* (below) and acting in a judicial manner (aka **acting judicially**) when making decisions, respectively. The **Area Judicial Forum (AJF)**, chaired by a circuit *judge,* is a wholly judicial mechanism whereby judges and magistrates can liaise with one another and as between the Crown Court and magistrates' court (and other *local* courts) re matters of common interest. It should be contrasted with a parallel **Judicial Leadership and Management Group (JLMG)** which enables discussion of judicial interests vis-à-vis *administration* by HM Court Service. Note also the existence of a more localised Justices' Interest Group (JIG)(see *magistrate*). Since 2005 a **Judicial Appointments Commission (JAC)** has been responsible for making recommendations to the *Justice Secretary* for the appointment of judges (and tribunal members). The **Judicial Communications Office (JCO)** works centrally to receive and disseminate *communications* with and between members of the judiciary nationwide. **Judicial decision-making** is the description for decisions by judges and magistrates (and possibly tribunal members); **judicial discretion** the application by them of their *discretion* to the facts and merits of an individual case, including fairness (see *fair/fairness*) and other **judicial principles**. **Judicial Office** refers to that of the *Lord Chief Justice* and senior judges via which interaction can take place, e.g. with other bodies and, in conjunction with *The Concordat,* which protects **judicial independence** (a form of *independence/interdependence* which insulates judicial decisions from undue influence) with, e.g. *Ministers of State* or officials. **Judicial policy** (which some see as a misnomer: as being in conflict with discretion) is the setting out of a broad approach to matters of *justice.* It is allied to *guidelines, Practice Directions* and the work of the *Sentencing Guidelines Council* (SGC). For **judicial review** see *appeal.* The **Judicial Studies Board (JSB)** provides training for full-time and part-time judges. A local Bench Training and Development Committee (BTDC and **Magistrates' Area Training Committee** (MATC) do the same re *magistrates.* The JSB publishes information across the spectrum of judicial decision-making, including an *Adult Court Benchbook, Youth Court Benchbook* and *Equal Treatment Benchbook*: all accessible at jsboard.co.uk For **Office for Judicial Complaints**, see *complaint.*

judiciary

Omnibus term for judges and magistrates of all ranks: one of the three 'great arms' of State re the *separation of powers.* The *Justice Secretary* has a duty to **protect the independence of the judiciary**: see, generally, *independence/interdependence.*

jurisdiction

(1) The extent of the power of a court, judge or magistrate to deal with a given matter, exercise authority, pass sentence, make orders, etc., with particular reference to its boundaries, including any territorial *restrictions*, *time limits* and maximum powers of sentence. For some other examples of provisions impacting on jurisdiction, see *appeal; Crown Court; either way offence; hack/hacking; higher courts; indictable offence; House of Lords; magistrate; summary offence; Supreme Court*. **(2)** The word is also used in other contexts to signify comparable powers/constraints re agencies/services or public officers. **Questions of jurisdiction** attract the *ultra vires* doctrine (beyond power) (and its opposite, *intra vires* (within power)). Hence also **inherent jurisdiction** (sometimes called inherent *discretion*): that which exists by virtue of the nature of a situation, task or role. Under longstanding *case law*, all formal rules are supplemented by the in built authority of judges, magistrates, police officers, etc. to adapt what they do to the circumstances and needs of individual situations. The *Home Secretary* also has certain inherent powers: see that entry.

juror/jury

The **jury** is the incarnation of the right of a *citizen* to be tried by his or her peers; presumed to stem from *Magna Carta* (1215) (see *Touchstones*). **Jurors** are chosen at random from the electoral roll. Since 2003, certain people such as judges and others concerned in the *administration of justice*, the clergy and others who formerly could not, or need not, perform **jury service** (known as **ineligibility**) are required to do so unless they have an acceptable *reason* (for what is termed **excusal**). They include: those over the age of 65, Members of Parliament, doctors, followers of certain *religions* and (in certain circumstances) members of the armed forces. Jurors are entitled to receive an attendance **allowance**, lunch vouchers, etc. for use in staff restaurants. A prosecutor can make a **jury challenge**, i.e object to an individual juror without putting forward a reason, by simply calling on him or her to 'stand by for the *Crown*', but this right of **peremptory challenge** is limited in its extent and rarely used in practice. Both prosecution and *defence* can make a **jury challenge for cause**, i.e. seek to reject a juror for good reason, e.g. because he or she is disqualified, ineligible, or biased. The **Juries Act 1974** (as amended in 2003) lists categories of people who are subject to **disqualification from jury service**, including those on *bail* or who have served, or are serving, *custodial sentences* or *community sentences* of certain types. For **election for trial by jury**, see *allocation and sending*. Each member of the jury swears a **juror's oath** (or makes a comparable *affirmation*): 'I will faithfully try the several issues joined between our Sovereign lady the Queen and the prisoner at the Bar, and give a true verdict according to the evidence'. There is a **Jury Central Summoning Bureau (JCSB)** (sponsored by the MOJ), which administers **jury summoning** on behalf of the Crown Court) and processes applications to be excused jury service; re which the *Justice Secretary* must issue *guidance*. **Jury trial** is a synonym for trial in the **Crown Court** (other than a judge-only trial: see *judge*). For the **role of the judge and jury**, see under *judge*. A **foreman of the jury** is elected by a simple vote of the jury in question and acts as spokesperson. **Speech to the jury** usually signifies an address by a *legal representative* at the start or end of a case; or by the judge at the very end of the case, aka **summing-up to the jury**: see *judge*/'roles of the judge and jury'. **Tampering with a jury**, e.g. bribery, threats, intimidation (including 'eye-balling' in the courtroom) is an offence (but see other uses of *tampering*) and a reason to **withdraw a case from a jury** and hold a judge-alone trial. 'Withdraw, etc.' is also used if a judge rules there is insufficient *evidence* for a trial to continue: see *judge*/'roles, etc.' For the backdrop to jury trial, see *The Criminal Jury Old and New: Jury Power from Early Times to the Present Day* (2007), Hostettler J, Waterside Press.

just See *fair/fairness*; *justice*; **just deserts** See *Touchstones*

justice

(1) 'Doing justice' or delivering justice is a central purpose and tenet of the CJS, meaning *criminal justice* predominantly. In the abstract, justice has various facets: doing things in a just manner and by taking only relevant matters into account: see, e.g. *equality*, *evidence*; *fair/fairness*, *human rights*, *Rule of Law*; so as to arrive at a **just outcome** based on sound *reasons*, consistently, following set procedures and avoiding arbitrariness: see also *accountability*; *guideline*; *openness*. Hence the maxim **justice is blind**: see *blind/blindness*. Justice-based references and derivatives include: **community justice**: see *community*; **Justice For All (2002)**: the White Paper that foreshadowed the *Criminal Justice Act 2003*; **justice gap**: see *reported crime*; **local justice**: see *local*; **perverting the course of justice** by, e.g. giving false or misleading information to the police or destroying *evidence*; **restorative justice**: see that entry; and **Royal justice** as dispensed by the sovereign until superseded by the authority of the judges following the Glorious Revolution of 1689. For **summary justice**, see *summary*. Note use of the formula **'justice for'** as a *campaign* slogan (or **4justice** as in Fathers4Justice: a group latterly taking direct action scaling buildings to unfurl banners urging better *responses* to their claimed rights). Similarly where people believe that there has been an **injustice**, or a **miscarriage of justice**: see in particular *Criminal Cases Review Commission* (CCRC) and the examples in *Touchstones* (including the landmark case of the *Birmingham Six*). **Smart justice** was a slogan used by New Labour to describe its crime policies from 1997 onwards; and is the name of a crime reduction *charity* which seeks 'to widen the public debate on crime and punishment and increase *confidence* in *community*-based solutions': see smartjustice.org (2) The word 'justice' also occurs in names, titles or descriptions, as with **High Court of Justice**: see *High Court*; **justice of the peace (JP)** aka *magistrate*. (3) The **Justice of the Peace Act 1361** was key to the evolution of the magistracy (and is still relied on re *binding over*). Note also **Supreme Court Justice**: see *Supreme Court*. (4) There are less structured ways in which 'justice' is used re which no short guide can do more mention, such as **moral justice**, **poetic justice** and **mob justice**. (5) JUSTICE is a leading, all party law *reform* and *human rights* organization: see justice.org.uk

justices' clerk (JC) The chief *legal* adviser to a bench of magistrates (including to a district *judge* (magistrates' courts); even though the judge will be a *lawyer*). Justices' clerks must be *barristers* or *solicitors* of at least five years standing. The role is fundamental to the system of volunteer *magistrates*. As only around 50 JCs remain (from 600 in the 1960s), everyday *advice* is provided by their teams of court *legal* advisers. The adviser is not party to decisions and the law circumscribes his or her role. The **Justices' Clerks' Society (JCS)** founded in 1839 is the professional body representing JCs and their legal advisers. Its aims include keeping relevant law under review, providing guidance to members and promoting improvements. See jc-society.co.uk

Justice Secretary (aka Secretary of State for Justice and Lord Chancellor) Since 2007, the responsible *Minister of State* at the MOJ. He or she need not be a *lawyer* (as was the convention until 2007). He or she is an elected politician appointed by the Prime Minister and a member of the Cabinet; and since 2005 no longer directly involved in the selection of judges or magistrates, or judicial *discipline*. Under the *Constitutional Reform Act 2005,* he or she must protect the independence of the judiciary. The first Justice Secretary was *Jack Straw* MP (a former *Home Secretary)* who on taking up that position asserted that this was his first *priority.*

juvenile

Someone below the age of 18. The name of the former **juvenile court** was changed to the *youth court* in 1991, but the term 'juvenile' rather than 'youth' appears to have largely continued in everyday speech. For some other key references re juveniles, see *appropriate adult; child; young person; Youth Justice Board; youth offending panel; youth offending team* (YOT); *warning and reprimand* and *welfare.*

K

keeping the peace

Fundamentally, criminal justice concerns **keeping the Queen's peace** (see also *Crown*). The need to do so by using *sanctions* against people who do not obey the criminal law is confirmed by societal needs ancient and modern, English and foreign. Few *communities* exist without such arrangements. The hue and cry of *Anglo-Saxon* times (see *Touchstones*) and *punishments* of former days are part of this same continuum of *controls;* which now find expression in forms of *imprisonment, fines* and *community sentences.* Ultimately *political,* the question remains, 'What should be done about lawbreakers?'; whereas the day-to-day functioning of the CJS is a *management*-related issue within various agencies/services. Hence, also, historically the **keepers of the peace** were the predecessors of the justices of the peace (JPs): see *magistrate.*

knife See *weapon;* **Koestler Trust** See *Touchstones*

L

label/labelling See *Touchstones*

law

It is important for CJS purposes: **(1)** to distinguish matters of law, i.e. of a *legal* nature and concerning the *interpretation* and/or application of **the law** as contained in *Acts of Parliament* (or delegated *legislation*) and the Common Law, from the facts and merits of cases, or, e.g. their *moral aspects* (see *Touchstones*); and **(2)** to note that the 'law' is used in a wide variety of other contexts, e.g. to signify the forces of **law and order.** This is the umbrella term under which *debates* on aspects of *crime* and *punishment* tend to take place. In practical terms it connotes the role of the Home Office, police and *border* guards in ensuring the *protection* of the public, public *safety* and *security,* and maintaining *public order.* **Law enforcement** encompasses the work of several hundred authorised bodies, aka **law enforcement agencies.** They include mainstream agencies/services such as the *CPS, Serious and Organized Crime Agency; British Transport Police,* Ministry of Defence Police; UK Atomic Energy Constabulary; *Serious Fraud Office;* HM *Revenue & Customs; Health and Safety Executive;* and *TV Licensing* as well as many other specialist or less well-known bodies charged with an *investigation* and/or *prosecution* function. The National Probation Service (see *probation*) also so describes itself. For other uses of *enforcement* see that entry.

The words 'lawful/unlawful' signify conduct, activities or events that comply with or contravene existing legal requirements (*civil* and/or *criminal*). A **Law Lord** (aka **Lord of Appeal in Ordinary**) is a judge of the House of Lords and life peer. By convention Law Lords were appointed from amongst holders of high *judicial* office or lawyers of long standing. (They will become *Supreme Court Justices* and appointments is now open to a wider range of suitably qualified people). Currently, they deal with *legal, judicial* or *constitutional* matters. Up to 12 in number, they sit as an Appellate Committee in a side room (i.e. not in the main chamber of the House) to hear appeals from the *Court of Appeal* and *High Court*; and give *rulings* (known as 'speeches'), which tend to carry great *weight* (see *Touchstones*). For **law officer** see *Attorney General; Solicitor General*. A **law report** is one written and in effect authenticated by a *barrister* (normally) and differs from a 'news report' in that respect. Law reports focus on *legal* matters and are a key tool in the operation of the doctrine of *precedent*. They are published in a various series such as the All England Law Reports, Weekly Law Reports, Criminal Appeal Reports (with a separate series on sentencing), Justice of the Peace Reports and Road Traffic Reports. They also appear, in summary form in *The Times* and *Independent*. **Lawyer** is a generic term for legal practitioners as a whole: see *barrister; solicitor; legal representative*. **'Laying down the law'** is a metaphor for 'pontificating' on a topic regardless of whether it has any true legal connotations.

Lawrence, Stephen See *Touchstones*

leave

Prior permission to do something (as is sometimes required by *law*), e.g: (**1**) **leave to appeal** as per certain *appeals* to the *Court of Appeal* or *House of Lords* (*Supreme Court*); or (**2**) appeal to those courts or the *Crown Court*; 'out of time', i.e. beyond the period normally allowed by law; or (**3**) to extend other **time limits** (see generally that entry); (**4**) **leave to bring a prosecution** as may have to be obtained from the *Attorney General;* (**5**) **leave to apply**, i.e. to make certain *applications*; or (**6**) **leave to remain in the UK**: see *asylum; border; immigration*.

legal

Appertaining to the *law* as opposed, e.g. to the facts, or *evidence, practice* standards or *moral aspects* (see *Touchstones* for the last of these). Hence, e.g. **legal advice** which is provided in the form of a **legal opinion** (see *opinion*) and, according to the context, by a *barrister, solicitor,* Crown prosecutor (see *Crown Prosecution Service*), justices' clerk (or court **legal adviser**)(lawyers as a whole being known as the **legal profession**), or from an 'advice centre' or Citizens Advice Bureau (see *advice*). In concept, **legal aid** allows any *citizen* to obtain **legal advice and representation**; under the auspices of the **Legal Services Commission (LSC)**. This is provided under a system which, historically, took both the *interests of justice* and financial circumstances of the applicant into account. The LSC replaced the Legal Aid Board in 2001 when the former assumed responsibility for funding. This *reform,* based on the *Access to Justice Act 1999* and *Criminal Defence Service* (Advice and Assistance Act) 2001, had various effects: 'legal aid' as such was replaced by **State-funded legal representation**; legal aid orders by **representation orders** granted in the *interests of justice*; and with free representation in magistrates' courts. Where a case ends in the *Crown Court,* the judge can order the accused person to pay some or all his or her legal aid costs, aka a 'recovery order'. Other reforms have involved *effectiveness and efficiency* savings in line with (some people say 'ahead of') those affecting the entire CJS; leading to claims that *access to justice* is in fact being curtailed and some solicitors leaving the scheme. See also *Community Legal Service* (CLS) and *Community Legal Advice*.

legislation

Omnibus term for that part of the *law* created by or under the authority of Parliament; as opposed to the *Common Law*. Hence also a distinction between **primary legislation**, i.e. *Acts of Parliament* (aka statutes) and **secondary legislation** or **delegated legislation** (aka statutory instruments (SIs); also styled *rules* and *regulations*), i.e. made under the authority of an Act (e.g. by a *Minister of State*; or a byelaw of a local or other public authority to whom such powers have been passed down). **Legislative process** signifies the related Parliamentary or other procedures; and **'The Legislature'** Parliament in this law-making capacity. See also *separation of powers*.

legitimacy

In a *democracy,* the idea that power and its use stem from *consent* of the people; which imports notions of its proper use within a context of *accountability* and *transparency.*

leniency

Sentencing someone in a lesser way than is dictated by the *seriousness* of an offence due to *mitigation,* the use of *discretion* and/or as an act of *mercy* (see those entries). Note also, in particular, the **unduly-lenient sentence**: see *Attorney General.*

liaison

Mutual contact with a view to sharing *information* and *concerns*, especially re *communication*, understanding and the carrying out of joint responsibilities. Examples appear within those entries in this work touching on criminal justice networks. Readers might like to note that it is only in modern times that many such arrangements have been truly developed, in conjunction with *partnership* and *working together.*

liberty

(1) A core feature of *democracy* and fundamental *rights* is the **liberty of the subject**. This is generally regarded by western-style *democracies* as something to be prized and not taken away lightly. The Declaration of Independence (USA) (1776) held certain truths to be self-evident, 'that all men are created equal, that they are endowed by their Creator with certain unalienable Rights [and] among these are Life, Liberty, and the pursuit of Happiness'. Similarly, 'Liberty, Equality, Fraternity' used in the *French Revolution* (see *Touchstones*); whose origins lie in earlier times and cultures. Re the UK, similar sentiments are encapsulated in *Magna Carta* (see *Touchstones*) and in modern times *human rights:* see Article 5 **'the right to liberty'**. For exceptions in practice, see, e.g. *arrest, detention*, refusal of *bail* and *imprisonment.* Many learned texts extol or seek to explain liberty in more abstract terms. Among better-known works are *On Liberty* (1859) by John Stuart Mill (Penguin English Library Series) and *Law, Liberty and Morality* (1963), Hart HLA, Oxford University Press. **(2)** More generally **civil liberties** is the description given to a swathe of basic rights that are assumed to be inherent within a liberal *democracy.* Hence also **(3) Liberty** (aka **National Council for Civil Liberties**): see *Touchstones.* Note also **(4)** the **Convention on Modern Liberty** launched in 2009 by Baroness Helena Kennedy QC and other penal *reformers*: an alliance of such groups whose aims include countering attacks on fundamental *rights, freedoms* and *safeguards*, etc. vis-à-vis the *State* and modern-day intrusions re such matters: see modernliberty.net According to one protagonist, Timothy Garton Ash 'Liberty in Britain is Facing Death by a Thousand Cuts' (*Guardian*, 19 February 2009). Note a counter notion of people who may wish to disparage such reformers that the latter may have been 'infected with' a **dangerous liberalism**; as identified by David Faulkner (himself a supporter of the need for sound underlying *values*) in 'Better Government: More Justice, Success and Failure in Criminal Justice, 1992-1998', Centre for Crime and Justice Studies (forthcoming 2009).

licence

A permission or authority that may be granted to an individual or a body. Hence, in particular, in a criminal justice context: a **pharmaceutical licence** to manufacture or supply drugs where this would otherwise be an offence: see, generally, *drugs*; en**dorsement of a driving licence:** see, generally, *road traffic; sentence/sentencing/* ancillary order'; **life licence:** see *life imprisonment*; **parole licence:** see *parole*. Note also licence in the sense of permission or *leave:* see that entry.

life imprisonment

A **sentence of life imprisonment**; and hence the term **lifer** for someone so sentenced. The number of prisoners serving such sentences (or other *indeterminate* sentences) increased from around 2,500 in the 1990s to over 10,000 by 2008. Lifers are subject to a **life sentence tariff** (see generally *tariff*) and ongoing *review* and *risk-assessment*. Depending on their progress, gradual downgrading of their security category will normally occur until they can enter open conditions (see *prison*) and begin the process of pre-*release* visits into the *community*, including in many instances on work-related schemes. Because of the time served under many life sentences (14 years on average and more re **mandatory life sentences for murder**) a chain of HM Prison Service and National Probation Service personnel (see *probation*) are involved in carrying out the *sentence plan* and in *reintegration and resettlement, education* and *assessment* processes. Typically, lifers complete a range of courses and may undertake longer-term educational or other projects. On release, they remain on licence for the rest of their natural lives and are subject to *recall* if they become a *danger* to the public. Hence, also, the terms **natural lifer**, i.e. those who have been told that 'life means life' (there are around 40 such prisoners in England and Wales including a number of *serial killers*); **discretionary lifers** (those sentenced to the maximum sentence when a life sentence is not *mandatory*); and **'two strikes' lifers** (see 'three strikes' in *Touch-stones*). For a general overview, see *Murderers and Life Imprisonment: Containment, Treatment, Safety and Risk* (1998), Cullen E and Newell T, Waterside Press.

list/listing

The scheduling (sometimes called 'allocation': but see also, e.g. *allocation and sending*) of cases at a court centre as between courtrooms, judges and magistrates - which occurs at both the *Crown Court* and in *magistrates' courts* as well as in the *higher courts;* as usually carried out by a **listing officer** (or **listing manager**) to avoid *delay* make optimum use of resources, and maximise 'judge time'. He or she will also consider the needs of the parties and witnesses. Cases can be listed (i.e. transferred) from one area to another if local sensitivities are involved, or for other good reasons.

live link See *video-link*; **'living instrument'** See *human rights*

local

One of the four main tiers of *administration*, i.e. local, area, regional and national. Hence the **local authority** which is charged with a range of (sole or *multi-agency*) *duties* and *responsibilities,* including re crime prevention/crime reduction, certain prosecutions and the *welfare* of *vulnerable* people, especially children, *youth justice,* the aged and those suffering from *mental impairment;* often via local *social services.* The idea that public affairs should be conducted locally where appropriate also has powerful criminal justice-related connotations in terms, e.g. of *access to justice,* history (criminal justice began when duties were placed on each 'hundred' and shire), ownership, public *confidence* and functionality (as with magistrates who know and are in touch with their own areas). The terms **local justice** and **local justice area (LJA)** (the basic unit of administration of the magistrates' court) also emphasise that as a matter of policy, *justice* in England and Wales has been dispensed locally, but is now under the nationwide *management* of HM *Court Service.* Despite a reduction in numbers from the 1960s onwards, under amalgamation and rationalisation, magistrates' courts sit on a daily basis in several hundred locations. The *Crown Court* also remains primarily 'locally' based; whilst **local policing** occurs through 43 'local' police forces; and often, e.g. via 'neighbourhood policing': see, generally, *police/policing.* See, also, e.g. *Criminal Justice Board/* **Local Criminal Justice Board (LCJB)'.**

lord

A title and rank used for various CJS purposes (so long as this continues), e.g. re **Law Lord**: see *law*, *House of Lords* (but note the change to a *Supreme Court* and Supreme Court Justices; **Lord Chancellor** (as now per *Justice Secretary* and Lord Chancellor) a historic role dating from medieval times; who, prior to the Constitutional Reform Act 2005, belonged to all three arms of *State* (see *separation of powers*) as a member of the *Cabinet* (and thus the Executive), speaker of the House of Lords (part of the Legislature) and head of the *judiciary.* The Lord Chancellor was also responsible for the efficient *administration of justice.* With the creation of the MOJ in 2007 some further vestiges of the role disappeared or became obscured by the new dual role. Hence, also, the former **Lord Chancellor's Department** (LCD) that became the Department of Constitutional Affairs (DCA) (2002) until taken over by the MOJ. The **Lord Chief Justice (LCJ)** is the head of the judiciary in England and Wales on whom statutory and other duties (*legal* and *administrative*) are cast; he or she often presides in the *Court of Appeal* and/or *High Court.* The LCJ has always been a powerful figure and defender of the *Rule of Law* and since 2005 heads various judicial bodies, including the Judicial Office (JO)(see also *Concordat*). For a history of the role, see *Lions Under the Throne* (1983), Mockler A, London: Muller. **Lord Justice (LJ)** is the rank of a judge of the *Court of Appeal*; not lords as such and they do not belong to/ sit in the House of Lords (unless otherwise entitled to). They number around 30; and are usually promoted from amongst *High Court judges* (who may deputise for LJs).

low-level behaviour, offending, etc.

Misbehaviour of a *petty* nature, of the least serious kind - sometimes called 'minor misdeeds'; that may amount to a criminal offence, but that is often deemed by the police, authorities, etc. to be worthy of minimal *priority* or *intervention* and that may thus be dealt with by a *warning* or *caution* (but possibly prosecution). Compare (un) *acceptable behaviour; anti-social behaviour* (ASB).

Macpherson Report See *Lawrence, Stephen* in *Touchstones*

magistrate

A **justice of the peace (JP)** (magistrate being a synonym), i.e. a *citizen* appointed to dispense justice in a **magistrates court** (below) as a form of voluntary public service and to carry out related duties. JPs first appeared in the 14th century when their role was fused with that of local administrator (see *administration/administrative*); but their origins can also be traced beyond the *Keepers of the Peace* appointed by Simon de Montfort (1264). In modern times, their work has been governed by a series of **Magistrates' Courts Acts** (MCAs), e.g. of 1952, 1957 and 1980. Property qualifications were abolished in 1905 in favour of seeking out people with the personal qualities for the role; since when the *bench* has become more broad-based. In 2005 the **administration** of magistrates' courts passed to HM *Court Service* (HMCS). Liaison **mechanisms** include such developments as a **Justices' Interest Group (JIG)** to enable HM Court Service (since 2005 responsible for the administration of such courts) to be aware of magistrates' views and concerns and allow for proposals from either side to be discussed; and **Area Judicial Forums (AJFs)** (see *judicial*).

Magistrates' court is a description for: **(1)** the decision-making tribunal which sits as a court of law to deal with cases under statutory powers and to dispense *summary justice*; **(2)** the building in which the court sits and where accused people, *barristers*, *solicitors* (mostly), *witnesses*, etc, attend court hearings, aka the **magistrates' courthouse**; and **(3)** technically speaking, all functions of JPs, in court or out, are discharged 'by a magistrates' court', e.g. when a *single justice* (below) signs a document. Magistrates' courts are inspected by *HM Inspectorate of Courts Administration* (HMICA); but not re *judicial* functions where *accountability* is via the *appeal* system. The **appointment** of lay magistrates occurs on behalf of the *Sovereign* following recommendations to the *Justice Secretary* by an independent **Advisory Committee on the Appointment of Magistrates**. Political views are not relevant except to ensure balance. They are appointed to a **Commission of the Peace**, have nationwide *jurisdiction* and retire at 70 years of age when they are normally placed on the 'supplemental list' following which they have few powers. They usually sit in court 'in threes': the legal minimum is two except when *legislation* states otherwise. There is an overall chair of the bench elected by colleagues. A 'bench chair' or 'day chair' usually presides on a rota basis. Only those approved by **Bench Training and Development Committees (BTDCs)** (of various kinds: often shortened, generically, to TDC) can act thus; linked to training, mentoring and 'competences'. The vast bulk of magistrates, some 30,000, are **lay magistrates**, i.e. unpaid volunteers given only a modest allowance for any loss of earnings, and travelling and subsistence allowances. They are not versed in law but advised by a *justices' clerk* (or court legal adviser). 'Lay' has in fact fallen from use: substantial training compensates for lack of qualifications, including via **Magistrates' Area Training Committees** and BTDCs (above). But contrast a professional **district judge (magistrates' court)**: see *judge*. Some decisions need only a **single justice**, e.g. *adjournments* and *remands*; as do many out-of-court duties. An **occasional court** (aka a **special court**) is one held outside normal hours, e.g. at a weekend. For **Magistrates' Association (MA)** see below.

The **magistrates' retiring room** is where JPs can discuss cases, including *verdict* and *sentence* in private. Legal rules, *guidelines* and a key *Practice Direction* on the role of legal advisers regulate when magistrates can (or sometimes should) be interrupted or informed that certain outcomes follow as a matter of law on given facts. Magistrates who serve in the *youth court* (or family court) have extra duties. For an overview, see *The Magistrates' Court: An Introduction* (2009), Gibson B, Waterside Press.

Magistrates' Association (MA) The MA was established in 1920 and incorporated by Royal Charter in 1962. It responds to Government on matters of mutual interest and initiates projects and proposals of its own. It publishes a regular journal, *The Magistrate* and, for many years, the 'Magistrates' Courts Sentencing Guidelines' (which have been superseded by comparable guidelines published after wide-ranging consultation by the *Sentencing Guidelines Council*). It has various committees, including an MA **Support, Training and Development Committee** (STDC). Most JPs subscribe to the MA and many are active in branches. Each branch elects a given number of representatives to a national council of some 100 members. A national secretariat is based in London. See, further, magistrates-association.org.uk

Magna Carta See *Touchstones*

management
The running, *supervision*, etc. of an agency/service, organization unit, team or body as noted under *administration/administrative*. But note especially here the terms **New Public Management (NPM)** (1980s onwards), involving, e.g. driving up *performance* through key performance indicators (KPIs) and *targets* whilst also promoting administrative *reform* and modernisation, which has affected the CJS as it has other public services. NPM has obvious links to *effectiveness and efficiency, value for money* and the *costs of criminal justice*. It can also cause tensions with regard to truly independent decision-making (see generally *independence/interdependence*). The idea of **managing offenders** has been in vogue from around that same time, the idea that crime cannot necessarily be eradicated but that it (and the offenders who commit it) can be managed so as to reduce its impact, in conjunction, e.g. with crime prevention/crime reduction initiatives. Hence also **integrated offender management** where various agencies/services are involved. Thus e.g. the **National Offender Management Service (NOMS)**: see *offender management*; and **offender managers** within the National Probation Service (NPS)(see *probation*). See also *Carter Report(s)* in *Touchstones*. The word 'management' is sometimes used to imply control: as with **anger management**. Note also terms such as **risk management**.

mandatory
Obligatory, not open to the use of *discretion* (except to the extent that it may be preserved by relevant *legislation*). For examples, see *sentence/sentencing; life imprisonment; road traffic*/'disqualification'; and the entry for *'three strikes'* in *Touchstones*.

manslaughter
An offence of homicide falling short of *murder* that can occur due to the existence of a lesser state of mind on the part of the accused or where a *defence* to murder such as provocation or diminished responsibility (see *mental impairment*) succeeds. In broad terms it is the killing of a human being by criminal negligence (or 'gross negligence' or a species of 'recklessness'): as to which see specialist works. Note also the present

Government review of homicide mentioned under *murder*. The maximum punishment for manslaughter is a discretionary sentence of *life imprisonment*. Modern-day cases involving the operation of the law of manslaughter include those of: (**1**) a teacher sentenced to imprisonment for 12 months after a ten-year-old from a group that the teacher had taken to the Lake District was swept away in a swollen stream (2003); (**2**) a number of similar cases involving failures of *supervision*; (**3**) a Nottingham doctor who ordered the wrong drug to be injected into a patient's spine and who received eight months imprisonment after his 18-year-old cancer patient died (2003); (**4**) two 16-year-olds convicted of manslaughter after pushing a 17-year-old with a water phobia from a bridge over the River Stour, Dorset; (**5**) a man at the helm of a 'grossly overcrowded' pleasure boat convicted of manslaughter at Birmingham Crown Court (2005); (**6**) gangmasters convicted after cocklepickers were 'cut off' by the incoming tide in Morecambe Bay (2006); and (**7**) the creator of a large inflatable artwork which 'took off' in a windstorm due to being insufficiently tied down (2006). There have been cases in which a charge of manslaughter has succeeded in circumstances akin to causing death by dangerous driving: see generally *road traffic*; or where there has been a breach of *health and safety* rules. The **Corporate Manslaughter and Corporate Homicide Act 2007** introduced a new offence under which companies and other organizations can be prosecuted where there has been a gross failing, throughout the organization, in the *management* of health and safety with fatal consequences: for further details, see justice.gov.uk under the heading for the 2007 Act.

McKenzie friend

Traditionally, an accused could take along to court someone other than a *lawyer* to *help and support* him or her; often termed a **McKenzie friend** (after *McKenzie v. McKenzie* [1970] 3 Weekly Law Reports 472. Strictly speaking, that case has been superseded. Such a person can still, with the *leave* of the court, assist the accused but cannot address the court as a *lawyer* can. Since the *Access to Justice Act 1999* courts have been discouraged from allowing any *abuse* of this mechanism, especially by 'unqualified *advocates*'. Historically, courts have also had an inherent *discretion* to hear from whomsoever they see fit (known as the rule in *O'Toole v Scott* [1965] AC 939).

media/press

'Media' nowadays signifies a range of *communications* systems for broadcasting and/or the publication of *information, data*, sound and/or images, including via TV, radio and the internet. By **'press'** is normally meant outlets for the printed word, especially newspapers, magazines, journals, pamphlets (and historically broadsheets, Penny Dreadfuls, etc). Governments have sometimes sought to censor or *silence* such activities, see, e.g. *Six Acts* in *Touchstones*; when the *risk* of unwarranted suppression and the *public interest* in *freedom of information* must be balanced against (a sometimes nebulous or unexplained) *national interest*. Hence great store is placed in **press freedom** and the role of the media/press as the **Fourth Estate** (alongside the Executive, Legislature and *Judiciary*). The police often use or cooperate with both, including via 'fly-on-the-wall' footage of *investigations, arrests, raids,* 'hot pursuit' and *surveillance*. See also *crime*/'Crimewatch'. The press can report court proceedings except in those few situations where *legislation* or a court order restricts this, e.g. *committal proceedings* before magistrates (when, normally, only a bare outline of the case can be published at that stage); or where the law allows a court to make a reporting *restriction*, e.g. to avoid a 'substantial *risk* of prejudice to the *administration of justice*' (which sometimes leads to 'evasive' or cryptic reporting). The Criminal Justice Act 2003 forbids publication of reports of *appeals* from evidentiary rulings. That restriction ends with the conclusion of the relevant trial. Other restrictions on what can be reported apply re the *youth court, children* (the court can prevent *identification* whenever a child appears in court, e.g. as a *witness*) and a limited range of other matters. Seats are normally reserved for the press in court, aka the **press bench** or **press gallery** and representatives can be present except in those rare instances when proceedings are held in camera (see *open court*). The *Court of Appeal* or the *House of Lords* can order a reporting restriction to be lifted, in its entirety or to a specified extent. Certain trials have 'collapsed' due to over-reporting or the publication of prejudicial information. A **D-notice** is one issued by Government to news editors asking them not publish certain items on grounds of national *security*; normally complied with by convention (see generally *self-regulation*). All reports should be fair and accurate. **Gagging order** is the term used to signify certain reporting restriction orders. In the context of criminal justice, a **media/press campaign** usually means one for *justice* re an individual or issue; including re a *miscarriage of justice*. See also press cooperation in *naming and shaming* in *Touchstones*. For a general overview, see *Media Law* (2007), Smartt, U, Sage. A **media panic** signifies the creation of alarm (by the **tabloid press** in particular), in response to a perceived societal ill, usually one not yet subject to *control* or *regulation*. **Media payments** to *witnesses*, victims, accused people or other participants in CJS proceedings (sometimes styled 'rewards') for their personal stories have caused controversy. A number of trials are reported to have resulted in *acquittals* due to such payments; whereby a voluntary *code* is now in operation. In one case the trial of a *gang* for kidnapping was abandoned after it transpired that the *News of the World* had paid a con man £10,000 and waited with TV cameras for events to unfold. The *Attorney General* later decided that the newspaper should not face prosecution for *contempt*; and the Press Complaints Commission (PCC) exonerated that newspaper. Yet, e.g. the *Guardian* was censured for paying a standard fee for an article written by a *prisoner* who served his sentence alongside Lord Jeffrey Archer (see *perjury*). See also the note re accounts by prisoners under *proceeds of crime*. The **media/ press release** is as much a device of CJS agencies/services as it is other undertakings and **press conferences** may be called by *Ministers of State* or an agency/service etc. Hence also police **media reconstructions** of an offence in order to encourage witnesses to come forward (and see also 'Crimewatch' mentioned under *Dando, Jill* in *Touchstones*). **Mediawatch UK** was founded by Mary Whitehouse (as the National Viewers and Listeners Association (NAVLA)(1960s)) to *campaign* against *obscenity*: see mediawatchuk.org.uk **Newsmaking criminology** refers to the efforts of certain *criminologists* to participate in the presentation of 'newsworthy items' so as to influence the crime and punishment agenda. The **Press Complaints Commission** (PCC) is charged with, among other things, *self-regulation* of reporting *standards*. **Trial by media** implies the *accusation* and prejudging of individuals, which leads to inevitable difficulties in terms of a fair trial (see *fair/fairness*), the outcome of which should be influenced solely by the *evidence* in the case; something to which sections of the media/press may have been particularly prone re high profile suspects in an 'age of celebrity'. See also *popular culture* in *Touchstones*.

mediation

Negotiation, arbitration, discussion, etc. usually meaning with the *help and support* of an intermediary with a view to resolution of a dispute or difference and/or ending or reducing conflicts. Mediation has many different guises and uses within *communities*. It is best-known in the CJS field re **victim-offender mediation**, often nowadays linked to aspects of *restorative justice*. Many such schemes exist, especially in *local* areas, to deal with what can be a sensitive and sometimes delicate area of CJS (and other) work. **Mediation UK** was for many years a leading umbrella organization for such groups, later superseded by **Conflict Practitioners UK** and related networks. Such approaches are in stark contrast to the formal, *adversarial system* of criminal justice noted in *Touchstones*. For an overview, see *Mediation in Context* (2000), Liebmenn M (ed), Jessica Kingsley. For other useful links, see restorativejustice.org.uk

medical aspects

Medical matters can touch on the CJS at any point, e.g. due to injuries to a victim or suspect; re the work of *Multi-agency Public Protection Arrangements* (MAPPAs) with regard to risk assessment, or the courts re fitness to plead or stand trial or other aspects of phyisical or mental impairment, with regard to sentencing and the work of HM Prison Service (HMPS) re prisoners, including within *allocation* processes, *healthcare, release* and parole. Similarly re the work of the National Probation Service (NPS), especially when a medical report is needed to accompany a pre-sentence report (PSR) (see *sentence/sentencing*). The *National Health Service* (NHS) and/or the *private sector* or *voluntary sector* provide a range of facilities to the CJS ranging from the medical examination of a suspect or victim at the *front end* of the criminal justice process to reports affecting *parole* and *release*. In addition, medical services prepare reports on the condition of defendants and or prisoners (including via a **Healthcare Service for Prisoners**: see *prison*) to assist the courts and/or the NPS re post-*custody* and other *community* supervision. See also *expert; mental impairment; opinion.*

membership organizations

Many membership organizations exist re parts of the CJS, including professional or reference bodies such as the Association of Chief Executives and Chief Officers of Probation (ACECOP); Association of Chief Police Officers (ACPO); Police Federation; Justices' Clerks' Society (JCS); Magistrates' Association; Prison Governors' Association (PGA); Napo and the Prison Officers Association (POA); as well as *campaign, reform* or *help and support* groups, and bodies or charities such as Action for Prisoners' Families; the Howard League for Penal Reform; Prison Reform Trust (PRT); Nacro; and Unlock. Related entries appear in various sections of this pocket book.

mens rea

The **mental element in an offence** as opposed to its physical aspects (see *actus reus*) and that covers a spectrum of states of mind from intention to recklessness to gross negligence and knowledge to 'failures' to specific states of mind as prescribed by *legislation* re a given offence (as with driving without reasonable consideration: see generally *road traffic*). In general in England and Wales, offenders are judged by reference to their own (often called 'subjective') intentions; but liability can depend on objective factors (see *objectivity/objective test*; and *Clapham omnibus* in *Touchstones*), especially if the allegation or *defence* involves questions of whether the accused person drew *reasonable* conclusions or acted reasonably in given circumstances. This can be a complex area re which specialist works on criminal law should be consulted.

mental impairment

People who have committed the most serious offences and who are mentally impaired are held in **special hospitals** in conditions of high *security* under the *supervision* and *control* of psychiatrists and other medical personnel (see *medical aspects; psychiatry/psychology*). But mental impairment can affect any criminal case at almost any point, including *diversion* from the criminal process altogether into hospital or other facilities. 'Duty psychiatrist' and *referral* schemes operate at many courts or police stations. They bring speedy professional advice which can also facilitate the (often difficult to obtain) admission of offenders to hospital in appropriate cases. An accused may be mentally **unfit to plead** (see further below). There is a defence of **insanity** although not commonly used today: at a time of *capital punishment* (see *Touchstones*) it was a way to avoid execution. See also especially *M'Naughten Rules* in that section.

There is also a defence of **diminished responsibility** that serves to reduce what would have been a *murder* conviction to one of *manslaughter*, thereby giving the judge a *discretion* re sentence (as opposed to the use of mandatory *life imprisonment*); based on the mental state of the accused at the time of the events in question. It was first enacted in the Homicide Act 1957 and is generally regarded as having been triggered by the execution of *Ruth Ellis* (see *Touchstones*). Where the accused is mentally impaired in what would have been a life sentence case, this will usually result in him or her being ordered to be detained for life or 'at *Her Majesty's pleasure*', i.e. without limit of time. In other cases, the **Mental Health Act 1983** and subsequent *legislation* allows courts to dispose of cases in a variety of ways including by **hospital orders** or **guardianship orders** (the latter usually supervised in the *community* by a *local authority*). Conditions of treatment for an offender's mental state can be a requirement of a generic *community sentence* or *release*. If an offender is sent to hospital, a Crown Court judge can, at the behest of doctors, make **an order restricting discharge**. A **discharged patient** is one discharged from a special hospital following his or her *detention* or a hospital in the community, e.g. after **being sectioned**: common parlance for admission to such a hospital after certification by a medical practitioner.

Fitness to plead covers either physical or mental fitness; when in either case it will not be possible to hold a trial if the accused is wholly unfit. The **Mental Health Act 2007** amended the **Mental Health Act 1983**, the *Domestic Violence, Crime and Victims Act 2004* and the **Mental Capacity Act 2005** in relation to mentally disordered people and for connected purposes: consult specialist works. A main purpose of the 2007 Act was to introduce *safeguards* concerning *restriction of liberty*; and to extend the rights of victims. The 1983 Act was largely concerned with the circumstances in which a person suffering from mental impairment could be detained for *treatment* without his or her *consent*; setting out processes to be followed and safeguards for patients to prevent inappropriate *detention*. A main purpose of all such *legislation* is to ensure that people with serious mental disorders which threaten their *health and safety* or the *safety* of the public can be treated irrespective of their consent where it is necessary to prevent them from causing *harm* to themselves or others. The changes in relation to the 2005 Act were in *response* to the 2004 European Court of Human Rights judgment in *HL v UK* (Application No.45508/99: aka the **Bournewood Hospital case**). It involved an autistic man kept at that hospital by doctors against the wishes of his carers. The European Court found that his admission to and retention in hospital under the Common Law of 'necessity' amounted to a breach of Article 5(1) of the European Convention on Human Rights (deprivation of *liberty*) and of Article 5(4) (the right to have lawfulness of *detention* reviewed by a court) (see *human rights*). The 2007 Act changed the way the 1983 Act defines **'mental disorder'**, so that a single definition applies, and abolished references to categories of disorder. These amendments complement changes to the criteria for detention; and introduced a new 'appropriate medical treatment' test re longer-term powers of detention. As a result, it will not be possible for patients to be compulsorily detained or their detention continued unless medical treatment which is appropriate to the patient's mental disorder and other circumstances of the case is available to that particular patient. An existing but dysfunctional 'treatability test' was abolished; and the Act broadened the group of practitioners who can take on the functions currently performed by approved *social workers* (ASWs) and responsible medical officers (RMOs). Other provisions gave patients the right to make an application to change (aka 'displace') designation of their 'nearest relative' so as to include, e.g. civil partners. Further to this, **supervised community treatment** (SCT) was introduced for patients following a period of detention in hospital; designed to counter *revolving door* syndrome (see *Touchstones*). It also introduced mechanisms to reduce the time before a case has to be referred to the **Mental Health Review Tribunal** by hospital managers and introduced extra safeguards re people under the age of 18 (see specialist works). The Act also placed a duty on relevant national authorities in England and Wales to make arrangements for help to be provided by **independent mental health advocates** (see generally *advocate*), re electro-convulsive *therapy* (ECT), and introduced further safeguards for patients. Changes to the 2005 Act provide for procedures to authorise the deprivation of *liberty* of someone who is resident in a hospital or care home who lacks the capacity to give personal *consent*. The MCA principles of supporting a person to make a decision whenever possible, and acting at all times in that person's best interests and in the least restrictive manner, now apply re all such procedures. Changes under the 2004 Act include new rights for victims of mentally disordered offenders not subject to *restrictions*: see specialist works. The *private sector* plays a significant role in all such matters. Leading *charities* from whom information is available include **Mind** (mind.org.uk) and the **Mental Health Foundation** (mentalhealth.org.uk).

mercy

The adage is that justice should be tempered with mercy, i.e. it is one thing to press for a conviction, quite another to be unduly punitive (see generally *punishment*), in some instances to be less so than the *seriousness* of the offence might suggest. Hence also the **prerogative of mercy**: see generally *Crown*. See also *suicide*/'mercy killing'.

Metropolitan Police Service (MPS)

The MPS was formed as the New Police for London in 1829, since when it has established a unique place in the history of policing and in modern-times a formidable reputation for being at the forefront of policing methods worldwide. Founded by Sir Robert Peel, the original 1,000 officers policed a seven-mile radius from Charing Cross and a population of less than two million. Today, the MPS employs over 30,000 police officers, 13,500 police staff, over 400 traffic wardens and 2,000 police community support officers (PCSOs). It covers an area of 620 square miles and a population of 7.2 million. It has also in modern times been at the centre of a range of controversies and at times at the centre of both *political* events and issues of national *security* (and see, e.g. *Lawrence, Stephen* and *Stockwell Shooting* in *Touchstones*). A wealth of information is available at metpolice.uk where it is also possible to sign up for regular MPS e-bulletins concerning the day to day activities of the service.

military

Justice within the military is dispensed by **court martial** to which dedicated rules and descriptions apply going beyond the scope of this work. The description **Judge Advocate** is given to a military officer authorised to preside as a judge at a court martial; which has no jury. There are **military prisons** on army land. Comparable arrangements exist re the Royal Navy and Royal Air Force. For the situations in which a court martial occurs rather than *discipline* by a commanding officer or an appearance in an ordinary criminal court, see army.mod.uk The term **military grade** is used to signify advanced *science, technology* or *weapons*, on the leading edge of developments, which may also be used by the police or *intelligence* services. Since 2003, the arrangements whereby service personnel can be asked to serve on a jury were revised making that possibility more likely. Historically in wartime, *summary trial* and execution (see generally *capital punishment* in *Touchstones*) by firing squad was a common feature ('to encourage the others'), e.g. for desertion in the face of the enemy; now recognised as often due to shell shock or trauma. Posthumous *pardons* were granted to large numbers of men in 2008. Note also historical use of the **militia** (see, e.g. *Peterloo Massacre* in *Touchstones*); and modern deployment of the army for policing purposes as in Northern Ireland during the *Troubles* (see *Touchstones*). 'Calling in the army' is perhaps viewed as a sign of a failure. It is conceivable nowadays that soldiers might be drafted in and serve in police uniform in order to 'swell police ranks' during in an *emergency*. Note also the existence of the **Ministry of Defence Police (MODP)**.

Minister of State

A political appointment by the Prime Minister normally from the party in power and referable to a government department (although there can be a *Minister Without Portfolio*) the holder of which office will be either a **Secretary of State** (such as the *Justice Secretary* or *Home Secretary*) or a **junior Minister**. Many rule-making and other powers are conferred on Secretaries of State, including under both primary and delegated *legislation* (see that entry). They also have certain *inherent powers*; but are accountable to Parliament and the democratic process (see *accountability, democracy*). Ministers can be from either House of Parliament and may or may not be of *Cabinet* rank.

Ministry of Justice (MOJ)

The MOJ was created in 2007, by transferring to this new government department the functions of the Department for Constitutional Affairs (DCA) (which it replaced), and adding certain *justice*-related responsibilities, some given up by the Home Office. The MOJ draws together various *justice*-related responsibilities within a remit which also extends to *constitutional* affairs. It works trilaterally with the Home Office and Department of the *Attorney General* to deliver a range of services; and re juveniles with the *Department For Children, Schools and Families* (DCSF). Its functions include those re: *HM Courts Service* (HMCS); the *judiciary* (including: liaison with the *Judicial Office* which falls under the *Lord Chief Justice*; the *Judicial Appointments Commission* (JAC); *Office for Judicial Complaints* (OJC); *Judicial Communications Office* (JCO); National Offender Management Service (NOMS) (see *offender management*) (and thereby the National Probation Service (see *probation*) and *HM Prison Service* (HMPS)); sponsorship of various *HM Inspectorates*; *Independent Monitoring Boards* (IMBs); the *Parole Board*; *Prisons and Probation Ombudsman*; *legal aid* and the *Community Legal Service* (CLS) (via the *Legal Services Commission* (LSC)); Government sentencing policy; sponsorship of: the *Sentencing Guidelines Council* (SGC), *Sentencing Advisory Panel* (SAP) and the *Law Commission*; hosting the *Office for Criminal Justice Reform* (OCJR); *Privy Council* Secretariat and Office of the Judicial Committee of the Privy Council; and *human rights*. The *management* of the MOJ was restructured in 2008 under various *Directors General*. For an overview, see *The New Ministry of Justice: An Introduction* (2nd edn. 2008), Gibson B, Waterside Press.

miscarriage of justice

A failure or breakdown of *justice*: usually meaning **a wrongful conviction**, but capable of meaning **a failure to bring someone to justice** where offences have been committed, or more loosely to ensure that a victim receives adequate and proper recompense, *reparation* or closure. It is the first of these with which the *Criminal Cases Review Commission* (CCRC) is concerned. See also various examples in *Touchstones*.

mistake

A **mistake of law** (sometimes described as **ignorance of the law**: albeit that this connotes lack of knowledge rather than a wrong interpretation) is not a defence or answer to an allegation of an offence. There is a *presumption* that everyone knows the law; a *rule* born of pragmatism and however difficult to reconcile with modern developments as to what and what is not prohibited: see the comments under *crime*. In contrast, a genuine mistake re the facts of a situation may amount to a *defence*; assuming that the person concerned has not been willfully blind: see *blind/blindness*. Either type of mistake may support *mitigation* depending on the circumstances.

mitigation

Facts or other information that will justify a court in reducing punishment when it comes to pass sentence. Hence the term **plea in mitigation** (often put forward on the offender's behalf by his or her *barrister* or *solicitor*) whereby the offender asks the court for *leniency* after being convicted; by emphasising that the offence is less *serious* than it might appear at first sight (known as **offence mitigation**); or in some instances it may relate to the special circumstances of the offender (known as **offender mitigation**). A considerable body of *law* and *precedents* cover what can and cannot amount to mitigation in given circumstances, the extent to which it should have any effect and what is expressly not mitigation. The term **mitigating circumstances** is used quite specifically re penalty points/totting-up procedures: see *road traffic*. Mitigation cannot affect a *mandatory* sentence, such as one of life imprisonment.

mixed fact and law

A reference to inter-related aspects of the *facts* as they are found to be by a court (ultimately) and the *law* as it will apply to that factual situation. This dynamic, cross-cutting feature is a frequent component of decision-making, when, e.g. a judge may need to carefully direct a jury: see generally *judge*/'role of the judge and jury'.

MI5 (Security Service)/MI6 (Intelligence Service)

MI5 is the short name for the home branch of what was the Secret Intelligence Services (SIS) and is nowadays aka the **Security Service**. It was originally 'Department 5' within the Directorate of Military Intelligence (DMI)(1916); a development re the even older Secret Intelligence Service (1909) and Secret Service Bureau (SSB) (late-1800s). It evolved via amalgamation with a Special Section at Scotland Yard (see generally *Touchstones*) involved in covert policing (1931). Apart from espionage, it has responsibility for the *protection* of the UK from threats to national *security*, *terrorism/terrorists*, sabotage and foreign agents within the UK; and any *threats* which would undermine the status quo of *democracy*, whether by *violence, political*, industrial or other means. In accordance with the Security Service Act 1989, MI5 also provides *advice* to bodies from the *public sector* and *private sector*; counters the amassing/proliferation of *weapons* and assists with crime prevention/crime reduction. It operates under the aegis of the *Home Secretary* (but is not part of the *Home Office*), is headed by a Director-General (DG), funded via the Single Intelligence Account (SIA) and is part of National Intelligence Machinery (NIM), coordinated by the Joint Intelligence Committee (JIC). Famous recruits have included Anthony Blunt (erstwhile Surveyor of the Queen's Pictures, later unmasked as a Communist spy) and authors A P Herbert and Ian Fleming (of James Bond fame). It is based at Thames House, Westminster.

MI6 is the short name for what was the foreign branch of the SIS; originally 'Department 6' within the DMI (1916); with responsibility for gathering *intelligence* abroad (and hence then and now called the **Intelligence Service**); that from 1909-1916 and finally by 1922 evolved as a separate service when the Foreign Secretary was given Ministerial responsibility for MI6. Its principal role is to produce secret intelligence in support of *security*, defence and foreign and economic policy within a framework laid down by the JIC; that it does by intelligence gathering, 'other tasks', via a range of 'sources', human, electronic and technological, as well as *liaison* with foreign security services. Key operations are subject to longstanding procedures for official and Ministerial clearance; but can be authorised retrospectively following the need for *emergency* action. Recruits have included the authors John Buchan, Somerset Maugham and Compton Mackenzie (later Sir). MI6 is based at Vauxhall Cross, London. MI5 and MI6 now recruit openly (rather than via 'a tap on the shoulder'/the Old Boy Network) and have useful web-sites: see mi5.gov.uk; mi6.gov..uk

mode of trial See *allocation and sending; either way offence.*

money
'The love of money is the root of all *evil*', so runs the adage; but many people would suggest other root *causes of crime* (and question whether 'evil' exists: see *Touchstones*). Many offences are of an acquisitive nature and thus 'about money' (or *value*), aka *proceeds of crime*. **Money laundering** involves the transmission or exchange of monetary value in such a way that there are no formal records or trace, e.g. to evade *taxation* or other liabilities. There have been 15 **anti-money laundering statutes** since 1993: see in particular *cash; gambling; organized crime; Revenue & Customs; suspicious activity report* (SAR; and note also *black economy* in *Touchstones*. Note also **monetary compensation** (see *compensation*) and **value for money (VFM)** (see *value/values*).

monitoring
(1) Checking or 'keeping tabs' on events, developments, people or other *targets*; and a word used to describe some forms of *research* or *inspection*. **(2)** Electronic **monitoring**: see that entry. **(3)** Similarly, monitoring of *children, vulnerable people, animals* or personal property to make, e.g. abduction, *assault* or *theft* more difficult. **(4)** For **Independent Monitoring Board** see that entry. **(5)** Surveillance: see *surveillance.*

moral aspects See *Touchstones*

motive/motivation
Motive can be defined as the reason or purpose that someone has for committing an offence; which may thus be *evidence* pointing towards guilt. such as personal benefit or gain, avarice, jealousy, revenge or to cover up a secret or misdeed. **Motivation** is what drives someone to achieve a particular end, whether as an offender (whose motive and motivation may well coincide), someone who is *'going straight'* or a CJS

practitioner, agency/service or reformer. Note also **lack of discernible motive** as per *Shipman, Harold* (see *Touchstones*) and **lack of motivation** that may occur when purpose or direction is unclear, confused or stems from indifferent *management*.

Mountbatten Report See *Touchstones*

multi-agency

A reference to any combination of agencies (see generally agency/service) usually implying a **multi-agency working,** working together and *partnership* in place of the relatively insular methods of earlier times. Note also **cross-agency** and **cross-cutting** to signify matters which transcend boundaries. Such approaches can raise questions of *independence/interdependence*, especially re extent to which the *judiciary* may be prepared to take part. **Multi-agency Public Protection Arrangements (MAPPAs)** seek to identify and manage potentially *dangerous offenders*, through *risk-assessments* and *referrals* to a range of agencies/services and resources, especially re *violence, sexual offences, children* and *vulnerable people.* They often work alongside, e.g. *Crime and Disorder Reduction Partnerships* and *Persistent Offender Schemes.*

murder

The **unlawful killing of a human being by another human being** accompanied by the legally required state of mind (see generally *mens rea*); sometimes, especially historically, called 'malice aforethought', in essence now an intention to kill or cause grievous bodily harm (see *assault*), or recklessness as to death (but see specialist works: murder also occurs, e.g. if excessive force is used in self-*defence* or and where a defence of provocation fails (assuming underlying *mens rea*). It is 'the most serious offence in the criminal *calender'* (see *Touchstones*); but defies categorisation due to the range of scenarios in which it occurs, e.g. *serial killing* (possibly accompanied by further *aggravating* features such as sadism, cannibalism); honour killing (described by one judge as an oxymoron: which occurs some 12 times per year in the UK in a cultural context); deaths from *domestic violence*; contract killing; assassination; *terrorism*; ritual killing; mercy killing (see *suicide*) and killings by juveniles (some 50 per year): see *Bulger case* in *Touchstones* and *Children Who Kill* (1996), Cavadino P, Waterside Press. For some sense of the variation, see the resources listed at muderorg.com There are over 900 murders a year by *adults* in the UK on average. Murder remains a Common Law offence although the *punishment*, a *mandatory* sentence of *life imprisonment* (formerly *capital punishment*: see *Touchstones*) is governed by *Act of Parliament*; as are 'partial *defences'* of diminished responsibility (see mental *impairment*) and provocation. Since 2007, the Government sought views on a *Law Commission* report, 'Murder, Manslaughter and Infanticide' (2004) (available at lawcom.gov.uk) as to placing murder on a *statutory* footing, setting out *defences,* the rules affecting complicity (especially re assisted *suicide*); and better procedures re infanticide (the killing of a child below 12 months old by its mother: attracting a lesser sentence, as first recognised by the Infanticide Act 1922: see specialist works). There have been other calls for the creation 'criminal homicide' to replace both murder and *manslaughter*, as well as abolition of the present *mandatory* sentence for murder to allow judges to reflect culpability. Notable developments have included the **Homicide Act 1957** (which introduced **degrees of murder**, since superseded, and diminished responsibility: see *mental impairment*), the **Murder (Abolition of the Death Penalty Act) 1969** and *statutory* sentencing principles re *tariffs* affecting *life imprisonment* (2003)). A key work is *With Malice Aforethought: A Study of the Crime and Punishment for Homicide* (2004), Blom Cooper L and Morris T, 2004, Hart Publishing. Special *prison/*'regimes' exist:

see *Murderers and Life Imprisonment: Containment, Safety, Treatment and Risk* (1998), Cullen E and Newell T, Waterside Press. **Mass murder** is a non-technical term for various types of murder when significant numbers of victims are killed. See, e.g. *Hungerford Massacre* in *Touchstones*. This can be contrasted with **genocide** or events such as the Nazi **Holocaust**. Police investigations is aided by a **Murder Manual**.

N

Nacro; naming and shaming; Napo See *Touchstones* for all three

narcotic

A drug. The term, its many derivatives or words pre-fixed **'narco-'** are of USA origin. See generally *drugs*. Hence **Narcotics Anonymous**: a non-profit fellowship of men and women for whom drugs have become a major problem. NA members are recovering addicts who help each other to 'stay clean'. The only requirement is the desire to stop using **narcotic substances**. See, further, www.ukna.org

national/nationwide

Terms used to signify an organization, agency/service, committee, activity, etc. that operates across the whole of *England and Wales* (see *Touchstones*)(or as applicable the UK, see, e.g. under *border*). Contrast *area, local* and note that some arrangements are regionally-based. Examples appear throughout this work, e.g. for **National Association for Youth Justice (NAYJ)**, see *Touchstones;* **National Crime Squad (NCS)**, see *Serious and Organized Crime Agency;* **National Criminal Intelligence Service (NCIS)**, ditto; **National Criminal Justice Board**, see *Criminal Justice Board;* **National Front**, see *front;* **National Health Service (NHS)**, see *health;* **National Identification Scheme (NIS)**, see *identification/identity*. The **national interest** is a criterion against which decisions may be made at the highest level to justify action that might otherwise be unlawful. Thus, e.g. under the European Convention On Human Rights (see *human rights*) a national government can derogate from certain Articles of the Convention (but not those involving absolute rights). The national interest is usually invoked when there is some major *threat* or *risk* to the UK or the public in general, as, e.g. re *terrorism/terrorist*. It has also been used to support the withholding of information that should otherwise rightly be in the public domain, especially given the Freedom of Information Act 1999 (see *freedom*). In the event of war proper, such matters are usually subsumed within special powers and *emergency legislation*. One problem is that 'the national interest' is a malleable concept which may be used re immediate events on a pragmatic 'act now, answer questions later' basis. Notoriously, in 2007-8, it was invoked in relation to the dropping of a prosecution in relation to *BAE Systems* (see *Touchstones*). For **National Offender Management Service (NOMS)**, see under *offender*. For **National Policing Improvement Agency (NPIA)** and **National Policing Plan (NPP)**, see under *police*. For **National Probation Service**, see *probation*. For **National security**, see *security*. The **National Society for the Prevention of Cruelty to Children (NSPCC)** (formerly The London Society founded in 1884) adopted the pre-fix 'National' in 1889. Its aims and purposes include the *protection* of children from cruelty, supporting *vulnerable families, reform*, raising awareness about such *abuse* and ending cruelty: see nspcc.org.uk For **National Victims Advisory Panel**, see *victim*.

natural justice See *fair/fairness*

Neighbourhood Watch (NW)(aka Home Watch)

'One of the biggest and most successful crime prevention initiatives' (Home Office), which is based on the simple idea of neighbours banding together so as to be on the look out for *burglars*, vandals (see *criminal damage*) and similar *threats* in a locality; which is linked to ideas of *community* policing, reassurance policing (see *police/policing*) and the benefits of 'closer communities'. It is also in the tradition of watches which have existed from the very earliest days: see *watch*. Variants of NW include **Boat Watch**, **Business Watch**, **Car Watch**, **Factory Watch**, **Farm Watch**, **Pub Watch**, **Horse Watch**, **Internet Watch**, **School Watch** and **Shop Watch**. Schemes are led by a co-ordinator and a committee and share *information* and *advice* with the police. Increasingly, they have joined together to ensure police force-wide *liaison*. An instructive 'model *constitution*' is accessible at neighbourhoodwatch.uk.com

Newton hearing

An example of the tendency to name self-contained procedures, etc. by the name of the *case* in which a *legal* challenge first arose; here with regard to a 'trial within a trial' (see *trial*), i.e. to determine the true facts in a situation where the accused enters a plea of guilty but then disagrees materially with some aspects of events as outlined by the prosecutor. From *R v Newton* (1983), *Criminal Law Review*, 198.

no/non/not

Words which may used as prefixes in order to stress negative aspects or sometimes for want of other suitable terminology. Hence, e.g. **no case to answer** to signify that there is no *prima facie* case against a suspect or accused person. In court, there will be no case to answer if the prosecutor fails to call (aka 'aduce') *evidence* of essential *ingredients* of the offence, e.g. that property said to to have been stolen was 'appropriated' as required by the law of *theft*; or when prosecution *witnesses* are deemed by the court to be so unreliable that no *reasonable* jury would convict. The case will then end at this point and the defendant will be *discharged*. Other examples include **no further action (NFA)** to describe a decision not to proceed with an *investigation* or *inquiry*; **no-go area** to point to a location re which there is a *risk*, e.g. due to a high potential for offences of *violence* in particular (whereas the government and police might deny that such places exist) or one where the police have put up a *cordon* (see *police/policing*); **no punishment without law**: see *human rights;* **no separate penalty**: see *sentence/sentencing;* **non-accidental injury**: see *injury*; **non-departmental public body (NDPB)**, i.e. a body in the public sector but not a *government* department; **non-police matter:** either: **(1)** beyond the remit of the police, e.g. because it is not an offence or otherwise attracting their *priorities* (as with, historically and wrongly, *domestic violence* and neighbour disputes); or **(2)** a matter falling to another, specialist *law enforcement agency* to deal with; **non-police court**: one dealing only with other kinds of *case*; **non-statutory**: not deriving from an *Act of Parliament* (as per non-statutory *codes* or *protocols*; or many *voluntary sector* bodies (and hence **non-statutory sector**: that part of the CJS, etc. lacking any underlying statutory basis). Similarly, **not conducive to the public good**: see *deportation;* **not guilty**: see *plea*.

nuisance

Policy-makers have always been somewhat ambivalent as to how far nuisance should be a criminal offence rather than a purely *civil* matter. It is however a form of *anti-*

social behaviour (ASB) and may be a **statutory nuisance** under dedicated *legislation* or bye-laws; as well as a **public nuisance** if of a gross kind: see the example given under *weapon* and see specialist texts on *criminal law*. Nuisance is also often an integral part of, e.g. *harassment,* intimidation and *domestic violence.*

oath

One of the two highest methods of asserting something (the other being an equivalent *affirmation*): a solemn vow by reference to a religious belief (see generally *religion*), e.g. that the person concerned will act truthfully, honestly and/or with 'true allegiance', that something he or she refers to did in fact exist, occur, etc, otherwise as to the correctness of something (such as the *identification* of a person or *exhibit*); as when giving *testimony* in a courtroom, aka a **witness oath**. Hence the terms **swearing on oath** to describe the formalities involved and **sworn on oath** to describe *evidence* that has been validated in this way. Oaths are made by reference to the religion of the person's choice except where this is impracticable when he or she can be required to affirm; which under the **Oaths Act 1978** he or she can do in any event. The essential point as to the criterion of validity is the degree to which a witness considers his or her conscience bound by the procedure. For a helpful guide, see jsboard. co.uk under 'Belief systems'. Police officers take an oath of attestation: see *police/policing*. For **juror's oath**: see *juror/jury*; **oath of allegiance**: see *Crown*. In contrast to the situation, e.g. in the USA, affidavits (sworn out-of-court written evidence) are not normally used in UK criminal proceedings (as opposed to *civil* ones) but they do have their place, e.g. in relation to certain High Court applications; whilst some written 'depositions' and/or *statements* are of a similar kind: see specialist works.

object

(1) As a noun, the aim or purpose of some strategy, tactic or activity; as per the aims, etc. of the CJS or one of its agencies/services. (2) As a verb, a challenge to given events. Note, however, that the much dramatised USA usage, 'Your honour, I object' (followed by lawyers approaching the bench in a huddle) has a less systemised place in the English CJS even if *lawyers* frequently make **objections** in the course of a case where they are of the *opinion* that something is incorrect or misleading. In certain instances this may lead to a formal *ruling* (see, e.g. *judges ruling; evidence*).

objectivity/objective test

The word **objectivity** is often used to signify detachment, neutrality and impartiality (as opposed to subjectivity); all traits that infuse CJS matters where close involvement with the subject matter can lead to bias. The term **objective test** is sometimes used as a synonym for a test of *reasonableness* (and in contrast with a 'subjective test': which looks to an actual state of mind, belief or knowledge: see generally *mens rea*); involving balance, disinterest, being away from the heat of events, without preconceptions as to *evidence, intelligence, data* and so on. See also *Clapham omnibus* in *Touchstones*.

obscene/obscenity

Various provisions prohibit obscenity and/or obscene publications, provide tests of obscenity, powers of *search* and *seizure*; including the **Obscene Publications Act 1959** (which introduced a *defence* of 'the public good') and **Obscene Publications**

Act 1964 ('An Act to strengthen the law for preventing the publication for gain of obscene matter and the publication of things intended for the production of obscene matter'). This is a specialist and highly sensitive area of criminal law particularly in an age of *civil liberties, human rights* changing social mores and the *internet*; re which see the work of the Internet Watch Foundation at iwf.org.uk (where the provisions are summarised and their interaction with other statutes such as the Sexual Offences Act 2003 and Police and Justice Act 2006 are readily accessible). The *Lady Chatterley's Lover* case noted in *Touchstones* is indicative of how obscenity moves with the times.

offender/offending

Words commonly used to describe people guilty of criminal offences and the conduct in question, respectively; as opposed to 'criminal' and 'criminal behaviour', in particular. Some commentators prefer 'offender' arguing that 'criminal' has potentially detrimental effects, such as *labelling* and (often vague and unspecified) *criminalisation* and long lasting effects (see *Touchstone* for both of these items and also the comments in *Spotting shades of meaning* on page xii of this work). Hence also the term **offending behaviour**, particularly amongst those involved in administering *community sentences, criminologists* and in *reform* circles. An **offending behaviour course** may be employed to deal with, e.g. *anger* management, *drug* and/or *alcohol* misuse, drink-driving (see *road traffic*) or life skills, debt and personal finance. Note also the *Sex Offender Treatment Programme* (SOTP). Similarly, **confronting offending behaviour** connotes the task of challenging offenders' precepts, ways and thinking skills with a view to **changing offending behaviour**, avoiding *risk* situations and *'going straight'*. Other derivatives include **dangerous offender, persistent offender, prolific offender, repeat offender** and **young offender**: see relevant entries. The **Offender Assessment System (OASys)** is a *risk-assessment* mechanism used by *probation officers* and in some prisons (and hence **eOASys** re *assessment* for *electronic monitoring*); a way of providing information so as to enable courts to ensure that offenders are given sentences which work. For the original 2003 launch materials, see probation.homeoffice.gov.uk (but note that the National Probation Service (NPS) is now allied to the MOJ rather than the Home Office). See also *'what works'* in *Touchstones*.

Use of the term **offender management** led to its use re a **National Offender Management Service (NOMS)** which is the umbrella body created in 2004 following the Carter Report of 2003 (see *Touchstones*) via which the MOJ 'commissions and provides the highest quality correctional services and *interventions*'. NOMS covers both HM Prison Service and the NPS. Under structures introduced in 2008, there is a strategic MOJ-related post of **Director General of Criminal Justice and Offender Management** and both services are run via a hierarchy of **offender managers**. Despite earlier suggestions that they be merged into a unified 'corrections service', the separate services and staff roles continue. NOMS has developed an **offender management (OM)** model in which a manager takes overall responsibility for each offender given *imprisonment* or *supervision* throughout their time in *custody* and on *licence* in the *community*. NOMS aims to apply the OM model to all offenders subject to relevant orders. For this and supplementary information, see noms.justice.gov.uk

office

(1) The office held by certain people of standing within the CJS, such as that of *Director of Public Prosecutions*. **(2)** A department, organization or unit of a public nature and which is generally so styled, e.g. **Cabinet Office**: see, *Cabinet*; **Home Office** See that entry; **Office for Criminal Justice Reform (OCJR)** See *reform*; **Office for Judicial Complaints (OJC)** See *complaint*; **Office for Security and Counter-Terrorism (OSCT)** See *terrorism*; **Office of the Attorney General** See *Attorney General*.

Old Bailey See *Touchstones;* **on the spot fine** See *fine*; **onus of proof**: see *evidence*.

open/openness

Openness is a key aim and *value* of all public services, along with *accountability* and *transparency*. The nature of certain decisions dictates that they, or at least the sensitive information relating to them, should be received behind closed doors and that it remain confidential; but this should be the exception. Hence the work of the Information Commissioner, see *freedom of information*. Re the principle of **open court** Article 6 of the European Convention on Human Rights (see generally *human rights*) states that: 'Judgement shall be pronounced publicly but the press and public may be excluded from all or part of the trial in the interests of morals, *public order* or national *security* in a democratic society, where the interests of juveniles or the *protection* of the private life of the parties so require, or to the extent strictly necessary in the opinion of the court in special circumstances where publicity would prejudice the interest of justice'. This accords with longstanding UK arrangements for members of the public and the *media/press* to observe court proceedings, subject to available space and appropriate behaviour (failing the latter they may be in *contempt of court*). In exceptional circumstances, criminal courts can sit in camera (i.e. 'behind closed doors'), e.g. in the interests of national *security* or if life and limb is at risk (a rare event in practice). Another exception occurs when a magistrates' court is considering whether to issue a warrant of further *detention*; but the suspect will usually be present. Special rules apply to *judicial* oversight in private of control orders (see *detention*); and evidentiary and other rulings by judges: see *evidence*; *judge's ruling*. Youth courts are not open to the public; but the *media/press* may attend although they must not publish the names of juveniles unless a court allows these to be disclosed in the *interests of justice*. A similar rule exists re child *participants* in cases of all kinds.

opinion

A view as opposed to an assertion of fact. Opinions, sometimes described as **considered opinions** or **expert opinion** (see further *witness/*'expert witness') are admissible in *evidence* provided that the court allows this, after satisfying itself as to the expert's credentials, qualifications, etc. The **opinions of non-experts** are not admissible; neither is one that goes directly to the question of guilt, which is for the jury or magistrates to decide. A **legal opinion** is one by a lawyer to his or her client or a court (e.g. during *representations* or legal *argument*). **Medical opinions** are regularly relied on across the CJS: see *medical aspects*. Opinions may be categorised as e.g. arguable, debatable, sound, tentative, definitive (as where a group of experts have considered a point), suspect or dubious. Some concern has existed re opinions given in *child protection* cases in particular: see the note on Meadows Law under *witness*.

organized crime

Crime carried out in a managed way, as if, e.g. by way of a legitimate business venture or a *military* or similar *campaign*; often meaning on an appreciable scale, possibly internationally. Examples include *drug* cartels; paedophile networks, *protection rackets* (often involving *blackmail*); *trafficking* and *organized crime*; all potentially a focus of the **Serious Organized Crime Agency (SOCA)** (see that entry), **Serious**

Organized Crime and Police Act 2005 (SOCPA); Organized Crime, Drugs and International Group (OCDIG) and attempts to counter *money laundering* via international *investigations*. The **Serious Crime Act 2007 (SCA)** *targets* such activities via offences of *assisting crime*; enables *data sharing* to prevent *fraud* or trace the *proceeds of crime*; enables *data matching* re *fraud* and for wider purposes; and transfers certain functions to SOCA. Other key connections are *black economy* and the *Underworld* (both in *Touchstones*) and the Prüm Treaty (see *global/international dimensions*).

P

paperwork

(1) The *case file* and/or other documents relating to it. (2) Any process conducted 'by way of the papers' rather than by a party appearing at some place (usually such as in a *courtroom* or judge's chambers) in person. Hence, also, e.g. **paper committal** re *allocation and sending*; **paper plea**: see *guilty plea/*written plea of guilty.'

parent/parental responsibility/parenting order

In modern times and in relation to *youth justice* or the *care* of children in particular, there has been an emphasis on **parental responsibility**. Hence in the *youth court*, parents or guardians can be ordered to pay the *fines*, etc. of juveniles or be made subject to **parenting orders**, i.e. to take part in related education and training. For a general overview, see direct.gov.uk and/or consult specialist works on *youth justice*. In broad terms such responsibilities include: providing a home for the child; having contact with and living with the child; protecting and maintaining the child; disciplining the child; choosing and providing for the child's *education;* determining the *religion* of the child; agreeing to the child's medical treatment; naming the child and agreeing to any change of the child's name; accompanying the child when outside the UK (and in particular agreeing to the any emigration plans); being responsible for the child's property; appointing a guardian for the child, if necessary; and allowing confidential information about the child to be disclosed.

Parkhurst Prison

One of three prisons on the Isle of Wight (with Albany and Camphill). It was, notoriously, at the the centre of CJS issues following the escape of three prisoners there in 1995; when *Home Secretary,* Michael Howard, categorised this as an operational matter for the director general of HM Prison Service, leading to the latter's departure and that of the *prison governor* John Marriott. Built as a *military* hospital (1805) it became 'a prison for boys' awaiting *deportation*, mainly to Australia, under the Parkhurst Act 1835. In 1847, a wing was added, built by prisoners, from 1863 to 1869 it was a women's prison, but has been a male prison since then. It was the first dispersal prison (1968): see *prison*. It remained a high *security* prison until the mid-1990s when it took on its current role housing those in the latter stages of *life imprisonment* and other long-term prisoners (plus local *remand* prisoners).

parole

The system for the early *release* of longer term prisoners; which operates under the **Parole Board (PB)**; subject to a **parole licences** and *recall* to prison for any breach of that licence, or other unfavourable *risk-assessment*. The PB is an independent, non-executive, non-departmental public body (NDPB), in particular of the MOJ (by which it is *administered*); but observes *directions* by the *Justice Secretary* containing release criteria and *procedures*. Following rulings of the European Court of Human Rights, these have been recognised as *guidelines* rather than instructions. It comprises a chair and around 80 members (some full-time). They include existing or former *judges, psychiatrists,* chief *probation* officers, *criminologists* and purely independent members; who meet in panels of three/four to consider **applications for parole**. The board publishes annual reports. See, further, paroleboard.gov.uk

partnership

An alliance between departments, agencies/services with a view to cooperation, *liaison* and 'working together' (see under *work*); a form of *multi-agency* working. Within the CJS, partnership is nowadays a key mechanism in forging a system rather than a process of justice, the latter typified by disconnected elements and stages (subject to retention of authority, decision-making, etc. where they properly reside). Depending on how matters are analysed or viewed, it can even be seen as extending, in a modified form and consistent with *judicial independence,* to the courts. The restructuring of government departments in 2007 led to a fresh impetus for partnership as between the MOJ, Home Office, Office of the *Attorney General* and (re juveniles) *Department For Children, Schools and Families* (DCSF) and re the agencies/services working within and alongside the CJS (see *wider criminal justice family* in *Touchstones*). The *Cabinet Committee on Crime and the Criminal Justice System* (CCCCJS) represents partnership at the highest level; which also occurs via *Criminal Justice Boards* and between *frontline* practitioners. This contrasts with former times when inter-agency suspicion, mistrust, issues of *jurisdiction,* territory and a lack of shared aims and effective *communication* inhibited progress. See, also, *independence/interdependence*.

party/parties

Words used to describe those people who are central to a *case*, in criminal proceedings meaning the prosecutor making the allegation and the accused person who either enters a *plea* of guilty or puts forward a *defence*. The same terms may be used in a looser and extended sense to refer to the *lawyers* involved 'on either side', or the prosecution or defence team. See generally *adversarial system* in *Touchstones*. Other people may be described as **participants**, e.g. the victim, *witnesses*, judges, magistrates, court and other CJS staff. Certain participants may have what is called *locus standi*, i.e. legal standing due to their direct interest in an outcome because it affects them; which may give them certain rights alongside those of the **main parties**, e.g. to make a *complaint* or seek a judicial review: see *appeal*.

payback See Touchstones; **peer** See *trial by peers*.

penal

Appertaining to *punishments*. Hence, e.g. the **Howard League for Penal Reform**: see *Touchstones*; **penal affairs**: the broad head under which such matters are usually debated; **Penal Affairs Consortium**: see *Touchstones*; **penal code**: see, e.g. *code*/'Indian Penal Code'; **penal colony**: see *Touchstones*/'transportation'; **penal laws**: see *religion*; **penology**: the scientific and/or theoretical study of punishments (often in the wider context of *criminology*); **penal populism**: popular views about punishments, which may be fallible: 'Penal populism does not work: two thirds ... believe crime is rising and blame the government; the other third rightly recognise that it is falling, but … give no credit at all to Ministers' (*Guardian* editorial, 26 August 2008) (see also generally *media/press* and *Touchstones/*'popular culture'); **penal reform**: the *reform* and potential abolition/replacement of punishments or of sentencing frameworks; **Penal Reform Trust** see: *Touchstones;* **penal servitude**: a form of *imprisonment* under the Penal Servitude Act 1853, served in the UK, that included *hard labour,* as an *alternative* to *transportation* (see *Touchstones* re the latter); three years to life, until abolished by the *Criminal Justice Act* 1948. For **automatic penalty** see *fine/*'administrative fine'; **death penalty** see *capital punishment* in *Touchstones*; **fixed penalty** see that entry; and **penalty points** see *road traffic*.

performance

Since the 1980s at least, the CJS and its component parts have been subject to various **performance indicators (PIs)**, including **key performance indicators (KPIs)**, often linked to *targets* and designed to improve *effectiveness and efficiency*, directed towards *administrative* matters and not touching on *judicial discretion*. PIs/KPIs vary re the agency/service in question. Examples can often be found by visiting their individual web-sites. They also change from time-to-time according to current *priorities*.

perjury

In broad terms, lying on *oath* (or *affirmation*) where this affects matters in a 'material particular'. Under the **Perjury Act 1911** it attracts a maximum sentence of ten years *imprisonment*. The integrity of the CJS and 'public *confidence*' in the administration of justice rests on people telling the *truth* and acting honestly, especially when giving *evidence*. Coincidentally, two of the best-known perjury trials of modern times involved politicians and the *media/press*: Lord (Jeffrey) Archer (former Tory MP and still a best-selling novelist) convicted in 2001 re false *evidence* given in a successful *civil* claim for defamation against the *Daily Star* in 1987 (when he received damages of £500,000), who served over two years' *imprisonment* for perjury and perverting the course of justice; and Jonathan Aitken (another Tory MP, now a penal *reformer*) who, in 1999, received an 18 month sentence re false evidence he gave against the *Guardian* newspaper re a claim, brought by him, in order, perversely, to wield 'the trusty sword of truth'. These cases also demonstrate that the offence can be committed in relation to an affidavit (which Aitken had sworn) as well as 'live' testimony in a courtroom; and that passage of time is no automatic bar to a prosecution (14 years in Archer's case). **Pious perjury** is a term used to describe perverse verdicts of juries (see *juror/jury*), i.e. those leading to an *acquittal* in the face of compelling evidence of guilt, or, e.g. a conviction of *manslaughter* to avoid a sentence of *capital punishment* for *murder*, or, in yet earlier times, by valuing *theft* below the level which attracted such punishment under the Bloody Code. See *The Criminal Jury Old and New: Jury Power from Ancient Times to the Modern Day* (2006), Hostettler J, Waterside Press.

persistent offender

One who perseveres with his or her offending, often (but not necessarily) committing similar offences, and despite, e.g. sentences and/or *warnings* as to the likely CJS consequences; and re whom: (**1**) a more severe sentence may be appropriate (**a**) as a matter of ordinary principle (see sentence/sentencing); or (**b**) under *legislation* designed to increase the severity of a sentence in specific situations; or (**2**) re whom special initiatives may be needed/justified, as per a national or local *multi-agency* **Persistent Offender Schemes (POSs)**. From 2001 a **Persistent Offender Task Force (POTF)** comprising senior representatives from the various CJS agencies, linked to a **Persist-**

ent Offender Project worked at 'catching, bringing to justice and rehabilitating offenders [who are] responsible for a disproportionate amount of crime'. It began as a step towards a Labour Government manifesto commitment to 'double the chance of persistent offenders being caught and punished by 2011'; leading, in 2004, to a replacement *prolific offender* strategy: see also that entry.

Phillips Commission See *Touchstones*

photography

(1) Photographic evidence, e.g of a *crime scene* is generally accepted in court by agreement, *admission* or, if need be, proof of the chain of *evidence* linking the taking of a photograph via its travels, processes and handling to its arrival at the trial. **(2)** For other general applications, see *CCTV; media/press; open court/*'in camera'; *road traffic/*speed camera'; *rogues gallery; surveillance; technology;* video/*'amateur camera-man'*. **(3) Photographing, drawing or recording proceedings** in or near a court-room is a *contempt of court* and/or prohibited by dedicated *legislation*. The 'artist's impressions' which appear in newspapers, etc. are created from memory from scenes observed first-hand in *open court*. Consistently, the Government and *judiciary* have resisted broadcasting proceedings of UK courts; albeit that in 2009 plans were announced for the filming of *judgements* delivered by the *Supreme Court* (but not of the earlier parts of such court proceedings). See also generally the entry for *video*.

piracy

(1) Historically, armed *raids* on ships for the purposes of *robbery* and sometimes *murder* were a considerable *threat* to travellers on the High Seas (albeit with seemingly more romantic connotations in *popular culture*: see *Touchstones*). Hence **Piracy Acts** such as those of 1717, 1721, 1724, 1837 and 1850; when the offence attracted *capital punishment* (see *Touchstones*) and was subject to UK *jurisdiction* wherever committed. This form of piracy has re-surfaced in modern times, e.g. off the coast of Somalia, as attacks on cruise liners and cargo vessels; linked to ransom demands by self-styled *vigilante* groups, bringing the policing of such matters to the fore re the United Nations (UN) and International Maritime Organization (IMO). **(2)** Also in modern times the term has been associated in particular with **software piracy** (and hence, e.g. **anti-piracy software**), **copyright piracy** (aka copyright *theft*), **film piracy** and **music piracy** in particular, i.e. by downloading such items from the internet and/or making illicit copies for distribution. In 2005 **'internet pirates'** from a UK-based group DrinkorDie prided themselves on being able to crack 'any *security code*' to make downloads available free to others; for 'the thrill' and to strike at trading giants (see *motive*). The prosecutor said they lived in a virtual world: 'They think of themselves as latter day *Robin Hoods'* (see *Touchstones*) [but] in reality it is a cover for *fraud*'. **Internet piracy** is fast growing and in 2009, Pirate Bay 'the world's most high-profile file-sharing site' was the subject of injunctions and prosecution (ongoing).

plea

The answer given by an accused person when he or he is asked: 'How do you plead, guilty or not guilty?' Following a **guilty plea** the procedure follows a regular pattern in all courts (increasingly so, due to the work of the *Criminal Procedure Rules Committee* (CPRC)). The court moves to the sentencing stage: see *sentence/sentencing*. A **not guilty plea** leads to a *trial* (see that entry). An **equivocal plea** occurs when the accused person admits that he or she committed the offence but gives an inconsistent explanation ('I stole the goods but I always intended to give them back'); which cannot be accepted. The case is put back for him or her to consider matters, take legal *advice*, etc. and, if necessary, for a trial to be held. For **fitness to plead** and **plea of insanity**, see *mental impairment*; and *M'Naughten Rules* in *Touchstones*. Note, also, **plea before venue**: see *allocation and sending*. For **written plea of guilty** (aka paper plea) see *paperwork*. For some historic forms of plea, see *A History of Criminal Justice in England and Wales* (2008), Hostettler J, Waterside Press. A **plea bargain** is an arrangement whereby an accused person agrees to plead guilty to a lesser/different matter to that originally charged in expectation of a lighter sentence; the corresponding 'bargain' for the CJS being that this will avoid wasting valuable resources.

police/policing

Terms normally referable to the (ordinary) *civil* police unless qualified by reference, e.g to special or non-geographic police forces such as the *British Transport Police* or *Ministry of Defence Police*. There are 43 *civil* police forces in England and Wales each covering a county or group of counties, except in London where there is one force for the City of London and the **Metropolitan Police Service (MPS)** covers the rest of the capital. The MPS also has nationwide responsibilities, e.g. re national *security*. A classic and enduring statement of the **aims of policing** was contained in the White Paper *Police Reform* (1993), i.e. to: fight and prevent crime; uphold the law; bring to justice people who break the law; protect, help and reassure the community; and provide *value for money*. Another insight can be gleaned from the form of **attestation** for police officers and special constables on appointment, i.e. 'I John Smith of the Blackshire Constabulary do solemnly and sincerely declare and affirm that I will well and truly serve the Queen in the office of constable, with fairness, integrity, diligence and impartiality, upholding fundamental human rights and according equal *respect* to all people; and that I will, to the best of my power, cause the peace to be kept and preserved and prevent all offences against people and property; and that while I continue to hold the said office I will, to the best of my skill and knowledge, discharge all the duties thereof faithfully according to law'. For a wide-ranging overview, see *Police and Policing: An Introduction* (2009), Villiers P, Waterside Press. The following selection is based on some of the more central and commonplace police-related items.

Police in the UK are not, routinely, **armed police** although they may be for specific purposes and high *risk* areas may be patrolled by, e.g. **armed response teams**, using guns or 'less lethal' *weapons* (see, e.g. *Taser-gun* in *Touchstones*). Other than in an *emergency*, they may need higher authority to draw arms. The **Basic Command Unit (BCU)** is a standard unit of command re the structures and *management* of police forces (within which each officer has 'original authority' and *discretion*. **'Bobbies on the beat'** connotes policemen on the streets operating visibly in *communities* and neighbourhoods; rather than responding from remote locations, via **control centres**. **Beat policing** (which stems from the earliest days of policing and *Bow Street Runners:* see *Touchstones*) occurs when a designated police officer is assigned to an area, such as a collection of streets. For **bent copper**, see *Touchstones*. A **chief constable** heads each of the 43 police forces except for the *Metropolitian Police Service* which has a **commissioner of police. Community policing** is a philosophy and method of policing based on the idea that police officers and private individuals *working together* can jointly solve problems of *law enforcement*: see also generally *community*; *Neighbourhood Watch*. A key focus of policing remains the **police station** albeit these are decreasing in number due to rationalisation. Some are **designated police sta-**

tions, i.e. nominated by the chief constable for the purposes of procedures under the *Police and Criminal Evidence Act 1984* (PACE) (below). A **custody sergeant** is also based at such a station, who collates and deals with matters arising from an *arrest* (assisted by other police officers of nominal rank and **custody officers**, in effect gaolers, who may be police or *civilians*, looking after people in **police cells**. For **police detention**, see *detention*; and also *bail*/'police bail' and *charge*. **Complaints against the police** may be resolved between the police and complainant informally, lead to an *investigation*, criminal, internal, or a *referral* to the *Independent Police Complaints Commission* (IPCC). **Covert policing** is a generic term for undercover work, the infiltration, e.g. of criminal networks, *drug* rings, *organized crime*, subversive groups and cultivation of *informers* (see especially the last entry).

Local **Criminal Investigations Departments (CIDs)** provide plain clothes **police detectives** (see *detection/detective*) as opposed to those in **police uniform** (see also *Touchstones*/'symbol'). CID work takes place separately and usually re more *serious offences* (but note also now the work of the *Serious Organized Crime Agency* (SOCA)). The **drugs squad** is one example of specialist operations; often carried out in teams or units (part of CID or mixed teams to which officers may be seconded). Increasingly, aspects of policing have taken on international or **global dimension. Europol,** the European Law Enforcement Organization, 'aims at improving the *effectiveness* and co-operation of the competent authorities in the member *States* in preventing and combating *terrorism*, unlawful *drug* trafficking and other *serious* forms of international *organized crime*': see further europol.europa.eu **Interpol** is the world's largest international police organization, with 187 member countries. Created in 1923 after an ad hoc meeting called by Prince Rainier in Monaco, it facilitates cross-border police co-operation, *help and support* to all organizations, authorities and services 'whose mission is to prevent or combat international crime'; even where diplomatic relations do not exist between countries; but within the limits of the national laws of different countries and the spirit of the Universal Declaration of Human Rights (see generally *human rights*). Its constitution prohibits 'any *intervention* or activities of a political, military, religious or racial character': see further interpol.int and *global/international dimensions*. For the relationship between policing and the **Home Office/ Home Secretary**, see those entries. **Intelligence-led policing** is police work based on *intelligence* as opposed to bare *information*: see the first of those entries for further distinctions. **Low visibility policing** takes place 'behind the scenes', away from the 'public gaze': painstaking work in support of diverse objectives or *targets*.

The **National Policing Improvement Agency (NPIA)** supports police forces to improve the way in which they work. It is a police owned and led organization which replaced or incorporated former national policing organizations such as the **Police Information Technology Organization** (PITO) and **CENTREX** (see *Bramshill* in *Touchstones*); as well as certain functions formerly carried out by the *Home Office* and Association of Chief Police Officers (ACPO) (below). Its origins lie in Home Office *responses* to suggestions by ACPO that an agency/service be established to support the implementation of *national standards*. It has a five-year rolling strategic plan (first published in 2004) and seeks 'to identify and plan ... for ... future challenges ... and [to] inform the *priority* and sequence of change programmes' using *evidence*-based methods and approaches. As its name implies, a central focus of its work is improving policing in England and Wales. Other functions include enhanced coordination of major national projects and the removal of duplication and waste; with *science* and *technology* to the fore. See further npia.police.uk For **police killers**, see *Touchstones*. A **'non-police matter'** is something outwith the responsibilities of the police; re which they may seek not to become involved. The term may also be used in the *courtroom* to signify a prosecution stemming from another *law enforcement agency*: see *no/non/not*. The **Police and Criminal Evidence Act (PACE)** is the key statute affecting all aspects of an *investigation* including *detention* without charge and police *interviews*. PACE and the **PACE codes of practice** govern when and for how long a suspect can be subjected to questioning. It sets out *time limits* (sometimes called **the PACE clock**) and the circumstances in which a case must be referred to a senior officer or court. PACE is reinforced by *best practice*, police training and *human rights*.

An autonomous **Association of Police Authorities (APA)** was formed in 1997 and works in *partnership* with the Local Government Association (LGA); one notable achievement being the creation of a **Statement of Common Purposes and Values (SOCPV).** This can be accessed at policesupers.com Chief constables are appointed by and report to their own police authority, which fixes the maximum strength of the force (subject to approval by central government) and provides buildings, equipment and other resources (subject to a government grant). It can advise a chief constable, e.g. on *law enforcement* priorities and the *allocation* of **police resources.** The **Police and Magistrates' Courts Act 1994** made police authorities free-standing bodies, reduced their size and introduced independent members (in addition to local councillors and magistrates). Further changes occurred in the Police Reform Act 2002 (below). For **police bail,** see *bail* and note *bail/*'street bail'. Since 2002, over 25,000 **police community support officers** (PCSOs) have been appointed, initially in London and, gradually nationwide. They wear uniforms, can detain people, but have no powers of arrest (neither do they make an oath of *attestation*: above). For **police detention**, see *detention*; **police discretion**, see *discretion*. The **Police Federation** is a staff association for police officers up to and including the rank of chief inspector; as created by the Police Act 1919, a year after a strike by the then unrecognised National Union of Police and Prison Officers (NUPPO): see further polfed.org The **Police National Computer (PNC)** is a secure nationwide *database* which since 1974 has been relied upon increasingly by the police and other authorised UK *law enforcement agencies*. It contains over one million records re people, vehicles, property, drivers and other matters and is a key resource. A PNC Code of Practice was issued by the Home Office in 2005. The PNC is now operated by the National Policing Improvement Agency (NPIA) (above). **Police officer's notebook** refers to a pocketbook in which daily events are recorded, to which the officer may refer, e.g. when giving *evidence*. Increasingly, electronic versions are in use. **Police procedures** is the generic term for rules affecting police work, including those of individual police forces.

The **Police Reform Act 2002** introduced an 'ambitious police policy [to] support the police service in tackling crime and *anti-social behaviour*' (Home Office); to ensure *effective* policing methods are used by all police forces and to tackle variations in *performance* as between forces, including: a National Policing Plan; powers enabling the *Home Secretary* to issues *codes of practice* and make *regulations* re the use of equipment, *procedure* or *practice*; and stronger powers of police authorities to remove chief officers in the interests of *effectiveness and efficiency*. Where a police force is 'manifestly failing in its duty' to protect and serve the public, the Home Secretary can intervene under the 2002 Act (see generally *intervention*). It conferred extra powers on *HM Inspectorate of Constabulary* (HMIC) created the *Independent Police Complaints Com-*

mission (IPCC); and allowed chief constables to confer police powers on a range of *civilians*; as well as further measures re *sex offender orders*; and re PCSOs (above). **Police Support Unit (PSU)** is a generic term for a 'back up unit' such as a **Firearms Support Unit (FSU)** (see generally *weapon*) or **rapid response unit (RRU)**. For **scenes of crime officer (SOCO)**, see *crime scene*. **A special constable** is a part-time unpaid volunteer police officer who assists full-time officers, usually for several hours per week, wears a *uniform* and is invested with police powers (contrast PCSOs above). **Policing by consent** is a theory of policing emphasising the fact that, ultimately, the police must maintain public *confidence* and support; that they act for *citizens* rather than 'police them'; and that broad public agreement is needed for the police to achieve their tasks: see the work by Peter Villiers referred to at the start of this entry. **Undercover policing** is a synonym for covert policing above. For **warrant card**, see *warrant*. See, also, *Commissioner of Police; Superintendents Association.*

policy/policy-making

Terms use to denote the aims and purposes of the overall arrangements re CJS matters and processes of decision-making; whereby a general stance is maintained, sometimes called **criminal justice policy**, e.g. what conduct should amount to an offence; maximum *punishments* and their place within the sentencing framework. For **political aspects**, see *Touchstones*. For **judicial policy** see under *judicial*. Compare *Strategy.*

possession

(1) With certain crimes the offence lies in possessing something, i.e. having personal custody or *control* of it, such a *drug*, an article for use re *terrorism/terrorist* or pornographic images of children (when, in the latter case, **mere possession** is enough to ground a conviction as opposed to active knowledge of their intrinsic nature). **Possession of an offensive weapon** (see *weapon*) may require *evidence* that the item was intended for such use as such, i.e. if not automatically a weapon (or 'weapon *per se*': such as a gun or knife as opposed to a bottle or piece of wood which is picked up and used to 'glass' or beat someone). Consult works on *criminal law* re the exact *mens rea* in each scenario. Note also: (2) **police powers to take possession** of items *during an arrest*; *raid*; or to preserve *evidence;* and (3) *prisoner/*'in possession'.

practice

(1) A word used to describe routine ways of discharging tasks, e.g. within an agency/ service and that is usually contrasted with *procedure* which is generally more akin to regulation and may involve *legislation* (as with *criminal procedure*). Hence also terms such as **best practice** (see further that entry), **good practice** (e.g. to a generally accepted standard but not necessarily, or proactively the 'very best') and **evidence-based** practice (see *evidence; research; 'what works'* (in *Touchstones*)). (2) A **Practice Direction (PD)** is a legal missive which is of a similar status and scope to a *ruling* of one of the *higher courts*, or *guideline* judgement, usually of a broad nature, giving *advice* on some aspect of **court practice**. PDs are normally issued by or on behalf of the *Lord Chief Justice,* or the head of a division of the *High Court.* The *Criminal Procedure Rules Committee* (CPRC) now covers some of this ground.

precedent

Rulings of the *higher courts* as published in *law reports*, verbatim accounts of the *opinions* of appeal judges, including dissenting views. They note the facts and set out the legal implications, together with the *reasons* for the judges' conclusions, focusing centrally, on the *law*. They are a subject of study by lawyers re their own *advice, arguments, opinions* and *representations*. In toto they represent a vast library of Common Law (contrast *legislation*). Decisions of the *Crown Court* or *magistrates' courts* do not set precedents, only rulings of the *higher courts*. Certain precedents are **persuasive only** (see *Privy Council*), others **binding precedents**, i.e. binding on a 'lower court'; of varying *weight* (see *Touchstones*) or authority depending on the seniority/reputation the judge concerned. Lawyers 'cite' precedents for or against a given proposition.

preliminary hearing/matters/stages

Pre-trial processes (and **pre-trial services** (PTS)) concentrate on clarifying the issues in a *case* and countering *delay*. There may be several stages between the start of criminal proceedings and the time when a case comes to trial. Certain cases may be 'fast-tracked', by the defendant being given the opportunity to enter an early guilty plea (which attracts a *statutory* discount: see *sentence/sentencing*); or indicate a 'plea before venue' (see *allocation and sending*). There may be a **criminal directions hearing (CDH)** at which, e.g. a timetable for the case, *disclosure* and other aspects of *case management* are raised. Legal *arguments* may be rehearsed in this context and the need for *legal* or other *research* identified; the purpose being to eliminate matters which might disrupt any trial. **National Probation Service pre-trial services** may include *assessments* re pre-sentence reports (PSRs) (see *sentence/sentencing*) being set in train, facilitating *bail support,* making *referrals* and ensuring that *victim impact statements* are available. Note also **early first hearing (EAH)** to signify the timely processing of matters essential to progress at the outset such as the arrangements for *legal aid*.

prerogative of mercy and **royal prerogative** See *Crown; mercy;* **pre-sentence report (PSR)** See *sentence/sentencing*; **press, media, etc.** See *media/press.*

presumption

A conclusion that follows as a matter of course once some underlying basis is established; and/or as a matter of entrenched principle. Hence, e.g. the **presumption of innocence**: the longstanding *rule* that an accused person is innocent unless and until found guilty by a court, or he or she voluntarily pleads guilty (now reinforced by Article 6 of the European Convention On Human Rights (ECHR)(see *human rights*)). This affects the way in which accused people are dealt with at all stages of the criminal process prior to conviction; and is, e.g. the reason why someone who is interviewed by the police is described as a 'suspect' rather than 'an offender'. In terms of *evidence*, presumptions may be **presumptions of fact** (e.g. re recurring phenomena such as darkness at night or daylight), **presumptions of law** (including that everyone is deemed to know the *law*: see also *ignorance*); **rebuttable presumptions** and **irrebuttable presumptions** re all of which see specialist texts on evidence.

previous conviction See *conviction; double jeopardy*

prima facie

'On the face of things'. Hence a **prima facie case** is one where on the basis of unanswered prosecution *evidence* there is sufficient *evidence* for a jury or magistrates to convict the accused; and in the absence of any further explanation or answer, usually meaning by the *defence,* may normally do so. But 'prima facie' does not mean conclusive. The court may or may not consider that he or she is guilty depending on all the circumstances, including the *weight* of the evidence (see *Touchstones*); any *defence* put forward; and the high criminal standard of proof: see *evidence*.

Prime Minister (PM)

PMs have sometimes played a prominent role in matters of criminal justice, including via *Cabinet committees*. Several held the post of *Home Secretary*, including Sir Robert Peel, Winston Churchill, Lloyd George and James Callaghan. The PM appoints the *Attorney General* and (subject to the work of the *Judicial Appointments Commission* (JAC)) still, it seems, as a matter of convention, is consulted re the very top judicial appointments (see, generally, *higher judiciary*). The PM Spencer Perceval was assassinated by John Bellingham (1812) after he was denied UK *compensation* for *imprisonment* in Russia, claiming it stemmed from British involvement so that he had the *right* to kill the top representative of his oppressors. Bellingham was executed in public a month after the *murder*, claims of insanity on his behalf being rejected (see generally *mental impairment*). Other UK PMs have faced assassination attempts; including Margaret Thatcher in the Brighton Bombing (1984) and John Major when a mortar was fired during a Cabinet meeting at No.10 Downing Street (1991) (both attributed to the Irish Republican Army (IRA)(see, generally, The *Troubles* in *Touchstones*)). There are many examples of the assassination of heads of State from around the world and across history. In the 1970s, Labour PM Harold Wilson complained that he was under *surveillance* by the *security services.* In 2007, Tony Blair was the first PM to be interviewed as a *witness* in a criminal *investigation* touching on his office (see *'cash for honours'* in *Touchstones*). The **Prime Minister's Strategy Unit** has been behind a number of CJS initiatives, see, e.g. *Carter Report(s)* in *Touchstones.*

priorities

Those set by government, an agency/service, *reform* group, etc. in line with aims, *objectives, resources, targets,* etc; which involve choices between competing *strategies*; whether nationally or locally according to the level of importance. Thus, e.g. the MOJ sets out its **main priorities** as follows: 'to strengthen *democracy, rights* and responsibilities, deliver fair and simple routes to *civil* and family justice [see generally *fair/fairness*]; protect the public [see *protection*] and reduce *reoffending*; ensure a more effective [see *effectiveness and efficiency*], transparent [see *transparency*] and responsive criminal justice system [see *response*] for victims and the public': see justice.gov.uk

prison

Until the 18th century, prisons were used mainly for people awaiting trial, *capital punishment, transportation* (see *Touchstones*), a visit by royal judges 'on *circuit*', or to enforce debts and other *civil* obligations. They were *private sector* undertakings (a form of 'lodgings') or an adjunct to power (e.g. in the dungeons of castles). The first truly public gaols were the **bridewells** (a word later appropriated as a nickname for police cells) and **houses of correction** as a *response* to petty offenders, vagrants (see *vagrancy*) and 'miscreants'; largely administered by *magistrates* (the then *local authority*). Their use for longer-term *imprisonment* and as symbols of *deterrence, shame* and *retribution* evolved slowly from the mid-1700s onwards. That they are now less draconian stems from the work of bodies such as the Howard League for Penal Reform; and Prison Reform Trust (PRT) (see *Touchstones* for those organizations and others). Leading texts include the *Oxford History of the Prison* (1998), Morris, M, Oxford University Press; *Prisons and the Process of Justice: The Reductionist Challenge* (1984), Rutherford R, Heinemann; and *Prison On Trial* (2005) (3rd. edn.), Mathiesen T, Waterside Press. *HM Prison Service* (HMPS) (see that entry) has been regulated by *legislation* since the early-20th century; and is now part of the National Offender Management Service (NOMS): see *offender management*. A small selection of prisons appear as *Main Entries* by way of illustration. Outline information about all prisons in England and Wales can be accessed via the 'Locate a Prison' facility at hmprison-service.gov.uk The following are amongst the more common prison-related terms.

Adjudication: see *discipline*, below; **allocation**: allocation to a prison(er) *category*, below (and see also that item for **assessment**). For **'the block'**, see prisoner/'segregation'. **CARATS** Counselling, Assessment, Referral, Advice and Throughcare Services: see *prisoner*. **Category**: following an assessment after being received into prison, a male prisoner is placed in one of four categories according to his *offence, sentence, sentence plan* and operational considerations. Both a prison and prisoners are frequently described by reference to their category. These are listed under *prisoner*, below. Each prison has a **chapel** and a prison **chaplain** (sometimes several from various faiths, such as Imams or Rabbis). Many chaplains are also involved in wider aspects of prisoner *welfare*. For **committal to prison**, see *imprisonment*. **Community prison** is a description given to those mainly local prisons (below) where the *community* is encouraged to become involved in prisoner *help and support, rehabilitation, reintegration* and mentoring, etc. For **control and restraint**, see *prisoner*. **Discipline** is shorthand for the internal HMPS system for maintaining 'good order and discipline' under the *Prison Rules* (below). Until 2002, *prison governors* (below) were responsible for adjudications (a quasi-court procedure) at which prisoners might receive added days (see, further, *prisoner*). This contravened Article 6 of the European Convention On Human Rights (see *human rights*; *fair/fairness*). Loss of *liberty* cases are now heard by visiting district *judges*, lesser day-to-day matters by prison staff. A **dispersal prison** is one for *serious* or high-*risk* offenders (see also *Touchstones*/'heavy end'). **Establishment** is the word used to describe any prison-related premises within 'the prison estate' (or a part of it managed by the *private sector*), including stores, warehouses and *hostels*. The **gate** (i.e. 'prison gate') is the single portal via which all traffic into and out of a prison must normally pass and where related checks and procedures occur, including re the reception of prisoners (below), their *release* and visits (see also below). See also *gate* in *Touchstones*. Each prison has its own **healthcare** arrangements and in many cases a **healthcare centre** with medical/nursing staff. It will also have a **library** which prisoners visit (often on a rota basis) and a **prison librarian**. A **local prison** is one that provides a service to local courts, usually by holding *remand* prisoners and those serving short sentences (and it may also be a *community prison,* above). **Minimum use of force tactical intervention (MUFTI)** is the description applied to measures to safeguard **security and control** (which are always *priorities*) including in an *emergency* or if appropriate in order to complete a search. Hence, also, **MUFTI** squad for that team (and note the jargon 'four (five, six) to unlock'). See also *prisoner*/'control and restraint'. An **open prison** is one without a secure perimeter where prisoners are 'free' within its grounds, some of whom hold their own keys. **Prison day** means the regular pattern of events in a given prison aka its daily regime: below. The term **prison governor** encompasses both the 'governing governor' (or 'No.1 governor', i.e. the top official in charge of an entire establishment: sometimes called **'a whole prison'**) and deputy or assistant governors of various grades. Governors wear plain clothes and also occupy various senior roles at HMPS headquarters. Hence, also, the **Prison Governors' Association (PGA)**, the main membership body for 'governor grades' which engages with the MOJ re prison-related matters, *policy* formation, *strategy* and day-to-day issues. It publishes a journal,

The Key. Governors can be contrasted with **prison officers** (and senior, principal and chief prison officers) who wear uniforms, act as guards and run aspects of the *regime* (below). The **Prison Officers' Association (POA)** describes itself as 'the largest union in the UK representing uniformed prison grades and staff working [within this field] with over 35,000 members in the public and private sectors'. It represents members across a range of professional issues, including: conditions of service, *education*, training, privatisation of prisons, *health and safety* and matters of *policy*.

Prison(er) overcrowding (which is discussed by reference variously to **prison(er) numbers** or **prison(er) population**) is the heading under which increases or decreases in the number of people: (**1**) in prison in England and Wales (and/or Scotland, Northern Ireland, or the UK as a whole as specified) at any given moment is discussed (in round figures) below 20,000 in 1948; 42,000 in 1993; 84,000 in 2008; 96,000 (projected for 2015 even though it is claimed that most forms of crime have fallen significantly over the past ten years: see *crime prevention/crime reduction*); or (**2**) similarly re a given prison. A **prison interview** can be: (**1**) one which takes place inside a prison as conducted by the police with a prisoner to *clear up* outstanding offences when it would be pointless bringing extra charges; or (**2**) any other interview in a prison-setting, e.g. with a *probation officer, psychiatrist* or *legal representative*. For **Prisons and Probation Ombudsman** see the separate entry below and for **Prison Reform Trust (PRT)**, *Touchstones*. The **Prisons Board** is the senior board of HMPS. For **prison sentence**, see *imprisonment*. The **prison van** is aka *transport* (see that entry) or colloquially 'meatwagon'. **Private prison** is shorthand for one built, constructed, financed and/or managed for HMPS by the *private sector*. **Reception** is: (**1**) the name of the prison office, usually by the *gate* (see *Touchstones*) which acts as the interface with the outside world; and (**2**) the process by which prisoners are received into a prison. The word **regime** signifies the daily schedule within an individual prison, including the times of locking-up/unlocking of prisoners, association, meals, exercise, education, visits to prisoners and religious worship (mostly dealt with under *prisoner*). There are **Basic, Standard** and **Enhanced Regimes**; and overall HMPS seeks to achieve **positive regimes**. For **release from prison**, see *release*. **Reports** for the *Parole Board*, etc. are prepared by prison governors, prison officers (above), *probation officers* and other people as part of 'integrated *offender management*', including making or collating *risk-assessments*. For **resettlement prison,** see *reintegration and resettlement.* **'Role change'** is used to describe the situation whereby a prison changes its function, e.g. from an establishment for lifers (see *life imprisonment*) to a training prison; and/or the category of prisoner it accepts. For **Rule 45**: see *prisoner*. **Vulnerable Prisoner Units** (VPUs) exist in many prisons and certain prisons are used wholly or mainly for this purpose. **Security and control** are watchwords for prison governors which stand above or are a pre-condition for other regime-related events: prisons must primarily be safe, secure, healthy and properly *controlled*. **Therapeutic community (TC)**: see *therapy*. **'Titan' prison** is the name given to each of three controversial, proposed prisons to hold 2,500 prisoners each in locations that are likely to be isolated from normal community contacts or family members. A **training prison** is one where (usually) long-term prisoners receive training with a view to gaining *employment*-related skills in readiness for *release*. **Wings and landings** is the omnibus term to describe the physical accommodation and its location within a prison (terms that may be used re actual wings of a single building and levels within those wings, or metaphorically; and which have a place within prison culture similar to 'gate' as noted in *Touchstones*). **Transport** is a name for the 'prison van': see also *transport*. For

women in prison/women's prisons, see *women; Holloway Prison.*

Prisons and Probation Ombudsman The final arbiter of grievances and *complaints* by *prisoners* or people subject to *community sentences*, etc. The PPO is wholly independent of HM Prison Service (HMPS), the National Probation Service (NPS) or *Justice Secretary* (by whom he or she is appointed (since 2007)). Complaints must have completed internal HMPS/NPS stages. Prisoners who failed to obtain satisfaction from the *prisoner*/'requests and complaints' system or people who are, or have been, under NPS *supervision* or housed in its accommodation, or had pre-sentence reports (PSRs) prepared on them (see *sentence*/'pre-sentence report') can (if eligible in other respects) apply to the ombudsman to review their cases. The ombudsman's *target* is to do so within 12 weeks of determining eligibility. He or she also deals with **fatal incident reports** (see also *deaths in custody* in *Touchstones*), undertakes **special investigations** and publishes an annual report. See further ppo.gov.uk

Prison Reform Trust (PRT) See *Touchstones*

prisoner

Either: **(1)** someone who is in custody awaiting trial or sentence, aka a **remand prisoner** (see *remand*) who may also be styled an **unconvicted prisoner** or **unsentenced prisoner** as appropriate; or **(2)** a **sentenced prisoner**: 'convict' is old terminology (and hence also historical references to a 'convict prison' or 'convict ship': see hulks in *Touchstones*). It still serves to distinguish people who have already been found guilty from those awaiting their trial; and a *civil* prisoner (below) from one held under a sentence following a criminal conviction. The items below are some of the more common prisoner-related words and terms.

Absconding describes a failure to return to prison, e.g. following home leave, or leaving the confines of an open prison without permission (in contrast to escaping from secure conditions. **Added days** are days added to a sentence for breach of the *Prison Rules* (see, also, *prison*/'discipline'). **Alcohol testing** is the procedure via which *HM Prison Service* (HMPS) checks to see whether prisoners have been using *alcohol* (see, generally, that entry and Counselling, Assessment, Referral, Advice and Throughcare Services (CARATS) noted below). **Allocation** to a particular prison or category (below) follows an HMPS **assessment** at the start of or during a sentence to determine which prison a sentence will be served inside (they may occur for a range of other purposes, e.g. participation in a course; treatment; *parole*) (hence also the omnibus term 'assessment and allocation'). **Association** is the period when prisoners are allowed to mix freely with one another outside of their cells.

Category (or 'cat') Prisoners and, correspondingly, prisons to which they are allocated by HMPS are categorised A-D. **Cat-A**: for those prisoners whose escape would be highly *dangerous* for the public, the police or the *security* of the *State*. Cat-A prisoners are normally allocated to a high security closed training prison (aka *dispersal prison*: see *prison*). See also *Touchstones*/'heavy end'; **Cat-B**: those for whom escape must be made very difficult; **Cat-C**: those who cannot be trusted in open conditions but do not have the will or resources to make a determined escape attempt; **Cat-D**: those who can reasonably be trusted in open conditions. Unsentenced prisoners are made Cat-B automatically, unless provisionally placed in Cat-A. Women and young offenders are categorised simply for open or closed conditions, apart from a few women prisoners who are treated as high-*risk* and as if in Cat-A. The decision is reviewed (at least) every 12 months. Prisoners tend to be moved to less secure conditions as they progress with their sentence plan/pre-release plan (both below). Otherwise, the precise *establishment* (see *prison*) to which an adult male sentenced prisoner is allocated depends on his offence, sentence, courses, etc. and available places.

There are some 1,000 **civil prisoners** at any one time serving under a separate regime but mostly within the same establishments as offenders (including those gaoled for *contempt*; and historically until the late-1960s for debt: hence old references to **debtors prisons** or the 'debtors' yard'). **Control and restraint (C&R)** is the head under which action is taken to maintain control, etc. in the event that there is a *risk* that it might be lost, due to the actions of prisoners: see, also, *prison/*'Minimum Use of Force Tactical Intervention ('MUFTI'). For **deaths in custody**: see that entry. Re **drug testing**, HMPS operates **mandatory drug testing (MDT)** and some prisoners submit to **voluntary drug testing (VDT)**. There are also a number of special schemes. **Counselling, Assessment, Referral, Advice and Throughcare Services (CARATS)** teams provide ongoing services of the kind referred to in their title across a wide range of alcohol and drug-related matters. For another useful perspective see *Drug Treatment in Prisons: An Evaluation of the RAPt Treatment Programme* (2000), Martin C and Player E, Waterside Press. Prison(er) **education** now centres (contentiously) on the acquisition of basic skills rather than advanced qualifications or the arts (but with opportunities to pursue activities funded independently by the prisoner or outside bodies); and there is a range of vocational training for longer-term prisoners. For an overview, see *Prison(er) Education: Stories of Change and Transformation* (2000), Wilson D and Reuss A, Waterside Press. The Prisoners' Education Trust concentrates on 'unlocking potential through education': see prisonerseducation.org. uk. **Escort** is the name given to the arrangements for taking prisoners to and from court, between prisons, on visits, e.g. to hospital, etc. now largely provided by the *private sector*. **Exercise** signifies walking around the prison yard at a scheduled time (always clockwise: 'with time not against it') or that in gyms or on sports fields, etc; some prisons being better equipped than others in this regard.

Action for Prisoners **Families and Friends** is the voice of and support mechanism for bodies working in this field (see prisonersfamilies.org.uk). There is special provision for **foreign prisoners** (some commentators claim more in theory than practice), including access to *interpreters* and contact with their embassy. '**Foreign prisoner crisis**' (2005) refers to the non-deportation of such prisoners at the end of their sentences following recommendations of the courts. See the note on Charles Clarke former *Home Secretary*. **Induction** is the process via which prisoners acclimatise to prison life; there being facilities, e.g. for 'first-nighters' in many prisons (linked to 'assessment and allocation' above). For **lifer**, see *life imprisonment*. **Listeners** are prisoners trained to listen to the concerns, worries and attitudes of other prisoners, talk with them and where appropriate relay concerns to HMPS. Prisoners may be allocated a **personal officer** to whom they then relate and respond, etc. **Possessions** signifies a prisoner's personal effects which are taken away from him or her and stored (often at **Branston**, Staffordshire) pending *release,* or, subject to *security* and other HMPS considerations, allowed to remain '**in possession**' (IP) (i.e. in his or her cell). **Prisoner of conscience** signifies someone imprisoned as a result of personal beliefs (right or wrong).

Prisoner population: see *prison*. **Purposeful activity** is a key aim of HMPS (and a key *performance* indicator), i.e. the idea that prisoners should be engaged in activity with some purpose, rather, e.g. than being idle or engaged in futile tasks (as they might be historically: such as moving bricks across the prison yard so that other prisoners could move them back again). For the **reception** of a prisoner into prison and **regime**, see *prison*. **Requests and complaints (R&C)** is the system by which everyday applications by prisoners are made to *prison governors* and *prison officers* and under which they (or HMPS headquarters) make decisions whether to grant or refuse the request. **Rule 45** (formerly 'Rule 43') is the *Prison Rule* (see generally *prison*) under which certain prisoners are segregated from the main body of prisoners, e.g. to prevent disturbances or for their own *protection*. See also *vulnerable prisoner* below. Hence the terms **segregation;** and **'the seg'** for the punishment block (aka **'the block'** and hence also being put **'down the block'**). Progressively, **sentence plans** are now drawn up for prisoners serving 12 months or more and *young offenders*. They seek to ensure that the prisoner's time in custody is spent positively and that problems underlying *offending behaviour* are addressed. Special provision exists re **sex offenders** in terms of *security, protection* and programmes, the **Sex Offender Treatment Programme (SOTP)** and its various levels of progression standing at the hub of this. The **suicide rate** and **suicide risk** in prisons is above the national average. For further details, visit inquest.org.uk **Throughcare** signifies *welfare* considerations re the whole of a prisoner's sentence, covering time spent in prison and in the *community* as part of an end-to-end sentence (see also *sentence/sentencing, rehabilitation; reintegration and resettlement; release*). **Training** is provided in a number of training prisons where longer-term prisoners can learn new skills, sometimes by 'working out' (below). **Visits to prisoners** are categorised (mostly informally), e.g. as an **outside visit** (sometimes styled a **local visit**) when the prisoner is allowed to meet someone outside the prison, e.g. a family member, or for *healthcare* or *interview* purposes; a **personal visit** (aka **social visit**) inside the prison by family, friends, etc; **legal visit** (or other **professional visit**) by a lawyer, etc; and **closed visit** in secure conditions as a *response* to *risk, security and control* (see under *prison*). Hence, also, **visitors centres** which now exist at or just outside many prisons where visitors can wait, buy refreshments and get information; and **visits room** (colloquially the 'fishtank' or 'goldfish bowl') from its lack of privacy. **Vulnerable prisoners** are those at-risk of attack, *bullying*, intimidation, etc. often an *informer*, juvenile, *sex offender*, paedophile, ex-police officer or someone who turned Queen's evidence (see *evidence*) or is suffering *mental impairment* and needing *protection* from other prisoners. self-*harm* or *suicide*. See also 'Rule 45' above. For **women prisoners**, see the entry for *women.* Payments to prisoners are usually discussed under the heading **work and pay**, signifying that many prisoners have an opportunity to work, e.g. in a prison **workshop,** farm or in some instances by **working out** in the community and returning to prison at night, earning commercial wages ready for *release, reintegration and resettlement.*

private

(1) A word used to distinguish events which occur in relation to the world of commerce rather than the *public sector* or, e.g. *voluntary sector*. The **private sector** is nowadays involved in widescale provision of many CJS-related services, e.g. the funding, construction and *management* of prisons; *prisoner* escort services; *electronic monitoring* (or tagging) of offenders; and the supply and installation of equipment of all kinds, including, e.g. vehicles, *technology*. See also *Carter Report(s)* in *Touchstones*. Note also, e.g. the status of the *Forensic Science Service* and the role of the private sector in producing programmes or treatment for offenders; as well as, e.g. work for prisoners in the *community* as part of *rehabilitation* or *reintegration and resettlement*. The *security* industry provides everything from *burglary* alarms and CCTV systems to *security guards,* bodyguards, security vans and *surveillance* equipment. (**2**) See also in particular, rights to **private and family life**: in *human rights*. (**3**) For examples of matters 'behind closed doors', see *informer; media/press;* national *security; open court.*

Privy Council (PC)

The PC advises on the exercise of the royal prerogative (see generally *Crown*) and, e.g. devolution; its secretariat coming under the *Cabinet Office* and MOJ. In 2009, the *civil liberties* group *Justice* (justice.org.uk) claimed that at 650 years-old and with a 'rag bag' of responsibilities it was long overdue for *reform*. It described it as a source of patronage and a *constitutional* loophole, including due to its power to make Orders in Council under the royal prerogative: 'It is difficult to see any place for the legislative role of the unelected and undemocratic Privy Council': the full text is available at justice.org.uk The **Judicial Committee of the Privy Council (JCPC)** (in effect an Appellate Committee of the *House of Lords* 'wearing another hat') sits in the **Privy Council Chamber**, Downing Street as a final court of *appeal* from Dominion territories (or former such territories) who allow this final avenue of appeal beyond their national systems, i.e. who have retained an appeal to Her Majesty in Council or, in the case of republics, direct to the JCPC; when foreign judges can be used/consulted. PC *rulings* are persuasive under the doctrine of *precedent* re courts in England and Wales (i.e. non-binding). JCPC functions move to the *Supreme Court* in October 2009.

probation

(**1**) 'On probation' is a status which may apply to various CJS employees during the early months of their work and pending confirmation of their permanent appointment. (**2**) In a sentencing context and since 2003, **probation for offenders** no longer exists, strictly speaking (although the term continues within the name of the National Probation Service below and re other items noted in this section). The former **probation order** and the idea of being **'on probation'** has metamorphosed into aspects of a generic *community sentence*. For some further background and references, see *Touchstones* under *Rainer Crime Concern.* A **National Probation Service (NPS)** was created in 2002 whose aims include the *protection* of the public; reducing *re-offending*; the proper *punishment* of offenders in the *community*; ensuring that offenders are aware of the effects of crime on *victims* of crime and the public; and the *rehabilitation* of offenders: see probation.justice.gov.uk It now operates as part of the National Offender Management Service (NOMS): see *offender management.* A **chief probation officer (CPO)** heads each **probation area**. CPOs have been appointed mainly from people who have worked their way up 'through the ranks'; but for some time it has been possible for appropriately qualified people to be appointed from outside the service. The former **Association of Chief Probation Officers (ACOP)** is now part of the **Association of Chief Executives and Chief Officers of Probation (ACECOP)**, reflecting other modern-day developments. The establishing of NOMS provided a fresh context for the NPS and 'Reducing Re-offending: A National Action Plan' (2004) emphasised the importance of an integrated approach to working with offenders via a range of government departments, agencies/services, the *voluntary sector* and *private sector*. The **probation centre** is a key resource: premises where programmes or projects for offenders on community sentences are provided. Similarly the **probation hostel**: now chiefly geared to *reintegration and resettlement.* From 2004 the 42 local **Probation Boards** were being replaced by independent

Probation Trusts under contract to NOMS to deliver **probation services**; each composed of representatives of the local *community* appointed by the *Justice Secretary*; as is the **chief probation officer (CPO)**, who is a member. The board/trust acts as the local employer as well as setting its own agenda against a backdrop of national *strategy*. The Justice Secretary has power to give *directions* to boards re the discharge of their responsibilities; and there are default powers (see generally *sanctions*) whereby he or she can remove and replace trusts/boards if they fail to perform effectively (see generally *effectiveness and efficiency*). Each also has a chief executive. A **Probation Association (PA)** replaced the former **Probation Boards Association** in 2008 to become the national employers' organization working with and on behalf of both boards and trusts: see probationboards.co.uk **Probation officer** is the description applied to members of the NPS below chief officer, chief executive and higher grade assistants, rising from **main grade probation officer** through **senior probation officer** to **principal probation officer**. Increasingly, senior posts may be styled 'manager'. *Frontline*, day-to-day work is carried out by probation officers holding at least a degree-level Diploma in Probation Studies (DipPS); assisted by **probation service officers (PSOs)**, re whom entry requirements are less demanding. The work encompasses *offender management*, fieldwork (visiting, interviewing, making professional contacts, etc.), attending court, *bail* information and support, writing pre-sentence reports (see *sentence/sentencing*) (and note also the *Offender Assessment System* (OASys), *supervision* of offenders on *community sentences*, *probation centre* work (above), running intensive courses for high-*risk* offenders (see also *Touchstones*/'heavy end') and other group work, supervising staff, managing *hostels*, selecting and supervising residents, and prison-related work alongside prison officers (aka 'throughcare'), early *release*, forging links with outside *supervisors, help and support* (see also, e.g. *Clinks* in *Touchstones*), and other aspects of *rehabilitation*. A central task is the *supervision* of offenders under generic *community sentences*, which often involves not simply basic *supervision* but arranging courses, programmes and resources to confront (aka 'challenge') *offending behaviour*. They also supervise people who are on *parole* or other forms of *licence* (aka **post custody supervision**) including taking *enforcement* action. Another focal point is the **risk assessment**, see *risk*. Where a probation officer routinely works in a prison he or she may be styled **prison probation officer**. Officers also work within *youth offending teams* (YOTs). Such work is governed by National Standards (see *standard*), *best practice* and NPS or (appropriate) MOJ *guidance*. The NPS employs support staff and specialists, e.g. re *research* and *technology*.

procedure

Ways of discharging particular duties, responsibilities, etc, usually implying a high level of direction, precision and/or detail as may, e.g. be laid down by *Act of Parliament*, *regulations* or in working manuals or instructions. Note in particular **criminal procedure** (see further that entry). Other uses include, e.g. **advised procedures** (see also *best practice*; *guideline*; *standard*), **approved procedures** (as where an authority, organization or profession has endorsed a particular way of doing things; **forensic procedures** and **police procedures**. See also generally *due process; human rights*. Hence also the twinning of **practice and procedure**: see further *practice*.

proceeds of crime

Any **revenue** or **assets** traceable to criminal offences. Hence in modern times the extensive duties placed on banks, lawyers, accountants and other people involved in monetary transactions to make *suspicious activity reports* (see that entry), particularly re potential *money laundering*, which has significant connections to *organized crime*, illegal *drugs*, the sex industry and *trafficking* of all kinds. There are various methods by which an offender can be made to surrender the proceeds of crime, including via a *civil* claim. The Proceeds of Crime Act 2002 introduced the short lived **Assets Recovery Agency (ARA)** to investigate and recover wealth accumulated through criminal activity. It consolidated and strengthened pre-existing arrangements re confiscation, civil recovery, *money laundering* and SARS (above); now part of the remit of the *Serious Organized Crime Agency* (SOCA)(including in conjunction with HM *Revenue & Customs*). Those surplus proceeds of crime which have been recovered have been channelled into a wide variety of crime prevention/crime reduction initiatives. Suggestions that more remote proceeds might be *targeted*, e.g. royalties from 'offender memoirs', foundered at first as being potentially unfair (see *fair/fairness*) or impractical, but resurfaced in a Criminal Justice Bill in 2009. See also generally *cash; money*.

profiling
A generic term for the creation of a synopsis, building on key/significant features from a mass of *data, samples, evidence, research*, etc. in order to produce an underlying picture: as with **offender profiling**, as practised by criminal psychologists (see *psychiatry/psychology*), i.e. generating a prediction of the kind of person who might commit a given type of offence; and the scientifically-based **DNA-profiling**: see *DNA*.

prolific offender
One who commits offences repeatedly and frequently (see also generally *habit/*'habitual offender'; *repeat offender*); it having been estimated that some ten per cent of the 'active offender population' are responsible for half of all criminal offences and that a small proportion of offenders (around 0.5%) are responsible for one in ten offences. The term may be reserved for more serious offenders, especially re a (possibly sudden) **spree of offences** (aka **spree offending**). Hence a national **Prolific and other Priority Offender (PPO)** strategy (2004 onwards) to provide end-to-end management of this this group of offenders: see crimereduction.homeoffice.gov.uk

proscribed organization See *terrorism/terrorist*

prosecution/prosecutor
Historically, the decision whether or not to bring a **prosecution** (an *accusation* in a criminal court of law: but note that 'prosecute' may also be used re a *civil* matter) was for the police (or other *law enforcement agency*). Individual officers brought their own *cases*; but in time, this was systemised and **prosecuting officers** (often of the rank of inspector) took over; and from 1945 **prosecuting solicitors** employed by police authorities (with private sector *solicitors* also being used as needed). The role passed to the CPS under the **Prosecution of Offences Act 1985**: see *Crown Prosecution Service*. Other **public prosecutors** include the *Serious Fraud Office* (SFO); HM *Revenue & Customs* or 'anyone specified in an order made by the Secretary of State'. A **private prosecution**, i.e. by any *citizen* remains possible except where prevented by law, or a consent or authority is required (see, e.g. *Attorney General*). A **private prosecutor** risks *costs* being awarded against him or her if the prosecution fails; an attempt to lay an *information and summons* may be rejected as vexatious or as an *abuse of process*; or that prosecution may be taken over by the CPS (and *discontinued* whatever the wishes of the would-be private prosecutor). A number of such prosecutions do occur every year, sometimes re *serious* matters: see, e.g. *Lawrence, Stephen* in *Touchstones*. The costs

of a successful private prosecution will be met from *public funds;* but there is no *legal aid* to prosecute. Other common uses include **case for the prosecution**: see *case; no case to answer; trial;* **prosecution discretion**: see *discretion;* **diversion from prosecution**: see *diversion;* and **summary of the prosecution case**: see *summary.*

protection

A word that arises in many CJS contexts, from *child protection* to that of other *vulnerable people.* It is also used in the context of *safeguards* and the preservation of *rights.* For some other main uses, see *health and safety; indeterminate sentence for public protection* (ISPP); *Multi-Agency Public Protection Arrangements* (MAPPAs); *public order; public protection; safety; sentence/sentencing.* For **protection racket** see *organized crime.*

protocol

(1) An addendum to the European Convention On Human Rights having a comparable status to an Article of the Convention: see *human rights.* **(2)** A (quasi-)formal agreement or understanding as between different organizations, agencies/services, etc. in which a procedure, method or approach is set down for reference. Protocols tend to exist especially where the parties are concerned about *independence/interdependence.*

psychiatry/psychology

A **psychiatric assessment** and associated **psychiatric report** (i.e. an expert *report* by a qualified psychiatrist) may be necessary to assess the extent of non-physical *injury* to a victim or the state of mind of a suspect; including his or her capacity to form *mens rea* or fitness to plead (see *plea*); or a *risk-assessment*, especially re a *dangerous* offender. In a CJS context, 'psychiatrist' is usually a reference to a **clinical psychiatrist** or **forensic psychiatrist** involved in a *case* as an *expert,* for either party, behind the scenes, in the courtroom or inside a prison. Hence **psychiatric hospital**, either in the *community* or a **special hospital**: see *mental impairment.* Similarly re **psychology** and terms such as **criminal psychologist** (as popularised by the ITV series 'Cracker') or **forensic psychologist**: experts involved, e.g. in making **psychological assessments**, offender *profiling* or *therapy.* The question whether certain offenders are 'mad or bad' pervades grand debates on crime and punishment; as do problems of 'irregular behaviour', 'personality disorder' and *Walter Mitty* syndrome (see *Touchstones*). For modern changes in relation to 'treatment', see *mental impairment.* These are all specialist areas of CJS work re which dedicated texts should be consulted. See, e.g. *Psychiatry and Criminal Culpability* (1997), Slovenko R, John Wiley; *Criminal Psychology* (2009), Pakes F and Pakes S, Willan Publishing.

public

Usually a reference to the **general public** (aka *citizens*) who among other things are entitled to **public protection** from *threats* and to live in a safe environment, as per the expression **public safety** (see *safety*); both key priorities of the Home Office. Hence also diverse connotations such as **reflecting public concern**: a general object/purpose of sentencing and a preoccupation of *Ministers of State*, especially in the face of specific *threats.* It is from **public funds** (aka the **public purse**) that most *costs* of the CJS come, including payments to an accused person following his or her *acquittal, legal aid* and those by the *Criminal Injuries Compensation Authority* (CICA). The **public interest** is a frequent point of reference, including re decisions of the *Attorney General*, CPS (and see, especially, *Crown Prosecution Service/* 'Code for

Crown Prosecutors'); and court-related contexts, as well as in terms of the *national interest*: see also that entry. **Public order** is the banner under which 'disorder' is usually discussed, ranging from disturbances, to riots to affray and *drunkenness* in a public place. The **Public Order Act 1936** which was a key development of *law and order* in this regard (see also *Cable Street* in *Touchstones*) and the **Public Order Act 1986 (POA)** created a range of modern-day offences and powers: see specialist works. For **public prosecutor**, see *prosecutor/prosecution*. For **public road**, see *road traffic*. For **public execution**, see *capital punishment* in *Touchstones*.

punishment

Crime and punishment go hand in hand in virtually all *communities*; the latter signifying a punitive *response* to breaches of the criminal law. It is, since 2003, a statutory purpose of sentencing. Historically, punishments were often brutal (for a summary, see *Punishments of Former Days* (1992), Pettifer E, Waterside Press); including the Bloody Code (see *capital punishment* in *Touchstones*) and corporal punishment which was only finally abolished in 1948. *Human rights* law forbids **'cruel and unusual punishments'** as did *Magna Carta* (see *Touchstones* for the latter). Modern thinking is that people are sent to prison **'as punishment'** not **'for punishment'** and *imprisonment* and other *custodial* sentences have been largely redefined in terms of *restriction of liberty* or 'humane containment' rather than *retribution* (see *Touchstones*), pain, vengeance or doing unpleasant things to people. *Restorative justice* combines punishment with more constructive approaches (in some incarnations eschews punishment altogether); as do *community sentences* (formerly styled **community punishments**). Note formulae such as **'punishment by way of a fine'** or other sentence. For some useful notes on types of punishment see 'National Archive' at learningcurve.gov.uk

purposes of sentencing See *sentence/sentencing*.

Q

qualified right See *human rights*; **quality and effectiveness (Q&E)** See *effectiveness and efficiency; standards; value*; **Q&E inspections** See e.g. *HM Inspectorate of Probation*; **Quarter Sessions** See *Assizes and Quarter Sessions* in *Touchstones*. For the main references to the **Queen** see *Crown*; *Regina/Rex*; *Sovereign*. **Queen's Bench Division** See *High Court*; **Queen's Counsel (QC)** See *barrister*; **Queen's evidence** See *evidence*; **Queen's peace** See *keeping the peace*.

R

race/racism

For 30 years or more, issues of **race** and **racism** have enjoyed increased *openness* re CJS matters, especially re *discrimination, disadvantage, equality* and *social exclusion*. They have often been at the centre of controversy or even events, see, e.g *Brixton Riots; Lawrence, Stephen* (the report of which found the *Metropolitan Police Service* (MPS) to be guilty of **institutional racism**; a charge which at various times since has been levied at and accepted by various other CJS agencies/services. In 2009 there were various conflicting reports and *research* studies re continued police failings or progress in this regard 'ten years on' from Lawrence; such that institutional racism could hardly be described as having 'a clean bill of health': see in particular *Policing and the Legacy of Lawrence* (2009), Hall N, Grieve J and Savage S P (eds.), Willan Publishing. **'Race and the Criminal Justice System'** is the title of a series of publications by the Home Office based on the work of its *research* department (1992 onwards) in *response* to **section 91 Criminal Justice Act 1991** (see that entry). The **Race Relations Act 1976** and **Race Relations (Amendment) Act 2000** contain key provisions, including offences to combat racism or discrimination on the basis of race-related factors in general and across public authorities as a whole: see also direct. gov.uk under **Racial Discrimination** and generally *aggravate/aggravation; hate crime; sentence/sentencing*. Matters are frequently complicated by an intertwining of underlying issues, see e.g. *Black Women's Experiences of Criminal Justice, Race Gender and Class: A Discourse on Disadvantage* (2003)(2nd. edn), Chigwada-Bailey R, Waterside Press. Many CJS issues are discussed by reference to their impact on *black and minority ethnic* (BME) people: a group *vulnerable* to unequal treatment generally. It would be impossible to chart all CJS events in this arena, but just four random examples of racial controversy occurring in one week in 2009 give little cause for complacency: **(1)** the MPS was being accused of **discouraging Black and Asian recruits** by fostering 'closed shops', especially re specialist units (see 'The Police and Racism: What Has Been Achieved in Ten Years since the Stephen Lawrence Inquiry' (2009), Equal Opportunities Commission); **(2) HRH Prince Charles**, heir to the throne (see *Crown*) being criticised for calling a longstanding friend 'Sooty' (said to be a term of affection, but referable to skin colour); **(3)** one of his sons, **Prince Harry** (third in line) facing *military* discipline for using the nickname 'Paki' re an Asian colleague (a term that has led to prosecution: see, e.g. under the heading *football*); and **(4)** twelve Tottenham Hotspur supporters being sentenced for **directing chants at a black player** from Portsmouth Football Club whilst he was on the field of play. The events occurred against a backdrop of more encouraging developments: the swearing-in of Barack Obama, the first black president of the United States of America.

raid

An unannounced police or other *law enforcement* visit, with a view, e.g. to *arrest, search, seizure* or the freeing of a hostage. Raids may occur at any time; but the **dawn raid** is a frequently reported practice, ostensibly because it allows the rest of the day to process any 'finds'. It has been criticised as 'Gestapo tactics' in some quarters; and often as lacking in proportionality. Raids may be styled **drug raid** (see generally *drug*), **a raid by the obscene publications squad (OPS)**, etc. according to the *target*. They are particularly visible re *smuggling, trafficking, handling stolen property, organized crime* and *terrorism/terrorists*. The police, etc. can impound or secure property believed to be the *proceeds of crime*, the subject of the offence, intended for use in committing crime (such as *weapons*, tools, keys, getaway vehicles, account books and forged documents (see generally *counterfeiting and forgery*)) or *evidence*. Processes exist for the return of 'police property' or *restitution* (see *sentence/sentencing* re the latter). In many instances, police need a court *warrant* re a *search* and/or advance authorisation by a senior officer: see generally those entries.

Rainer Crime Concern; RAPt See *Touchstones* for both; **rape** See *sexual offence*.

reasonableness

Reasonableness or **'acting reasonably'** is a guiding principle for decision-makers that may also have *legal* ramifications. Practitioners, agencies/services, courts, etc. are expected or often specifically required by law to act in such a way. Reasonableness may also imply *fairness*; the idea that decisions should be impartial, balanced, supported by the facts, *data, evidence, intelligence* and relevant considerations. Failing this they may be subject to challenge under *human rights* law or by way of judicial review (see *appeal*). There are **offences based on unreasonableness**, such as **driving without reasonable consideration** for other road users: see generally *road traffic*. The *defence* of mistake of fact requires there to have been a genuine and **reasonable mistake**: see specialist works on *criminal law*. Reasonableness is also the cornerstone of **the objective test**: see *objective/objectivity* and also *Clapham omnibus* in *Touchstones*.

reasons for decisions

A key strand of development re the modern-day CJS is the extent to which judges, practitioners, etc. must explain themselves as a matter of routine. The position under UK national law was that criminal courts need not give or announce **reasons for decisions** unless compelled to do so by *legislation*. They might also need to be disclosed in a **statement of reasons** re certain kinds of *appeal*. The practice of the *higher courts* has always been to give reasons for their *rulings* which are a key aspect of the Common Law and doctrine of *precedent*; but the regular giving of reasons by judges or magistrates is of relatively modern origin (largely 1980s onwards). A *jury* does not give its reasons: a matter which has sometimes been debated given the potential impact of their *verdict*. Examples of **requirements to give reasons** by statute include when a court (summarised): does not award *compensation*; uses *imprisonment*; does not activate a suspended sentence of *imprisonment*; refuses *bail or* or grants conditional bail. Requirements of the European Convention On Human Rights (see *fair/fairness; human rights*) require 'judgements [to be] pronounced publicly': interpreted as requiring a **reasoned explanation**. The *Criminal Justice Act 2003* contains a general provision placing a duty on courts to give reasons for sentences and **an explanation in ordinary language** (except re *mandatory* sentences); adding substantially to the individual situations already noted. For **grounds and reasons**, see *bail*.

rebalancing See *Touchstones*; **recall** See *release*; **recidivism** See *reoffending*.

recognizance

(1) An undertaking to a court that a sum of money may be forfeited to the *Crown* in event of a particular occurrence: as with *binding over to keep the peace*; a bail/'surety'. **(2)** A **recognizance mission** to establish 'the lie of the land', e.g. by the police, *security services*, offenders or terrorists (see *terrorism/terrorist*).

record

Many CJS activities are recorded in writing or electronically as a matter of good practice or by *law*. Courts may be described as **courts of record** (but not the magistrates' court: though, naturally, it keeps copious records); meaning that their proceedings are recorded in a word-for-word ('verbatim') transcript, stored in archives and are *evidence* of what occurred. **Recorded crime** of certain *categories* must be routinely counted by the police: see the explanation under *report*. Contrast 'surveyed crime' as charted by initiatives such as the *British Crime Survey*. For previous **previous record** see under *conviction*. See also **Criminal Records Bureau (CRB)**.

recorder/assistant recorder See *judge*

rectification

Correcting an error; usually implying without the need for formal action such as an *appeal* or litigation, especially where the *mistake* is quickly discovered. In a *judicial* context, the underlying principle is that once a decision has been announced a court cannot go back on it: known as the doctrine of *functus officio*. Magistrates' courts can correct their own sentences, orders and errors in limited circumstances, known as **section 142 rectification** (i.e. under the Magistrates' Courts Act 1980). Crown Court judges have traditionally altered their decisions if they realised in good time that a mistake had been made. See, also, *road traffic*/'vehicle rectification scheme'.

redemption, 'Reducing Crime: Changing Lives'

redemption, **'Reducing Crime: Changing Lives'** See *Touchstones* for both; **re-examination** See *evidence*/'cross examination'

referral/reference

Words signifying: (**1**) the passing from one person, body or specialist to another of a *case*, problem or issue, including to a **referral agency** (see also *drug; psychiatry/psychology)*; usually in the expectation of an *assessment, report*, etc; (**2**) referral of a juvenile by the *youth court* to a **referral order panel**, aka *youth offending panel* within the *Youth Justice System* (and distinguish a **youth referral order (YRO)**); or (**3**) a **referral to a higher/different authority** as, e.g. with an **Attorney General's reference** or one by the **Criminal Cases Review Commission (CCRC)** (see those entries) or *Law Commission*; (**4**) a **case reference**, i.e. to a *law report* re a *ruling* of one of the *higher courts* (as, e.g. may be cited by a *barrister* or *solicitor*); or (**5**) by analogy, an **academic reference** or **technical reference** in a text, thesis, dissertation or manual.

reform

In a CJS context, a word used to describe: (**1**) attempts to change aspects of criminal justice, via *campaigns*, etc. and ostensibly for the better, but involving enlightened or punitive shifts according to the perspective of the would-be **reformer**. Hence, e.g. the work of the *Law Commission*; **penal reform** through individuals and **reform groups** (see, e.g. *Howard League for Penal Reform* and *Penal Reform Trust* (PRT) in *Touchstones*). Note also the **Office for Criminal Justice Reform (OCJR)** sponsored by the MOJ: a cross-departmental arrangement to support agencies 'working together to provide an improved service to the public ... and deliver the National *Criminal Justice Board's* (NCJB's) vision [for criminal justice]', including by providing **Criminal Justice Boards** with 'an overall *framework* and *guidance*': cjsonline.gov.uk There are also bodies with more specific aims and purposes, focusing, e.g. on **police reform** or **procedural reform**; (**2**) allied reforms such as **reform of the House of Lords**: see *House of Lords*; and (**3**) **reform of the offender** which has always been regarded as central to CJS aims and sentencing in particular.

refreshing memory See *witness*

regulation

(**1**) A form of *legislation*, usually meaning 'secondary legislation', often containing *rules*, but possibly 'primary legislation' as per the **Regulation of Investigatory Powers Act 2000 (RIPA)**: see *informer*; **Road Traffic Regulations Acts**: see *road traffic*. (**2**) Any form of governance, e.g. as contained in the *rules, instructions* or *standards* of a agency/service. (**3**) Other forms of **self-regulation**, e.g. arrangements for matters of *discipline* with regards to a body, profession or defined group, but essentially separate and apart from any CJS *sanctions*. Hence also **self-regulating communities** which may occur in a range of contexts and that are of interest to *criminologists*, etc, including ethnic groups such as gypsies/Romanies (and note the national Gypsy Council: see nationalarchives.gov.uk); but also extreme examples such as *gangland*, those re The *Troubles* or the *Underworld* (see *Touchstones* for the last two entries).

rehabilitation

(1) Restoring an ex-offender, especially an ex-*prisoner* (but essentially anyone whose ties with his or her *community* have been disrupted), so as to enable a fresh start, including via *reintegration and resettlement, education, employment, treatment,* training and *help and support,* especially after a long spell in prison; when he or she may have been 'institutionalised', i.e. reliant on other people for his or her daily needs. For an entertaining account of such trials and tribulations, see *I'm Still Standing* (2002), Turney B, Waterside Press. (2) The *welfare*-oriented **rehabilitative ideal** came into vogue after the Second World War and lost ground in the 'prison works' era (see *'what works'* in *Touchstones*), but has been revived to an extent. Note also in particular: (3) **alcohol rehabilitation, drug rehabilitation**; and 'rehab' to describe a place or the practice of rehabilitation of recovering alcoholics (see *alcohol*) or *drug* users; (2) the **Rehabilitation of Offenders Act 1974** which allows certain convictions to be treated as 'spent' after a set number of years; so that the offender need not make *disclosure* other than in situations described in that Act (and later *legislation*)(e.g. re sentencing or in *security*-related situations); when these *time limits* also depend on the length and type of sentence; and (3) the **youth rehabilitation order (YRO)**: see *youth court.*

reintegration and resettlement

Closely associated with *rehabilitation,* processes of re-assimilation into a *community*; the underlying aims including 'seamlessness', closure (re victim, offender and *community*), *normalisation* (see *Touchstones*) and *'going straight'*. In effect, 'settling back' into accommodation, employment, etc. and becoming part of a community once again. Within a prison setting, resettlement may involve 'working out' (e.g. on day *release*) in readiness for *release*. Hence also a **resettlement prison**: see *prison.*

release

(1) The process whereby prisoners are freed from prison at the end of their sentence, or temporarily (as per **compassionate release, day release, weekend leave** or other **temporary release**), usually after serving a portion of a sentence. This may include release for regime-related activities such as *community* projects, outside *employment*, training or *education*. The *Criminal Justice Act 2003* revised the **statutory release provisions**, which vary according to the sentence given (see the brief notes under *imprisonment* and *imprisonment for public protection* (ISPP) (which also deal with the extended sentence for public protection (ESPP)). Beyond this consult specialist works. Standard sentences usually involve: (a) a *custodial* part served in prison; followed by (b) the remainder being served in the community following 'early release', whether on *parole* or some other form of **release licence** (or for older forms of sentence and until these are exhausted what is known as **automatic conditional release** or **discretionary conditional release**). Certain release arrangements involve consideration of *risk*-assessments and the offenders' progress in prison, including re any *sentence plan* or courses attended. There are National Stand-

ards (see *standard*) for **post-release supervision** by the National Probation Service, the aims of which include: the *protection of the public*; the prevention of re-offending (see *crime prevention/crime reduction*); and successful *reintegration and resettlement*. An adult prisoner (here meaning someone over 21 years of age) serving a sentence of under four years may be released under **home detention curfew** (see that entry). In many instances, prisoners remain subject to **prison recall** (often just '**recall**'). From 2007, under an **end of custody scheme** in *response* to prison(er) overcrowding (see *prison*) many short-term *prisoners* were released 18 days before their formal release date. See also *prisoner/*'sentence plan' and note the use of such terms as **earliest date of release (EDR)** or **normal release date (NDR)**; both of which may be affected by *prison/*'discipline'. **(2) Release** the longstanding *charity*: see *drug*.

religion/religious aspects

The idea that faith was a matter of personal choice emerged only gradually against a backdrop of early Paganism and later *criminalisation* (see *Touchstones*) of, e.g. blasphemy, heresy and dissent. 'Enforced beliefs' or 'religious divides' have frequently distorted the criminal process and its *priorities* as evidenced by medieval purges (including burning heretics). Similarly by an intermingling of religious issues with allegiance, protest, uprising, *witch hunts* (see *Touchstones*), *terrorism/terrorists* (see especially *The Troubles* and *September 11* in *Touchstones*) and the interests of the *Crown* (itself at times contended on religious bases). Note especially **penal laws** passed for the *protection* of the established church (the Church of England: now, following acceptance by its General Synod in 2009, scheduled for de-establishment after almost 500 years) against Catholics following the break with Rome; and the many 'no-popery'-related events of which the Gunpowder Plot (1605) is perhaps the best-known; the rise in anti-Semitism across Europe in the early 1900s; and anti-Muslim feeling today. Another example of many acts of **religious repression** is the *imprisonment* of the author and non conformist preacher John Bunyan (1628-1688). Minority faith groups such as the Quakers, have played a large part in criminal justice *reform*; whilst the the *Probation Service* emerged from mainstream church-based initiatives (see *Rainer Crime Concern* in *Touchstones*). Article 9 of the European Convention on Human Rights protects **freedom of thought, conscience and religion** (see generally *human rights*), leading to greater tolerance; some critics claim, silencing (see *silence*) of criticism or analysis. Prisons often have **multi-faith** chapels and teams of chaplains, rabbis and imams, etc. and 'worship' is a feature of all *prison/*'regimes' (there have also been reports of **religious demarcation** by *gangs,* etc.). In 2005, the Government claimed its Race and Religious Hatred Bill would prevent anti-Muslim disturbances (see generally *public order*) such as had occurred in Bradford, Burnley and Oldham, sparked by 'right-wing elements', especially problematic post-September 11. Proposals in 2009 that would prevent Muslim **religious extremism** (seen as linked to the 'raising of the Black Flag of Islam' as a symbol of domination or promoting Sharia law) have proved equally controversial; albeit some commentators trace such problems to the **religious Crusades** of the 11th century onwards when Muslim countries were invaded due to Christian zeal. An ancient convention whereby places of worship were *'no-go areas'* for *law enforcement*, places of sanctuary, no longer exists. They have been subject to *raids* and *searches*, Finsbury Park Mosque, North London (closed for a time under post-September 11 terrorism powers) becoming an iconic reference point after Muslims continued worshipping on the street outside. The Anti-terrorism, Crime and Security Act 2001 extended *hate crime* to cover religious hatred, see also generally *aggravate/aggravation.* **Religious belief is no defence** to a criminal charge (a belief, e.g. in a religion which permits polygamy would no defence to a charge of bigamy); but in some other circumstances might fall to be taken into account, e.g. re whether *mens rea* existed, re *motive* or in *mitigation* (compare *moral aspects* in *Touchstones*). See also *oath* (in *Main Entries*) and *benefit of clergy* and *redemption* (in *Touchstones*).

remand/remand centre

The terms **remand on bail**, **remand in custody** and **remand and adjournment** derive from those CJS processes which take place, initially at a magistrates' court and later possibly at the *Crown Court*, whereby decisions are made as to whether or not an accused person should be held in *custody* (police cells or normally a prison for periods beyond 24 hours) or be allowed *bail*. Similar processes occur after conviction when an offender is **remanded for sentence** during an *adjournment*, e.g. for a pre-sentence report: see sentence/sentencing. **Remand centre (RC)** is the name for part of a prison, or *young offender institution* (YOI) (holding young people below 21 years of age mainly) for people who are **on remand**, as e.g. **HM YOI and RC Reading**.

remorse See *naming and shaming* in *Touchstones*; *reparation*.

re-offending

Committing a **further offence**, usually meaning after being convicted and sentenced by a court for an earlier offence; or whilst on *bail* after being charged and awaiting trial or sentence. Hence crime reduction/crime prevention initiatives to tackle what is aka **recidivism**; some 80 per cent of younger prisoners re-offending within two years of their *release,* possibly repeatedly. Others may predict only a marginal increase, if any, in their sentence by 'clocking up' more offences once they have been caught. However, offending whilst on bail is a statutory basis for a higher sentence.

reparation

(1) 'Making good' or 'putting right' the *harm* done by an offence, via active, financial or other means. Hence **reparation schemes** whereby offenders do so in a *controlled* way (also a rationale of unpaid work: see *community sentence*). **Voluntary reparation** may indicate remorse, a 'mending of ways' which can be *mitigation*. Reparation is a *statutory* purpose of sentencing; and one reason for *sentence*/'deferment of sentence'. **(2) Reparation orders** in the *youth court* help juveniles to see the consequences of their offending and take responsibility; by requiring them to repair *harm* caused by their offence(s), directly to the victim (including via victim/offender *mediation* if both parties agree) or indirectly to the *community*, e.g. removing graffiti. **(3)** Reparation is strongly associated with *restorative justice*. **(4)** 'Making reparations' is used in a grander sense to indicate damages paid by one nation to another following conflict.

repeat offender/repeat offending

Terms applied to people who offend a second, third, fourth, etc. time; usually meaning after they have been warned re their behaviour, especially by a court. See in particular the entry for *prolific offender* (but note that 'repeat offending' may involve one recurrence as opposed to a chain of reoffending, or a *revolving door* (see *Touchstones*).

report

A formal (usually meaning a written) *response,* in the form of a narrative, *data*, information and/or conclusions, as per, e.g. an **annual report**; **government report**;

pre-sentence report: see *sentence/sentencing*; **psychiatric report**: see *mental impairment; psychiatry/psychology*; **Report of a Royal Commission**; **report of an inquiry** (see, e.g. *Lawrence, Stephen* in *Touchstones. etc.*); or **report to Parliament** by a *Minister of State* (see *accountability*). **Reported crime** is that reported to the police, etc. by victims, bystanders, *informants*, neighbours, *witnesses,* etc. which is recorded within given categories. Hence also the term **recorded crime**. Both form the basis of *Criminal Statistics* prepared by the Home Office showing crime rates, trends, changing patterns of crime and clear up rates: see *clear up/clear up rate*. Reporting, recording and categorisation have sometimes proved controversial due to differing practices, methods, misallocation and lack of precise comparisons over time. It has long been acknowledged that there is a big difference between the volume of crime which actually occurs and that which is reported and recorded; more so between crimes and convictions. The total of all crimes which somehow 'fall by the wayside' is reflected in the 'attrition rate', which some people put at over 90 per cent (depending on the type of crime). The difference between reported crime and that which is cleared up is known as the 'justice gap' (but care is needed as this term may be applied to other 'voids'). Some commentators point out that the true extent of offending lies hidden, raising basic questions, e.g. re *law enforcement*, crackdowns, blitzes, the purposes of sentencing, the rationale of *deterrence* and *punishment*, and, ultimately of the CJS itself. For **reporting restriction** see *media/press*.

representation/representations

Words used when a case, proposition or objection is being put forward, especially in the context of public affairs or on someone's behalf. See, e.g. *legal representation.*

reprimand See *warnings and reprimands*; **requirement** See *community sentence; condition; licence*; **requisition** See *charge and requisition*; **resettlement** See *reintegration and resettlement.*

respect

(1) A state of human and or social relationships in which people of whatever background or view make allowances, tolerate, allow for and freely acknowledge the stance of others, even if they may differ. Hence the government's **Respect Agenda** (2003) which has been closely associated with discouraging *anti-social behaviour*: see respect.gov.uk **(2)** 'Respect' is a form of greeting in some *communities*.

response

A word that occurs repeatedly within the CJS to signify, e.g: **(1)** broad **responses to crime** or CJS-related events by Government or agencies/services, i.e. how they react to and deal with crime, especially the responses of the police and courts; **(2)** **response times**: such as those of the police in attending an incident, or other *waiting times*: see *Touchstones*; **(3)** the **responses of offenders** to crime prevention/crime reduction initiatives and/or sentences; **(4)** similarly by to a potential victim to a *threat* or in his or her *defence*/'self defence'; **(5)** **media/press responses**: see *media/press* or those of the general *public* to *policy* announcements, etc; or **(6)** **responses to a consultation**, etc. whether by or to Government or a *campaign* group or focus group.

restitution See *sentence*/ 'ancillary order'

restorative justice (or Restorative Justice) (RJ)

A form of *justice* which focuses on repairing *harm* rather than aspects of legal or other processes which enhance conflict, distress, pain, formality, etc. In a criminal justice context it does so by marking the *seriousness* of the offence (using *punishment* and/or shaming: see *naming and shaming* in *Touchstones*), but mixes this with *reparation*, *rehabilitation* and *reintegration* rather than *retribution* (see *Touchstones*). RJ has no set definition: it concentrates on **restoration**, so far as possible, of the situation which existed before the offence took place (or *status quo ante*); sometimes described as **'restoring harmony'**. It can be traced to the 12th century at least; and is often linked to sentencing circles (especially those in New Zealand, Australia and the Middle-East) and the idea that the breach between offender and community is best tackled 'in the round'; building on an acknowledgement of wrongdoing, public demonstration of remorse and re-acceptance into the fold. Whereas conventional sentences tend to be exclusionary by nature (particularly *custody*), RJ is inclusionary (compare also *community justice*; but contrast *social exclusion*). RJ started to permeate mainstream CJS thinking in the UK from the mid-1990s; becoming a theme of official pronouncements, initially re juveniles. Some adherents see it as capable of reducing (even eliminating) *punishment* in favour of problem-solving solutions, but with dangerous offenders being 'contained' out of necessity. For an overview, see *Doing Justice Better: The Politics of Restorative Justice* (2008), Cornwell D J, Waterside Press; and re the use of RJ in prisons, *Restorative Justice in Prisons: A Guide to Making It Happen* (2006), Newell T and Edgar K, Waterside Press. Pure RJ remains an ideal and the whole notion contrasts markedly with the *adversarial system* (see *Touchstones*); but it is a force to be reckoned due partly to the *voluntary sector* and *reform* groups. The **Restorative Justice Consortium (RJC)** is a nationwide collective of RJ-based organizations. It describes RJ as 'processes [that] give victims the chance to tell offenders the real impact of their crime, to get answers ... and to receive an apology ...[It] holds offenders to account ... and helps victims to get on with their lives'. Restorative processes occur in other contexts, e.g. *schools*, workplaces and public services. See further restorativejustice.org.uk and compare *relational justice* in *Touchstones*. RJ features strongly in relation to *youth justice* in particular.

restraining order See *harassment*

restriction

A word with various CJS connotations: the lawful **denial of liberty** re lawbreakers has existed since the Roman era (possibly longer), but it is only within the last 200 years or so that *prisons* and similar establishments became places holding *prisoners* serving terms of *imprisonment* ordered by courts. In modern times, **restriction of liberty** has become a central tenet re sentencing, especially re a *community sentence*, and also by way of a **restriction order**, e.g. preventing someone from certain activities such as foreign travel (but note that the term is also applied to certain *civil* court orders and *bankruptcy*). A hospital order may be accompanied by an **order restricting discharge** (sometimes also referred to as a 'restriction order'): see *mental impairment*; a judge or magistrate may impose **reporting restrictions** pending the outcome of a trial or concerning a juvenile: see *media/press*. The term is also to be found in a many contexts within other entries in this work ranging from **legal restrictions** to **physical restriction** or 'restraint' (see, e.g. *prison*/'control and restraint').

retribution See *Touchstones*

Revenue & Customs (R&C)

HMR&C describes itself as 'one of the UK's biggest businesses, with annual revenue of £457 billion ... as well as collecting tax, we administer benefit payments, help to protect *national interests* and carry out ... wide ranging work that helps to keep Britain in the black. We pay out tax credits and check travellers aren't bringing anything into the country that they shouldn't'. It has an *investigations* branch and a *prosecution* arm; dealing with tax evasion and related matters; often under its own wide-ranging powers to demand *disclosure,* answers to specific questions (by way of an exception to the *rule* against self-incrimination), seize *cash* or assets and levy penalties (see *fine/* 'administrative fine') and punitive surcharges. Whilst subject to the control of the courts (in which revenue claims can also be enforced) its own decision-making processes are administrative (see *administration/administrative*) not basically *judicial*; under an **Inspector of Taxes** or the Commissioners of R&C. In 2007, that part of HMR&C dealing with customs at ports/airports became part of the *Border Agency*.

review

The reappraisal or revisiting of events, usually by an *independent* and/or higher or specially appointed authority that may exercise related powers or make recommendations. Hence, e.g. the **Criminal Cases Review Commission**: see that entry; review by a **Crown prosecutor**: see *Crown Prosecution Service;* **review of police detention**: see *detention;* **judicial review**: see *appeal*; **Review of the Criminal Courts**: see *Auld Report* in *Touchstones*; **Review of the Sentencing Framework**: see *Halliday Report* in *Touchstones;* **reviewable sentence**: see *sentence/sentencing*.

rights (and responsibilities)

Questions and issues of rights pervade the criminal justice process (and other contexts). **Rights** are often viewed as being balanced by responsibilities, to the extent, e.g. that it has been mooted whether there might be a 'Bill of **Rights and Responsibilities**' (R&R) covering citizens and others; albeit controversy about how such a balance might be struck against a backdrop of existing provision, including re **human rights**: see further that entry. This has also been linked to (contentious) issues of *Britishness* (see *Touchstones*). **Responsibility** is often equated with 'duty' and 'obligation' all of which arise in both legal and other forms, such as 'moral responsibility' (see *moral aspects* in *Touchstones*). Both R&R apply to *judicial* officers, *public* officers and the *State* on the one hand (many duties are cast, e.g. on *Ministers of State*, the police and courts) and *citizens* or organizations on the other; whether generally or in a given situation. Examples appear across this work. For the **right to silence** see *silence.*

risk

A word that permeates CJS tasks and decision-making, especially re public *safety, violence* and *sexual offences*. Hence, e.g. **at-risk** to describe *children* or other *vulnerable people* in need of *protection*; or those who are **at-risk of offending**, particularly juveniles and young offenders; or to signal *danger/dangerousness*. Many processes involve making **risk-assessments**: see, e.g. *Multi-agency Public Protection Arrangements* (MAPPAs); *parole*. **Risk management** acknowledges the existence of risk and seeks to *control* it through sound *management, intelligence, assessments* and *best practice*, etc. Hence also the term **risk aversion** to describe a 'shying away' from **risk-taking** (risk, it is argued by some commentators, being an unavoidable facet of some CJS tasks). Risk aversion has featured re debates around a number of tragic outcomes such as the *Stockwell shooting*, the case of *Victoria Climbie* (see *Touchstones* for both) and the *murder* of Naomi Bryant in Winchester, Hampshire in 2005 by convicted *sex offender* Anthony Rice, nine months after he was released on *parole*.

road traffic

Motor vehicle traffic: for the main part meaning 'on public roads'. Hence **road traffic law** which encompasses myriad **road traffic offences** (RTOs) (since the first such *legislation* in the early-1900s). RTOs touch on all (often minute and detailed) aspects of the manufacture, construction and use of vehicles. Everyday examples include **speeding, careless driving, dangerous driving, defective brakes, lights and steering, dangerous driving** and **excess alcohol** (driving whilst above the statutory alcohol limit as discerned by a **roadside breath test** (aka 'breathaliser') and an **intoximeter** at a police station), **driving whilst under the influence of drugs** (where scientific developments are likely to lead to roadside drug tests), together with *aggravated* or extended forms of offence such as causing death by careless driving (if linked to excess alcohol) or causing death by dangerous driving (in any circumstances). Some more serious RTOs attract *imprisonment*; whilst many lesser ones are dealt with by *fixed penalty notices,* e.g. when motorists are 'caught' by speed cameras often operated by **road safety partnerships** between the police and *local authorities* and/or the *private sector* (aka **Safety Camera Partnerships**); usually linked to **automated number plate recognition (ANPR)**). Hence a number of **Road Traffic Acts, Road Safety Acts, Road Traffic Regulations Acts** and allied *regulations* (see, generally, *legislation*). **Vehicle rectification schemes** are operated by the *police* as an *alternative to prosecution* (when the offender will have his or her vehicle repaired and take it to a **police vehicle examiner** or produce a certificate of repair from the garage. A central feature of road traffic law is *mandatory* or *discretionary* **disqualification** and/or **endorsement** of a driving licence by courts with **penalty points.** These are accumulated until they trigger a **totting up** disqualification, when 12 points are reached. Offences attract a given number of points or a range of points from which courts may choose at their *discretion*. Some disqualifications, such as that for excess alcohol, can be avoided if the court finds **special reasons** re the offence; or re totting up if it finds **mitigating circumstances** re the offence or offender. Records are kept at the **Driver and Vehicle Licensing Centre (DVLA)** (aka Swansea: its main base in Wales). In *response* to deaths on roads, the government intends increasing maximum *punishments* for some RTOs. The leading practitioner work is *Wilkinson's Road Traffic Offences* (23rd edn. 2008), Swift K and Wallis P, Sweet & Maxwell.

robbery

The offence under section 8 of the *Theft Act* 1968 which basically consists of *theft* (or other underlying offences) accompanied by force or putting someone in *fear* that force will be used. Many *burglaries* are misdescribed as robberies in popular speech. It extends to modern-day forms of robbery such as **muggings** (a popular term for **street robbery** of an individual victim). Historical forms of robbery include **garrotting** and **highway robbery**: see *Touchstones* under 'garrotting', 'Great Train Robbery', 'Ratcliffe Highway', 'Robin Hood' and 'Turpin, Dick'.

rogue

A term that can in modern times serve to place a gloss on offending as per a long tradition as demonstrated by *Brewer's Rogues, Villains and Eccentrics: An A-Z of Roguish Britons Through the Ages* (2002), Donaldson W, Cassell and *The Oxford Book of Vil-*

lains (1992), Mortimer J, Oxford University Press; but which also points to the kind of person *targeted* by the Vagrancy Acts of 1824 and 1837 that penalise **rogues and vagabonds**. **Rogues gallery**: (**1**) an album of photographs of offenders or suspects (aka **mugshots**: full-face and side profiles) kept by the police and through which a victim or *witness* can leaf in the hope of recognising an assailant, burglar, robber, etc. (see also generally *identification/identity*); a process that is nowadays increasingly computer-based; or (**2**) anyone deemed to be acting in a dubious (i.e. **'roguish'**) and possibly criminal way. Hence also the oxymoron **'loveable rogue'** to describe an offender whose personality serves to distance or obscure his or her crimes.

rule

Usually a reference to: (**1**) a **statutory rule** (often aka a **regulation**), e.g. re *criminal procedure, health and safety* (and other 'regulatory offences'). Such measures are myriad and often complex even though *ignorance of the law* is no excuse. They are often made by a *Minister of State* under delegated *legislation* with minimal real scrutiny. Hence, also, e.g. the **Prison Rules** and in particular **Rule 45** (see *prison*); (**2**) rules of the Common Law; and/or (**3**) stemming from *rulings* of the *higher courts*; or (**4**) **non-statutory rules** or **non-legal rules** which govern, e.g. *best practice* or the day-to-day affairs of CJS agencies/services. (**5**) The **Rule of Law** is adhered to by liberal democratic *States* (see generally *constitution/constitutional; democracy*). It stems from the work of jurists and philosophers of the 18th century onwards. There is no standard definition: essentially, it holds that no-one is above the law and that everyone is bound by it and entitled to its *protection* in *equal* measure. The law should be observed and enforced universally; and there should, e.g. not be any *'no-go' areas*, whether controlled by criminal *gangs*, sectarian interests or the dictats of the powerful. Exceptions or inroads include the *Crown;* diplomatic immunity (see specialist works); and certain *informers*. The Constitutional Reform Act 2005 requires the *Justice Secretary* to **respect the Rule of Law**. For a modern-day **appeal to the Rule of Law**, see *BAE Systems* in *Touchstones*. (**6**) Note also the use of rules in other walks of life and popular expressions such as 'throwing **the rule book**' at someone (launching a large, possibly oppressive, number of charges). **Ruling** is the term for a finding by: (**1**) a *judge* or *magistrates* in the course of a *case*; (**2**) the *higher courts* on *appeal* (when the ruling may be described as having the force of *law*); or (**3**) a public officer such as the *Attorney-General* (e.g. that something is in the *national interest*) or the *Independent Police Complaints Commission* (IPCC) (as to whether a complaint is admissible).

S

safe/safeguard/safety

The **safety of the public** is one of the first priorities of any *State*; as can be seen in the UK from the responsibilities of the Home Office (HO) in particular, including re the *police/policing; law enforcement; border control* and *terrorism/terrorists*. More generally, the HO and other government departments are concerned to ensure *safety* within communities and hence, e.g. a **Safer Communities** initiative which has provided £20 million for *Crime and Disorder Reduction Partnerships* to pursue *targets* and priorities: see crimereduction.homeoffice.gov.uk/safercommunities. *Legislation* may *target* aspects of public safety, e.g. re **health and safety** (see that entry) or **road safety** and **safety camera partnerships** (see road *traffic*); whilst other developments encourage a **safe environment**, including in prison. A **safety interview** can be conducted with a suspect in an *emergency* by-passing normal *rights,* and *procedures:* see Codes C and H under the *Police and Criminal Evidence Act 1984* (PACE). **Safeguards** are an intrinsic part of *human rights.* They also act as a bulwark in a range of contexts to help ensure *rights* and *protections* (see e.g. *juvenile; presumption of innocence; trading standards; welfare*). Another general aim is **safeguarding the public**, i.e. in terms of its overall *protection* and *security.* Note also **safeguarding identity**: see *Home Office; identification/identity;* and **safety at sportsgrounds**: see *football.*

sample
(1) A portion or section of physical material, a substance, body tissue or bodily fluid, etc. such as may be suitable for *forensic analysis;* and that may thus become *evidence* or a basis for an *opinion.* Hence an **intimate sample** is one taken from an intimate part of the human body re which special *restrictions* apply. (2) Similarly a **representative sample** or 'cohort' for *research;* from which wider conclusions may be drawn.

sanction
A word commonly used in CJS circles to denote *controls* of various kinds, especially re *policing,* sentence, etc, *enforcement* or similar arrangements, such as *prison/*'discipline' or aspects of *self-regulation, restriction* or restraint (see, e.g. *prisoner/*'control and restraint'). It is sometimes said that a feature of the criminal law is that it prohibits conduct, etc. by the application of **criminal sanctions;** but many non-criminal controls also involve **applying other sanctions:** such as parking tickets, administrative fines (see *fine*), *anti-social behaviour orders* (ASBOs) and *civil behaviour orders* (CBOs)).

Scanning Analysis Response Assessment (SARA)
SARA is a methodical process for solving problems; as used by the police but that can be of use to other CJS practitioners where a problem needs to be identified and tackled, avoiding waste of time or resources. It is in common use within UK police forces (and also in the USA). It has four stages: **scanning**: spotting problems using, e.g. knowledge, basic *data* and electronic maps; **analysis**: using hunches and *technology* to look deep into the characteristics of a problem and its causes; **response**: devising a solution, working with the community whenever possible; and **assessment**: looking back to see if the solution worked and noting any lessons to be learned.

school
Schooling and *education* is a central feature of and influence on anyone's formative years and can be seen as a place where youngsters can 'slip into crime' due, e.g. to lack of attainment, achievement, *guidance* or self-esteem. Many factors were identified by Angela Devlin in *Criminal Classes: Offenders at School* (1991), Waterside Press based on the first-hand accounts of people who went on to become *adult* offenders. Other recurring motifs in the lives of such people included *bullying* and truancy. The following is no more than a selection (in alphabetical order) of school-related CJS items.

Teachers have suffered from **abusive parents** and pupils, including physical and verbal *abuse* or intimidation; some 220 reporting *assaults* on them in 2006; when the National Association of Head Teachers (NAHT) urged a change to the law to allow them to exclude from school children whose parents resort to extreme or unacceptable behaviour (see generally *acceptable behaviour*); citing instances of one headteacher who received a *threat* to kill, four *assaulted* by parents using *violence* 'as a first resort' and another forced from the road whilst driving. The **approved school** was a form of educational provision introduced by the *Children and Young Persons Act 1933* (CYPA) whereby *education* and accommodation for juveniles 'in trouble' were provided on (usually) the same premises and (often) in a secure setting. The approved school replaced the **Industrial School** and **Reformatory School**; and was the precursor of the *community* home with education (CHE) and similar forms of local authority accommodation. It fell from favour following the Carlton Approved School Inquiry (1959) and serious incidents at other such schools, alongside adverse *media/press* coverage; all triggers for the predominantly care-oriented regime for younger children of the CYPA 1969. **Arson of school premises** is one example of a recurring offence. In 2006, Zurich Insurance reported that during the last year the *value* of property so damaged by pupils had doubled since 2000 to £83 million. The *Department For Children, Schools and Families* (DCSF) is the relevant Government department re schools and is also now the foremost re *youth justice*; under which many *social services* and education services operate and overlap. Problematic **drug use** has led to a formal anti-drugs policies at individual schools; some schools resorting to the use of police sniffer dogs. **Education welfare officer** (EWO) is a name often given to a member of *local authority* staff with responsibility for ensuring aspects of a child's education, including re attendance at school (as to which there may also be a designated **'school attendance officer'** from either the local authority and/or the police). **Failing to ensure regular attendance** is an offence by a *parent* or guardian (re which several parents have been sentenced to *imprisonment* in modern times).

'Good schools' tend to support, coach, mentor and 'look after' disruptive pupils as would a parent, normally, as described by Andrew Rutherford in *Growing Out of Crime: The New Era* (2002) (3rd edn.), Waterside Press. Apart from their widescale responsibilities in running a school, **headteachers** (and others) have power, under the Education and Inspections Act 2006, to issue *fixed penalty notices* to parents, etc. re non-attendance. There have been suggestions that schools are ideally placed to identify potential offenders and single out those who might benefit from *intervention*. With regard to *weapons*, **knives carried by pupils** have been of particular **concern**, as in the *community* generally; the **Philip Lawrence Awards** being a reminder of this as well as a memorial to a head teacher (and posthumous winner of the Queen's Gallantry Medal) who was stabbed to death outside the gates of his school by a pupil in 1995: for further background see 4children.org.uk There have been suggestions that airport-style *security* might be used 'at the school gate'. **Pre-emptive education** is designed to anticipate and prevent offending (see, generally, *crime prevention/crime reduction*). In the UK, **public school** is a misnomer for 'private school', i.e. one operated for profit (if sometime charitably so) by the *private sector*, of which longstanding schools such as Eton, Harrow, Rugby and Winchester College have reputations greater than many 'minor public schools'. In 2005, England's top public schools narrowly escaped prosecution for operating a cartel to keep up fees. Significant numbers of the higher judiciary attended such establishments, if likely to reduce with the creation of the *Judicial Appointments Commission* (for a historical survey, see, e.g. *The Politics of the Judiciary* (1997) (5th edn. revised), Griffith J A G, HarperCollins. **Safer Saner Schools** is a multi-national initiative devoted to implementing restorative practices in schools: see www.safersanerschools.org and generally *restorative justice*. **Truancy** (aka 'bunking-off') is non-attendance at school on the part of the child. There are conflicting arguments about whether truancy and offending are connected although most commentators would probably agree that offending (if often of a *low-level* kind) whilst truanting can occur due., e.g. to opportunity, the already subversive nature of events and an inbuilt lack of lawful things to become involved in. From 1997 to 2005, government spent a reported £1 billion trying to 'tackle' truancy; including through new schemes such as 'electronic registration' in some places; and fast-tracking of prosecutions of parents (in the same period the number of truants rose by one-third). The *youth court, youth referral panel* and *youth offending teams* (YOTS) may receive **school reports**, usually as compiled by a headteacher. Their nature, content and style have altered since a Nacro report, 'Must Do Better' (1986), Ball C (ed.), pointed to their potentially disproportionate impact on decision-making, especially at that time due to their containing pejorative but unsubstantiated remarks. **Teachers** occupy a position of trust vis-à-vis the children they teach and stand 'in the place of parents or guardians' whilst the child is on school premises or, e.g. attending school outings or 'away' sporting events (aka *in loco parentis*, often shortened to 'in loco'). There have been tensions due to allegations made by children, their parents or in some instances school governors re offences and/or *abuse* by teachers, or of dishonesty (and in certain instances convictions). Vetting, *Criminal Records Bureau* (CRB) checks, the inhibiting effects of *health and safety* considerations and (in the perception of some) constraints of *human rights* have discouraged some from joining or remaining with the profession; and there are a significant number of cases in which teachers have been *victims* (see earlier above). The **'turnaround school'** was suggested by the Tory Opposition to replace *referrals* to **'sin-bin' schools** or individual tuition for excluded pupils (often in their own homes: see also *social exclusion*).

science

Along with developments in *technology* those in the scientific field have revolutionised CJS work, especially that of police; who rely on the **Forensic Science Service** (see that entry) (or similar providers of such services). For examples, see *DNA*; and *fingerprint* in *Touchstones*. The potential of scientific development to tackle crime has perhaps only just begun; especially for those who claim that science and genetics have a role to play in validly predicting who is likely to offend. Scientific development is a key interest of the *Home Office* (HO) and its **Scientific Development Branch** to 'provide advice, support, innovative technology and capability to help the HO achieve its key *objectives* of protecting the public [see generally *protection*], reducing crime, especially *drug*-related and violent crime [see *violence*], and managing migration [see *immigration*]'. For further details, see scienceandresearch.homeoffice.gov.uk.

scrutiny

The integrity of the CJS is protected by a range of independent arrangements to audit, examine, monitor or investigate its activities. See, e.g. various *HM Inspectorates*. For other examples, see *Criminal Cases Review Commission* (CCRC); *Independent Police Complaints Commission* (IPCC); *Prisons and Probation Ombudsman* (PPO) and *Independent Monitoring Board* (IMB). Scrutiny also occurs at other levels, as when the Audit Commission is asked to examine some aspect of the CJS or an individual travels as an observer in relation to a prisoner who is being deported. Scope for scrutiny also exists via internal procedures such as *best practice* and arrangements for reporting *abuse, corruption, discrimination*, etc. See also *value/values*.

search

The searching of a person, premises, vehicle, boat, aircraft, etc. for the purpose of an *investigation* and/or to secure *evidence*, make an *arrest*, or otherwise in the interests of crime prevention/crime reduction; whether under a court *warrant* or *police powers*. See, also, *raid; seizure*. Hence **stop and search**, i.e. the stopping and searching of someone in the street or some other public place, e.g. re *drugs, weapons*, stolen property, aka **'sus'**. The **sus laws** have frequently been criticised for their discriminatory application by police officers (see generally *discrimination*) who, it is said, tend to *target* those who 'look as if they might be offenders' (see *stereotype/stereotyping* in *Touchstones*); rather than people they actually believe to be so; especially black people. Nonetheless, the sus laws have been extended and *safeguards* relaxed re *terrorism/terrorists*; with the effect that anyone can be searched on the merest pretext.

section 95 (Criminal Justice Act 1991) See *costs; discrimination; race/racism.*

security

A word of diverse CJS uses. The term **security of the person** refers to the *protection* of the individual from events which might impact on his or her physical (or possibly emotional) integrity and is a principle sanctioned by *human rights* (see Article 5 of the European Convention On Human Rights). Hence he or she ought not to go in *fear* of attack or *assault*, due to the existence of a safe environment (see *safety*), which extends to protecting the entire nation from external threats or, e.g. subversion from **'the enemy within'**. Hence terms such as **homeland security** which is a responsibility of the *Home Office,* and **National Security** (or sometimes **State security**) which is a *priority* of Government in general (and part of the remit of the *Metropolitan Police Service* (MPS)). It is also a basis on which it is possible to depart from the ordinary *rules* for the greater good of the nation, to counter a *threat* to the interests of the *State* (and hence an **Office for Security and Counter-Terrorism (OSCT)**. Such departures are permitted by *human rights* law; but may sometimes have occurred in situations which defy acceptable explanation, leading to considerable concerns. Nations may pass *emergency legislation*, e.g. in time of *war*, or to counter *terrorism/terrorists*. One problem is that 'national security' is a flexible concept capable of *abuse* in the wrong hands. See also questions raised by the *BAE Systems* case noted in *Touchstones*. Note also *media/press/*'D-notice'. For **Security Service** and **Intelligence Service** see *MI5/MI6, etc.* Anyone can *ask* to see his or her **security file**; but this may be refused. 'Security' arises especially re prisons where **security and control** is a key priority; and there are **security categories**: see *prison* for both. Other common uses are **security device**, e.g. a bicycle lock or *burglar* alarm; **security for bail**, see *bail*; and **security guard**: usually a reference to a *private sector* guard at commercial or other premises or, e.g. re *cash-in-transit*. Hence also the **security industry** which develops and markets a range of its products, e.g. to the police and *military*. **Security level**: see *threat* level. **Social security** is routine shorthand for *welfare* benefits.

seizure

The taking and impounding of items which are, e.g. the subject or *proceeds of crime*, *evidence*, materials or substances, etc. that may become exhibits in a trial. The police enjoy wide powers of *search* and seizure; including special powers in relation to *terrorism/terrorists*; or may be authorised to seize items under a court *warrant*.

self-esteem See 'going straight'; *school*; and *broken windows* in *Touchstones*; **self-harm** See *harm*; **self-incrimination** See *silence/*'right to silence'; **self regulation** See *regulation;* **sending (to the Crown Court)** See *allocation and sending.*

sentence/sentencing

Sentencing, the imposition on offenders of *punishments* or *sanctions* by way of a court order, is usually treated as a specialist area of study although it links unavoidably to many of the items noted in other entries. Punishment is sometimes described as **restriction of liberty** and is obviously an interference with *liberty*, but legitimately so provided that it does not involve torture, cruel and unusual punishments or other unlawful intrusions on fundamental rights (see *human rights*). The extent to which it goes hand-in-hand with *welfare*-related aspects, as per expressions such as **punishment and rehabilitation** (see *rehabilitation*) has varied through history and according to the political or *judicial* temperature, or pressure for **reform** (as touched on in various sections of this book). Sentencing is dealt with in *legislation* (see now, in particular, the *Criminal Justice Act 2003*), other **sentencing law** (the rulings of the *Court of Appeal* or other *higher courts* as reported, e.g. in the dedicated **Criminal Appeal Reports (Sentencing)**) and learned texts. It is a special part of the training of judges and magistrates. The *Sentencing Guidelines Council* (SGC) (see the separate entry below) is now key to understanding developments in this field. Following conviction, the facts are outlined to the **sentencing court** (the judge or magistrates) by the prosecutor and the defendant is invited to make *representations* and any **plea in mitigation** (see *mitigation*). He or she is then sentenced, taking into account any sentencing guidelines (below) and any prior **indication of sentence** by the judge or magistrates. A **list of any previous convictions** (see *conviction*) is handed to the court by the prosecutor, along with a note re the defendant's *character and antecedents*. There may also be a list of other offences to be taken into consideration (see *TIC*). With all the more serious matters there will be a **pre-sentence report** (below).

For **appeal against sentence** see *appeal*. A **commensurate sentence** is one equating with the *seriousness* of the offence in terms of its proportionality and ensuring 'just deserts' (see *Touchstones*). For **committal to the Crown Court for sentence**, see *either way offence*; and for the special **life imprisonment** provisions, see that entry. Discharges can be used where punishment is 'inexpedient'. An **absolute discharge (AD)** marks offending but involves the offender in no further liability (other than that it counts, as all sentences do, towards a *criminal record*). Under a **conditional discharge (CD)** there is no punishment provided that the offender does not commit another offence within a period of up to three years (chosen by the court). The CD lapses provided that there is no such offence. Otherwise, the offender can be sentenced for both the new offence and that re which the conditional discharge was made. **Ancillary orders** are regularly made to run alongside a sentence, depending on the circumstances and sometimes the level of court, they include *costs, compensation*, *disqualification*, **confiscation, forfeiture, destruction** or **seizure** of items, *assets, cash, weapons, drugs*, forged documents (see *counterfeiting and forgery*), tools used to commit or attempt crime, and **restitution** of stolen, etc. property, i.e. return to its owner. A **restraining order** can be made re *harassment* in particular. From the late-1990s, the *anti-social behaviour order* (ASBO) has been used to avert immediate criminal *sanctions*. The similarly preventative **criminal anti-social behaviour order** (or CRASBO) can be made as an ancillary order. Re a foreign national, **deportation** to his or her country of origin can be recommended by a court to the *Justice Secretary*, for consideration as the offender's *release* from a UK prison approaches (or sometimes deportation can occur before that). An *attendance centre* order can be made re a someone aged 15-21 (now as part of a *community sentence*), i.e. for attendance at premises in the *community* for a mix of instruction and rigorous physical activity. Sentences, e.g. of *imprisonment* can be **consecutive sentences** (i.e. that follow one after another) or **concurrent sentences** (which 'run' side-by-side in time).

Credit for a timely guilty plea The principle and legal duty of giving such credit, aka a **sentencing discount,** to reflect the fact that an offender has, e.g. speedily submitted himself or herself to *justice* and this saved time, expense, resources and did not put a victim or witnesses through the ordeal of giving *evidence* in a trial is nowadays embedded in *legislation* and the appropriate level of reduction by *sentencing guidelines*: see sentencing-guidelines.gov.uk The court must take into account the stage in the proceedings when the intention to plead guilty was indicated and its circumstances. With 'required' *custodial* sentences it is 'not prevented' from making a reduction if the outcome does not fall below 80 per cent of that set by law.

Crown Court sentencing powers The **maximum sentences** by the *Crown Court* range up to *life imprisonment,* which is the **mandatory sentence** for *murder* (and in certain other situations), and a **discretionary sentence**, e.g. for *manslaughter.* The maximum sentence for an offence is laid down in *legislation.* Many more serious offences attract a maximum sentence of 14 years *imprisonment* or an *indeterminate sentence for public protection* (ISPP). The Crown Court has unlimited powers to fine offender, subject to *reasonableness, fairness* and proportionality. In contrast, **maximum imprisonment in the magistrates' court** per (imprisonable) offence is six months; or 12 months in aggregate. An unimplemented regime of **custody plus** and **intermittent custody** (aka colloquially 'week-day imprisonment' or 'weekend gaol') contained in the *Criminal Justice Act 2003* would affect this and also allow sentences of 12 months per offence. Custody plus and intermittent custody involve sentences served partly in prison, partly in the community; but whether these will now be brought into effect remains to be seen. For details, see *Criminal Justice Act 2003: A Guide to the New Procedures and Sentencing* (2004), Gibson B, Waterside Press. Fines and compensation have a ceiling of £5,000 each per offence in magistrates' courts (subject in relation to fines to ceilings set by five statutory **fine levels**).

Deferment of sentence is the postponing of a sentence to allow a court to have regard to the offender's conduct, situation, efforts re *'going straight'* and making *reparation*, etc. and any changes to his or her circumstances. The arrangements were revised in 2003 to allow certain activities by the offender to occur during the period of deferment and for the court to consider 'how well the offender complied'. Sentence can be deferred (for up to six months) but only if the offender *consents* and undertakes to abide by any *requirements*. Deferment must be in the *interests of justice*. The court may appoint a *supervisor* (a *probation officer* or anyone it sees fit) to monitor compliance. It can deal with the offender before the end of the period of deferment if satisfied that he or she has failed to comply with one or more requirements or if he or she commits another offence. **Discount for a guilty plea**: see *credit for a timely guilty plea* above. **End-to-end sentence/sentencing** are terms used to describe the coordination of sentences, *release* and *parole*, etc. as between the National Probation Service (see *probation*) and HM Prison Service (aka a **seamless sentence** as part of integrated *offender management*); via mechanisms to ensure continuity and cohesion of *work* with an offender inside *prison* and in the *community*. This may, e.g. involve setting-up links and *referrals* re *drug, alcohol* or *sex offending* programmes in prison and in the *community, communication, monitoring* and post-custody *supervision*.

For **enforcement of sentences, etc.** See *enforcement*; **fines (and other financial orders)** See *fine*; **framework for sentencing** See *sentencing framework* below. **General objects/purposes of sentencing** is the description given to a range of sentencing aims, now largely superseded by statutory purposes of sentencing (below). They included matters such as marking public *concern* and at one stage *retribution*.

Generic community sentence See *community sentence;* **indeterminate sentence for public protection (ISPP)** See that entry; **imprisonment** See that entry. An **indication of sentence** is one by a court: (**1**) at the time when the accused person is deciding whether or not to plead guilty (including re 'plea before venue': see *allocation and sending*; *plea*; or (**2**) following, when calling for a pre-sentence report (below) so that the offender can better prepare *mitigation*. For **life sentence**, see *life imprisonment*. Originally, the only **mandatory sentence** was *capital punishment* (see *Touchstones*), latterly just for *murder*, replaced from 1965 by a **mandatory life sentence** (see *life imprisonment*). Parliament has since passed various measures that curtail the *discretion* of the *judges*: these include mandatory sentences of imprisonment under a **'three strikes' law** (see *Touchstones*) and *indeterminate sentences for public protection* (ISPPs); leading to tensions between the Government, Parliament and the *judiciary*. Magistrates must sometimes make mandatory orders, see. e.g. *road traffic*. **No separate penalty (NSP)** is a device sometimes used once a sufficient overall sentence has been imposed worked out and sentencing for residual matters would make little or no practical difference; usually re lesser or *summary offences*.

Pre-sentence reports (PSRs) are routinely obtained in all the more *serious* cases. They can be requested by a sentencing court from a *probation officer*, member of a *youth offending team* (YOT) or *social worker* (re a juvenile) where a *community sentence*, *custody* or some other concern is in mind (e.g. *mental impairment*: when a *psychiatrist* may also be asked to prepare an *assessment/*). Sentencing is then adjourned for the report to be prepared (see *adjournment*). A PSR may be: a **standard delivery report (SDR)**, which usually takes 15 working days, is used in more serious cases, and is likely to be in writing; or a **fast delivery report (FDR)**, more focused when some relatively straightforward community sentence option is in mind, which is provided in a matter of days, and may well be delivered orally. (The latter were formerly called **specific sentence reports (SSRs)**). PSRs can be 'dispensed with' if the court considers that one is unnecessary. Their content is the subject of National Standards (see *standard*). They are confidential but since the **Pre-Sentence Report (Prescription of Prosecutors) Order 1998**, Crown prosecutors are entitled to see a copy, whilst there can be *disclosure* to other *public prosecutors* at the *discretion* by the court. A copy is normally provided to the offender or its contents brought to his or her attention by the writer of the report; and a copy is given to the offender's *legal representative*. Typically, a PSR contains basic information re the offence and offender, a note of the sources used and steps taken to validate *data*. It will include relevant information about the offender's background, day-to-day activities, abilities, associates, attitudes, responsibilities and any known problems, e.g. re *drugs, alcohol, mental impairment*, employment (or lack of it) and debt; and a *risk assessment* re potential future *harm* to the public and the likelihood of *re-offending*. It may contain a sentence proposal.

For **racial, religious, etc., motivation** and sentencing, see *aggravate/aggravation; hate crime; race/racism*. A **reviewable sentence** is one where the court retains an interest in checking to see that it is being complied with and re which it may exercise certain statutory powers if the sentence is not being satisfactorily complied with. **Seamless sentence** See end-to-end sentence above. **Sentence plan** See *prisoner*.

The **Sentencing Advisory Panel (SAP)** was originally set up under the Crime and Disorder Act 1998 and now supports the *Sentencing Guidelines Council* (SGC), below. It is appointed by the *Justice Secretary* in consultation with the *Lord Chief Justice*; who also appoints its chair. It is responsible for **research into sentencing** (see generally *research*), producing *reports* and information. Its findings are passed to the SCG together with related materials. The SAP may make proposals to the SGC which the SGC must consider. In turn, the SGC must notify the SAP of any proposed or revised Sentencing Guidelines (below) and the SAP must consult various people and respond. The **Sentencing Commission** is a proposed independent body, hence a **Sentencing Commission Working Group (SCWG)** is seeking views on how a structured sentencing framework (below) could be adapted for England and Wales, drawing references from experiences in the USA. **Sentencing framework** is the description given to the first comprehensive statutory sentencing framework contained in the *Criminal Justice Act 1991;* as replaced by that of the Criminal Justice Act 2003. In summary, it contains different **levels of sentence** and the **thresholds for sentences** of different levels by way of a *discharge, fine, community sentence* or *imprisonment*. **Sentencing guidelines** contain considered advice and, e.g. suggested starting points for sentences in given situations, such as those of the *Court of Appeal* or nowadays principally as issued by the **Sentencing Guidelines Council (SGC)**. The SGC is headed by the *Lord Chief Justice*. It promulgates *advice* and *guidance* to all judges and magistrates on a range of sentencing matters. It has seven further *judicial* members, four non-judicial ones. Established by the *Criminal Justice Act 2003,* it reports annually to the *Justice Secretary*. It has a secretariat which is the *liaison* point for interested parties. Once the SGC decides that a guideline is a **definitive sentencing guideline**, then all courts must observe it, or explain why they have departed from it in an individual case. The *Justice Secretary* consults with the SGC at arms-length, can appoint an observer and can put forward proposals.

Statutory purposes of sentencing now exist in relation to both: *youth justice*, where a **principal statutory purpose of sentencing** was enacted in 1998 (revised 2008), i.e. preventing offending; and, since the *Criminal Justice Act 2003* (see 142 of that Act), *adults*: (a) the *punishment* of offenders; (b) the reduction of crime (including through *deterrence*); (c) the *reform* and *rehabilitation* of offenders; (d) the *protection* of the *public*; and (e) *reparation* by offenders to people affected by the offence(s) for which he or she is being sentenced. **Suspended sentence of imprisonment** See *imprisonment*. The **totality principle** is that under which, if several sentences are to be imposed on the same occasion, the court should look at the overall effect on the offender. For **unduly lenient sentence**, see *Attorney General*.

separation of powers

A key doctrine of constitutional law (see generally *constitution/constitutional*) of fundamental significance re matters of *justice*. Centrally, it holds that within a *democracy* the functions of the Executive, Legislature and *Judiciary* should operate independently of one another. See, also, *independence/interdependence; judicial decision-making*.

September 11 (9/11) See *Touchstones*

serial offender

Informal description for someone who commits a particular kind of offence periodically, on separate occasions, possibly at shortening intervals and at a potentially escalating level of *seriousness*. Whilst the term can be applied to any offender, it is usually reserved for those committing *violence* or *sexual offences*, such as a **serial rapist** or **serial killer**. Such offenders may also be 'spree offenders' who commit their offences in a sudden burst of activity over a short time span; as with the 'Ipswich *murders*' (Suffolk) (late 2006) of five women over a matter of weeks by an offender with no record of this kind of behaviour (albeit such events always invite further *investigation* and the notion offenders may have carried out undiscovered offences in the past). In his comprehensive survey of serial killers post-Second-World War, *criminologist* Professor David Wilson notes that *vulnerable people* are the main *targets*: the elderly, women involved in prostitution (see *street offences* in *Touchstones*), gay men, runaways, 'throwaways', *children* and 'kids moving from place to place': see *Serial Killers: Hunting Britons and Their Victims 1945 -2006* (2008), Wilson D, Waterside Press lists known *victims* within that timeframe. Some notorious UK serial killers are noted under *baby farm, Cromwell Street, Moors Murders, Shipman, Harold* and *Yorkshire Ripper* in *Touchstones*. Contrast several victims on one occasion (see, e.g. *Hungerford Massacre* in *Touchstones*); mass murder and genocide: see *murder*.

serious/seriousness

Terms which are constant points of reference for CJS practitioners: the **seriousness of the offence** affecting *priorities*, *responses* and sentencing in particular. In determining 'seriousness', a court must consider: the offender's culpability re the offence in question together with any *harm* caused, or intended, by it, or which might foreseeably have been caused. Sometimes a court must treat an offence as **more serious** than normal, e.g. if it was committed whilst on *bail*, involved certain *aggravating* features, or if the offender has previous *convictions*. In general terms, whether an offence is serious is a question of fact and degree, but some offences are generally so regarded, e.g. *violence, sexual offences,* those involving *terrorism/terrorists, weapons* or, naturally and by definition, **serious fraud** (see *fraud*). For **serious arrestable offence**, see *arrest*; and for the **serious enough** and **so serious** threshold tests, *community sentence* and *imprisonment*, respectively. The **Serious Crime Act 2007 (SCA)** contains lists of serious offences for the purposes of that Act. It introduced (among other things) the *civil* **serious crime prevention order** as described under *anti-social behaviour/*'gangster asbo'. It also replaced Common Law offences of *incitement*, etc, enabled *data sharing* and *data matching* to prevent *fraud* or trace *proceeds of crime*, and transferred the functions of the Assets Recovery Agency to the **Serious Organised Crime Agency (SOCA)** (below) and introduced measures re *investigations, cash* recovery, *search warrants, stop and search* and **serious violence** (see *violence*). SOCA also acquired some powers from, or that now operate alongside, those of HM *Revenue & Customs*.

Serious Fraud Office (SFO) The SFO is an independent government department responsible for the *investigation* and *prosecution* of serious or complex fraud. It is headed by a director who is appointed by and accountable to the *Attorney General*. It has four divisions, each headed by an assistant director and made up of multi-disciplinary *case* teams of *lawyers*, financial investigators and support staff covering different geographical areas. However, many SFO cases originate in London and are 'farmed out'. There is an Accountancy Support and Forensic Computing division which links to the UK *Internet Crime Forum*. Key **SFO criteria** for taking on a case include whether:

the suspected fraud seems to have been **so serious or complex** as to demand SFO specialisms and knowledge (e.g. of financial markets); its *value* exceeds £1 million; there is a significant international dimension; it is likely to be of widespread public concern; or requires the use of special SFO powers (including of obligatory *disclosure* and obligatory answers to questions: contrast the rights to *silence*). The SFO has sometimes attracted controversy, not least when expensive prosecutions have failed. But commentators point out that such a *risk* is unavoidable when pursuing complex matters. Notoriously, the SFO became embroiled in the machinations re the *BAE Systems case* (see *Touchstones*), but was ultimately backed by the *House of Lords*.

The **Serious and Organized Crime Agency (SOCA)** was launched in 2006 under the **Serious Organized Crime and Police Act 2005 (SOCPA)**; an aim being 'to reduce the harm caused ... by serious *organized crime*'; estimated by government at more than £20 billion per year. SOCA brought together the former National Crime Squad (NCS), National Criminal Intelligence Service (NCIS), parts of HM *Revenue & Customs* (those dealing with *drug*-trafficking, criminal finance) and the UK Immigration Service (now part of the Border Agency: see *border; immigration*). A key SOCA responsibility is the recovery of the *proceeds of crime* and *money laundering*; using increasingly sophisticated ways of *monitoring* transactions; such that it is now virtually impossible for people to conduct any substantial financial transaction without there being some trace of it which SOCA can gain access to. See also, e.g. *suspicious activity report* (SAR). SOCA is an executive *non-departmental public body* (NDPB) sponsored by, but operationally independent of, the *Home Office*. It is led by a board with a majority of non-executive members who are responsible for ensuring that SOCA discharges its responsibilities and meets priorities set by the *Home Secretary*. Under the 2005 Act, SOCA must publish an annual plan and report. Note also **SOCA Online**: a secure system for use by people submitting SARS (above).

service

A word which: **(1)** is largely synonymous with 'agency': see mainly the entry for *agency/service*; but that **(2)** also features in terms such as **service delivery** or **quality of service**, when the emphasis is mainly on *effectiveness and efficiency*.

sex/sexual

As with *violence*, special considerations apply to **sexual offences** in terms, e.g. of policing, *targeting, record*-keeping and sentencing. The informal *label* **sex industry** is often used to signify a range of commercially-based activities, legal, illegal, dubious or criminal, the last of these often linked to *abuse, drugs,* people-*trafficking, obscene* publications, *organized crime,* prostitution (see *street offences* in *Touchstones*) and/or kidnapping; and the **sexual exploitation** of children, women or other *vulnerable people* in particular. Key statutes include the **Sex Offenders Act 1997** (see further below) and **Sexual Offences Act 2003** which re-defined many sexual offences such as rape (where less than seven per cent of *complaints* led to convictions in 2008) and **sexual assault** and created new ones such as **sexual voyeurism** and offences based on **under-age sexual intimacy**: see specialist works. The **Sex Offender Treatment Programme (SOTP)** operates on various levels of progression in *prisons* or the *community*. Parallel developments include the *Child Exploitation and Online Protection Centre* (CEOP); *Multi-agency Public Protection Arrangements (*MAPPAs); and *indeterminate sentence for public protection* (ISPP). Hence terms such as **sex offender, sexual offence** and **sex offender register** (as created by the 1997 Act which imposed a *requirement* on most sex offenders to register with the police follow-ing their conviction by giving their name, address and personal details). The Crime and Disorder Act 1998 introduced **sex offender orders** on the application of the police, placing existing offenders under a similar duty. The Police Reform Act 2002 (see, generally, *police*) allowed these to run UK-wide and as an interim measure in urgent situations. A **sexual offences prevention order** under the 2003 Act, a *civil* construct (a variant of which can be made if someone is convicted of a sexually-relat-ed offence), is a preventative measure, breach becoming an offence, i.e. at the *enforce-ment* stage; or it can be made re people convicted of violent (non-sexual) offences if a court thinks this necessary for the *protection* of the public from serious *harm* from the offender. Actions or events aimed against someone's **sexual orientation** are a basis of *hate crime* and/or for increasing the severity of a sentence (see generally *aggravate/aggravation*). They also contravene *discrimination* laws.

shaming See *naming and shaming* in *Touchstones*

silence
(1) The historic **right to silence** in the face of an *accusation* or *investigation* was always regarded as a fundamental right, on the basis that no-one should be obliged to convict himself or herself 'out of his or her own mouth' (aka **self-incrimination**) (hence, also, the USA's *Fifth Amendment*: see *Touchstones*); and to discourage *abuse, corruption* and *torture* (there being no want of *miscarriage of justice* cases to demon-strate how easily a *'confession'* can be wrung out of someone: see, e.g. *Birmingham Six*; *Kisko, Stephen* in *Touchstones*). Its dilution, if not outright abolition, occurred in the Criminal Justice and Public Order Act 1994, following which a court is permitted to draw inferences where an accused person does not mention something when charged, or later in his or her *defence*, including a trial, which he or she then seeks to rely on. This has become an integral part of the police *caution* on *arrest*. Other statutes place an obligation on suspects to answer given questions, including re certain *investigations* by the *Serious Fraud Office*, HM *Revenue & Customs* and as a result of modern defence *disclosure* rules. **(2)** 'Silence in court' is the traditional cry of the court usher when a judge or magistrates enter a courtroom, or to quell potential *contempt* of court. **(3)** Si-lencing is a dubious process whereby dissent, protest or democratic engagement (see *democracy*), etc. are curtailed by subtle or ingenious means: see *Silently Silenced: The Creation of Acquiescence in Modern Society* (2004), Mathiesen T, Waterside Press.

single justice See *justice*

sit/sitting
Words related to the holding of a court hearing, i.e. when judges or magistrates **sit on the bench** in a courtroom during what is known as 'a sitting'. But note also 'in chambers' and/or 'in camera' (i.e. **sitting 'behind closed doors'**: see *open court*).

Smith and Hogan See *Touchstones*

social exclusion (SE)
A term used to signify the **exclusion of people from mainstream involvement** in *communities* (or in some instances from geographical locations) as evidenced by factors such as: unemployment (see *employment*), low skills, below average incomes, unfair *discrimination*, inadequate housing (see, also, *homelessness*), ill-*health*, family

breakdown and lack of opportunity or democratic engagement (see *democracy*). This may be linked to high *crime rates*. SE also occurs through *banishment, imprisonment* or other forms of *displacement*; leading to a vicious circle of *disadvantage*. Hence a **Social Exclusion Unit** (SEU) was set up in 1997 to create 'joined up solutions to joined up problems' and work across government departments. In 2001, this became a responsibility of the *Cabinet Office* from which various initiatives have stemmed, including 'Reducing Re-offending by Ex-prisoners' which noted that *imprisonment* does not in itself succeed in turning the majority of offenders away from crime and that it can make matters worse; whereas it is necessary to tackle *causes of crime*. But 'What actually happened was that they cherry-picked the most politically acceptable and convenient actions, and rubbished the rest' (Julian Corner, *Safer Society,* 2004). **Tackling SE** remains central to CJS *strategy* and is inter-related, e.g. with regeneration schemes and ideas of *community* cohesion. It is also intertwined with issues of *equality, fairness* and *democracy*. See also, e.g. *broken windows* in *Touchstones*.

social services

Usually a reference to *local authority* social services and their various departments, units or staff (aka **social workers; social work managers**, etc.) who deal with young people (especially *children*) and old or other *vulnerable people*, including those in poor *health* or suffering *mental impairment* (see also *guardianship*). This work is often carried out independently of the CJS proper under legal duties cast on local authorities; often nowadays in conjunction with *education* responsibilities. It may also be an integral part of CJS work, e.g. re *child protection* or where social workers or *youth workers* are members of *youth offending teams* (YOTs) or *Multi-agency Public Protection Arrangements* (MAPPAs). Parallel responsibilities of *local authorities* in relation to Crime and Disorder Reduction Partnerships (CDRPs) are noted under *partnership*.

solicitor

In a CJS context, a *lawyer* who advises clients on legal matters and who may provide *legal representation* for them in the magistrates' court and/or prepare cases for a *barrister* to present in the *Crown Court* or the *higher courts*; including for both private clients and those who are in receipt of *legal aid*. The **Law Society** is the representative body for solicitors in England and Wales which negotiates with and lobbies that profession's independent regulators, government and others, and provides training and *advice* to solicitors. For further information, see lawsociety.org.uk Hence, also, **Solicitor General**: one of the Government's *law officers* (a role dating from the 1500s) within the Office of the *Attorney General*: see further attorneygeneral.gov.uk

sovereign For *Main Entries* affecting the sovereign, see *Crown*; *constitution/constitutional*; *Rule of Law*. **special constable** See *police/policing*; **special court** See *magistrate*; **specific sentence report** See *sentence/sentencing*.

speech/speeches

Usually a reference to: **(1)** those by *legal representatives* or *judges*, variously described as a **speech to the jury** (or magistrates), **opening speech** or **closing speech** according to the situation; or where appropriate, a **judge's summing-up** (see *judge/*'role of the judge and jury'). Similarly, re legal or other *representations* within the course of a trial; **(2)** explanations given by Law Lords in the **House of Lords, which** are/were known as speeches rather than *judgements*; or **(3)** those of *Ministers of State* and other key CJS figures on public occasions, e.g. concerning *policy, strategy*.

sponsorship of agencies, etc.

A good deal of CJS provision is sponsored by government rather than part of it. For a list of justice-related bodies which are sponsored by the MOJ, see *The New Ministry of Justice: An Introduction* (2008) (2nd. edn.), Gibson B, Waterside Press.

standard/standards

Increasingly, agencies/services are governed by standards created by themselves or where appropriate government or other public entities, including in some instances via delegated *legislation*. The term **National Standard** is sometimes used, as re those for the National Probation Service (NPS) and *National Policing Improvement Agency* (NPIA); or **performance standard** to signify one geared to *targets* and/or particular *outcomes*. For **standard of proof**, see *evidence*. Note also especially, **standards in public life**: by which civil servants and other public officers are guided (see *Poulson, John* in *Touchstones* for part of the background to these which are also intended to counter 'sleaze' and ensure the integrity of public services). For the **Parliamentary Commissioner for Standards**, see parliament.uk Similarly, in other contexts, such matters as **parenting standards**: see generally *parent, etc*; **standard conditions** or **standard requirements**, e.g. re *bail* or as part of a *community sentence* or *parole*; and **standard of care**, i.e. that by which levels of care are judged re offences involving failure or negligence (or failings of an agency/service). See also *Trading standards*.

State

References in this work to 'the State' are to the Government in all its manifestations or relevant public authorities as a whole according to the context. Similarly, e.g. a reference to national *security* might equally be one to **'State security'**. For a general treatment of the inter-relationship between the *citizen*, the State and the CJS, see *Crime, State and Citizen: A Field Full of Folk* (2006) (2nd. edn), Faulkner D, Waterside Press. For **Minister of State**, see that entry. For **State funded legal representation**, see *legal aid*. Note also the *monitoring* work of **Statewatch**: see statewatch.org

statement

(**1**) A formal pronouncement, e.g. by a *Minister of State* such as the *Justice Secretary* or *Home Secretary* (in the House of Commons or elsewhere but usually meaning in public or in writing). (**2**) Similarly, by the head of an agency/service, by someone who has secured an *acquittal*, or a victim. (**3**) A **statement of facts** is integral to the procedures for a *written plea of guilty* and also an *appeal* by way of case stated. (**4**) According to the context, a **statement of reasons** may be made by a court, a police officer or other public official as appropriate, or, e.g. by the *Criminal Cases Review Commission* (and see generally *reason*). (**5**) For **witness statement**, see *witness*.

statute

(**1**) A synonym for Act of Parliament. Hence **Statute Book** is a metaphor for the entire body of law enacted by Parliament (aka *legislation*), which may extend to other forms of **statutory legislation**, including **statutory instruments** (SIs), sometimes aka **statutory regulation** or **statutory rule**: see *regulation*; *rule*. The word 'statutory' is also commonly used to describe anything done or provided for by statute, as where, e.g. a court or police officer exercises **statutory powers** or an accused person relies on a **statutory defence**, i.e. one provided for by the **statutory provision** creating the offence or associated legislation (usually and sometimes called a 'special *defence*'). For **statutory declaration**, see *declaration*. (**2**) Sometimes the **statutes of an organization**, corporation or society, i.e. internal rules, regulations and *procedures* and having no direct correlation with statutes of the kind described in (1).

Stephen Lawrence See *Lawrence, Stephen* in *Touchstones*; **Stockwell shooting** and **Stone's Justices' Manual** See *Touchstones;* **stop and search** See *search.*

strategy/strategic direction/strategic planning

Direction, planning, etc. at the highest level which also connotes the promulgation of strategy to other levels, including, e.g. *management* (see also generally *administration/administrative*) and the *front line* where the strategy will be put into effect. **CJS strategy** is the responsibility of the MOJ and Home Office in conjunction with its partners in government and via the *Cabinet Committee on Crime and the Criminal Justice System* (CCCCJS). Agencies/services also set their own individual strategies for achieving aims and objectives, subject to any legitimate overall direction.

street See *Touchstones*

suicide

Suicide (or rather **an attempt to commit suicide**) is no longer a crime, but assisting suicide and associated offences are so due to the **Suicide Act 1961**. The UK has always (thus far) resisted *decriminalisation* of such events which would permit *help and support* re **euthanasia**; albeit that in modern times prosecutions have dwindled to the point where, despite some 100 cases referred to the CPS (2008) re people travelling abroad to specialist clinics in places such as Switzerland, no prosecutions have followed; the CPS indicating that it has no policy against prosecution, each case being decided on its merits. Seemingly, cases would be prosecuted where there is *evidence* of pressure being brought to bear on *vulnerable people* rather than the primary *motivation* stemming from the person committing suicide. Various organizations hold competing views: the **Voluntary Euthanasia Society** pressing for a relaxation to allow, e.g. terminally-ill people suffering extreme pain to accelerate their own deaths; various pro-life bodies being strongly against change. In terms of *human rights*, commentators are equivocal re whether, e.g. the right to life in Article 2 of the European Convention On Human Rights should include a personal right to end one's life with *help and support* (the European Court of Human Rights having ruled that it does not re an English woman, Diane Pretty, who died in 2002). In 2008, an **assisted suicide** was broadcast by Sky TV; and an *investigation* was triggered by a suicide broadcast live on the internet. **Suicides in prison** occur at approximately four times the rate for the population in general: see generally *deaths in custody*; and note **suicide watch** whereby prisoners thought to be at *risk* are checked every 15 minutes or so.

summary

A word used in various contexts, most significantly re **summary justice**, usually meaning: (**1**) in a technical sense, *justice* in the magistrates' court which can also be quite correctly described as a **court of summary jurisdiction**; (**2**) similarly in relation to *military* discipline in particular or that under the Prison Rules (see *prison*/'discipline'); (**3**) justice meted out speedily, simply and untrammelled by complex *procedures* or *rules*, whether in a court or, e.g. by way of a *caution, diversion* from prosecution, *fixed penalty notice*, 'on the spot *fine*', *referral order* or *warning and reprimand*; the term having been adopted in particular in modern times to describe 'justice' dispensed directly via police or *administrative* action rather than the courts. (**4**) More loosely, any form of 'justice' which occurs speedily and whether officially (and lawfully) or not e.g. by a kangaroo court, retaliation, including within the *Underworld* (see *Touchstones*), or a punishment beating (as meted out in Northern Ireland during The *Troubles:* see *Touchstones*). See also generally *vigilante*. Hence re (1) above, **summary offence** means one triable only in the magistrates' court. These must normally be prosecuted within six months but *jurisdiction* is now nationwide. Many summary cases involve little more than transgressions or *low-level* offences, even if technically *criminal offences*. Everyday examples of **'purely summary'** or **'summary only'** matters are: speeding and many other *road traffic* offences; using a TV without a licence; lesser *public order* offences; common *assault*; *criminal damage* if the *value* is low; some social security offences; and those against bye-laws. Many become *'paperwork cases'*. **Summary trial** follows the same broad rules of *criminal procedure,* etc. as for more serious offences (see generally *trial*). The maximum penalty for such offences is laid down by Act of Parliament, often the one creating the offence (see generally *sentence/ sentencing*); usually a *fine,* but some more serious summary offences attract up to six months *imprisonment.* Other common uses of 'summary' include: (**5**) **summary of the prosecution (or defence) case**, i.e. the outline given at the start of a trial or when making *disclosure*; or (**6**) any synopsis or brief version of events. Note also (**7**) the **Simple, Speedy, Summary Justice** initiative which seeks to improve *case management* and goes by the acronym **CJSSS**: see further at cjsonline.gov.uk

summing-up See *judge/*'role of the judge and jury'; **summons** See *information and summons;* **supergrass** See *informer.*

superintendent

A rank or title usually reserved for **police superintendents**, or e.g. those in charge of an institution or hostel, or in the fire service. Hence the **Police Superintendent's Association (PSA)** representing some 1,600 superintendents and chief superintendents working in England and Wales, the Isle of Man and non-geographic forces. Its objectives are to: 'lead and develop the police service to improve quality of *service delivery* to local *communities*; influence *practice, policy*, and decision-making at chief officer and government level; and to provide appropriate support and *advice* to members regarding conditions of service'. See further policesupers.com

supervision

That by: (**1**) the National Probation Service (see *probation*) or a *youth justice team* as a requirement of a *community sentence, parole* or other *release* licence; (**2**) by a mentor, warden or superintendent of a *hostel*, etc; or (**3**) of a practitioner whilst 'on probation', under *discipline*, etc. Note also **intensive supervision (and support) (ISS)** (usually meaning whilst subject to a *community sentence*); **close supervision** (re a high-risk offender in prison); and **post-custody supervision:** see *release*

support See *bail support; help and support; Victim Support; witness support.*

Supreme Court

The UK's first **Supreme Court of Justice (SCJ)** in the sense of it being the highest UK court was created by the Constitutional Reform Act 2005 and begins work in October 2009; taking over the *judicial* functions of the *House of Lords*. It will hear *appeals* on points of *law* of general public importance. The SCJ is being housed in the Middlesex Guildhall, Westminster. Its president is a senior *Law Lord*, Lord Judge, *Lord Chief Justice,* having been designated for that role. In balancing *independence* with ministerial *accountability* there are links with the *Justice Secretary* and MOJ of the kind envisaged by The *Concordat.* The SCJ will also assume the *judicial* role of the *Privy Council.* Re *administration, management* and oversight of the SCJ, the president and a chief executive are responsible for its day-to-day running and operation; supported by 'Supreme Court Staff' (civil servants). Existing Law Lords become **Supreme Court Justices** automatically and they remain (non-debating) members of the House of Lords, but new SC justices are appointed directly to the SCJ and do not become members of the House of Lords (i.e. in their *judicial* capacity: it is conceivable that they may be members independently). In 2009 the first SCJ interviews were held involving applicants from a wider background than has been the case historically for Law Lords (and other judges), due to the 'opening up of the judiciary'.

surety See under *bail*

surveillance

Keeping watch over *citizens* including by **covert surveillance**: see *police/policing/*'covert policing'. Much modern-day surveillance is more overt, as with *CCTV.* The term is now regularly applied to forms of **retrospective surveillance** or **duty-led surveillance** as where the records of a supermarket, bank or emails are accessed or in certain instances, must be disclosed (see *suspicion/*'suspicious activity report') under various powers, e.g. re *money laundering, serious crime* and *terrorism/terrorists*; or **surveillance by automated law enforcement** as with speed cameras (see *road traffic; fixed penalty notice*) or automated number plate recognition (ANPR): see generally *technology. Civil liberties* groups argue that the UK is the most 'watched over' country in the world (estimates that anyone may be photographed hundreds of times a day abound) and commentators point to what they claim is an **endemic surveillance society**; exacerbated by concerns about the large number of *law enforcement agencies* who are authorised to use or access such facilities, including under the pretext that they are exercising (widely drawn) *crime prevention/crime reduction* functions or dealing with *terrorism/terrorists*. See also *Big Brother* in *Touchstones*. The opening-up of files under the *Freedom of Information Act 2000* has disclosed how much in the past the police or *security services* have been involved in reinforcing the *political* priorities of Governments by keeping *watch* on people's activities.

suspect/suspicion

Before and until the conviction of any person there is a *presumption of innocence.* Only following conviction (if and when this occurs) does a suspect become an *offender* or, as some people, media reports and pronouncements prefer it, a 'criminal'. Hence also the **reporting of suspicions** to the police; including by way of the **suspicious activity report (SAR)** *targeting* the *proceeds of crime* and *money laundering* via, e.g. banks, lawyers, accountants and businesses who may meet such offences when dealing with clients/customers; now enhanced by provisions allowing any police officer to seize *cash* above a statutory amount in the absence of a satisfactory explanation for carrying it; and associated CPS procedures.

suspended sentence of imprisonment See under *imprisonment*; **system** See *Criminal Justice System; Youth Justice System.*

tag/tagging See *monitoring*; **taken into consideration** See *TIC*.

tampering

(1) tampering with a motor vehicle, e.g. interfering with the operation of its brakes, steering or to gain entry to it. **(2) Tampering with a jury** See *jury*. **(3)** Informally, any similar *offending behaviour* involving 'interference', e.g. with *children*.

target

(1) The focus of an *investigation*, project, operation, budget, *time limit*, etc; when the suspect, aim or purpose may be called '**a target**'. There is, e.g. a modern emphasis on **targeting the proceeds of crime**. Similarly, offences such as *cybercrime* (see *Touchstones*), *drug-misuse, paedophilia, unfit food* and *domestic violence* or at a lesser level of *seriousness, road traffic* offences, *TV Licensing* or *anti-social behaviour*. **(2)** The intended victim of an offence, especially that of a hit-man, predatory offender or someone engaged in *fraud* or *deception*. **(3)** One set by government, an agency/service, etc, such as **a target to achieve a given level of service** or throughput. Some such targets have proved controversial, especially if they invite fast-tracking of a kind that might place *justice* at risk. Hence, also, **hard target** and **soft target** (and **target hardening/softening**) to signify difficult or easy targets (a tighter/looser focus).

tariff

(1) A period set by a judge as the minimum time to be served in prison before the offender can be considered for *release* from an *indeterminate sentence* or *life imprisonment*. The *Attorney General* can refer to the *Court of Appeal* the tariff set re a life sentence for *murder*. **(2)** A *guideline* punishment, 'the going rate'/starting point, provided any such 'tariff' is not taken as hindering judicial *discretion*.

taxation/taxing

(1) The formal, quasi-judicial process for **assessing a bill of costs** to make sure that correct and justifiable amounts have been charged by a *lawyer* (see *costs*; *Crown Court*), whereby the correct amount for payment from *public funds* or as between the parties is certified. **(2) Taxation by the government** when failure to pay tax, make a tax return and related matters are offences; but frequently dealt with out of court, see HM *Revenue & Customs*; *fine*/'administrative fine', surcharge etc. **(3)** 'Relieving' a *victim* of his or her property, i.e. *theft* or *robbery* (often called 'mugging'), e.g. by blocking his or her path, hindering progress (especially in *prison*). **(4)** A 'levy' by someone running a *protection racket*, especially re the *Underworld* (see *Touchstones*).

technology

As with progress generally, technological advances have led to new ways of committing offences and equally of their *detection, investigation,* etc. Hence, the (former) **Police Information Technology Organization (PITO)** (now part of the *Serious and Organized Crime Agency*). Such developments are primarily a responsibility of the *Home Office* but other agencies/services have **technology departments**. Modern advances include *CCTV* (extending to 'talking cameras' that can issue a *warning, Big Brother*-style (see *Touchstones*)) and other *surveillance*, automated number plate recognition (ANPR), biometrics, rapid *communications* systems (see also *Scanning Analysis Response Assessment* (SARA)), advanced *data*-sharing, internet-based *investigations*, retrieval of 'deleted' e-*data*, *monitoring* of people, traffic, animals or property, heat imaging and *global satellite positioning* (GSP) (via mobile telephones), *video* recording (and 'real time video analysis'), face recognition, cameras in police vehicles or police officers' helmets, *DNA*-testing (aka 'genetic fingerprinting'), initiatives re *drug*-testing devices and non-lethal force (see *Taser-gun* in *Touchstones*). See also *science*.

terrorism/terrorist

Terms referable to a wide-ranging topic that until modern times has tended to be dealt with as a separate and discrete strand of policing due to its sensitive and political nature and the fact that it touches on national *security*. Hence for many years *The Troubles* in Northern Ireland, but since *September 11* in particular al-Qaeda (see *Touchstones* for a brief note and also for *July 7* and *Stockwell shooting*). It seems to be generally agreed that the overall challenges to national *security* have radically changed since the days of the Cold War and Irish Republican Army. The topic has become more intertwined with criminal justice and attracted greater *openness* in general due to a range of factors: the **Terrorism Act 2000** (and a number of subsequent **Terrorism Acts**); the fact that these have impacted on *citizens* generally on the UK mainland (terrorism is a UK-wide responsibility); the potential for *function creep* (see *Touchstones*); extended powers of *search*/'stop and search'; the global and sometimes hidden nature of the *threat*; extensive *media*/*press* coverage; and *human rights* considerations (see, e.g. *detention without trial*). The Criminal Justice and Immigration Act 2008 created a new *immigration* status for people seeking to enter the UK who have been involved in terrorism or *serious crime*. A **Joint Terrorism Analysis Centre (JTAC)** was established in 2003 as part of the development of co-ordinated arrangements for *handling* and disseminating *intelligence* in *response* to **global terrorist threats**; a *multi-agency* unit, staffed by members of several agencies/services including: the Defence Intelligence Staff (DIS) and representatives from the Home Office, Foreign and Commonwealth Office and the police. It sets *threat levels* and issues threat *warnings* (re international terrorism) and provides in-depth *reports* on trends and terrorist capabilities. Its head reports directly to the Director General of the Security Service, who reports to the Joint Intelligence Committee (JIC). An Oversight Board is chaired by the *Cabinet Office* and there are arrangements to fast-track meetings and decision-making at the highest level (see further intelligence.gov.uk). Hence an **Office for Security and Counter-Terrorism (OSCT)**. **The Terrorism Act 2000** was the first of a series of such Acts that have been passed in modern times, mostly in the wake of September 11 as set out in *Police and Policing: An Introduction* (2009), Villiers P, Waterside Press. A **proscribed organization** is one listed by Government which it then becomes an offence to join, take part in or support; re which exists a **Proscribed Organizations Appeal Commission (POAC)** to deal with *appeals* in cases where the *Home Secretary* refuses to de-proscribe an organization that is believed by him or her to be involved in terrorism: for details, see siac.tribunals.gov.uk/poac

testimony

The oral *evidence* of a *witness* in the *courtroom* or when making a sworn *statement* out of court under certain *procedures*. **Testimony in the witness box**: that given on *oath* or *affirmation* by a witness; which attracts *cross-examination*, etc. see *evidence*.

theft

The offence of theft as defined in sections 1 to 7 **Theft Act 1968** (as amended); an *Act of Parliament* which created a range of acquisitive (or similar) offences, such as *blackmail, burglary, deception, handling* and *robbery*. Theft occurs when someone dishonestly appropriates property belonging to another with the intention of permanently depriving that person of it of it, it being immaterial whether this is with 'a view to gain'. Theft is an *either way* offence whose maximum sentence is *imprisonment* for seven years. Certain things cannot be stolen, e.g. flowers picked whist growing wild. Note also the offence of **going equipped for theft,** e.g. with a tool (such as a jemmy), key or appliance (section 25). Common forms of theft include 'shoplifting'. The offence of taking a motor vehicle without consent (section 12) (and later *aggravated* forms of this offence) was created to overcome difficulties in proving an intention to 'permanently deprive' (see *mens rea*). See generally specialist works on *criminal law*.

therapy

A form of *treatment* of physical, mental or behavioural disorders meant to cure or rehabilitate people (see *rehabilitation*); and hence **psychoanalysis** and **psychotherapy** seek to resolve such problems via *medical* approaches (see also *mental impairment; psychiatry/psychology*). A **therapeutic community (TC)** is one in the *community* or prison which uses therapeutic approaches, via groups (aka 'communities'), self-*help and support, guidance* and counselling. **Grendon Prison** in Buckinghamshire became well-known from the 1960s for its innovative therapeutic *prison/*'regime'. It was later the model for other such regimes, including at Dovegate Prison, Staffordshire. Accounts include *The Frying Pan,* Parker T (1960), Penguin; and *Grendon Tales: Stories from a Theraapeutic Community,* Smartt U (2002), Waterside Press. Hence also **electro convulsive therapy (ECT)**: see *mental impairment*.

threat

(1) Crime is sometimes assessed in terms of its general level of *seriousness* and need to be made a *priority* by the extent to which it creates a **threat to the safety of the general public** and/or national *security*. The real threat of crime may be less than might appear due to *fear* of crime. Hence development of **threat levels**, including re *terrorism/terrorists;* designed to enable a broad indication/*assessment* of the extent and likelihood of the threat of an attack; based on a range of factors including current *intelligence* and recent events. **Threat assessments** are also produced as events unfold. There are five **threat levels** which inform decisions re the *security* needed to protect the UK's Critical National Infrastructure (CNI): Low (an attack is unlikely); Moderate (possible, but not likely); Substantial (a strong possibility); Severe (highly likely) and Critical (expected imminently). (2) **Making a threat** and/or **threatening behaviour** which can occur in a wide range of contexts, from *domestic violence* to *public order* to **hoax threats** or terrorism, is an offence under sundry *legislation* as is, specifically, a **threat to kill**, oral or in writing: see works on *criminal law*.

three strikes See *Touchstones*

threshold/threshold test/criteria

A **legal hurdle** or **practice-based** hurdle which must be surmounted before a power can be exercised, e.g. sentencing criteria re a *community sentence* or *imprisonment*; tests used by the CPS (which include a **threshold test**): see *Crown Prosecution Service*.

Such test normally involve **threshold criteria**, i.e. a list of factors or circumstances which must be taken into to determine whether a threshold has been reached.

TIC (take/taken into consideration)

After someone is convicted of an offence he or she can ask the court to **take into consideration** other offences which he or she admits but with which he or she has not been charged, i.e. in deciding on the appropriate level of sentence for the offence of which he or she stands convicted. Hence a **list of TICs** produced by the prosecutor and agreed by the offender. Once an offence has been properly **TIC'd** it cannot be the subject of a later prosecution. There has been controversy re the false 'trading' of TICs as between *prisoners* and police to *'clear up'* offences; now subject to closer scrutiny.

ticket

Colloquial term for: **(1)** a *fixed penalty notice*; **(2)** a *parole* or other licence re *release* from prison, etc; aka a **'ticket of leave'**, especially with regard to temporary release; and hence also **'ticket of leave man/woman'** for the person concerned.

time limit/timetable

Time limits apply (or may be applied) to some CJS processes, e.g. commencing *summary* proceedings; lodging an *appeal*; a **custody time limit**: see *custody*; and *disclosure*. A **timetable** is normally a reference to one set: **(1)** by a judge, magistrate or *justices' clerk* with a view to progressing a criminal case, especially at a *directions* hearing or as part of *case management*; or **(2)** for other CJS purpose, e.g. the Police and Criminal Evidence Act 1984 (PACE) (hence 'PACE clock'), the preparation of a pre-sentence report (PSR)(normally 21 days)(see s*entence/sentencing*), or a prisoner/*'sentence plan'*.

Titan prison See *prison;* **tough/toughness** See *Touchstones.*

trading standards

Standards set by *law* and *practice* and enforced (see generally *enforcement*) where these create offences via local government **Trading Standards Departments**; aided by **Trading Standards Central (TSC)**, a modern incarnation of UK government responsibility in this field. TSC aims to provide a 'one stop shop' for information about **consumer protection** in the UK. There is also a **Trading Standards Institute (TSI)**. For further information about this specialist field, see trading standards.gov. uk A failure to meet trading standards may also involve *fraud* (possibly largescale) or *organized crime*; triggering the involvement of the police, Serious Fraud Office (SFO) (see *fraud*) or *Serious and Organized Crime Agency*. At a lesser level there are arrangements for alternative dispute resolution (ADR) as between consumers and traders, suppliers, etc. A European Consumer Network (ECN) allows people to pursue *rights* across the European Union and/or obtain information re European consumer law.

trafficking

A term commonly applied to the illicit transfer of items, especially across national *borders*, particularly **drug trafficking** (see further *drugs*), **people trafficking** (see also *immigration*), **trafficking in contraband goods** or, e.g. in relation to *fraud* (such as a 'carousel fraud')(see *Touchstones*). Increasingly the authorities, including the police, UK *Border Agency* and HM *Revenue & Customs*. have sought to *target* such activities, which may be linked to *organized crime*. A major criticism of UK *law enforcement* in this area is that it frequently *targets* the 'foot soldiers' rather than the main culprits, i.e. its directing mind (hence, e.g. corresponding expression such as 'drug mule'); although there have been some initiatives to treat some *low-level* offenders as *victims* rather than culprits under *welfare* and *protection* schemes; as where women trafficked for prostitution (see *street offences* in *Touchstones*) have been given refuge. Often such victims are dependent on, e.g. *'gangmasters'*, or *fear* reprisals, *blackmail* and extortion; including against family members in their country of origin.

transparency

In order to ensure *accountability*, public affairs and matters of *justice* in particular should so far as possible be *open* and visible without the need to overcome excessive hurdles, as encapsulated in the principles of *open court,* giving of *reasons* and *freedom of information.* Certain matters may need to remain undisclosed in the interests of national *security*, or, e.g. to *protect* a *juvenile*. But this should not affect a principle requiring as much openness as possible and the need for an adequate explanation in those situations where it is less than clear to observers what is happening.

transport/transportation

(1) Road transport as regulated by *road traffic* law, especially that part of it which applies to heavy goods vehicles (HGVs). **(2)** **'The transport'** is used to describe the prison van (see also *prisoner*/escort) (aka 'the meatwagon' or, re the police, 'black maria'). **(3)** **'Transports'** has dark undertones due to its use to describe railway transports of Jewish people and others to Nazi concentration camps in the 1930s and 1940s: see an article about those transports at watersidepress.co.uk **(4) Transportation of offenders** to *penal* colonies: see *Touchstones* (and also for *Tolpuddle Martyrs*).

treason See *Touchstones*

treatment

Particularly from the 1970s, the idea that some offenders required treatment (as if suffering from a medical condition) or that there was a need to resolve 'social deficits' was to the fore. Although not entirely abandoned, especially re **drug treatment** (see *drugs*), *mental impairment, sex offending, welfare*-based approaches, aspects of the rehabilitative ideal (see *rehabilitation*) and *therapy*, 'treatment' now plays a more muted role and the **medicalisation of offending** tends to attract criticism. Hence debates as to whether courts should follow a **treatment model** as opposed to a *punishment* model, or whether there are even better forms of *offender management* whilst people 'recover' and stop offending. See, e.g. *Offender Rehabilitation and Treatment: Effective Programmes and Policies to Reduce Re-offending* (2002), McGuire J, John Wiley.

trial

The central stage within the CJS process is the **trial of an alleged offender**, i.e. by a judge (aka **trial judge**) and jury at the *Crown Court* or by magistrates. Hence **trial court** (aka 'court of first instance') as opposed to *appeal* court. A trial follows the same pattern in both types of court, increasingly so with a bringing into line of *criminal procedure*: see that entry. The accused is asked to enter a plea to each count in the *indictment* or to each *charge*. The *presumption of innocence* applies and there must be a **fair trial**: see *fair/fairness; human rights*. The prosecutor must prove the allegation to the required standard of proof: see *evidence*; failing which the accused must be discharged. He or she is not obliged to give *evidence* in his or her own *defence* but a court may nowadays draw appropriate *inferences* if he or she declines to explain matters: see *silence*/'right to silence'. Many cases turn into guilty pleas once they reach court: hence the expression **'cracked trial'** to describe one that 'caves in' at a late stage (whether following the procrastinations of the accused or, e.g. because a *witness* may have disappeared, died or been intimidated); thus disrupting the court *list/listing*. Hence initiatives to avoid such an outcome; including *case management* and credit for a timely guilty plea (see *sentence/sentencing*). Attempts are made to expedite trials, but in some places there can still be an appreciable delay before a trial starts, especially in larger Crown Court centres. For **election for trial**: see *allocation and sending*; **judge-only trial**: see *judge*; **jury trial** (aka **trial by jury**): see *jury*. **Re-trial** means either: **(1)** a second trial where this has been ordered by an *appeal* court, usually by the *Court of Appeal* or *High Court*; or **(2)** in some cases after the accused has secured an earlier *acquittal*: see *double jeopardy*. **Trial by peers** signifies trial in the Crown Court by a jury of ordinary *citizens* or by magistrates as their representatives. The exceptions are **trial by a district judge** and a **judge-only trial**: see *judge* for both; and **trial by peers**, i.e. before the *House of Lords,* which any member charged with offences can demand, even if this might now be unlikely to survive *human rights* or other challenges. There are no modern instances of such an occurrence. For sentence of death passed by the House on one of its members, see *Ferrers, Earl* in *Touchstones*. **Trial Unit**: see *Crown Prosecution Service*. **Trial within a trial**: aspects of the trial determined by the judge/magistrates separate to the main issue, i.e. of guilt (when the **trial proper** is placed on hold). Examples are evidentiary rulings (see *evidence*), issues of *mental impairment* and *Newton hearings* (see *Touchstones*). For **mode of trial**, see *allocation and sending*. For **pre-trial matters**, see *case management; direction*.

truth

Witnesses swear (see *oath*) or affirm (see *affirmation*) to 'tell the truth, the whole truth and nothing but the truth'; but the English trial process is not a search for truth as such, rather an encounter between opponents: see *adversarial system* in *Touchstones*. Deliberately failing to be truthful in some 'material particular', i.e. one germane to the *case* or *evidence* being given may amount to the offence of *perjury*. Note also the idea of **truth and reconciliation** as originally practised in South Africa and that has been a model for repairing *harm* and achieving closure in a number of places since, including Northern Ireland where it continues re The *Troubles* (see *Touchstones*).

TV Licensing (TVL)

The licensing authority with regard to TV licence offences and the authorised public *prosecutor* in this regard: see *prosecutor/prosecution* and tvlicensing.co.uk

'two strikes' See *Three strikes* in *Touchstones*.

U

unduly lenient sentence

The *Attorney General* (AG) may refer what he or she believes to be such a sentence to the *Court of Appeal* (CA). The power is restricted to certain more *serious* offences as gradually extended over the years. It applies to all those which are *indictable only* and to some *either way offences* specified in delegated *legislation*. The sentence must 'fall outside the range of sentences which the judge, applying his or her mind to all the relevant factors, could reasonably consider appropriate'. Such factors have been fleshed out by CA *rulings*. Requests to consider referring a sentence may stem, e.g. from the prosecuting authority, the victim or his or her family, Members of Parliament, *campaign* groups or *citizens*. There is a *time limit* of 28 days from the date of sentence for the AG to apply to the CA to allow for the necessary court papers to be obtained and the *legal* situation to be considered.

unfit

Unfit for the purpose is a phrase used: (**1**) to describe goods, etc. that do not meet *trading standards* due to their poor quality or state; which if **unfit food** or certain other items may also be 'condemned' by officials or a court (known as a 'destruction order') as well as leading to prosecution; (**2**) by *Home Secretary*, John Reid on becoming Home Secretary (2006) to describe the Home Office; that triggered a review leading to the creation of the MOJ and splitting-off of Home Office responsibilities in 2007. **Unfit to plead**: not mentally fit to enter a plea to a charge: see *mental impairment*. **Unfit to stand trial**, i.e. to withstand the rigours of trial and possible punishment. It is rare for someone to fall into this category, the more serious the offence the more circumspect the courts are likely to be (in the *Crown Court* the matter is one for the judge rather than the jury). **Unfit for further punishment** when compassionate release may be granted (as occurred re Ernest Saunders, one of the *Guinness Four*: see *Touchstones*). Provisions of *road traffic* law make it an offence to drive whilst **unfit through drink or drugs**; or use an **unfit vehicle** on a public road. The term is also used (**3**) in a looser sense to signify failings and describe people thought to be unfit for a given role, such as an **'unfit mother'** (see generally *child protection*) or someone who is deemed to be **'unfit to keep an animal'** (see *animal*).

United Kingdom (UK)

The **prefix UK** is used re various authorities, powers and responsibilities which apply across **the whole of the UK**, including Scotland and Northern Ireland, rather than just *England and Wales* (see *Touchstones*); such as national *security*. The UK should also be contrasted with (the broader) Britain, the Channel Islands and the Isle of Man. Care is sometimes need as definitions can vary in scope geographically re different legislative measures. Examples of UK wide functions include the **UK Atomic Energy Authority/Constabulary (UKAEA/C); UK Immigration Service (UKIS)** responsible for the *detection* of *immigration* offences and related *law enforcement* operating mainly at ports as part of the UK *Border Agency*; **UK Internet Crime Forum**: see *cybercrime* in *Touchstones*; and **UK Visas**: see *Border Agency*.

Unlock See *Touchstones*; **unused prosecution material** See *disclosure*.

V

value/values

(**1**) Other things being equal, the **financial value of an offence**, i.e. the loss caused by an offence such as *theft*, *fraud* or *criminal damage* will affect its *seriousness* and mode of trial (see *allocation and sending*); and similarly the notional value of an *in-*

jury, i.e. its extent (see also *compensation*). (**2**) Note, also, **value for money (VFM)**: the principle that expenditure should be matched by 'sound value' or 'best value'; which has operated re public services from the 1980s onwards, ultimately spreading to the CJS; where it has impacted to differing extents according to the agency/service concerned (and consistent with *justice*-based considerations); generally by comparison of outcomes over time linked to cost-benefit *data*. (**3**) The values of CJS practitioners are one key to sustaining *confidence* in that system and preventing abuse. They include such things as decency, *equality of treatment*, ethics, honesty, human dignity, integrity, propriety and in a *human rights* era, fairness (see *fair/fairness*). For a classic account of their importance, see *Criminal Justice and the Pursuit of Decency* (1994), Rutherford A; *Police Ethics* (2nd. edn 2006), Miller S et al (both Waterside Press). (**4**) Similarly the values (or lack thereof) of offenders and the idea of **instilling values**.

vehicle rectification scheme (VRS) See *road traffic*

vendetta

(**1**) Non-technical term for retaliation based on revenge or the need to obtain some kind of (usually unlawful) 'payback'; that may be of longstanding origins, have 'simmered', and might involve a *gang*, feud with a neighbour, or *organized crime*. (**2**) More loosely, any lawful, age-old reprisals after a stand-off or difference of view.

venue/plea before venue See *allocation and sending*

verdict

(**1**) The outcome of a criminal trial, i.e. a **jury verdict**, that of the judge in a **judge-only trial** (see judge) or a **verdict of magistrates**, i.e. whether the accused person is guilty or not guilty. (**2**) Similarly, the outcome of other proceedings like an *inquest*, i.e. a **coroner's verdict** (or the **verdict of an inquest jury**). (**3**) More loosely, any decision arrived at after considering competing versions of events, priorities, arguments, etc. Hence, re (1): **alternative verdict** which can be returned in certain situations by a jury or occasionally magistrates, i.e. conviction for an offence other than that originally set out in the *indictment* or charge usually of a lesser and/or similar offence; **majority verdict**: a jury must be unanimous, but the judge can accept a majority verdict if at least ten of 12 jurors are agreed (adjusted re a reduced jury). This can happen if the jury has had time to reach unanimity and the judge thinks this will not occur. Magistrates decide by a majority and any disagreement is not made public. For **medial verdict** and other historical verdicts: see *The Criminal Jury Old and New: Jury Power from Early Times to the Present Day* (2004), Hostettler J, Waterside Press.

victim

Anyone who suffers directly as a result of a criminal offence, i.e. the person injured or whose property is stolen, damaged, destroyed or lost. Hence, also, the (non-technical) term **secondary victim** for someone who suffers at one remove, such as a family member, which is also used where they lose income when, e.g. a partner is sent to prison, or the offender has an *addiction*. Note also the idea of **grooming a victim** (as someone might coax an animal), especially re sexual offences and/or *vulnerable people*. A **victim liaison officer (VLO)** is a *police* officer (usually) who is a go-between re the victim and officers involved in *investigation* or *prosecution*. A **victim personal statement (VPS)** (aka **victim impact statement**) is one made by the victim for the attention of the judge or magistrates at the sentencing stage which describes the effect that the offence had on the victim and his or her family, including the anger, anxiety and stress that it caused and/or the extent of any physical, mental, emotional or financial *harm*. This does not affect the sentence, but ensures that the victim is not excluded from the criminal justice process. The **Victims Charter** (1990) was the original, Government-led initiative, which helped to trigger improvements. There is a **Victims' Advisory Panel/Commissioner** (yet to be fully implemented); and a **victims' surcharge** (£15 per case in 2008) which is added to each *fine* imposed by a court in England and Wales; to fund improved services for victims and *compensation* schemes. Re *domestic violence* or *abuse,* victims may be called 'survivors'. Central to the **victims' movement** is **Victim Support (VS)**: a key example of the work of the *voluntary sector* and *volunteers.* VS is an independent *charity* helping people affected by crime. It provides free, confidential support to *help* victims deal with their crime-related experience, whether or not the crime is *reported*. Victims are contacted by members of local branches who can provide them, their family and friends with *guidance. Citizens* can also use **Victim Supportline** and/or volunteer to assist VS by way of practical *help and support*, making a donation or shopping online. VS also employs full-time staff. From 2008, various local member charities across England and Wales began merging to form a single, nationwide body. VS is in contact with over 1.25 million victims and witnesses each year. See, further, www.victimsupport.org.uk

video
(1) A **video link** is a real-time TV link, usually meaning from a cell to a courtroom; but also between other separate locations. Live links are regularly used for the purposes of certain *remand* hearings; as well as in cases involving *children* or where a *witness* is abroad. **(2)** A number of offences have been solved or prosecuted as a result of the **videos of amateur cameramen**. Examples include: the case of a police officer with 24 years' service who was initially sentenced to two months *imprisonment* after being filmed on video kicking and punching a young man in the street (reduced to a *community sentence* on *appeal* to the Crown Court following a 500 signature local petition)(2002); that of a Leeds police officer who was imprisoned for 21 months after being filmed punching a man in the stomach (2003); and incidents of 'happy-slapping' when an offender or associate has filmed random physical attacks, in one instance involving *manslaughter* (2008). **(3)** The online **virtual viral video** is a means of spreading a computer virus, see generally *hacking*. **(4)** **Video parades** and **Video Identity Parade Electronic Recording** is transforming police *identification* parades.

vigilante/vigilance
A **vigilante** is someone 'on the look out' for offences and offenders (i.e. exercising **vigilance**); a risk being that he or she may 'overstep the mark' and take the law into his or her own hands, possibly leading to *violence* or 'mob violence'; such has occurred in the UK in modern times, e.g. re some known paedophiles. It may also occur in a slightly different context when formalised but unlawful *summary justice* is meted out (see, e.g. the reference to 'punishment beatings' within The *Troubles* in *Touchstones*). The **Guardian Angels**, a self-styled USA street patrol group, found it within its 'remit' to visit the UK and offer its services some years ago. For an illustration of excess, see **Ku Klux Klan (KKK)** (and **lynch law** in that entry) in *Touchstones*. The CJS renders this kind of **vigilantism** unnecessary and involves *citizens* in legitimate crime prevention/crime reduction initiatives, *Neighbourhood Watch* and similar schemes. Note also the rationale behind Rule 45 (see *prison*) and *witness protection* schemes.

violence

Provisions exist concerning various aspects of the CJS re violent offenders (and, similarly, *sex offenders*). There is no offence of 'violence' as such, rather a range of *assaults, murder, manslaughter,* etc. Statutes such as the Criminal Justice Act 2003 contain lists of such offences for given statutory purposes. For some other related entries see, e.g. *danger/dangerousness; domestic violence; Multi-Agency Public Protection Arrangements; indeterminate sentence for public protection* (ISPP); *risk*; and *serial killer.* The Criminal Justice and Immigration Act 2008 introduced a **violent offender order (VVO)**. This is a *civil* 'preventative order' based on qualifying offences re which an application can also be made for its variation, renewal or discharge. The Act lists the kind of conditions which can be made part of VVO or **interim VVO** and sets out the duties of people subject to such an order, e.g. to notify the police of personal details and changes to them. As with other *civil behaviour orders* (CBOs), non-compliance is an offence.

visibility See *accountability; openness; police/*'covert policing'; *transparency*

visit

(1) One to see a prisoner: see *Independent Monitoring Board; prisoner.* **(2)** a *euphemism* (see *Touchstones*) for a *raid* by the police, etc. **(3)** One by a *burglar*, etc.

voluntary/volunteer

The **voluntary bill of indictment** is a now largely outmoded (but extant) way of *commencing criminal proceedings* in the Crown Court. In broad terms, the **voluntary sector** is that part of the *wider criminal justice family* (see *Touchstones*) that largely involves non-*statutory* organizations, *charities* and the like. Contrast the use of the term **volunteer** which may imply unpaid involvement but with statutory or government sponsored elements, e.g. *magistrates, police/*'special constables', members of *Independent Monitoring Boards, Victim Support* or the *Witness Service.* **Voluntary drug-testing**: see *drug; prisoner.*

vulnerable people, witnesses, etc

CJS strategies encompass various measures for the *protection* of **vulnerable people**, e.g. *witnesses, informers,* children, those troubled with *mental impairment* or *domestic violence.* Hence also **vulnerable prisoner/Vulnerable Prisoner Unit** see *prison; prisoner.* There are schemes to *target* **vulnerable families**: see, e.g. nspcc.org.uk

W

waiting time

That between events or stages within the criminal justice process (in some instances aka **'response times'**); by reference to which the *interests of justice, good practice, service delivery, effectiveness and efficiency, standards* or *delay* can be measured. Examples include the time between: **(1)** a *citizen* making an *emergency call* and police attending a *crime scene*; **(2)** someone *reporting* an offence and an *investigation*; **(3)** the time taken for the CPS to make a decision concerning prosecution; **(4)** *commencing criminal proceedings* and the trial and/or conclusion of such proceedings (note, also, **fast-tracking** mentioned under *preliminary hearing*); **(5)** that between a *referral* and an *assessment, report,* etc; **(6)** reception into prison and *prisoner/*'allocation' or a *prisoner*/'sentence plan'; (**7**) an *appeal, complaint* or application and it being dealt with, e.g. to the *Parole Board* or *Prisons and Probation Ombudsman* (PPO).

Wandsworth Prison

The largest prison in London which can hold just over 1450 prisoners. It has a separate *vulnerable prisoner unit* (VPU) (the **Onslow Centre**) holding some 330 prisoners. Outside London, only Liverpool Prison compares in size, both being amongst the largest prisons in Western Europe (but see *prison*/'Titan prison'). It was built in 1851 (see generally *Victorian aspects* in *Touchstones*). The cells/main residential areas (see *prison*/'wings and landing') are still housed in the original buildings; albeit with extensive refurbishment, including in-cell sanitation, privacy screens for cells occupied by more than one prisoner and in-cell electricity. The five wings of the main **Heathfield Centre** are used variously for: over 100 prisoners serving *life imprisonment* (or related *remand* prisoners); *drug-free* prisoners; induction into prison and 'first-nighters'; *prisoner*/'assessment'; and *prisoner*/'allocation'. Wandsworth was the venue for some high profile executions (see generally *capital punishment* in *Touchstones* and, e.g. *Bentley, Derek* there); and was the last UK prison at which a gallows facility was formerly 'mothballed'. Outline information about all prisons in England and Wales is available via a 'Locate a Prison' facility at hmprisonservice.gov.uk

war

A state of war (or other *emergency*) may allow certain offences to thrive, due e.g. to fast-moving events, shifting *priorities*, secrecy, opportunities to obscure *motives*, increased mobility, access to *weapons* and exposure to *violence*. It may also (be used to) justify *summary* powers and, e.g. general *restrictions of liberty* (such as a curfew) and the internment of aliens or dissenters. Economic *controls* (such as rationing) may boost the *black economy* (see *Touchstones*); and encourage racketeering or looting. Periods following wars may be 'lawless'. The Napoleonic Wars led to vagrancy and unemployment amongst impoverished and often lame soldiers returning home to a depressed economy. It is often said that the Second World War led to a loosening of *values* and hardening of attitudes, and judges 'cracking down' on *violence* especially (see *Bentley, Derek* in *Touchstones* which can be viewed as a landmark in this regard). Surviving offenders against the *Crown* during the English Civil War (1641-1652) were later 'rounded-up' and executed following the Restoration of the monarchy: see, e.g. *The Tyrannicide Brief: The Story of the Man who sent Charles I to the Scaffold* (2005), Roberstons G, Chatto & Windus (which also tells the story of radical *lawyer* John Cook). Notoriously, the **Iraq War** (or 'conflict': see *euphemism* in *Touchstones*) has left ongoing questions re its fundamental legality. **War crimes** include: (**1**) any offence so styled committed under cover of war, e.g. involving genocide or 'crimes against humanity', whereby those in charge of events or carrying out atrocities are fixed with criminal responsibility, before a national court, special tribunal or, increasingly, the *International Criminal Court* (see further *global/international aspects*). A key point of reference is the **Geneva Convention(s)**: as to which see specialist works; or (**2**) in the UK, offences under the **War Crimes Act 1991** when courts have extra-territorial *jurisdiction,* which is unlimited in time. Only one prosecution has run its course, of Anthony Sawoniuk, a 78-year-old former railway worker who in 1991 was sentenced to *life imprisonment* for *murdering* of two Jewish women in 1942 (he died in prison in 2005: see *deaths in custody*). Note also **war terminology** (aka 'battle terminology') as when CJS aims are couched in such language, e.g. **'fighting crime',** 'war on drugs' or 'enemy within' (see also *demonisation* in *Touchstones*).

warning

(1) The idea of **warning an offender** (or potential offender) is as old as *policing* itself. From the 1970s onwards, the **formal police warning** became the *caution*. The police continue giving warnings (or advice) 'on the street' (see generally *street* in *Touchstones*). Since 1998, for juveniles, there has been a separate system of **warnings and reprimands**, used progressively, as an *alternative to prosecution*, possibly linked to *referrals* to appropriate agencies/services. But note also the 'higher level' system of conditional *cautions* for young people introduced by the Criminal Justice and Immigration Act 2008. (2) A **public warning** is a general warning, e.g. re a hazard, *threat, health and safety* when an *emergency* exists or, e.g. not to approach a *dangerous offender*, or to be aware of a given type of offence that is becoming prevalent (see *vigilance*), or re the effects of the perils of *drugs, alcohol, gambling* or driving (see *road traffic*).

warrant

(1) A document containing an order for the physical arrest of a person or for his or premises to be searched and/or items to be seized; and addressed, e.g 'To all police constables'; or (2) otherwise containing the details of a court order, e.g. a warrant committing someone to prison and ordering the *prison governor* to hold the person concerned for a fixed period, aka a **committal warrant**. Various types of warrants can be issued by magistrates or judges (the latter being known as **'bench warrants'**). Hence, e.g. terms such as **warrant of arrest** and **search warrant**, the latter, e.g. to search premises, e.g. for *drugs*, contraband, stolen property (see generally *theft*), etc. **Warrant 'backed' for bail**: when issuing a warrant of arrest (below) a court can also order that, once the person concerned has been arrested, he or she must be given *bail* in accordance with terms specified by the court and **endorsed on the warrant** (i.e. written on it, usually or metaphorically on the reverse or 'back'). The arresting officer must make an appropriate record when executing any warrant. A **warrant card** is a special form of *identity card* issued to police officers and which should be shown whenever authority is exercised unless the officer is already known or in uniform. Provided that the offence carries a possible sentence of *imprisonment* a warrant of arrest can be issued in some circumstances; usually if other methods would prove unproductive (e.g. if the accused has no fixed abode (NFA), lacks *community* ties, or has failed to surrender to *bail*). There are similar powers re a **witness warrant**, albeit rarely used, but sometimes necessary. A **warrant in the first instance** is one issued at the outset of a case, not, e.g. in *response* to a failure to attend court.

weapon

Quite apart from any offence which may be committed with a weapon, such as grievous bodily harm (see *assault*) or *murder,* there is an offence of **carrying an offensive weapon** (without lawful excuse: it would not apply e.g. to the *military* or an **authorised firearms officer**), attracting a maximum penalty of 14 years *imprisonment*. Some weapons are offensive without further proof (i.e. 'offensive *per se*'), such as a gun or dagger. Virtually anything can become an offensive weapon such as a pole or a kitchen knife (a question of fact depending on the intention of the user: see generally *mens rea*). The police tend to regard some items as attracting suspicion, such as bolt-cutters, chains and screwdrivers. Weapons are often associated with *gangs*. **Gun crime** is regulated by a sequence of **Firearms Acts** and varying levels of prohibition or *restriction*, extending from the outright banning of 'high end' automatic weapons to the use of certain guns in controlled environments such as gun clubs, down to the use of air pistols on private property by people above a fixed *age*. Note also the impact of the *Hungerford Massacre* (see *Touchstones*). Similarly, there are severe restrictions on **replica firearms** re which there have been various convictions for operating **gun factories** offering 'conversion services', i.e. into real guns. **Knives** have also been a cause of increasing *concern*, being carried by young people (including schoolchildren: see *school*) in particular. See, e.g. antiknifecrime.co.uk. Certain **bladed weapons** are specifically banned, such as machetes, combat knives and (from 2008) Samurai swords. All such measures are reinforced by the Violent Crime Reduction Act 2007 and similar *legislation*: see homeoffice.gov.uk under 'gun-and-knife-powers'. Note also self-*help and support* bodies such as **Mothers Against Knives** founded in 2005 by two concerned Middlesbrough parents, Barbara Lesley Dunne and Councillor Joan McTigue: see mothersagainstknives.tripod.com **Biological weapons** can spread disease (e.g. by releasing a virus). When in 2005, one of several 'ricin plots' to 'destabilise society' was interrupted in Manchester, detective constable Stephen Oake was stabbed. Kamel Bourgass (an illegal *immigrant*) was convicted of murder (2004) and later *conspiracy* to cause a public *nuisance by* using poison and explosives: see also generally *Police Memorial* in *Touchstones*. Dedicated provisions also *control* **radiological weapons** and substances: see specialist works. Note also the use of **dogs as weapons**, especially by *gangs,* Dangerous Dogs Act 1991 (and later *legislation*) outlawing *dangerous* breeds such as the pit bull terrier, Japanesae tosa and Dogo.

welfare

The welfare of victims, witnesses, offenders, people who are at-risk of offending (and to an extent those working within the CJS, including in terms of their *health and safety*) has always been a consideration and has come to the fore from time-to-time in different contexts. It was the rationale for the formation of the Probation Service (see *Rainer Crime Concern* in *Touchstones*) and is a guiding, fundamental and longstanding principle in relation to *children* and *young persons* (see *welfare principle*, below). Certain agencies may be referred to as 'welfare services', particularly *social services* (even though they may nowadays have some *law enforcement* functions); whilst many charities and *help and support* groups may also be characterised in this way. The **welfare principle** is the guiding principle of *youth justice* and child care that now operates alongside statutory purposes of sentencing. It is contained in the (still extant) section 44 Children and Young Persons Act 1933 (CYPA 1933) (and whether, e.g. the juvenile concerned appears as a defendant or as a witness and in whatever court, not simply the youth court). It states that: 'Every court in dealing with a child or young person … either as an offender or otherwise shall have regard to the welfare of the child or young person'. This must now be reconciled with the principal statutory purpose of youth justice (see under *youth justice*) in the Crime and Disorder Act 1998 (as reaffirmed in 2008) and various strands of official *guidance*.

white collar crime See *Touchstones*

witness

Someone who has observed given events and can give *evidence* about them to the police and a court, i.e. concerning the facts and who may be styled a **lay witness** (an ordinary member of the public); **prosecution witness**: see generally prosecution;

defence witness: see generally, *defence*; or **police witness** (a police officer giving evidence obtained in that capacity; but this term may be used for prosecution witnesses more generally). All these can only give evidence of facts whereas an **expert witness** (see further *expert*) can express his or her *opinion* concerning material issues in a case that he or she is qualified to hold, e.g. in the fields of medicine (see *medical aspects, pathology, forensics, science* or *technology*; with the prior *leave* of the court. A police officer may be an acceptable expert, e.g. re the state of a vehicle where he or she is a professional *road traffic examiner*. Expert witnesses have been the subject of criticism in modern times, including due to the case of Sir Roy Meadows, an expert in paediatrics whose explanations of the causes of injuries to or deaths of children contributed to a number of *miscarriages of justice*. Expert evidence is not relied on when a jury or magistrates can properly draw their own conclusion. **Interfering with a witness** (aka **tampering**) is an offence (as is *obstructing the course of justice*); and also a ground for refusing *bail*. In the courtroom, witnesses can use notes or a previous statement for the purposes of **refreshing their memory** although how and why a witness recalls events is likely to affect his or her general credibility. Some witnesses do not not **come up to proof** (give the evidence or version of it that it was anticipated they would); others may be **hostile witnesses** i.e. technically 'hostile' rather than physically or verbally so; although they can sometimes be the latter as well. A hostile witness is one who acts counter to and inconsistently with an earlier account and who thereby shows a form of *bias*: see texts on *evidence*. **Testimony** is short for **witness testimony**: see *testimony*. **Witness care** involves witnesses being properly treated and looked after whilst performing a public duty. Hence the **Witness Service (WS)**: a nationwide service catering for the needs of witnesses under the auspices of *Victim Support*, which states that many witnesses 'feel worried about going to court, regardless of whether or not they were the victim of the crime'. WS gives care, information and *help and support* to witnesses, victims, their families and friends when they go to court; whether to give evidence for the *prosecution* or *defence*; special care being provided for **child witnesses**. WS operates via full-time paid and volunteer staff who provide and facilitate *help and support* to witnesses by arranging: someone to talk to in confidence; a chance to see the courtroom before a case starts; information about CJS procedures; a quiet place for witnesses to wait; someone to accompany a witness into the courtroom; practical assistance (e.g. with expense forms); access to people who can answer questions; and debriefing after the experience of being in court. The service is free and independent of the police, courts, etc. Police **witness protection schemes** operate if an *assessment* shows that a witness would suffer *threats,* intimidation*, harassment, violence* or other unlawful pressures and in advanced situations *video-links* may be used, safe houses, armed guards, a change of *identity*, or if the witness is in prison arrangements for him or her to be on *prison*/'Rule 45'. Note also the special arrangements that exist in relation to an *informer*. Reasonably incurred **witness costs and expenses** are reimbursed from *public funds* re prosecution witnesses and, where there is an *acquittal, defence* witnesses (otherwise the defence normally pays for its own witnesses and may be ordered to repay to the public purse the full *costs* of the prosecution). **Witness statement** is the description given to one made by a witness, usually meaning out-of-court and in writing. It is signed by the witness stating that its contents are true. Subject to certain conditions it is admissible in *evidence*; or it may be an **agreed witness statement**, or possibly incorporated in a formal *admission*. Such statements are often used re non-contentious matters.

women

Many issues of criminal justice have focused on or around women: in relation to issues of gender (see *discrimination*), over-representation amongst *prisoners*, under representation in the CJS, or unfair or unequal treatment (see *fair/fairness; equality*). Women figure amongst the leading penal reformers (see *reform*), as with Beatrice Webb and Elizabeth Fry; but it was 2007 before there was a woman *Home Secretary*, Jacqui Smith and Attorney General, Baroness Scotland. There have been several other CJS-oriented women junior *Ministers of State*. Dame Barbara Mills QC was the Director of Public Prosecutions (DPP) from 1992–98 and previously Director of the Serious Fraud Office (SFO)(see *fraud*)(and has held other senior offices); believed to be the first woman in such a senior position. Women magistrates, judges, solicitors, barristers and other CJS practitioners have all increased in number significantly in modern times. The first woman *Law Lord* was Lady Hale (2004). The first woman chief constable was Della Cannings (2002) in North Yorkshire. Julia Hodson was appointed in Nottingham in 2008. The first in Scotland was Norma Graham (Fife, 2008). Certain agencies/services such as HM Prison Service (HMPS) and the police are regarded as still having macho cultures and 'glass ceilings' despite increases in their complements of women. Some commentators have argued that women's issues tend to lie hidden, see, e.g. *Invisible Women: What's Wrong with Women's Prisons?* (1998), Devlin A, Waterside Press which criticised **regimes for women prisoners** (see, generally, *prison*) as 'a female version of those for men'. Leading commentators include Professor Betsy Stanko who worked for the *Metropolitan Police Service* (MPS) on studies such as 'Violence and Risk' and Professor Pat Carlen's whose books include *Women and Punishment: Gender, Crime and Justice* (1987) (with Anne Worrall), Open University Press; and *Analysing Women's Imprisonment* (2004) (with Anne Worrall), Willan Publishing. In *Eve Was Framed: Women and British Justice* (1993), Helena (Baroness) Kennedy offered a critique of the British legal system focusing on the treatment of women by courts; looking also at the prejudices of judges, the misconceptions of jurors, labyrinths of procedures and *media/press* influence. For further examples, see *Black Women's Experiences of Criminal Justice, Race, Gender and Class: A Discourse on Disadvantage* (2nd. edn 2003), Chigwada-Bailey, R, Waterside Press. **Women in Prison (WIP)** is a *charity* working with women at *risk* of *imprisonment*, in prison or undergoing *reintegration and resettlement*, *education* and training and/or development. It seeks to educate *citizens* and policy-makers re women in the CJS and promotes *alternatives to custody* for women, in particular: see womeninprison.org.uk

Woolf Report; **Woolmington v. DPP**: See *Touchstones* for both entries

work/working/works

Unemployment is a key *cause of crime* and hence many work-related training schemes in *prison* and in the *community*. For **'what works'**, See *Touchstones*. **Work and pensions** is shorthand for *Department of Work and Pensions,* which has its own *law enforcement* and *prosecution* functions. **Working together** is another way of describing *partnership* and a clue to its origins, which lie in various forms of *multi-agency* working. Hence also **'Working Together to Cut Crime and Deliver Justice: A Strategic Plan for 2008 -20011'** (Cm 7247, 2007): the title of a plan produced by the Office for Criminal Justice Reform (OCJR) (see *reform*) on behalf of the Home Office, MOJ and Office of the Attorney General. A copy of the plan, which is regularly updated, is available at cjsonline.gov.uk

Wormwood Scrubs

Example of a large, busy London prison which, like many of the UK's older prison establishments, was constructed mainly in Victorian times (see generally *Victorian aspects* in *Touchstones*), mainly between 1875 and 1891. In 1902 its last woman prisoner (see generally *women*) was transferred to *Holloway Prison*. In 1922, one wing was turned into a *borstal* (see *Touchstones*). During World War II, Wormwood Scrubs was used by the War Department. A hospital wing (see *prison*/'healthcare') was opened in 1994 and, in 1996, two main wings were refurbished and a fifth wing added (see generally *prison*/'wings and landings'). It has an operational capacity of just under 1,300 prisoners as a local category B prison accepting 'all suitable male prisoners over 21 from courts within [its] catchment area', whether as *remand* prisoners or those serving terms of *imprisonment*. Brief information re all prisons in England and Wales is available via a 'Locate a Prison' facility at hmprisonservice.gov.uk.

wrap

Drug wrap See *drugs*; **'on a wrap'**: a colloquial term for 'charged with an offence': see *arrest; charge;* **'take the wrap'**: be punished, usually whilst others evade this.

written plea of guilty See *plea*; **written statement** See *witness statement*

Y

young

A word that can signify different things in different contexts. Hence **young offender: (1)** strictly speaking, one aged 18 or more but less than 21 years of age; or **(2)** more informally anyone below 21 years of age, extending to older juvenile offenders below the age of 18 in particular; **young offender institution (YOI)**: the standard form of *custodial* provision for offenders aged 15 to 21 (with a secure training centre (STC) for younger offenders: see specialist works); other than where they are/can lawfully be held in a *prison*. YOIs are scheduled for replacement but this appears to be 'on hold'; **young people** (as a whole): informal term used in CJS, YJS and other circles without reference to any specific age group; usually when discussing issues, services, etc. in relation to children and and younger *adults* in general; **young person**: someone aged 14 to 17 years inclusive: (one of the two categories of juvenile under the *Children and Young Persons Act 1969*; the other being a child aged 10 to 13).

youth

(1) For many purposes, 'youth' is synonymous with 'juvenile' (the latter term having survived changes in statutory terminology although both are in general use). **(2)** A word that is sometimes used imprecisely (as in **youth worker**) to refer to **young people as a whole** (see, further, above), i.e. without regard to close definition or legality. **Youth court**: that to which alleged juvenile offenders are brought and whose *administration* occurs under the umbrella of the magistrates' court (but separately from it). The youth court replaced the juvenile court in 1991; when the upper age-limit for someone being brought before this court rather than the adult court was raised from 17 to 18. Hence also **Youth Court Benchbook**: see *Judicial Studies Board*. The court consists of specially trained magistrates who belong to a statutory **youth court panel**. Most first time juvenile offenders are now dealt with under the scheme of *warnings and reprimands* or, if they do appear in the youth court, a *referral* *order* to a *youth offending panel* (YOP)(below); unless (in broad terms) the offence is too *serious*. Youth court panel magistrates are appointed by local Bench Training and Development Committees (BTDCs) (with a comparable arrangement in London). **Youth court sentences** are dedicated sentences re which the Criminal Justice and Immigration Act 2008 introduced **youth rehabilitations orders (YROs)**, a new replacement generic *community sentence* within which a range of requirements can be attached. For these sentences, **youth custody** (instead of *imprisonment* for those aged 15 or over) and a number of pending and significant changes, see readily accessible information at yjb.gov.uk Note also the role of the **youth offending team (YOT)** (below). Maximum fines are linked to age and have lower ceilings. Often, a *parent* or *guardian* can be held to account, e.g. to ensure a fine is paid; and see *parenting order.* Certain *grave crimes* are dealt with by the *Crown Court.*

Youth Crime Action Plan (YCAP) (sometimes Y-cap) is a government plan to tackle youth crime that has appeared in various forms, including from 2008 as a comprehensive strategy-cum-consultation paper: 'a cross-government analysis of what further we need to do to tackle youth crime'. It sets out a 'triple track' approach of *enforcement* and *punishment* re unacceptable behaviour (see generally *acceptable behaviour*), 'non-negotiable support and challenge where it is most needed', and better and earlier crime prevention. The 2008 YCAP emphasised a *welfare* approach, centring on proposals to: expand family *intervention* to some 20,000 families; remove *high risk* children from the streets at night; after-*school* patrols; democratic involvement in *reparation* projects; holding *parents* to account through *penal* sanctions if their children do not complete a sentence; placing a duty on *local authorities* to fund the *education* of young people in *custody* (hence giving them an incentive to find ways to reduce the number going to custody); and better support after *release* (see dcsf.gov.uk/publications/youthcrimeactionplan). YCAPs are prepared jointly by the MOJ, *Department For Children, Schools and Families* (DCSF) (see *children*) and Home Office with input from No.10 Downing Street. There also are duties placed on local areas to create and publish their own YCAPs. For the Independent Commission on Youth Crime and Anti-social Behaviour see police-foundation.org.uk (and its own website in due course).

Youth justice is the umbrella term for this area of CJS work (and also for wider matters of *fairness* and *justice* relating to young people: below); whilst **Youth Justice System** (YJS) describes that part of the CJS which operates in relation to *juveniles* as opposed to *adults.* Youth justice is sometimes regarded as extending beyond the YJS to cover any item affecting the development, education, upbringing and protection of young people, especially from *abuse* or exploitation; with an emphasis on training, personal development and *access to justice* as well as other public services. The YJS rests on the same broad tenets, structures and general laws as the adult CJS, with analogous approaches to *anti-social behaviour* though with many special provision, powers and variations. Sentencing has the same underlying rationale as for *adults* but is subject to special statutory purposes and more progressive, *tolerant* or *restorative* departures, methods and *welfare* considerations (see also earlier above). The **youth offending panel (YOP)** (aka 'referral order panel') is a local *statutory* panel which is responsible for devising an *action plan* in relation to a juvenile referred to it by the youth court, or otherwise because he or she is *at-risk.* The YOP operates under the auspices of a youth offending team (YOT) (below). It is comprised of **youth offending team** (see below) members and other people appointed to it, either generally or for a specific purpose. Its responsibilities include devising an *action plan* (sometimes called an '*intervention* plan') for the juvenile, and counselling him or her in the interests of crime prevention/crime reduction. The YOP deals with juveniles referred to it (see generally *referral*) by the *youth court* or other cases by way of *diversion* from the YJS, or generally in the interests of crime prevention/crime reduction. The action plan which it devises (above) may involve various forms of *intervention*, activities, treatment and further referrals to other agencies/services. Where a court-based referral fails (in effect if the juvenile is in breach of the order), the matter can be sent back to the youth court for sentencing in the ordinary way. **Youth justice team** is **(1)** A loose synonym for *youth offending team* below; or **(2)** a description applied to a wider group of practitioners involved in youth work.

Youth Justice Board (YJB)

The **YJB** is an executive non-departmental public body (NDPB); created by the *Crime and Disorder Act 1998*. Its 12 members are appointed by the *Justice Secretary*. It operates in conjunction with the MOJ, the *Department For Children, Schools and Families* (DCSF) and, as appropriate, the Home Office (its pre-2007 sponsor) (e.g. re *drugs; guns; knives*). It oversees the *Youth Justice System* (YJS), working to prevent offending and *re-offending* and to 'ensure that *custody* for [people under 18 years of age] is safe, secure, and addresses the causes of their *offending behaviour*'. It advises *Ministers of State* on the operation and standards of the YJS; monitors *performance*; purchases *custodial* places; identifies/promotes effective practice (see *effectiveness and efficiency*); makes grants to local authorities/others; commissions *research* and publishes information. YJB strategy is based on '*evidence*, where this exists', sound leadership, *partnership*, teamwork, *openness, respect* and trust. Its vision is of a YJS through which 'more offenders are caught, held to account and stop offending'; where juveniles receive support to lead crime-free lives; victims are better treated; and there is public *confidence*. The YJB has no power vis-a-vis the *youth court*.

youth offending team (YOT)

The local **YOT** (sometimes informally referred to as a **youth justice team (YJT)**) is the focus for *frontline, multi-agency* work with *juvenile* offenders or those at-*risk* of offending. It comprises representatives from the *Youth Justice System* (YJS) working in *partnership*: in *response* to orders of and *referrals* by the *youth court*. It works with young people as they mature into *adults*, by tackling *offending behaviour*, creating *action plans*, engaging as well in crime prevention/crime reduction and preparing youth-focused *assessments* using **ASSET** and now **ONSET** frameworks. The latter covers referral and assessment. It was designed by the Centre for Criminology at Oxford University and is fully described at yjb.gov.uk The YOT also arranges programmes and *resources* and manages or provides *community sentences, bail support* and *reparation* schemes. Each **YOT includes** a *social worker; probation officer; police officer*; nominees of the *health* authority and *education* authority; and other people and specialists as and when appropriate. It must perform various functions assigned to it in the local *Youth Justice Plan*. It organizes/co-ordinates referrals by courts to the *youth offending panel* (YOP). It is not directly involved in *warnings and reprimands*.

Z

zero tolerance and **Zito Trust** See *Touchstones* for both

The Waterside Press A-Z of Criminal Justice

If you found this *Pocket A-Z of Criminal Justice* useful you may also be interested in the larger work on which it is based. It contains separate sections on each of the major areas of criminal justice and includes some 25,000 entries and cross-references.

The Waterside Press A-Z of Criminal Justice

Bryan Gibson Consultants David Faulkner, Deborah Cheney, John Harding and Nick Stevens

The essential guide to **crime, punishment and criminal justice**. With entries spanning the entire realm of **crime, justice and penal affairs** – plus a Timeline of **events, laws, methods and trends** from 500 AD to date.

A **TOUCHSTONE** for practitioners, criminologists, lawyers, judges, magistrates, social historians, teachers, students, researchers and others who want to know about the bigger picture of criminal justice, that ranges from basic information to detailed analysis and points of reference.

A **UNIQUE HANDBOOK** that is encyclopaedic yet concise, contemporary and historical, practical, scientific and expert. An ideal fact-finder for libraries and readers right across the English-speaking and Common Law worlds.

A WORK THAT RANGES ACROSS THE CRIMINAL JUSTICE SPECTRUM from basic explanations to fundamental issues of crime and punishment.

A WEALTH OF INFORMATION which exists nowhere else in this readily accessible format and style. Among other things it covers:

abbreviations, acronyms, approaches, associations, barbarity, brutality, cases, codes, commentators, cultures, data, dates, debates, definitions, descriptions, developments, drugs, events, evidence, euphemisms, examples, experts, facts, frameworks, general principles, government departments, ground breaking advances, groups, guidelines, history, human rights, icons, ideas, initiatives, issues, judges, justice, juveniles, language, law, law and order, lawbreakers, lawyers, legislation, metaphors, media, methods, notoriety, offences, offenders, organized crime, outlaws, parole, policing, politicians, popular culture, practitioners, prisons, prisoners, probation, projects, proposals, punishments, questions, references, rules, regulations, restorative justice, sentencing, slang, shifts, statutes, symbols, systems, terms, terminology, texts, thinking, trailblazers, trials, tyrants, utterances, vice, victims, views and opinions, witnesses, working together, young offenders, youths, z-cars, zealots and zero-tolerance.

Details from WatersidePress.co.uk or email enquiries@watersidepress.co.uk

Acronyms and Abbreviations

The following list contains a selection of common short forms of words etc. Some of these can be extended using a prefix, suffix or inserting another letter, e.g. **C** for **community**, **J** for **joint**, **L** for **liaison**, **N** for **national**, **P** for **police**, **T** for **task**, **team** or **traffic**, **U** for **unit** and **UK** for **United Kingdom**. Numbers may signify 'second, etc. generation' as with **Holmes 2** and **MNTI2**. Usages may vary from place to place. Names may be used to signify a report, case, text or concept: see, e.g. the entries for **Archbold**; **Woolf**; **Woolmington**; **Bulger** and **Lawrence** in *Touchstones*. The italicised references below are to *Main Entries*. Most other items can also be found in their full form in that section except where the reader is directed to *Touchstones*.

AA (1) Alcoholics Anonymous; **(2)** appropriate adult; **(3)** double A-man, i.e. high-*risk* in terms of escaping from prison etc, and thus possibly wearing distinctive clothing.

ABC acceptable behaviour contract

ABH actual bodily harm

ACC assistant chief constable

accused (1) (used as a verb) accused of a criminal offence; **(2)** (used as a noun) the accused person.

ACECOP Association of Chief Executives and Chief Officers of Probation

ACPO Association of Chief Police Officers for England, Wales and Northern Ireland; Note also **ACPO(S)** where S = Scotland.

ACR (1) automatic conditional *release* from prison (being phased out); **(2)** automated crime recording, i.e. by the police.

ACRO the **ACPO** Criminal Records Office

Act Act of Parliament

AD absolute discharge

ADs added days (re *prison*/discipline')

AEAC Atomic Energy Authority Constabulary (or **UKAEAC**): see ukaea.org.uk

AEO attachment of earnings order

AFR automated fingerprint recognition

AG (or A-G) Attorney General (-General)

AIT Asylum and Immigration Tribunal

AJF Area Judicial Forum: see *judicial*

AJU Administration of Justice Unit

allocation various meanings: *Main Entries*

Altaris a police command and control system and 'management IT solution'

AMP Association of Muslim Police

ANPR automated number plate recognition

APA Association of Police Authorities

APFF Action for Prisoners Families and Friends: see prisonersfamilies.org.uk

ARA Assets Recovery Agency (former)

Archbold See *Touchstones*

ASB/O anti-social behaviour/order

ASSET See *youth offending team*

AUR automatic unconditional *release*

A&S allocation and sending

BA Border Agency (aka 'Border Force') (often in the fuller form **UKBA**)

backed for bail a *warrant* on which has been written an instruction from the issuing court that the person arrested under it be released on *bail* (originally 'on its back')

BAWP British Association of Women in Policing: see bawp.org

bill/Bill (1) bill of indictment; **(2)** bill of costs; **(3)** Parliamentary Bill

BCS British Crime Survey

BCU (1) Basic Command Unit; **(2)** Borough Command Unit (both police usage).

bench various usages: *Main Entries*

BME black and minority ethnic

Bramshill Bramshill Police College (see-*Touchstones*), now part of the **NPIA**

Branston the main **HMPS** stores located in a depot at Branston, Staffordshire

BTDC Bench Training and Development Committee (see *magistrate*)

BTP/A British Transport Police/Authority

Bulger See *Bulger case* in *Touchstones*

CA (or C of A) Court of Appeal

C&A character and antecedents

CAB Citizens Advice Bureau: see *advice*

CARATS Counselling, Assessment, Referral, Advice and Throughcare Services: see *drug*

case stated Short for appeal by way of case stated: see *Main Entries* under *appeal*

cat (1) category; **(2)** cat o'nine tails: see *whipping* in *Touchstones*.

caution various usages: see *Main Entries*

CB Courts Board: see *court*

CBO (1) civil behaviour order; **(2)** community beat officer (police).

CBRN/I chemical, biological, radiological or nuclear/incident

CC (1) chief constable; **(2)** (police or other) communications centre.

CCCCJS Cabinet Committee on Crime and the Criminal Justice System

CCJS Centre for Crime and Justice Studies: see *Touchstones*

CCMF Criminal Cases Management Framework (within **HMCS**: see *case management*)

CCRC Criminal Cases Review Commission

CCTV closed circuit television

CCU (1) Complex Crime Unit (usually meaning of the police, **CPS** or **SFO**); (2) Computer Crime Unit (similarly).

CD (1) conditional discharge; (2) criminal damage; (3) compact disc (as in popular speech; also for storing *data, evidence,* etc.)

CDH criminal *directions hearing*

CDRP Crime and Disorder Reduction Partnership

CDS Criminal Defence Service

CEO (1) chief executive officer; (2) court enforcement officer.

CEOP Child Exploitation and Online Protection Centre

CGT criminal geographic targeting

CHE community home with education

Cheltenham See **GCHQ**

CHIS covert human intelligence source: see *Main Entries* under *informer*

CICB/C/P/S Criminal Injuries Compensation Board/Commission/Panel/Scheme

CID Criminal Investigations Department, i.e. in a local police area: see *police/policing*

CJ (1) *criminal justice.* Hence, e.g. **CJA** Criminal Justice Act; **CJB** Criminal Justice Board (see also **LCJB** and **NCJB**); **CJS** Criminal Justice System; **CJSP** Criminal Justice Strategic Plan; **CJSSS**: Simple, Speedy, *Summary* Justice; **CJU** Criminal Justice Unit (of the **CPS**/police). (2) CJ is also sometimes used for *community justice.*

Clinks Community Links: see *Touchstones*

CLS Community Legal Service

CO (1) community order; (2) custody officer (see *police/policing*); (3) Cabinet Office; (4) commanding officer: of *military* origin but sometimes used by police re someone in charge, e.g. of an operation, raid, etc. Note also police use of 'commander' for such a person or as a senior rank.

code various usages: see *Main Entries*

commissioner various usages: *Main Entries*

comp compensation. Note and contrast 'fully comp' re motor vehicle insurance

consent various usages: see *Main Entries*

contempt (1) contempt of court; (2) blatant disregard for the law or other people.

contract various usages: see *Main Entries*

cordon a police, etc. cordon at a *crime scene,* incident or around a 'no-go' area

CPA (1) crime pattern analysis; (2) Child Protection Agency.

CPF Correctional Policy Framework

CPIA Criminal Procedure and Investigations Act 1996

CPNI Centre for the Protection of the National Infrastructure: see cpni.gov.uk

CPO (1) chief probation officer; (2) crime prevention officer; (3) *child protection* officer; (4) community punishment order (historical: now a requirement of unpaid work within a *community sentence*).

CPRC Criminal Procedure Rule Committee

CPS Crown Prosecution Service

CPU Child Protection Unit

CRA Constitutional Reform Act 2005

CRASBO criminal anti-social behaviour order: compare **ASBO** and see generally *anti-social behaviour* (ASB)

CRB (1) Criminal Records Bureau; (2) Crime Reporting Bureau.

CRO (1) Criminal Records Office; (2) crime reduction officer.

CRP crime reduction programme

C&R (1) control and restraint in *prison* (contrast **R&C** there); (2) charge and requisition: see *commencing criminal proceedings.*

CS (1) community sentence; (2) criminal statistics; (3) community service (historical: now a requirement of unpaid work within a *community sentence*); (4) *crime scene* (hence also see **CSI** and **CSM** below); (5) CS gas; (6) custody sergeant.

CSAB/CSAP Correctional Services Accreditation Board/Panel

CSI/M *crime scene* investigation/management (or 'manager')

CSO (1) (police) community support officer aka **PCSO** below; (2) community service order (historical: see note at **CS** above)

CSR confidential source register (re a **CHIS**). See *informer.*

CSU (police/**CPS**) Court Support Unit

CT counter-terrorism/terrorist; hence **CTC** = CT check; **CTS** = **CT** search.

CTL custody time limit: see *custodial/custody*

CTO central ticket office (i.e. re a **FPN/D**)

CYPA Children and Young Persons Act

DAG Diversity Action Group

DAT Drug Action Team

DC (1) Divisional Court; (2) detective constable; (3) detention centre.

DCA Department for Constitutional Affairs (now replaced by the **MOJ**)

DCC deputy chief constable

DCSF Department For Children, Schools and Families: see dcsf.gov.uk

DCI detective chief inspector

declaration various usages: *Main Entries*

deferment deferment of sentence

DG Director General

DI detective inspector

DIC (1) drunk in charge; (2) driver improvement centre/course (and **DIS** for Driver Improvement Scheme): see *road traffic.*

disclosure various usages: *Main Entries*

DIU Divisional Intelligence Unit

DJ(MC) district *judge* (magistrates' courts)

DNA deoxyribonucleic acid

domestic (1) a domestic dispute; (2) national as opposed to international; (3) events within an agency/service or family, etc.

DPC Data Protection Commissioner

DPG Diplomatic Protection Group

DPP Director of Public Prosecutions

DPS designated police station

DR diminished responsibility: see *mental impairment*

DS (1) duty solicitor; (2) detective sergeant.

DSU (police) Divisional Support Unit

DTTO drug testing and treatment order

DV/C/L/O (1) domestic violence; (2) developed vetting. Re both where C = **coordinator;** L = **liaison;** O = **officer.**

DVLA/C Driver and Vehicle Licensing Agency/Centre (aka **Swansea**)

EAH early administrative hearing, see *case management* and *preliminary hearing*

ECHR (1) European Convention on Human Rights; (2) European Court of Human Rights (often written as **Eur. Ct. HR**)

ECT electro convulsive therapy: see *mental impairment*

EDR (or **ERD**) earliest date of *release* (earliest release date), i.e. from prison

eFIT electronic photofit

EM electronic monitoring

ESPP extended sentence for public protection

ETA/D estimated (or earliest) time of arrival/departure at a *crime scene, emergency,* etc.

Europol a Europe wide policing arrangement: see *police/policing*

EWO either way offence

FBI Federal Bureau of Investigation (USA). Hence **FBI-style** methods, etc.

FBO football banning order

FDR fast delivery report for *sentencing*

FIU (1) (police) Force Intelligence Unit; (2) (police) Football Intelligence Unit.

FLO (1) family liaison officer; (2) football liaison officer; (3) force liaison officer.

FOI freedom of information

form previous form: a criminal record

FPN/D fixed penalty notice/for disorder

FPS Fraud Prosecution Service (of the **CPS** rather than the **SFO**: see *fraud*)

FPT/Fpt fingerprint

FSS/L Forensic Science Service/Laboratory (the latter not necessarily FSS-related)

FSU (1) (police) Force Support Unit; (2) (police) Firearms Support Unit.

FTA fail to appear (at a police station or court, e.g. in answer to bail)

FTD fit to detain (police usage)

GA Gamblers Anonymous

GBH grievous bodily harm

GHB gamma-hydroxybutryate (a hard *drug*)

GCHQ Government Communications Headquarters aka **Cheltenham** (Gloucestershire)

GOAD good order and discipline (in prison)

GovCo a *private sector* undertaking initiated by government, e.g. **FSS** Ltd

G&R grounds and reasons, i.e. usually for refusing to grant *bail*

hate crime various usages: see *Main Entries*

HCJ High Court of Justice

HDC home detention curfew

HGV heavy goods vehicle

HL (1) House of Lords; (2) Howard League for Penal Reform: see *Touchstones.*

HM Her Majesty's. Hence, e.g. **HMCI** HM Chief Inspector (re several see *Main Entries*); **HMCS** HM Court Service; **HMI** HM Inspector (again see *Main Entries* for **HMIC** = Constabulary; **HMICS** = Court Services; **HMI Prisons**; and **HMI Probation**). **HMP** is used for: (1) Her Majesty's prison; or (2) Her Majesty's pleasure. **HMPS** = Prison Service; **HMRC** (or **HMR&C**) = *Revenue & Customs*; **HMSO** = Stationery Office, but see now **TSO.**

HO (1) Home Office. Hence also, e.g. **HOC** = HO circular; **HO guidance**; (2) hospital order: see *mental impairment*. Note also **HOPO**: an HO production order, i.e for a prisoner to be 'produced from prison' (which is now an MOJ responsibility)

'holding centre' a synonym for *immigration* detention centre

Holmes/Holmes 2 See *Touchstones*

HR/HRA human rights/Human Rights Act 1998

HS Home Secretary

H&S health and safety; **HSE** H&S Executive

IAA Immigrant Appellant Authority

IC intermittent custody

ICC Interception of Communications Commissioner

ICP incident control point

ICVA Independent Custody Visitors Association (re police cells, etc.): see icva.org.uk

ID *identification/identity*

IMB Independent Monitoring Board

IMCA Independent Mental Capacity Advocate (see *advocate; mental impairment*)

Interpol an international policing arrangement: see *police/policing*

IO (**1**) indictable offence; (**2**) investigating officer, meaning one from the police or some other *law enforcement* agency

IOC interception of communications. Hence also **IOCA** = Act; and **'intercept'** which is used both as a noun or verb.

IOJ *interests of justice*

IOM integrated offender management

IP 'in possession': see *prisoner*

IPA International Police Association

IPCC Independent Police Complaints Commission (formerly simply the **PCA**, i.e. not 'Independent'; where A = Authority)

IPP imprisonment for public protection (but note also use of **ISPP** below)

IPS Identity and Passport Service (sometimes in its full form, **UKIPS**)

IPTF International Police Task Force

IS Immigration Service (sometimes **UKIS**) and now subsumed within the **BA/UKBA**

ISPP *indeterminate sentence for public protection* (sometimes just **IPP**)

IT (**1**) intermediate treatment (for juveniles, historically); (**2**) information technology; and note **PITO** (now part of the **NPIA**).

IWF Internet Watch Foundation

J (**1**) 'Mr Justice' (i.e. a judge of the High Court), usually J in writing; (**2**) a Justice of the Supreme Court (when in being); (**3**) the pre-fix **joint**.

JAC/O Judicial Appointments Commission/ Ombudsman

JC (**1**) Judges Council; (**2**) justices' clerk.

JCO Judicial Communications Office

JCS Justices' Clerks' Society

JCSB Jury Central Summoning Bureau

JIC joint intelligence committee/coordinator

JIG Justices' Interests Group: see *magistrate*

JLMG Judicial Leadership and Management Group (**HMCS** inspired)

JO Judicial Office (effectively of the **LCJ**)

JP justice of the peace

JR judicial review: see *appeal*

JS (**1**) Justice Secretary; (**2**) judgement summons (as used in *civil* proceedings).

JSB Judical Studies Board

JTAC Joint Threat (or alternatively Terrorism) Analysis Centre (national)

KPI key performance indicator

LA legal aid

LAGLO lesbians and gays liaison officer

Lawrence See *Touchstones*

LC Law Commission

LCD Lord Chancellor's Department (former)

LCh Lord Chancellor: see *Justice Secretary*

LCJ Lord Chief Justice

LCJB Local Criminal Justice Board

League ('The League') Howard League for Penal Reform: see *Touchstones*

LGA (**1**) Local Government Association: see lga.gov.uk; (**2**) local government area.

Liberty See *Touchstones*

licence various usages: *Main Entries*

lifer someone serving a sentence of *life imprisonment*. Hence, e.g. **mandatory lifer**, **discretionary lifer**, **two strikes lifer** according to the sentence under which he or she is serving *life imprisonment*.

LIO (police) local intelligence officer

LJ Lord Justice

LJA local justice area

LO liason officer: and see **FLO, LAGLO, VLO**.

LSC Legal Services Commission

MA Magistrates' Association

mags/court magistrates/magistrates' court

MAPPA Multi-agency Public Protection Arrangements

MATC Magistrates' Area Training Committee

MC magistrates' court. Hence **MCA** = (**1**) Magistrates Courts Act; or (**2**) magistrates' court area (now restyled as an **LJA**)

MC/I/T Major Crime/Investigation/Team

MDA Misuse of Drugs Act (various)

MDP alternative for **MODP**

MDT mandatory drug test/testing

MFH missing from home (and note also in this context police use of **'misper'**)

MHA Mental Health Act (various dates)

MID Motor Insurance Database

miscarriage miscarriage of justice

'misper' missing person (police usage)

MI/S/T/U Major Incident/Support/Team/ Unit, etc.

mitigation a plea in mitigation

MNTI Magistrates National Training Initiative (now **MNTI2**) ('Minty Two')

MO *modus operandi* (an operating style, re an offender or **CJS** practitioners)

MODP Ministry of Defence/Police

MOJ Ministry of Justice

MP (1) Member of Parliament; **(2)** military police/policeman/woman.

MPA Metropolitan Police Authority

MPB Missing Persons Bureau (national)

MPS Metropolitan Police Service

MPSO money payment supervision order, i.e. to enforce a *fines and financial orders*

MSU (police) Mobile Support Unit

MUFTI minimum use of force tactical intervention (**HMPS** usage)

N general pre-fix for 'national'. Hence, e.g. **NI** = national interest; **NFIU** = (police) National Football Intelligence Unit; **NIM** = (police) National Intelligence Model; **NIS** National Identification Service (or sometimes **NI Scheme**).

NA Narcotics Anonymous

Nacro See *Touchstones*

NAFIS National Automated Fingerprint Identification System

NAHT National Association of Head Teachers (see *school*)

NAI non-accidental injury. i.e. unexplained and may well be a cause for suspicion

Napo See *Touchstones*

NAYJ National Association for Youth Justice: see *Touchstones*

NBCF National Bench Chairmen's Forum (re *magistrates*)

NCCL National Council for Civil Liberties (aka *Liberty*: see *Touchstones*)

NCF (1) National Crime Faculty; **(2)** National Competency Framework.

NCIS National Criminal Intelligence Service (now part of **SOCA**)

NCJB National Criminal Justice Board

NCRS National Crime Reporting Standard

NCS National Crime Squad (now part of **SOCA**)

NDPB Non-departmental Public Body

NDR normal *release* date

NFA no **(1)** further action; **(2)** fixed abode.

NG not guilty

NIM National Intelligence Model

no case 'no case to answer'

NOMS National Offender Management Service

NPIA National Policing Improvement Agency

NPP National Policing Plan

NPS (1) National Probation Service; **(2)** National Policing Strategy.

NPT (1) Neighbourhood Policing Team; **(2)** National Police Training (now superseded by arrangements under the **NPIA**)

NS (1) National Standards (see *standard*); **(2)** national *security* (and hence **NSAP** for National Security Appeals Panel).

NSP no separate penalty, when a court passes sentence for several offences and taking matters 'in the round' considers that, overall, there is 'enough punishment'.

NSPCC National Society for the Prevention of Cruelty to Children

NSY New *Scotland Yard*: see *Touchstones*

NUPPO National Union of Police and Prison Officers (historical, see *police/policing*)

NVC non-verbal communication

NW Neighbourhood Watch. Hence, e.g. **BW** = Boat Watch/Business Watch, **FW** = Factory Watch/Farm Watch, **HW** = Horse Watch; **IW** = Internet Watch; **PW** = Pub Watch, **SW** = School Watch/Shop Watch.

OAPA Offences Against the Person Act 1861

OAsys offender assessment system

OCJR Office for Criminal Justice Reform

OCU Operational Command Unit

OIC officer in charge/command (also **OIOC** where **O** = overall)

OJC Office for Judicial Complaints

ONSET See *youth offending team*

operation a police or other manoeuvre

OPS Obscene Publications Squad

OPSI Office for Public Sector Information: see opsi.gov.uk

OPSU (police) Operational Support Unit

OSC Office of the Surveillance Commissioners

OSCT Office for Security and Counter-Terrorism

OSU (police) Operational Support Unit

PAB Police Advisory Board

PAC Penal Affairs Consortium: *Touchstones*

PACE Police and Criminal Evidence Act 1984. Hence also **PACE codes** under it.

PB (1) Parole Board; **(2)** Prisons Board; **(3)** Probation Board.

PBA Associations re any of the above

PC (1) police constable; **(2)** previous convictions; **(3)** Privy Council; **(4)** probation centre; **(5)** politically correct (general usage: and see the comments on p.ix).

PCA (1) Proceeds of Crime Act 2000; **(2)** Police Complaints Authority (now **IPCC**).

PCSO police community support officer (frequently shortened to **CSO**)

PD Practice Direction: see *practice*

PDA personal digital assistant (a hand-held device such as a Blackberry), especially as used by lawyers or increasingly the police

PDH plea and directions hearing

PDO potentially dangerous offender

PER prisoner escort record

PF Police Federation

PGA Prison Governors Association

PII public interest immunity: see *informer*

PIO (1) principal investigating officer; **(2)** Public Information Office (see also **OPSI**)

PITO Police Information Technology Organization (now part of **SOCA**)

PM (1) post mortem; **(2)** Prime Minister.

PNC/B Police National Computer/Bureau

PN/D See **FPN/D**

PO (1) public order; **(2)** probation officer; hence **CPO**, ACPO (assistant chief), **PPO** and SPO (senior); **(3)** persistent (or prolific) offender; hence **POTF** Persistent Offender Task Force; and **PYO** (below).

POA (1) Public Order Act (various years); **(2)** Prison Officers Association.

POCA Proceeds of Crime Act 2000

POLSA police search adviser

POU Public Order Unit

PPO (1) Prisons and Probation Ombudsman; **(2)** principal probation officer; **(3)** prolific and other priority offender.

PQ Parliamentary Question

PRA Police Reform Act 2002

previous previous convictions aka **form**

PRIME problem-solving in *multi-agency* environments

PRT Prison Reform Trust: see *Touchstones*

PSA (1) prison service area; **(2)** Police Superintendents Association; **(3)** petty sessions area (formerly PSD = division and now an LJA'); **(4)** Public Service Agreement.

PSNI Police Service of Northern Ireland

PSO probation service officer: see the explanation under *probation* in *Main Entries*

PSR pre-sentence report, usually meaning by the **NPS** or a **YOT**

PSU Police Support Unit

PTS pre-trial services

PVC/I police vehicle collision/incident

PYO persistent/prolific young offender

QBD Queen's Bench Division: *High Court*

QC Queen's Counsel (aka **'silk'**), i.e. a senior barrister who wears a silk gown

Q&E quality and *effectiveness*

QGM Queen's Gallantry Medal

QPM (1) Queen's Police Medal (or sometimes **Queen's policeman**); **(2)** quality performance management.

R Regina (or Rex): see *Crown*

RAPt (lower case 't') Rehabilitation For Addicted Prisoners Trust: see *Touchstones*

RC remand centre

R&C (1) *Revenue & Customs*; **(2)** requests and complaints in prison (contrast **C&R**)

RCC Rainer Crime Concern: see *Touchstones*

reasons i.e. for a decision; including **G&R**

referral See explanation in *Main Entries*

RE racial equality. Hence **RES** where S = scheme or system.

recorder (1) part-time circuit *judge* (but Recorder of London = the senior such judge there); **(2)** Recorder of the **MPS**: historic name for London's police paymaster.

regime (1) usually that in an individual *prison*; or **(2)** possibly a reference to a prevailing administration or authority.

Regina/Rex See *Crown*

restriction various usages: *Main Entries*

review various usages: see *Main Entries*

RIC remand in custody

RIPA ('reaper') Regulation of Investigatory Powers Act 2000

RJ restorative justice (or Restorative Justice)

RJC Restorative Justice Consortium.

RMP Royal Military Police

ROSH risk of serious harm

ROSPA Royal Society for the Prevention of Accidents

Royal Courts Royal Courts of Justice

RSI roadside interview

RSO (1) road safety officer; **(2)** registered sex offender.

RSPB Royal Society for the Protection of Birds

RSPCA Royal Society for the Prevention of Cruelty to Animals

RT road traffic. Hence, e.g. **RTA** = Road Traffic Act or road traffic accident; **RTI** = road traffic incident; **RTO** = road traffic offence; **RTRA** = Road Traffic Regulations Act.

RUC Royal Ulster Constabulary (now replaced by the **PSNI**)

Rule 45 See *prisoner* 'Rule 45'

RVP rendezvous point

SAMM Support After Murder and Manslaughter: see *Touchstones*

SAP Sentencing Advisory Panel

SAR suspicious activity report, i.e. by a bank, lawyer, business, etc.

SARA Scanning Analysis Response Assessment: see the explanation in *Main Entries*

SASO Special *Advocates* Support Office

SB Special Branch

SC Supreme Court (or **SCJ** where J = Justice)

S&C security and control (in prison)

Scarman See *Brixton riots* in *Touchstones*

SCWG Sentencing Commission Working Group

SDR standard delivery report for *sentencing*

SE social exclusion. Hence also **SEU** for Social Exclusion Unit

section See uses of this word in *Touchstones*

SEG special escort group, e.g. re a hazardous load on the highway, perhaps by **MOD/P**

sending part of **A&S**

SFO Serious Fraud Office (and see **FPS**)

SGC Sentencing Guidelines Council

SI Statutory Instrument: see *legislation*

SIAC Special Immigration Appeals Panel

silk See **QC**

SIO senior investigating officer

SIS Secret Intelligence Service

SO (**1**) summary offence; (**2**) standing order, e.g. of the police, **HMPS**, other agencies/ services and bodies.

SOA Sexual Offences Act (various)

SOCA Serious Organized Crime Agency

SOCO scenes of crime officer

SOCPA Serious Organized Crime and Police Act 2005

SOCVP Statement of Common Purposes and Values: see *police/policing*

SOTP Sex Offender Treatment Programme

source (**1**) a police information or intelligence source (see, also, **CHIS**); (**2**) any general source of information, etc.

speech various usages: *Main Entries*

SS (**1**) Social Services; (**2**) suspended sentence, i.e. of *imprisonment*

SSR specific sentence report

SSU Scientific Support Unit

ST summary trial, i.e. by magistrates

statement various usages: *Main Entries*

STDC Support, Training and Development Committee: see *Magistrates Association*

Stone See *Touchstones*

STOP name for various 'opposition' or '**stop campaigns**'. 'Stop and search', see **sus**.

summary various usages: see *Main Entries*

sus 'suspicion'. Hence **sus laws** allowing police to stop and search people 'on suspicion' or at random re *terrorism/terrorists.*

suspended sentence (**1**) i.e. of imprisonment; (**2**) a *hanging* pun: see *Touchstones.*

Swansea See **DVLA/C** above

tag various usages: see *Main Entries*

tampering various usages: see *Main Entries*

TAR traffic accident record

target various usages: see *Main Entries*

tariff various usages: see *Main Entries*

Taser Taser-gun: see *Touchstones*

TC therapeutic community

TFO transfer of fine order, i.e. from one area to another for *enforcement* (but magistrates now have nationwide *jurisdiction*)

TFT/U Tactical Firearms Team/Unit

'three strikes' See *Touchstones*

TIC take(n) into consideration

ticket various usages: see *Main Entries*

TSO The Stationery Office: see tso.co.uk

TU Trial Unit (**CPS**/police)

TVL *TV Licensing*

TWC (alternatively '**twocking**'): taking a conveyance without consent of the owner

UKAEC United Kingdom Atomic Energy Constabulary: see ukaea.org.uk

UK Borders UK Border Agency (aka **UKBA**)

UKIS UK Immigration Service

unfit various usages: see *Main Entries*

Unlock: see *Touchstones*

VASCAR Visual Average Speed Calculator (alternatively Camera) and Recorder

VDR/S Vehicle Defect Rectification/ Scheme

VDT voluntary drug-testing (in *prison*)

VEL vehicle excise licence. Hence the offence of having **no VEL**.

verdict various usages: see *Main Entries*

VFM value for money

VGT Virtual Global Task Force

VIPER Video Identity Parade Electronic Recording

VODS vehicle online descriptive search

VOO violent offender order

VP vulnerable person/prisoner. Hence **VPU/W** = VP Unit/Wing.

VPS victim personal statement

VRS vehicle rectification scheme

VS (**1**) Victim Support; and hence also **VSS** = VS scheme; (**2**) voluntary service.

wanted wanted for questioning about an offence, in effect as a suspect

warrant various usages: *Main Entries*; and note that **WFD** = warrant of further detention: see *detention* in *Main Entries*

WIP Women in Prison: see *women*

Woolf See *Touchstones*

Woolmington See *Touchstones*

WS Witness Service

YC youth custody

YCAP (or **Y-cap**) youth crime action plan (national or local: see *Main Entries*)

YJ youth justice. Hence also, e.g. **YJB** = Youth Justice Board; **YJS** = Youth Justice System; **YJT** = Youth Justice Team.

YOI young offender institution

YOP Youth Offending Panel

YOT Youth Offending Team

YP (**1**) young person (14-17); (**2**) young prisoner (18-21).

YRO youth referral order

ZT zero tolerance

Touchstones and Curiosities

CJS practitioners and criminologists tend to navigate by landmarks, key concepts, telling illustrations, famous cases, turning points or vivid (sometimes) extreme examples. The following selection is abridged from the *Waterside Press A-Z of Criminal Justice*.

Italicised items refer to *Main Entries* (purple section) unless stated otherwise.

addiction A state whereby the person concerned ('**the addict'**) becomes dependent on, e.g. an activity, substance or routine, to the extent that it comes to dominate his or her life, leading to a distortion of *values*, priorities, thinking, *responses*, etc. This can involve subterfuge, lies, *denial* (below) and possibly lead to offending (especially if there are financial implications in **fuelling addiction**, or loss of *self-control*. Contributory factors may include personality or psychological disorders related to obsession, compulsion or mania. Note also **addiction to crime**: for 'the buzz' which offending may give; and common forms of dependence on *alcohol, drugs* and *gambling*. Addiction attracts often conflicting medical and popular definitions which no short work can even begin to deal with. Consult specialist works.

adversarial system A system of justice in which opposing parties use *forensic* tactics to 'win' their case; primarily a contest rather than a search for the *truth*. Hence there may be criticism if an accused escapes on a technicality; there is a 'cracked trial' (see *trial*); or aggressive cross-examination (see *evidence*), especially of a vulnerable *witness*. Contrast inquisitorial approaches of some European *jurisdictions* (and Scotland) when a judicial officer (examining magistrate/procurator fiscal, etc.) oversees the *investigation* from an early stage. For the key role of **adversarial methods** in the development of criminal justice in England and Wales (and some of its more positive aspects) see *Fighting For Justice: The Origins and History of Adversary Trial* (2006), Hostettler J, Waterside Press.

Allen, Peter Anthony and **Evans, Gwynne Owen** The last people to be executed in the UK; by simultaneous *hanging* (below) at Liverpool Prison (Allen) and Strangeways Prison, Manchester (Evans) on 13 August 1964. Both dairymen, Evans (25) lodged with Allen (21) and his family in Preston, Lancashire. They visited a John West 'to borrow money'; stabbed and killed him and stole bank books and a watch. By mischance, Evans left behind a raincoat in the pocket of which was a medallion bearing his name. 'It would be difficult to imagine a more brutal *murder*': Lord Parker, *Lord Chief Justice*.

amnesty A moratorium in relation to prosecution at the *discretion* of the police or other *law enforcement agencies*, usually with a view to some particular end, such as a **knife amnesty** or **gun amnesty** to facilitate the surrendering of *weapons* (i.e. with 'no questions asked'); or less usually a **general amnesty** when past offences are 'written-off', usually meaning by *legislation*. Similarly, where punishments are cancelled or reduced. Widespread amnesties followed the Civil War (1651)(in 1660, e.g. an **Act of Oblivion** absolved many 'regicides', those responsible for the death of the king) and two rebellions (1715 and 1745). An analogous situation arose when certain prisoners were released to join the armed forces on the outbreak of war (1939). Similarly re *terrorism/terrorists* linked to the Good Friday Agreement (see, generally, The *Troubles* below). There have, since the 1980s, been a number of 'so-called amnesties', e.g. re weapons (above) and *asylum* seekers; and what has been dubbed '**amnesty by stealth'** when, e.g. particular kinds of prisoners have been *released* early, or police forces have decided not to enforce *drug* laws. Note also **Amnesty International (AI)**, a movement which 'stands up for humans wherever *justice, freedom* and *truth* are denied', including re prisoners of conscience worldwide: see amnesty.org.uk

anecdote A brief tale or yarn that may or may not have a basis of *fact, evidence, data* or *intelligence*; ranging from stories about the unguarded remarks of judges to those, e.g. re the naivety of the CJS outsider who mistakenly thinks that a Justice of the Peas is the person who tends the court allotment. Two of the best-known collections are the *Oxford Book of Legal Anecdote* (1986), Gilbert M (ed.), Oxford University Press; and *Miscellany at Law* (2006), Megarry, R E, Wildy, Simmonds and Hill.

Anglo-Saxon origins of criminal justice

Crime and *punishment* in England and Wales can be traced back to the 'dooms' (laws) of Anglo-Saxon times (600 AD onwards); beyond which records are scant or nonexistent; and folklore, myth or legend intertwine with reality. For a comprehensive account from that time to the present day, see *A History of Criminal Justice in England and Wales,* Hostettler, J (2008), Waterside Press.

Archbold *Archbold's Criminal Pleading and Practice.* The leading work on *evidence, practice* and *procedure* in the *Crown Court* (in particular); first published in 1825 and now annually with updates by Sweet & Maxwell.

Armstrong, Herbert Rowse The only solicitor to be executed for murder (in 1922 aged 55); who was also *justices' clerk* for Hay-on-Wye, Powys. His wife's body was exhumed after he tried to poison a lawyer rival. The case is the subject of *Exhumation of a Murder: The Life and Times of Major Armstrong* (2006), Odell, R, Mandrake (among other works) and remains a landmark re similar fact *evidence.* His last words were: 'I am innocent of the crime for which I am about to die'. In 1920, Harold Greenwood, another solicitor, obtained an *acquittal* in comparable circumstances; some commentators advancing *conspiracy theories* re how history was not going to be allowed to repeat itself in 1922. In modern times a number of CJS personnel have been convicted of *murder* and sentenced to *life imprisonment.*

Assizes and Quarter Sessions The former criminal courts of first instance above the level of the magistrates' court which could try and sentence people accused of *serious offences*; until the *Beeching Report* (below) and the Courts Act 1971, which created the *Crown Court.* See, e.g. *Farewell to Assizes* (1972), Neil, Sir B, Garnstone Press. Quarter Sessions was aka 'The Follies'.

Auld Report That by Lord Justice Sir Robin Auld (2001) concerning the future administration of the criminal courts; certain recommendations from which were acted upon (others rejected) re the present arrangements

whereby the *Crown Court* and magistrates' court are both administered by HM *Court Service*; and the streamlining of procedures to ensure greater consistency of approach. See criminal-courts-review.org.uk

baby farm A phenomenon of the 1800s (mainly) whereby parents unable to look after their infant *children* 'farmed them out' to the *private sector*; often little more than a family rearing tens of *children*; leading to the Infant Life Preservation Act 1872 and *legislation* on adoption. In 1870, in London, Margaret Cowan was convicted of the *murder* of an illegitimate child by poisoning and neglect; having taken in 40 children, for trivial amounts, many dying. In 1879, John and Catherine Barns of Tranmere, Merseyside were convicted of *manslaughter* in 'a gross case'; and as late as 1907 Rhoda Willis (aka Leslie James) was executed at Cardiff Prison (see generally *capital punishment* below) for killing a one day old child. The most notorious case is that of '**Reading Baby Farmer**', Amelia Elizabeth Dyer (possibly Britain's most prolific *serial killer* ahead of Harold *Shipman* below) who murdered an unknown number of children over 15 years. In 1895, she moved to Reading, Berkshire where three children were found strangled in the River Thames. Seven more bodies bore similar white tape. Arrested for killing Doris Marmon (four months), entrusted to Dyer for £10, Dyer made a *confession*, saying that her *motive* was the fees she charged after the deaths. Convicted at The *Old Bailey* (below) on a single count, Dyer was hanged at *Newgate Prison* (below) aged 57 (one of the oldest *women* to be executed). These events occurred despite earlier initiatives such as the **Foundling Hospital**, London (1739) (for abandoned, etc. children) founded by philanthropist Thomas Coram (1668-1751). See Thomas Coram Foundation: coram.org.uk

BAE Systems A modern-day case involving discussion of the *Rule of Law.* In 2007, a long-running *investigation* into bribery and *corruption* at this major UK company involving commercial deals with Saudi Arabia (and other *States*) was halted by the Director of the Serious Fraud Office (SFO) (see *fraud*) after the UK government claimed that prosecution was 'not in the *national interest*'; Saudi Arabia being a key anti-terrorism partner (see generally *terrorism/terrorist*) and large scale purchaser of planes, weapons and other exports; causing Lord Taylor, a former *Lord Chief Justice,* to suggest government *intervention* served to undermine the *Rule of Law.*

basket justice From the 16th century, *justice* (so-called) was dispensed by certain magistrates after placing a basket in front of their *bench,* into which 'offerings' might be paid by people facing trial or sentence. It was only in the late-18th century that the idea that 'justice is not for sale' took increasing hold and this practice was finally eradicated. See now *fair/fairness*

Beeching Report The Report of the Royal Commission on Assizes and Quarter Sessions, 1966-1969 (aka the **Report of the Beeching Commission**) (HMSO, 1969; Cm. 4) into the workings of the criminal courts; chaired by 'axe-man' industrialist Dr (later Lord) Richard Beeching (ex-chair of the British Railways Board at a time of branch line closures; before and afterwards with Imperial Chemical Industries (ICI)). The report focused on centres for *administrative* purposes and *circuit* boundaries. It led to the replacement of *Assizes and Quarter Sessions* (above) by the *Crown Court* and its various 'tiers'.

benefit of clergy A medieval form of immunity from prosecution in the ordinary courts; first bestowed on clergymen by Henry II entitling them to be tried in the ecclesiastical courts (with a tendency to *mercy*); whose origins lay in the *murder* of Thomas à Becket in Canterbury Cathedral (1170); but that eventually became a device whereby anyone could avoid *punishment* after an *Act* of 1352 stated that: 'all manner of clerks, as well secular as religious [see, generally, *religious aspects*] … shall freely have and enjoy the privileges of the Holy Church'. This was interpreted by *judges* so as to include 'anyone who could read'. Men, generally, could avoid *punishment,* except re *treason* or *witchcraft* (both in *Touchstones* below), by reciting the '**neck verse**', i.e. to save their necks (see *hanging* below), which became the sole literacy test. The preamble to an Act of 1489 complained that this allowed *serious offences* to be committed with impunity. It restricted the circumstances in which and number of times that '**clergy**' could be pleaded where the offender was not in holy orders (accompanied by branding to allow future *identification*). By one bizarre twist, people *assisting crime* could be punished even where

the principal offender might claim clergy; whilst the Transportation Act 1718 made *hanging* partially redundant. In 1624, 'clergy' was partially extended to *women*; in 1691 fully extended. It was abolished in 1827.

bent copper A term commonly applied to police officers who commit criminal offences, particularly of *corruption*; confirming the notion that there is 'a rotten apple in every barrel'. For a collection that includes key instances from the earliest times of policing and including 'The Trial of the Detectives' (1877) to the dubious investigative techniques of CIDs of the 1970s in particular, see *Bent Coppers: A Survey of Police Corruption* (1993), Morton J, Little Brown. **Noble cause corruption** implies acting with 'good' if misguided intention, e.g. to win over a jury by falsifying *evidence*. The Harry ('Tanky') Challoner case (1964) is often cited as a prime example: in which a brave but deranged detective became 'the scourge of the Soho *Underworld*' (below); then planted a brick (i.e. a missile) on a demonstrator who he deemed to be insulting foreign royalty.

Bentley, Derek A young adult, possibly suffering from *mental impairment* (certainly of a mental age of eleven) who was sentenced to *capital punishment* (below) and executed in 1953 at *Wandsworth Prison,* one of the most disturbing incidents in English CJS history. He was the accomplice (see *assisting crime*) of a juvenile gunman, Christopher Craig, who was below the *age* for such a sentence. Craig shot dead police constable Sydney George Miles, on a factory roof in Croydon, south London during a foiled (largely pathetic) burglary of commercial premises. Various issues arose re the true nature of the enterprise; including whether Bentley knew of or had agreed to the use of a *weapon* by Craig; and, in particular, the interpretation to be placed on Bentley's equivocal exhortation to Craig, 'Let him have it' (i.e. 'hand over the gun' or 'shoot'). There was general disquiet re the conduct of the trial by *Lord Chief Justice* Goddard at a time of *violence* by young men post-Second World War; and re the refusal by the *Home Secretary* to grant a reprieve. The execution was a landmark along the route to the abolition of the death penalty. Bentley was granted a posthumous *pardon* after the *Court of Appeal* quashed his conviction in 1998 on the grounds that the original trial judge was biased against the defendants and misdirected the jury. Scientific evidence also showed that three police officers who asserted that Bentley had cried out 'Let him have it' must have fabricated that *evidence*. For an early account, see *To Encourage the Others* (1971), Yallop, D, W H Allen.

Big Brother A metaphor for the *surveillance* society as envisaged by George Orwell in his futuristic novel *1984* (1949); in which no-one can hide from the all-seeing eye of the telescreen and each move is open to forms of *criminalisation* (below), especially re subversion and ill-defined 'thoughtcrime'. Some commentators see echoes of a **Big Brother mentality** re events in the UK today. The work also portrays an institutionalised form of *demonisation* (below), manipulation of *hate* and describes 'newspeak' (a language of government/public institutions in particular that is notorious for creative terms which serve to ensure social *control*).

Birmingham Six One of the earliest, modern-day *miscarriage of justice* cases; particularly important for the impact it had on a somewhat complacent CJS; in which six people wrongly served 16 years *imprisonment* each for the 1974 IRA bombing of the Mulberry Bush public house, Birmingham and the *murders* of 21 people. Those convictions were found by the *Court of Appeal* to be unsafe (1991). Events had until then been typified by institutionalised *denial* (below). The case was one of the factors leading to the *Royal Commission on Criminal Justice* of 1991-3 (see *Crown*); and both the *Criminal Cases Review Commission* (CCRC) and *Police and Criminal Evidence Act 1984* (PACE).

black economy An informal, largely hidden economy (aka the **black market**) which functions, beyond official control, alongside the mainstream economy. It encompasses activities from moonlighting for undeclared income (perhaps linked to benefit or other *fraud*) to *organized crime,* including trading in **black market goods**. It may involve *theft, handling,* evasion of *taxation, counterfeiting, smuggling, drug* dealing and aspects of the sex industry. Its impact causes intrinsic *harm* to (and 'skews') the market economy; and is a magnet for *corruption,* intimidation, *money laundering, protection* rackets, *threats, blackmail,* employment of illegal immigrants (see *immigration*), *trafficking, violence,* etc. Difficult to measure or police, the **UK** black

economy is generally put at some ten per cent of General Domestic Product (GDP) varying with formal economic conditions. In some countries it can be as high as 50 per cent and is seen as a necessary *evil,* below. See, e.g. *Wages of Crime: Black Markets, Illegal Finance, and the Underworld Economy* (2004), Naylor R T, Cornell University Press.

Black Panther Description applied to Donald Nielson (a 'natural lifer') who was given five sentences of *life imprisonment* at Oxford Crown Court in 1976 for the *murder* of three sub-postmasters and the abduction of heiress Leslie Whittle. He was also convicted of causing grievous bodily harm (GBH)(see *assault*) to a sub-postmistress; and associated *serious offences.* Events began with a *robbery* at Jump, South Yorkshire (1971) and escalated to include shootings (see *weapon*) from 1974 onwards at Harrogate, Yorkshire, Accrington. Lancashire and Langley, West Midlands. The Post Office offered a then record reward of £25,000 for information leading to his arrest and conviction. Lesley Whittle was found dead in the underground drainage system at Bathpool Park, Kidsgrove, Staffordshire after a ransom demand of £50,000 went awry. Despite a huge manhunt and police operation (Operation Basket), Nielson was stopped by chance due to a random *road traffic* check. Misreading the situation, he kidnapped two police officers and forced them to drive 20 miles at gunpoint. Only a crash prevented an audacious getaway.

Blackstone, Sir William (or just **Blackstone**) (1723-80) Judge, jurist, writer, professor of law at Oxford University and a judge of the Court of Common Pleas; noted for his *Commentaries on the Laws of England* (1765-69) which had a profound impact on the development of the Common Law and the criminal law in particular (and which are still cited in court on occasion). His remarks include: 'It is better that ten guilty persons escape than that one innocent suffers'; 'Public wrongs [are a] violation of rights and duties to the whole community [striking] at the very being of Society'. '**Blackstone**' is also the name of a series of legal texts published by Oxford University Press: see oup.co.uk

blame culture One where there is a tendency to attach or apportion individual/institutional blame/fault rather than seek conflict free solutions and to focus on maintaining harmony. Contrast, e.g. *restorative justice*.

Borstal A village near Rochester, Kent where the first 'experiment' in indeterminate training for young offenders aged 15-21 (23 from 1930) began; that gave its name to **borstal training** (1902 -1982); attributed to prison commissioner Sir Evelyn Ruggles-Brise (1857-1935). The play 'Borstal Boy' (1958) (and film 2002) by Irish playwright and one-time *juvenile* republican *terrorist* Brendan Behan (1923-1964) is set in a borstal and highlights the by then inherent brutality (Behan evaded *capital punishment*, below, only due to his *age*). In the short story, *The Loneliness of the Long Distance Runner* (1958) by Alan Sillitoe (and film 1962) a *disadvantaged* youth who turned to crime 'for relief' survives the **borstal regime** by pandering to the governor via athletic prowess; but deliberately stops short of the winning line in a key race: a metaphor for disaffected youth.

Bottomley, Horatio William (1860-1933) Fraudster (see *fraud*), self-publicist and rabble-rouser, who 'relieved' investors via *high-profile* enterprises, including Victory Bonds (1919). Founder of the *Financial Times* and *John Bull* (a symbol of *Britishness* below), he was twice MP for Hackney until allegations by a former associate led to his *falling from grace* (below). Notorious for quaffing champagne, including at court during his trial, he received seven years' *penal servitude*; after which, reduced to appearing in vaudeville at the Windmill Theatre and other dubious venues, he died in penury.

Bow Street London address immortalised in the annals of crime and punishment due to its central location and historic associations; many famous/notorious cases passing through **Bow Street Magistrates' Court**, making it one of the best-known in England; until it closed in 2007. It was originally presided over by novelist stipendiary (i.e. paid) magistrate *Henry Fielding*, below. The **Bow Street Runners** (1749-1839) were an embryonic police force and a blueprint for the New Police (1829). They operated from the court and later the equally famous and iconic **Bow Street Police Station**.

Bramshill Location of the National Police College at Bramshill House, Hampshire which after being re-styled as part of CEN-

TREX (a 'centre of excellence') became part of the *National Policing Improvement Agency* (NPIA) in 2005; whose work includes training police leaders across the UK and internationally. Other notable police colleges exist at Hendon (re the *Metropolitan Police Service*), Wakefield, Yorkshire, Tulliallan, Scotland (see tulliallan.police.uk) and Cookstown, Northern Ireland (see psni.police.uk)

Bridgewater Three (or sometime 'Four') A long-running *miscarriage of justice* case in which three men were imprisoned for 18 years each following their 1979 convictions for the *murder* of newspaper boy Carl Bridgewater at Yew Tree Farm, Stourbridge, Staffordshire. They were released by the *Court of Appeal* in 1997, their convictions being unsafe; after six police-led inquiries and three *appeals*. An example of the labelling of cases by numbers, especially after a *campaign* begins. Compare **Birmingham Six** (above), **Guinness Four**, **Maguire Seven** (see *Guildford pub bombings*), **Tottenham Three** (see *Broadwater Farm*)(all below).

Britishness Prevailing ideas of multiculturalism – in which diversity, difference and a variety of cultures are encouraged – have been challenged as potentially divisive; leading to a resurgence of notions of 'Britishness' (also linked in part to *crime prevention/crime reduction*). In 2007, before becoming Prime Minister, Gordon Brown said: 'I want to discuss ... how important being British is to [our] *identity*, what [British people] think [are] British *values* ... how we better integrate our ethnic communities ... [and] respond to Muslim fundamentalism ... our role in Europe ... and whether global challenges demand a stronger sense of national purpose'. This became a focus of the Green Paper, *The Governance of Britain* (2007; Cm 7170). Some commentators warn that an excess of patriotism (with its potential for xenophobia, a 'fortress mentality' and so on) can also lead to counter-productive rifts, gulfs, splits and segregation of *communities*.

Brixton Riots Public order disturbances and *violence* linked to *race/racism* in various parts of the UK in the early-1980s; which reached their peak in Brixton, South London in April 1981: **the first serious urban riots of the 20th century**, of a *seriousness* not until then seen by the *Metropolitan Police Service* (MPS). 'Operation Swamp 81' led to stops and *searches* of black youths; confrontations with police; an incident in which six officers were injured; rumours of aggressive policing and routine searches of black people. In the worst riot, Molotov cocktails (crude petrol bombs) were thrown; 100 police cars/other vehicles damaged, 135 premises looted; the fire brigade attacked; and 300 police officers and 70 civilians injured. The Scarman Report ('The Brixton Disorders 10-12 April 1981') by senior Law Lord, Lord Scarman focussed on policing methods rather than root causes. It stressed: that the police, *community* and their leaders shared responsibility for *communication*; that police should be better organized and equipped; and noted the impact of un*employment* and *discrimination*.

Broadwater Farm Location of a riot in Tottenham, north London (1985); in which extensive damage was caused and police officer **Keith Blakelock** hacked to death by a mob whilst trying to protect the fire brigade from attack (one week after a *Brixton riot*, above). He was ambushed and attacked with machetes, knives and other weapons. Winston Silcott, Engin Raghip and Mark Braithwaite, were convicted of *murder* and sentenced to *life imprisonment*; despite 'a wall of *silence*'. The 'Tottenham Three are Innocent' and 'Broadwater Farm Defence' *campaigns* led to their being freed by the *Court of Appeal* in 1989 after *forensic evidence* showed that *interview* records had been tampered with (see generally *tampering*). A senior officer was later cleared of *perjury*.

Broken windows (1) A tactic employed by *political* and other demonstrators (see generally *radical heritage* below), especially around the turn of the 20th century (including by Suffragettes), i.e. of **throwing a brick through a window**; re which in the past there may sometimes have been a level of *tolerance*. The practice re-appeared in modern times in the UK re protests by animal activists against Huntingdon Life Sciences (a laboratory) and McDonalds (the burger chain). **(2)** An **environmentally-based theory of criminology** attributed to James Q Wilson and George Kelling (USA) (1960s) that crime, *fear* of crime and poor *law enforcement* are more likely to occur and be accepted as the norm in badly maintained areas, where **'windows get broken and and remain so'**, due, e.g. to low levels of *respect*, *self-esteem*, *concern* or *motivation*.

Bronson, Charles (or just **Bronson**) Often cited as Britain's most *dangerous* prisoner, Michael Gordon Peterson (b.1952) (Bronson being his 'fighting name'; after the USA 'tough guy' actor). He has spent over 30 years in prison for armed *robbery*; often in segregation (see *prison/*'the block'). His reputation as a monster, hostage-taker, victim, artist, raconteur and eccentric is explained in his autobiography, *Bronson* (2000), Blake Publications: 'I've been on more [prison] roofs than Santa Claus, eaten more *porridge* [below] than The Three Bears and taken more hostages than Saddam Hussein'.

B-Specials Often cited as an example of 'all that can go wrong' in policing, the part-time, Protestant reservist **Ulster Special Constabulary** (or **B-men**) formed in Ireland following the *Easter Rising* (below) (and disbanded in 1970) (see generally *The Troubles* (below)). They were poorly paid, aggressive and biased against Catholics. The earlier **Black and Tans** (1920-22) (also the name of a Tipperary hound pack) were a British-sponsored quasi-military reservist force, distinguished by their police-cum-military attire.

'Building Communities, Beating Crime: A Better Police Force for the 21st Century' Title of a White Paper (2004; Cm 6360) concerning future developments in policing (see, generally, *police/policing*) and law and order generally. It spoke of 'revitalising' policing, enhancements to neighbourhood policing, sustained *reform*, a reduction in bureaucracy and re-examined the aims of the police and their 'responsiveness'; leading to a more visible, accessible police presence. It is available at www.homeoffice.gov.uk

Bulger case In 1992, James Patrick **Bulger**, a two year old child, was abducted and *murdered* in Liverpool, Merseyside by ten-year-olds **Jon Venables** and **Robert Thompson**; leading to a public outcry across the UK and especially locally where events were reminiscent of the *hue and cry* (below); triggering a firm new line on *law and order* and leading to increasing politicisation of criminal justice (see further *political aspects*; *tough/toughness* below). Bulger disappeared from New Strand Shopping Centre. His mutilated body was found on a railway line at Bootle. The accused (whose identities were *disclosed* in the *interests of justice*) were convicted at Preston Crown Court (1993) and ordered to be detained during *Her Majesty's pleasure*, with a *judicial* recommendation that they serve 'very, very many years'. Lord Taylor, Lord Chief Justice, then ruled that they should serve at least ten years. *Media/press* reaction (including a *campaign* by *The Sun* newspaper) led 300,000 people to petition *Home Secretary* Michael Howard. In 1995 he said that they should serve at least 15 years; but in 1997 the *Court of Appeal* found this unlawful and after *appeals* to the European Court of Human Rights (ECHR) (see *human rights*), the Home Secretary lost to the *judges* the power to set *tariffs* for 'lifers' under 18 (and later *adults*: both, since 2007, MOJ-linked matters). Thompson and Venables were *released* after eight years. An injunction safeguards their *identities* and locations. The case led to changes in the way trials of *children* at the *Crown Court* occur, then a highly formal way. There are more such cases than most people realise; another landmark case being that of **Mary Bell** (1968). For a survey, see *Children Who Kill* (1996), Cavadino P (Ed.), Waterside Press.

Butler Trust An independent *charity* which recognises 'excellence and innovation' by people working with offenders in the UK. Through its annual **Butler Trust Award Scheme** and associated **Development Programme** it helps to develop *effective* care for offenders by: identifying and promoting excellence and innovation by a range of criminal justice staff, contractors and volunteers; developing and disseminating *best practice* in the care and *resettlement* of offenders; and providing professional and personal development opportunities for award-winning staff. For further details, see thebutlertrust.org.uk

Cable Street A street in the East End of London that became the scene of *public order* disturbances in the 1930s; hence the **Battle of Cable Street** as commemorated by a blue plaque: 'The people of East London rallied [here] on 4 October 1936 and forced back the march of the fascist Oswald Mosley and his Blackshirts … "They shall not pass"' (as per the Spanish civil war slogan 'No pasaran'). London's Jewish population of 185,000 lived around Stepney. The British Union of Fascists (BUF) believed that Jews were involved in a conspiracy of world domination; whilst anti-semitism was sweeping across Europe (notoriously in Nazi Germany). The Blackshirts sought to show

their strength and solidarity, but left-wing opposition led to escalation, riots and *assault*; paving the way for the *Public Order Act 1936*, a ban on the wearing of *military-style* uniforms for *civilian* purposes and a crackdown on extremism, from the left or right.

calendar The **criminal calendar** is a description applied to the entire catalogue of criminal offences, many now beyond the immediate comprehension of *citizens* or lawyers, of which *murder* is generally regarded as being **the worst offence in the criminal calendar**. Some 3,000 crimes have been added to this calendar since 1997. **Calendars for prisoners** are a growth industry; time having always been of the essence of a prison sentence and thus a preoccupation. In a different vein, the **Newgate Calendar** is the title of a publication: see *Newgate* below.

canteen culture An informal tag for the conservative, potentially *discriminatory* attitudes of criminal justice practitioners; especially sections of the police as brought to prominence by filmmaker Roger Graef in his TV documentary, *Thames Valley* (1970): the interchanges of police officers when amongst their own, 'cheek-by-jowl', in the privacy of their canteen, social clubs or patrol cars. Pragmatic tips may be passed re methods and short-cuts, working the system, 'ticking the boxes'. Comparable events occur in other CJS settings, e.g. on *prison* landings or in the Inns of Court (see *barrister*). For a more positive view of such interaction, see 'Police (Canteen) Culture: An Appreciation' (1999), Waddington, PAJ, *British Journal of Criminology*, 39, 287-309. More generally, the 'barrack room culture' of the *military* was, even in 2009, being associated with bad attitudes to *race/racism* and *foreigners* (below).

capital punishment Capital punishment (aka the **death penalty**), latterly by *hanging* (below), was abolished in the UK in 1969 (after being suspended in 1965); and was for all practical purposes made impossible when the UK eventually ratified the Sixth Protocol to the European Convention On Human Rights in 2004. See generally *human rights*. For other landmarks, see *Allen, Peter Anthony and Evans, Gwynne Owen; Ellis, Ruth; Evans, Timothy* and *Hanratty, James* (all in *Touchstones*); and entries in the section on *Key dates and events*. From medieval times England was famed for its **Bloody Code**

of several hundred **capital offences**, many minor in nature; when London was the **City of the Gallows**. Abolition is associated with the singlemindedness of Sidney Silverman MP and the Campaign for the Abolition of the Death Penalty. For a minutely observed account, see *Hanging in the Balance: A History of the Abolition of Capital Punishment in Britain* (1997), Block BP and Hostettler J, Waterside Press. Capital punishment continues in many countries: China, Iran, Pakistan, Saudi Arabia and the USA account for 88 per cent of executions. For this global perspective, see *The Death Penalty: A Worldwide Perspective* (4th. edn. 2008), Hood R and Hoyle C, Oxford University Press. There is a **Centre for Capital Punishment Studies** at the University of Westminster: see relevant pages at wmin.ac.uk/law **Clive Stafford Smith** (b.1960) is a British born lawyer and director of the Louisiana Crisis Assistance Centre, New Orleans, USA. A leading champion of *human rights* he has devoted his career to the *legal representation* of impoverished defendants (see generally *causes of crime*) including via regular *appeals* from 'Death Row'. His pioneering work received global recognition as long ago as the 1980s following Paul Hamann's award-winning TV documentary 'Fourteen Days in May' (BBC, 1987). A similar programme from Death Row was broadcast in 2003 (BBC 2). He is the founder of **Reprieve**: see reprieve.org.uk

carousel fraud An ingenious form of *white collar crime* (below), or possibly *organized crime*, aka **'missing trader fraud'**, i.e. missing trader intra-European community (MTIEC), involving the creaming off of *value* added tax (VAT) in a situation where it is chargeable in one country but not payable in another. The fact that VAT was charged is then obscured by (possibly repeated) import and export transactions ('the carousel'). Of considerable dimensions in modern times, it has led to long sentences and the pursuit of *proceeds of crime*, sometimes by wholesale freezing of bank accounts and assets by HM *Revenue & Customs* during an *investigation*.

Carter Report(s) Those by **Lord Patrick Carter** as commissioned by government but otherwise independent. The first *A Review of Correctional Services in England and Wales, Managing Offenders, Reducing Crime* (2003), Carter P, Prime Minister's Strategy Unit, led to changes in the way correctional

services are provided and managed and also the *National Offender Management Service* (NOMS). It focussed on 'contestability' so as to open up competition and produce the most *effective* sentences 'whoever delivers them'; government stating that it intended to encourage the *private sector* and 'not for profit' sector in this regard: 'We want to encourage *partnerships* between ... providers ... which harness their respective strengths'. The second Carter Report, *Securing the Future: Proposals for the Efficient and Sustainable Use of Custody in England and Wales* (2007), Carter P, MOJ accepted as inevitable certain increases in the *prison(er) population* and proposed Titan prisons (see *prison*), a *Sentencing Commission* and a possible sentencing 'grid' for *judges* to match sentencing demands and resources. Sentencing grids in which aggravating and mitigating factors are geared to levels of *punishment* have existed for many years, including within the *Probation Service*. One of the first to be developed was the Minnesota Grid (USA, 1980; 1989). Others are styled 'sentencing matrix': see, e.g. law.jrank.org under 'Sentencing Guideline'.

Casement, Roger (1864-1916) (later Sir) British diplomat, Irish nationalist, republican and activist, who was executed for *treason* (below) at *Wandsworth Prison* re events linked to the *Easter Rising* (below); turning on legal niceties of nationality and allegiance; events overshadowed by Casement's 'Black Diaries' recording (then illegal) homosexual encounters and his taste for lowlife; which were circulated in order to undermine an *appeal* for clemency (see *mercy*). A Special Commission in Ireland (2002) found that the diaries (once thought to be a *forgery* by the security services) were genuine. A painting of related events in the *Court of Appeal* by Sir John Lavery hangs in the National Portrait Gallery, London. According to the poet W B Yeats: 'Upon the British Empire/ Upon the Church of Christ/ The ghost of Roger Casement/Is beating on the door'. His body was reinterred in Dublin in 1965.

'cash for honours' (1) An *investigation* of 2007 into allegations that honours, e.g. knighthoods and peerages (see *peer*), were being traded by government, its *Ministers of State* or high-ranking party members in return for party-political financial support (see also *political aspects* below); after which the Crown Prosecution Service (CPS) decided against prosecution. At one stage the events involved dawn *raids* on the homes of 10 Downing Street staff; and led to Prime Minister Tony Blair being interviewed by the police as a *witness*. **(2)** Comparable events of the 1920s in which Prime Minister Lloyd George was embroiled, leading to the *imprisonment* of Maundy Gregory and the Honours (Abuses) Act 1922 which first made the practice a specific criminal offence.

Centre for Crime and Justice Studies (CCJS) An independent charity based at King's College London (KCL) that informs and educates re all aspects of crime and the CJS: 'Our vision is of a society in which everyone benefits from justice, safety, economic and social security. Our mission is to promote just and effective *responses* to crime and related harms by informing and educating through critical analysis, research and public debate'. The CCJS publishes a journal, *Criminal Justice Matters* and makes an annual **Una Padel Award** in memory of a former director. See crimeandjustice.org.uk

centre stage Expression used from time-to-time when an agency/service has sought an enhanced CJS role as, e.g. when the *Probation Service* said in the 1990s that it would be 'moving centre stage'; an expression other agencies have also used since that time.

Chartists The last 'near-revolution' in the UK in response to a 'People's Charter' (1838) setting out radical demands in the wake of the Reform Act 1832. The Chartists were an alliance of 'well-to-do' southerners, artisans, trade unionists and 'discontented masses' from the industrial North. Their activities began in London, Birmingham and Leeds, leading to riots, disturbances, debates, propaganda, insurrection, disorder and a suggestion of impending Civil War (with events in the South more moderate). Large numbers of people were sentenced to *imprisonment* or *transportation* (below). For their final March (1848), 170,000 police officers manned barricades in central London; but the day passed without major incident as protest subsided.

churning Routinely putting-off making a decision rather than progressing a case towards its outcome, e.g. where it is adjourned *repeatedly* without any advances being made.

Clapham omnibus 'Man/woman on the Clapham omnibus' is a metaphor for *reasonableness*; connoting the thoughts, beliefs and actions of the 'ordinary person', who travels on a Clapham, South London, bus. He or she features mainly in *civil* cases but is not unknown to the CJS. The *law reports* abound with references to this disinterested bystander even if situations found to be reasonable have, as one judge once put it, credited him or her with 'the agility of an acrobat and the foresight of a Hebrew prophet'.

Climbié, Victoria The case of Victoria Climbié ranks as one of the most tragic child *abuse* cases in the UK. Victoria, aged eight, from the Ivory Coast, was *murdered* in London in 2000. There were over 100 injury marks on her wasted body. Marie Therese Kauao (her great aunt) and Carl Manning (Kauao's partner) were each sentenced to *life imprisonment* in 2001. The **Laming Report** ('The Victoria Climbié Inquiry: Report of an Inquiry by Lord Laming' (2003), Cm 5730) set out lessons to be learned from the 'lamentable' *administrative, management* and professional failures in which *social workers*, *health* visitors, police and National Health Service staff repeatedly missed the signs or opportunities to save her. It condemned 'buck-passing' by senior officials; and said *discipline* of subordinates served to deflect higher responsibility and *accountability*. See victoria-climbie-inquiry.org.uk The case led to 'the biggest shake up' of children's services for 30 years. Afterwards, an appeal was launched so as to build a school in the Ivory Coast in Victoria's memory. The case is one of a number before and since of which those of **Maria Coldwell** (1973, Isle of Wight) and **Baby P** (2007, Haringey) are landmarks.

Clinks Short for **Community Links**; established in 1998 to strengthen and develop *partnerships* between *voluntary* and *community*-based organizations and *HM Prison Service* and the *Probation Service*. It now has an additional strand focussing on developments relating to the National Offender Management Service (NOMs) (see *offender management*). Clinks has developed a diverse network of agencies which contribute to the *rehabilitation* of offenders and building safer and more inclusive communities (see also *social exclusion*). It is also a contact point for bodies providing services to offenders and/or their families. See www.clinks.org and for an overview, *Prisons and the Voluntary Sector: A Bridge Into the Community* (2002), Bryans S, Martin C and Walker R, Waterside Press.

clip around the ear The early-to-mid 20th century practice whereby *low-level* offenders (typically *juveniles*) were cuffed about the ears by a police officer as a warning. Aka **cuffing**, this remains a metaphor for *cautions, warnings and reprimands* or police *advice*. Hence the Opposition's 'new generation clip around the ear' and *tough* (below) action following a poor *response* by the offender (2009) (contrast its approach to *hoodies* below in 2006).

cold case An unsolved crime re which the *case file* was closed and *investigation* suspended; which is later revived. Systems exist for periodic *review* by **cold case review teams**; often re *high profile* matters (below) or persistently worrying ones. With developments in *DNA*-profiling, over 500 such reviews led to 120 convictions for *murder* or other *serious offences* between 2000 and 2008; or resolution of an alleged *miscarriage of justice*: see, e.g. *Hanratty, James*, below. In a landmark case, the Dearne Valley rapist (aka 'shoe rapist' from his habit of storing victims' shoes), *serial offender*, James Lloyd (aged 50) was convicted at Sheffield Crown Court in 2006 of rapes and other sexual offences committed 20 years before, and given sentences of *life imprisonment*; the first offender to be traced using scientifically enhanced familial *DNA*; that of his sister who had been arrested for the *road traffic* offence of 'excess alcohol'. One of oldest outstanding investigation (of a 1946 murder) is taking place in Penllergaer, Wales. In 2009, Surrey Police were reported to be investigating a murder case from 1926.

criminalisation A term of various connotations, focusing around the idea of 'turning people into criminals' or 'making criminals out of people'; either due to the way in which the law itself impacts on *citizens*, or the way that the CJS treats them, e.g. through *targeting* offences or *law enforcement* priorities. The term is also associated with the creation of an excessive number of *crimes*; as well as poverty, *disadvantage* and people 'on the margins' (see *marginal* below and *social exclusion* in *Main Entries*); who are also vulnerable to *net widening* (below). Such tactics are inherently malleable, tending to focus on those who are perceived to be 'in

need of attention'. The process is also nowadays associated with *anti-social behaviour* (ASB) (and *civil* behaviour orders (CBOs)), where behaviour which is not intrinsically criminal is criminalised at a 'second stage', i.e. if there is a breach of the original order; and where the chain of events may not have attracted *safeguards* normally associated with criminal cases. Contrast *decriminalisation*.

Cromwell Street Murder location and an example of the description of events by reference to place, i.e. **25 Cromwell Street, Gloucester** (subsequently like 10 Rillington Place, London: the home of John Christie: see *Evans, Timothy*) demolished to avoid morbid sight-seeing. It was the home of husband and wife (predatory) *serial killers* Frederick (Fred) and Rosemary (Rose) West who took in vulnerable, rootless, young women/girls (although West Family members also became victims). Their home became an 'open house' where pornography, *alcohol* and *drugs* were available. Several bodies were buried in the garden and beneath the house. Fred committed suicide in 1995 in Gloucester Prison whilst awaiting trial (see generally *deaths in custody* earlier in this section) whilst Rose was convicted of ten murders and sentenced to *life imprisonment*; Fred began by killing his first wife. Several victims were *tortured* and/or made to participate in sexual *abuse*, sometimes video-recorded; causing criticism a when materials 'surplus to requirements' were auctioned by the Official Solicitor under a duty to raise funds for Fred's estate; excerpts being broadcast by Channel 4 TV after the *Attorney General* declined to intervene as guardian of the *public interest*. Allegedly, there were other murders: an assertion common re such offenders.

cybercrime Description which has been applied to various types of crime committed 'in cyberspace', i.e. due to the existence of the internet, e.g. internet *fraud* (especially that based around identity fraud: see *identification/identity*), *hacking* and making indecent images of *children*. Hence initiatives to counter such offences aka **cyberpolicing**, including via a **Virtual Global Taskforce**: see generally *global dimensions*. Some people limit cybercrime to that which 'could not be committed but for the internet' as opposed to existing offences which can nowadays be committed in a novel way by using it, such as *harassment* or *hate crime* by email.

Dando, Jill Co-presenter of the long-running BBC TV 'Crimewatch' programme (see *crime*) which *appeals* for *information* about unsolved crimes; shot dead on the doorstep of her Fulham, South London (1999). In 2008, Barry George's conviction for her *murder* was quashed by the *Court of Appeal* after he had served six years of a sentence of *life imprisonment*. Aka Barry Bulsara (after the late-lead singer of the rock group Queen), he was a loner, obsessed by celebrity, with a habit of 'following women'. Neither this, other eccentric traits nor dubious *evidence* was deemed by the Court of Appeal to be enough and his conviction was held unsafe. For a prediction of and reasoning for this, see *Wanted* (2005), Turney B, Waterside Press.

dark matters Criminal justice can be a **dark topic**. An insight into this, ranging across matters such as *murder*, *suicide*, genocide and the Holocaust can be accessed at dark-tourism.org.uk which describes itself as 'the premier online academic resource facility' in this field. For fascination with **dark locations** of the kind noted in other entries, see *An Infamous Address* (1989), Wilkes R, Grafton Books; *The Murder Guide to London* (1990), Fido, M, Chicago: Academy Press.

deaths in custody Generic head under which deaths in prison, police or other official *custody* (or *detention*) are discussed; extending from death from natural causes to *suicide*, accident (see also, e.g. *health and safety*; prison/'safe prison') or ill-treatment. Some 100 deaths per year are involved; the annual total acting as a broad barometer of improvements or failings. Many cases have become rallying points, including those of: **Joy Gardner** (enforced deportation) (d.1993), **Roger Sylvester** (prone restraint at a psychiatric hospital)(d.1999); **Christopher Edwards** (killed in 1994 by his cell-mate whilst on *remand* to prison: the European Court of Human Rights holding that the UK authorities were responsible for several shortcomings: see also *No Truth, No Justice: A David and Goliath Story of a Mother's Successful Struggle Against the Public Authorities to Secure Justice for her Son Murdered While in their Care* (2002), Edwards, A, Waterside Press; **Zahid Mubarek** (d.1997) re whom a public inquiry made over 150 recommendations for improvements following his being killed by a cell-mate at Feltham *Young Offender Institution* the day before that

scheduled for Mubarek's *release*); and **Adam Rickwood** (d.2004 aged 14) the youngest person to die in custody in the UK, at Hassockfield *Secure Training Centre*, County Durham (operated by the *private sector*), a *suicide* following restraint re which a fresh inquest was ordered in 2009. Further information about this topic generally is available from the leading organization **INQUEST** (inquest.gn.apc.org). All deaths in prison automatically lead to *investigation* by the *Prisons and Probation Ombudsman*; police-related deaths a *referral* to the *Independent Police Complaints Commission* (IPCC).

demonisation Styling, *labelling* or *stereotyping* (both below) individuals, or groups, as people whom the public should *fear* (who, in some cases, may be dubbed *evil*, below); such as *hoodies* (below), *immigrants* (see *Main Entries*), paedophiles and *marginal* people (below). Similarly, views or opinions, may be demonised (an extreme form of **'bad mouthing'**); and 'monsters' may be created by the *media/press* and in *popular culture* (the latter below). The process may have *political aspects* (as when those engaged in the Miners' Strike of 1984 were dubbed **'the enemy within'**); and has connections to *hate* crime, *discrimination* and *social exclusion*. It may be a socio-psychological phenomenon that communities need their 'demons', failing which they will invent them; which can affect international relations as it can a local *witch* hunt (and note in particular the reference to *Demonologie* within that entry below).

denial A term with stronger CJS connotations than in ordinary speech: signifying a form of self-delusion re, e.g. whether something occurred or re personal responsibility. For example a sex offender may wrongly deny that matters were as *serious* as described by a *witness* etc, claim that the *victim* was the instigator, or insist that it was 'normal' behaviour (see also *normalisation* below). Denial features in many contexts from *domestic violence* to *serial offences* and *addiction* (the last of these above). Similarly, offenders convicted by a court following a *plea* of 'not guilty' may remain **in denial** in the face of hard *evidence*; including via spurious *appeals* or claims of a *miscarriage of justice*; due to an inability to face the *truth*; making it harder to discern genuine cases. A similar scenario can exist re the CJS and its practitioners as a form of *blindness*: see e.g. *Birmingham Six* (above). Traditionally, *HM Prison Service* has made no allowance for denials by convicted prisoners; partly for pragmatic reasons but also because its duty is to carry out court sentences in a humane way. The word denial is also used to signify **denial of liberty**.

Dickens, Charles (1812-1870) Novelist and social commentator; including re poverty, *disadvantage* and other *causes of crime*, e.g. in *Nicholas Nickleby*, whose youthful experiences brings him into contact with the *Underworld* (below). After attending the public executions of Maria and Frederick Manning (1849), Dickens wrote to *The Times* urging that such events take place inside prison, describing the ribaldry at the gallows as 'a sight so inconceivably awful ... the wickedness and levity of the immense crowd ... could be imagined by no man, and ... [or be] presented by no heathen land under the sun'. *The Times* disagreed, admitting that executions were '*judicial* slaughter' - but a 'useful terror and a convenient humility'. Dickens also wrote about debtors prisons in which his father was for a time imprisoned.

doli incapax rule A *rule* of the Common Law whereby someone between the ages of 10-14 could not be guilty of an offence unless, in addition to ordinary *mens rea*, he or she knew that what he or she did was seriously wrong. This rule was abolished by the Crime and Disorder Act 1998 (but the statutory rule that a child under ten does not have the capacity to commit crime survives).

Dudley and Stephens A celebrated case, that of *R. v. Dudley and Stephens* (1884) 14 QBD 273, in which shipwrecked mariners killed and ate their cabin boy; pleading necessity as a *defence*. The jury agreed that if they had not so acted they would most probably have perished; and that the boy, being in the weakest condition, would have died first. The sailors were found guilty of *murder* and sentenced to *capital punishment* (above), albeit the judge did not don the standard black cap when passing sentence; a *signal* (below) to the *Crown*, which reduced this to six months' imprisonment apiece. The case remains influential re the *defence* of necessity. For an account, see *The Custom of the Sea: The Shocking True Tale of Shipwreck, Murder and the Last Taboo* (2000), Hanson N, Corgi.

Easter Rising The last armed rebellion in British history, in Dublin, Ireland (then part of Britain) in 1916: an abortive, sustained insurrection that began on Easter Monday, an attempt by republicans to seize *control* of Ireland and independence from Britain. It lasted from April 24-30, during which the Irish Citizen(s) Army (ICA) supported by Irish Volunteers, led by *barrister* and teacher, Pádraig Pearse, took strategic locations, including the General Post Office (GPO) and Dublin Castle, reading out a proclamation of 'an Irish Republic free of the British *Crown*'. The rising is also notable for the huge *military* response of the British; and executions by firing squad at Dublin's Kilmainham Gaol (now a museum) of 14 of its leaders for *treason* (below) and see generally *capital punishment* (above); plus the internment of thousands of Irish people (many held in England). See also *Casement, Roger* above.

Ellis, John (1874-1932) Public executioner (1901-1924) who hanged 203 people (see *hanging* below) then committed *suicide*; possibly due to stress. His 'victims' included Dr. Hawley Harvey Crippen (1910); Sir Roger *Casement* (1916) (above); Herbert Rowse *Armstrong* (above) (1922); and Edith Thompson (1923), amidst disturbing scenes: see *Criminal Justice: The True Story of Edith Thompson* (1988), Weis, R, Hamish Hamilton. He resigned on health grounds (partly due to *alcohol* use); and wrote *Diary of a Hangman* (1996 reissue), Forum Press.

Ellis, Ruth The last woman to suffer *capital punishment* (above) in the UK (and see *hanging* below), aged 28, at *Holloway Prison* on 13 July 1955; variously described as a manageress, West End club hostess, good-time girl and prostitute. She was convicted of the *murder* by shooting of her lover, racing driver David Blakey, outside the Magdela Tavern, Hampstead, London. The last of six shots injured a bystander from a ricochet. There was no precedent for a *defence* based on diminished responsibility (see *mental impairment*). Ellis showed subdued if not passive interest in her fate, or in answering the charge; refused to *appeal* or (until the eleventh hour) ask for *mercy*; and declined to say who supplied the gun until it was too late for this to countermand the *political* imperative driving *Home Secretary* Sir David Maxwell-Fyffe who declined a reprieve.

England For legal purposes (and hence for descriptive purposes in many texts) England includes Wales: Interpretation Act 1978.

euphemism The CJS has produced many euphemisms, not least those used by prisoners to re-define their plight, e.g. as **guests of Her Majesty** or **time out**. *Capital punishment* (above) produced many euphemisms, such as **take a ride up Holborn Hill**, i.e. on a hurdle (a kind of trolley without wheels) to the gallows (murderers being unworthy to walk on God's earth); and **dancing in the air**. They also occur in terms such as **helping the police with their enquiries**, i.e. often meaning as a potential suspect in police *detention* rather than an independent *witness*; and **easing the passing**, i.e. euthanasia or *mercy killing* (see the reference to John Bodkin Adams under *Shipman, Harold* below). Note also use of **'The Troubles'** below.

Evans, Timothy A key case along the route to the abolition of *capital punishment* (above); and the first clearly identifiable major post-Second World War *miscarriage of justice*; when an innocent man was hanged. Evans, of low IQ, was convicted due to his false *'confession'* to the *murder* of his wife and daughter (1950). Following official procrastination, he was granted a posthumous pardon (1966); after the conviction of *serial killer* John Reginald Christie (Evan's landlord and a former special constable) for one of the 'Evans murders' (1953) failed to trigger this sooner. See *Miscarriages of Justice* (1987), Woofinden, B, Trafalgar Square.

evil Discussion abounds re the nature of evil, whether it exists at all, in pure or abstract form, as a natural phenomenon or as a by-product of upbringing, environment, etc. Similarly, whether there are **necessary evils** (or **lesser evils**); as when *national security* or the *safety* of the *community* is placed ahead of that of an individual. People may be perceived to be driven by satanic impulses and hence demonised as **'evil monsters'** (see *demonisation* above). The word 'evil' is sometimes used by judges when sentencing someone deemed to be, say, **evil and depraved** but generally has little or no place in CJS discourse. At Common Law, particularly historically, certain offences were treated as **evil in themselves** (*malum in se*), such as *murder*. Relevant works include *Evil Minds: Understanding and Responding to Violent Predators* (2004), Meadows R and Kuehnel J, Pearson Education and *Knowledge of Evil: Child Prostitution and Child Sexual Abuse in Twentieth-century England* (2002), Brown, A and Barrett D, Willan Publishing. Examples of the use of the word 'evil' also appear occasionally within other entries in this work.

falling from grace The converse of *'going straight'*. The annals of crime and *punishment* contain countless examples of people of status, wealth, talent or fame who have ended up on the wrong side of the law: a puzzle for those commentators who seek to explain crime as a by-product of *disadvantage*, *broken windows* (above), etc; and too commonplace to be mere exceptions to the rule. For a selection, see *Brewer's Rogues, Villains and Eccentrics: An A-Z of Roguish Britons Through the Ages* (2002), Donaldson, W, Cassell.

Fanny Adams A girl aged eight from Alton, Hampshire who was *murdered* in 1812 (by a *solicitor's* clerk) and cut to pieces. Hence the expression **'sweet FA'** to signify 'worthlessness' (of naval origin possibly in nearby Portsmouth) that evolved into **'sweet fuckall'**. There is an Australian variant (the crime itself occurred in London in 1874): **Harriet Lane**, a colloquial term for corned beef.

Ferrers, Earl *Peer* of the realm who stood trial before his 'equals' (see generally *trial by peers*) in the House of Lords for the *murder* of a servant. He was executed at *Tyburn* (below) in 1760 before an immense crowd; and was possibly the first person to experience *hanging* (below) by means of the 'drop' (falling through a trapdoor: in his case a primitive version) rather than strangulation. By a quirk of history, Earl Ferrers (a descendant) was Minister of State at the Home Office (1990-93) in charge of *criminal policy*.

felonies and misdemeanours The historic classification of *serious offences* (felonies) and lesser offences (misdemeanours) is no longer of practical significance in England (having been abolished by the Criminal Law Act 1967) but still exists in the USA. The terms also survive in popular speech. Hence, in particular, informal use of the word **felon** for a *serious* offender and the expression **high crimes and misdemeanours** to describe, e.g. *treason* (below) or crimes in high places. The distinction affected (what is now) *allocation and sending* and maximum *punishments*.

Fielding, (Sir) Henry (1707-1754) Leading figure with regard to the development of the English novel and social reformer (see generally *reform*) who wrote *Tom Jones* (1749); *An Enquiry into the Causes of the Late Increase in Robbers* (1751) (arguing that the *motive* was greed not luxury nor need); and *Amelia* (1751) describing 'lawless' times. See, also, *Wild, Jonathan,* below. Fielding was appointed 'police court' magistrate at *Bow Street* (above)(1748) (and also served in Westminster and Middlesex) where he created a policing blueprint using thief takers, later *Bow Street Runners* (above); as developed by *Sir Robert Peel* (below) from the 1820s onwards. He used the *media/press* to persuade *citizens* to volunteer *suspicions*, and started embryonic criminal records (see, now, *Criminal Records Bureau*). The success of the runners convinced government to sponsor Fielding (via the Secret Service Fund) to *research* the case for a nationwide force. He was partly responsible for the Licensing Act 1737 (under which the Lord Chamberlain censored plays until 1968) after ridiculing the Prime Minister at a public reading. He was succeeded by his blind half-brother and assistant, **(Sir) John Fielding** (1721-80).

Fifth Amendment A key provision of the USA Constitution, containing various basic *citizens'* rights including that country's rule against self-incrimination (hence **'pleading the Fifth Amendment'** which is also sometimes heard in the UK in popular speech), i.e. declining to answer formal/official questions on the ground that the person concerned might incriminate himself or herself); *double jeopardy;* and *due process* (all 1791). It states: 'No person shall be held to answer for a capital, or otherwise infamous crime, unless on a presentment or indictment of a grand jury ... nor shall any person be subject for the same offence to be twice put in jeopardy of life or limb; nor ... be compelled ... to be a witness against himself, nor be deprived of life, liberty, or property, without due process of law; nor shall private property be taken for public use, without just compensation'. For UK comparisons, see *human rights; silence/* 'right to silence'.

fingerprint The unique impression left by a human finger on contact with a surface or materials capable of retaining such a mark. The *identification* of suspects by their fingerprints (aka **'dabs'**) has long been an everyday event, to the extent that hand-held electronic fingerprinting devices are in use linked to *databases*. Prints can connect suspects to offences as part of a chain of *evidence*. The discovery that prints could be 'lifted' is credited to Henry Faulds (around 1880); *effective* use depending on a system of classifications developed by Sir Edward Henry, Commissioner of Police for London and implemented by Scotland Yard (1901). The first high profile use was re a *murder* by Alfred and Albert Stratton (1905). In 2006, some doubt was cast on the reliability of such evidence by Shirley McKie, a woman police constable (WPC) from Kilmarnock, Scotland, cleared of *perjury* after four experts from the Scottish Criminal Records Office (SCRO) wrongly stated that a print at a *crime scene* belonged to her. Hence, in modern-times **genetic fingerprint**: see *DNA*; and a **National Automated Fingerprint Identification System (NAFIS)** (part of the *National Identification Service* (NIS)); which examines 850,000 sets of **arrest fingerprints** a year and 40,000 **prisoner fingerprints**. **Palm prints** are a variant (first mass use 1955). Prints can be taken from other parts of the body.

foreigner If a foreign national, someone who is not a *citizen* of the UK, is convicted by a court in England and Wales and sent to prison, he or she will normally be taken to an English, etc. prison to serve out his or her sentence; and *release* occurs under the same general arrangements as for UK nationals; subject to any recommendation for *deportation*. International arrangements do exist for the transfer/exchange of prisoners as between *States*; when the sentence can then be served in the foreign country concerned. Similarly, *community sentences* are carried out in the UK; but foreigners may be at a 'disadvantage': a court may think that *imprisonment* is a safer option, i.e. because he or she might otherwise quit the *jurisdiction*. Similarly, re *fine enforcement* when imprisonment in default may be triggered more readily than re a resident UK national with a fixed address. Certain 'reciprocal', inter-State *enforcement* arrangements do exist; said to be improving. Under the Criminal Justice and Immigration Act 2008 **'foreign criminals'** are effectively deprived of any right they might have to enter or stay in the UK. There is a long history of foreigners being treated with *suspicion* or in *marginal* ways (below). Questions of nationality fall to the *Home Office*; admission to the UK to the UK *Border Agency*. For related areas, see *asylum, deportation, immigration*.

French Revolution Events in France from 1789-99 when diverse *communities* in French Society, influenced by thinkers such as Rousseau, found common cause to oppose feudal structures and a discredited monarchy; in which, initially, the Girondists overthrew the Bourbon Crown, stormed the Bastille Prison and formed a ruling States General (National Assembly); events that reverberated across Europe and had a considerable impact on *law enforcement* in Britain, leading to repressive measures, lack of tolerance and harsh *responses* to signs of uprising (including, notably, in Ireland). With the rise of the Jacobins, the French regime progressed to beheading King Louis XIV (1793), Queen Marie Antoinette and leading members of the aristocracy; triggering the **Reign of Terror** (September 1793-July 1794: aka 'The Terror') when events turned yet more radical under a Committee on Public Safety (see generally *euphemism* above). A Revolutionary Tribunal was created, from which there was no *appeal*; that from mid-1794, used only *capital punishment* (above) (by guillotine) leading by May 1795 to some 2,600 executions, including of the tribunal's one-time protagonist/prosecutor, Robespierre. 'The Directory', its final genesis, was displaced by Napoleon Bonaparte (1799).

function creep (aka 'mission creep') A phenomenon whereby *legislation*, power or authority created for one purpose is adapted for wider purposes (often after assurances that 'necessary' new powers will be used in a just a minority of cases). Striking examples exist re *serious crime, terrorism* and *anti-social behaviour* (ASB). Similarly 'creeping' use by *Ministers of State* of delegated *legislation* re the burgeoning stock of new criminal offences (nearly 100 carrying *imprisonment* in 2007: a figure obtained under the *Freedom of Information Act 2000* and quoted by Baroness Stern in Parliament in 2009).

Garden House Riot *Politically* motivated riot stemming from a 'rolling demonstration' outside the Garden House Hotel, Cambridge (1970) which led to the *imprisonment* of several university students. A 'Greek Week' in support of the 'Colonels' regime' in Greece led to protests that escalated over several days until over 400 students gathered to

dissuade people from entering the hotel for a celebration dinner; when they tried to drown out the speeches with noise. The dinner was invaded, parts of the hotel wrecked (see, generally, *criminal damage*) and *violence* flared on both sides. Nine students were charged with *incitement* to riotous assembly.

garrotting Strangling someone by placing a thin wire, rope or scarf around the victim's throat and tightening it quickly; rendering that person unconscious, possibly the victim of *murder*. Numerous such *assaults* occurred in 1862-3 in London linked to *theft* and *robbery* (hence **'Garrotte tip'**: a *euphemism* for the *proceeds* of such crimes). This led to the **'Garrotting Act' 1863** and *punishment* by flogging, which was claimed to be *effective* in terms of *deterrence* when this spate of offending ceased. A 'silent' method of killing, garotting has also been favoured by security forces. **The Garrote** was a device used in Spain re *capital punishment* (1812-1974); as well as in other *jurisdictions* from time-to-time.

gate A word of diverse CJS application (of which the following are indicative): **(1)** the **prison gate** has iconic resonances for prisoners and prison staff as the interface with the world outside, including 'reception' (see *prison*) and *release*; **(2) gatelodge** is a description of: **(a)** the 'gatehouse' cum residence historically attached to some prisons; and **(b)** *Gatelodge* the journal of the Prison Officers Association (POA)(poauk.org.uk); **(3) gating** equates with *restriction of liberty*, especially re *children*, often meaning under parental control; **(3) garden gate** was **(a)** a slang term for police officer (1800s): the equivalent of 'yokel' after recruitment brought unemployed agricultural labourers to London; and **(b)** rhyming slang for *magistrate* (1800s); **(5)** gate is commonly used as a suffix to imply *corruption* or *deception*: after **Watergate** the 1970s bugging scandal that ultimately unseated USA president, Richard Nixon. Examples from 2008/2009 include: **Crowngate** when the BBC had to apologise to the Sovereign re misleading film footage; and events involving payments by lobbying groups to members of the House of Lords (aka 'cash for influence') being styled **Ermingate**. Other usages include: **(6) gate money** (aka 'garnish money'): **(a)** a form of *protection* money paid to warders, 'senior prisoners' or old hands by a newcomer on reception into prison (particularly at *Newgate*

Prison below); abolished under George IV; or **(b)** money paid to get out of prison following *acquittal,* basically for 'rent' owed; that ended in the 1780s due to the efforts of John Howard (see *Howard League* below); **(7) 'clang of the prison gate'**: the (questionable) notion that a 'taste of prison' is good for first-time offenders, on grounds of *deterrence* (i.e. the metaphorical or actual sound of a cell door closing behind a prisoner. In 2002, Lord Woolf, Lord Chief Justice whilst giving a *guideline judgement* re *burglary* stated: 'We fully accept that there are ... cases where the clang of the prison cell door for the first time may have a deterrent effect but the statistics of re-offending suggest that the numbers who will be deterred by their first experience of incarceration are not substantial'; **(8)** the informal term **gatekeeping** re events at any stage of the CJS, i.e. a mechanism for keeping people away from severe outcomes such as *custody,* or *risks* associated with ready *intervention* or *treatment* (especially from the 1980s onwards); and **(9) gate fever**: a quasi-medical condition suffered by prisoners as their *release* date approaches.

Gordon Riots (aka 'no popery riots').Major riots of 1780 triggered by the zeal of **Lord George Gordon**. In January he handed in a petition to Parliament by the Protestant Association, complaining of 'indulgences' to Roman Catholics (concessions conferring some equal rights with Protestants). In June, he led a 40,000 strong march from St George's Fields to Westminster with another petition; but the event became a mob riot, involving arson, looting and destruction of Catholic property (with the Bank of England and four prisons being 'opened-up') (hence **St George's Fields Massacre**). Using reinforcements from armed associations, the Horse Guards, Foot Guards and the militia of several counties, the authorities launched a massive *response*, resulting in 210 rioters being killed, 248 wounded (of whom 75 died later in hospital) and subjected to *capital punishment* (above). Lord Gordon was tried for High Treason but secured an *acquittal.* Alderman Kennett was found guilty of 'dereliction of duty'. The *value* of the damage was some £180,000 (at 1780s prices).

Great Train Robbery (GTR) (1) A major *robbery* (aka 'heist') when the Glasgow to Watford, London mail train was stopped by a *gang* acting with *military* precision and

over £2 million in 'used notes' was taken (largely unrecovered) (1963); that became a benchmark for such crimes. The ringleaders received (the then) unusually long sentences of 25-30 years *imprisonment* on the basis of *deterrence*. Several became household names: leader Bruce Reynolds; Ronald Biggs (who escaped to Brazil and evaded re-capture for 20 years then returned to complete his sentence); Thomas Wisbey (*murdered*); and Buster Edwards (who sold flowers by Waterloo Station, London). Modern comparisons are with the **Brinks Mat Bullion Robbery** (1998): £40 million pounds in gold (again largely unrecovered; and **Northern Bank Robbery**, Belfast (2004): £22 million, reputedly the work of the Irish Republican Army (IRA); whilst some city *frauds* or via the internet are estimated in terms of billions of pounds. **(2) An earlier GTR** (1855) of hundredweights of gold ingots led by speculator Edward Agar, 'a misapplied genius'; and **(3) similar GTRs** at other times worldwide.

grey crime Offences committed by older people (imprecisely defined). With greater life expectancy there is an ageing *prison(er) population*; re which it has been urged there should be special provision (which there is re some people serving *life imprisonment*; and programmes, regimes and *healthcare* facilities in prison may have been responding. Some prisoners in their 70s and 80s may have been incarcerated late in life (and will maybe die naturally in prison: see generally *deaths in custody*, above); others, younger when sentenced, have 'grown old' there. Grey crime is said to be prevalent re such offences as shoplifting, benefit or insurance *fraud* and HM *Revenue & Customs* offences. It has also been suggested that some pensioners seek to compensate for 'being sold short' after a long, decent working life. It has been estimated that some 50 per cent of *sex offenders* in prison are over 60. Older people have also been sent to prison for not paying their council tax (some due to *civil disobedience* in refusing to pay) or *anti-social behaviour* (extending to 'feeding the birds'). The *Prison Reform Trust* (below) suggests that the majority of **grey offenders** should be dealt with in the *community*; and for the few who are *dangerous* there ought to be purpose-built establishments.

Guildford pub bombings Explosions at the Horse and Groom and Seven Stars public houses ('army pubs': Guildford, Surrey being close to Aldershot, Hampshire, which houses a '*military* town') by an active service unit (ASU) of the Irish Republican Army (IRA)(1974) at the height of The *Troubles* (below); when five people were *murdered* and 60 maimed/seriously injured. Hence the **Guildford Four** (Gerry Conlon, Paul Hill, Patrick Armstrong and Carole Richardson); the alleged culprits who were convicted then *released* after 17 years when their convictions were found to be unsafe by the *Court of Appeal* (see generally *miscarriage of justice*). Their false '*confessions*' were obtained by *torture* and potentially critical *prosecution* material was not disclosed (see now *disclosure*). In a connected miscarriage of justice case the **Maguire Seven** were convicted of possessing nitroglycerine, allegedly for IRA bomb-making, after a *raid* in Kilburn, north London (1976). Both cases have links to the **Balcombe Street Siege** (1975) (the 'Balcombe Street gang' claiming responsibility re both). The events were the backdrop for a feature film, 'In The Name of the Father' (1993) (centring on the Guildford bombings). For an account, see *Trial and Error: The Maguires, the Guildford Pub Bombings and British Justice* (1989), Kee R, Penguin. Compare *Birmingham Six* (above).

Guinness Four Ernest Saunders, Gerald Ronson, Anthony Parnes and Jack Lyons who were convicted at The *Old Bailey* (below) of involvement in a *conspiracy* to drive up the *value* of Guinness brewing shares during its £2.6 billion takeover bid for Distillers (1986). Each was sentenced to *imprisonment* (ranging from two to four years). In 2002, their *appeals* to the *House of Lords* were rejected. They had argued that even before the European Convention On Human Rights was part of English law (see *human rights*) UK courts were obliged under international law to take account of *rulings* of the European Court of Human Rights, in particular re *fair/fairness*. Five Law Lords upheld the prosecutor's contention that English law (as it stood at the time of their 1990 trial) 'could not be trumped' by Europe. The European Court had found that the four were deprived of their right against *self-incrimination* (see generally *silence*/'right to silence' and *Fifth Amendment* (above)); but noted that they would later have fallen under an exception vis-à-vis that right due to more recent UK *legislation* by which they would have been compelled to give *evidence* to Department of Trade inspectors. The Law Lords said it was 'well-established' that international treaties are not part of English law and UK courts have no *jurisdiction* to interpret/apply them.

habeus corpus A Latin tag meaning 'You may have the body'. The **writ of habeus corpus** is the ultimate mechanism of the UK's *higher courts* with which to *safeguard* the *liberty* of the individual; within and beyond the realm. It is a flexible, potentially wide-ranging (*civil*) remedy, whereby, e.g. an order can be made against a gaoler to produce his or her prisoner to the High Court for it to determine whether or not the latter is being lawfully held; when it may order *release*; as it can when e.g. there has been an abduction, false imprisonment or hostage-taking. The first measure 'for the better securing of the liberty of the subject', aka the **Writ of Right** (1679), stemmed from a hard-won campaign against *abuse of power*. *Blackstone* (above) noted that habeus corpus 'may be suspended by Parliament for a specified time when the *emergency* is extreme … [when] the nation parts with a portion of its liberty to secure its own permanent *welfare*, and [suspects] may then be arrested without cause or purpose being assigned'. Habeus corpus has in fact been suspended many times; automatically viewed as a failing. Otherwise, 'No man is to be imprisoned except by judgement of the King's courts or whilst awaiting trial … This *freedom* is … safeguarded by the most famous writ in England' (Lord Denning, Hamlyn Lecture, 1949). The Common Law and vestiges of ancient statutes are reinforced by the Bail Act 1976 (see *bail*), Police and Criminal Evidence Act 1984 and Article 5 of the European Convention On Human Rights ('right to liberty of the person': see generally *human rights*).

Halliday Report That by John Halliday (a former senior *Home Office* official), 'Making Punishments Work: A Review of the Sentencing Framework for England and Wales' (2001) (available at homeoffice.gov.uk/documents/halliday-report). It concluded that 'There is no "right" *sentencing framework*, suitable for all places in all circumstances at all times' and urged one that 'appears to suit present and foreseeable circumstances . . .'. Many of the recommendations were enacted in the *Criminal Justice Act 2003*.

hanging Hanging by the neck until dead was the main form of *capital punishment* (above) in the UK from Anglo-Saxon times; although guillotines were used in Scotland ('The Maiden') and certain English towns, e.g. Hull (as in European countries such as France and Germany). It reached its zenith with England's **Bloody Code** of several hundred capital offences in the 18th century. Before the trap was invented (see also *Ferrers, Earl* above), a horse and cart were placed under the gallows (or 'gallows tree') and a noose around the condemned person's neck. The horse was made to bolt, leaving the offender **hanging in the air** (or 'dancing in the air': per *Wilde, Oscar* below); resulting in strangulation; or the condemned person stood on a ladder which was turned about and hence the term **'turning off'** (as per *Wild, Jonathan,* below). From the late-1800s the practice became more scientific, leading to the spring-loaded trap (to catch the trap-door so that it did not swing back to break the condemned person's legs); and a Home Office **Table of Drops** was devised whereby physique was taken into account to decide on the length of rope necessary to achieve instant death by breaking the neck (though errors still happened). Hanging still occurs in some countries; though largely superseded by lethal injection. See, also, *Pierrepoint, Albert* below. A **hanger and flogger** is a 'hardliner' who prefers to see severe *punishments* as also per *whipping* (below). He or she may be categorised as politically 'to the right' (sometimes of Ghenghis Khan, punitive ruler of the Mongol peoples from 1206). Hanging also features prominently re *suicide* (including re *deaths in custody* above); see also lynch law within *Ku Klux Klan* below.

Hanratty, James (1936-1962) One of the last people to be executed in the UK, for shooting dead Michael Gregston (he also raped and shot Valerie Storey, who survived) at Deadman's Hill, Bedfordshire on the A6 (hence aka the **A6 murder**). His conviction turned on Storey's *identification* of him as the killer to the jury at Bedford Assizes, who rejected his *alibi* that he was in Llandudno, north Wales. A *campaign* to clear his name persists despite modern *DNA*-tests linking Hanratty to the exhibits (his supporters argue that there may have been cross-contamination in storage). As with the case of *Ruth Ellis* (above) this one was a landmark along the route to *capital punishment*

(above). Key texts include: The *A6 Murder—Regina v. James Hanratty: The Semblance of Truth* (1963), Blom-Cooper, L, Penguin; *Who Killed Hanratty?* (1971), Foot, P, Cape (1988), Penguin; and *Hanratty: The Final Verdict* (1997), Woofinden, B, MacMillan.

hard A word that occurs repeatedly in a CJS context, including vis-à-vis the Victorian prison era of **hard bed, hard board, hard fare**: see *Key Dates and Events*/1865; **hard drug**: see *drug*; **hard evidence**: see *evidence*; **hard fact**: see *fact*; **hard labour**: see *preventive detention*; and **hard target/target hardening**: see *target*. Other usages include **hard-nosed copper** for a seasoned officer not readily given to explanations, having 'seen it all before' and possibly disillusioned.

harvesting Working through a mass of *data* looking for offences 'ripe' for prosecution (aka **trawling**: a 'fishing expedition'; or **mining**, i.e. 'a potentially rich seam'). Computers can nowadays be programmed to search for *evidence*, e.g. of *tax evasion, money laundering* or other *suspicious activity*. They can also identify inconsistencies and areas for *investigation*. Conventionally, such work began once there was some reason to think that an offence had occurred, or was about to occur, except, e.g. for test-purchases re breach of *trading standards* or licensing laws, or infiltration by undercover officers in anticipation of offences, see, e.g. *informer*. With harvesting, etc. there is a straightforward search on the assumption that within any tranche of data a proportion of offences will 'turn up'.

heavy A word that occurs repeatedly in a CJS context as with **heavy crime**, i.e. *serious* crime (which tends to be concentrated mostly in the larger cities/urban centres); **heavy policing** (aka 'swamping') by the *allocation* of large numbers of police officers to a task, or 'aggressive policing': a tough, macho, or **heavy-handed** *response*; and **heavy sentence**, i.e. a (possibly unexpectedly) long one. Hence also **heavy end offender** aka 'high end offender' and 'high *risk* offender'): one at the upper end of the offending scale in terms of *seriousness* who may well also be a *dangerous offender*; re whom precautions are needed such as close or intensive *supervision*, e.g. in prison, by *Multi-agency Public Protection Arrangements* (MAPPAs), *parole officers*.

high profile matter One in the public-eye (see also generally *media/press*) because, e.g. it involves a particularly *serious*, notorious or noticeable offence; or which was committed by or against someone who is already in the public eye. Contrast **high profile offender** which is a term used to describe an offender who repeatedly comes to the notice of the police or the other CJS agencies/services.

Holmes (or **HOLMES**) The Home Office Large Major Enquiry System (now Holmes 2). A *data* entering and *management* system used in relation to all major *investigations*/inquiries; which was partly a *response* to the long-running and chaotic 1970s *Yorkshire Ripper* investigation (below). The name is also a nod in the direction of **Sherlock Holmes**, the methodical, deductive (some people say inductive) private investigator created by novelist and amateur *criminologist* Sir Arthur Conan-Doyle (1859-1930).

hoodie A phenomenon of the 2000s: a youth (typically) who wears a hooded top and who is thus hard to recognise or identify facially or at a glance (see *identification/identity*) and re whom people may thus go in *fear*, especially if accompanied by negative *media/press* coverage; and who could be an offender but is more likely a law-abiding *citizen* sporting a modern fashion. Hence at one stage (ill-conceived) government plans to *target* the wearing of such clothing; countered by a 2006 Opposition '**hug a hoodie**' *campaign* (as it was dubbed by government). Clothing and lifestyle accoutrements have often been associated with similar *stereotypes* (below), including, e.g. re Teddy Boys (1950s); Mods and Rockers (1960s) and Chavs (1990s).

hooligan Originally a 'rough-and-tumble sort of person' or ruffian; not necessarily involved in offending; but gradually a term for a lawless person. In modern times the term has been informally applied to a range of offenders, especially *young offenders* involved, e.g. in riots, *public order offences* or *anti-social behaviour* (ASB); including, e.g. **football hooligans** (see generally *football*). The word first appeared in *popular culture* (below) in the late-19th century re a boisterous Gypsy family, the Houlihans, Irish people living in London in the 1890s; who feature in *The Hooligan Nights: Being the Life and Opinions of a Young and Impertinent Criminal* (1899), Rook, C, Victorian London Publications.

Hosein brothers A notorious case in which two Indian brothers and Moslems, Arthur (aged 34) (aka 'The King') and Nizamodeen (22) (who was dominated by Arthur) were convicted at The *Old Bailey* (below) in 1970 of the 1968 murder of Muriel McKay, of her abduction and *blackmail*. Mrs. McKay (whose body was never found) was the wife of the then deputy chair of the *News of the World*, Alick McKay. She was taken from her London home by mistake: her captors believing her to be the wife of that newspaper's Australian owner, Rupert Murdoch (after a company Rolls Royce was followed to the wrong address). Ransom demands of £1 million (today some £10 million) were made over several weeks, coupled to *threats to kill* her if not paid. The brothers were eventually traced after their car was seen in the vicinity of an abortive ransom collection point; an exercise book used re demands being found later at their home, Rooks Farm, Stocking Pelham, Hertfordshire. It has been generally assumed that her body was fed to pigs there. Each was sentenced to *life imprisonment*.

Howard League for penal reform
A leading UK penal *reform* organization taking its name from the 18th century prison reformer **John Howard** (1726-1790). Aka '**The League**', it is the oldest such body in the UK, dating from 1866. It is independent of government and other spheres of influence; and is funded by donations. Its core aims/beliefs include (paraphrased): a safe society where fewer people are victims of crime; where offenders should make amends for their offences/change their ways; and where *community sentences* should be used to make people take responsibility. John Howard's influential works include *The State of the Prisons in England and Wales with Preliminary Observations, and an Account of Some Foreign Prisons and Hospitals* (1794), which describes his visits to prisons at home and abroad and contains reports on their conditions; re which extensive extracts can be found on the internet. He died of 'gaol fever'. See generally howardleague.org

hue and cry A process of Anglo-Saxon times by which bystanders were required to join in the hunt and apprehension of offenders; as later formalised by the Statute of Westminster (1285) which required that anyone who witnessed a crime must make and maintain such a pursuit, effectively in the form of a local posse, against offenders fleeing from place to place. If a local hundred failed to do so it could become liable for certain offences; whilst **raising a false hue and cry** was an offence. **The Hue and Cry** was a police weekly journal of the 1800s. The term continues in popular use re any police chase.

hulk A ship used as a floating prison, mainly in the 1600s and 1700s; when 'The Hulks' were moored on the River Thames at Wapping, London (near Execution Dock), off Hull, Yorkshire, Portsmouth, Hampshire and other seaports. In the 1990s, *HM Prison Service* (HMPS) used a former USA transport ship, The Weare, as a prison ship at Portland, Dorset (under *private sector* management). Periodically, rumours circulate that particular ships have been earmarked by HMPS as a precaution against an otherwise uncontrollable rise in the *prison(er) population*.

Hungerford Massacre Events of 18 August 1987, when 15 people were randomly *murdered* and 14 injured on the streets of Hungerford, Berkshire after Michael Ryan (aged 27) ran amok with a Kalashnikov rifle and Beretta pistol (see, generally, *weapon*). Those killed included strangers, neighbours, his mother and passers-by (including the *justices' clerk* for nearby Newbury, Ian Playle). After barricading himself in a school for several hours, Ryan committed *suicide*. The case had a deep effect on UK gun control (as did comparable events at a school in Dunblane, Scotland in 1996) as well as on police *communication* and *responses*. For an account, see *Hungerford: One Man's Massacre* (1993), Josephs, J, Smith Gryphon Publishers.

John Doe (and in politically correct times **Jane Doe**). Names, American in origin, given to unidentified corpses. In the UK, descriptions such as A (or, e.g. Adam), B, C, etc. seem to be preferred; or descriptive ones, such as 'Mr Seagull' after a body was found washed up on a Dorset beach in 2002.

Julie (Operation Julie) A covert (but ultimately *high profile*, above) police operation of 1976-7 to disrupt the main UK (and to some extent global) production and supply of the *drug* LSD (aka 'acid'); ending in co-ordinated *raids* by 800 police officers nationwide; but centring on a remote farmhouse at Tregaron, Wales, a mansion at nearby Carno and Seymour Road, West London - all drugs

factories-cum-laboratories producing pure, potent LSD on a commercial scale - that led to the *seizure* of large quantities of the drug in microdots (miniature tablets) plus the ingredients for some four million 'hits'; causing the price to escalate from 50p to £1 per tablet overnight (see *black economy* above). This was 'the beginning of the end' of the prevailing LSD counter-culture. By chance, the vehicle of a main *suspect*, Richard Kemp was impounded and *searched* following a fatal accident, revealing fragments of a drug production-related wrapper. He and various premises were placed under *surveillance*. In all, 17 people were sentenced to *imprisonment* for a total of 170 year. Actions in the *civil* courts failed to deprive the offenders of their gains; hence powers in later Drug Trafficking Offences Acts (DTOAs) and, eventually, the *Proceeds of Crime Act 2002*. The operation was *codenamed* after Woman Police Constable (WPC) Julie Taylor.

July 7 in 2005. The day of the **London bombings** in which 52 people were killed on London's transport system, on the Underground and a London bus, by a series of explosions caused by *suicide bombers*; generally accepted as being the work of al-Qaeda; which acted as the trigger for an increase in *emergency* powers to deal with *terrorism/ terrorists*. July 7 is also the backdrop for the *Stockwell shooting* (below). It is sometimes described as the day when *September 11* (below) was brought home to the UK, with similar effects in terms of increased vigilance, levels of policing and *fears* for public *safety*.

Just deserts The Old Testament principle of 'an eye-for-an-eye, a tooth-for-a-tooth' as recompense for injury or loss, meaning equivalent *value*; as translated into proportionality and which became an underlying rationale of the **just deserts sentencing framework** of the *Criminal Justice Act 1991*.

Kisko, Stefan Notorious *miscarriage of justice case* in which semen found on a child *victim's* underwear (Lesley Moleseed) was the subject of non-*disclosure* by the prosecution at a 1976 trial for her *murder*. It was later found that Kisko, who protested his innocence throughout a sentence of *life imprisonment*, was medically incapable of producing semen. He died in 1993, a year after his *release*, without seeing the later conviction of another man for the offence (compare *Evans*,

Timothy above). The events were the basis for a TV drama, 'A Life for A Life' (1998), ITV.

Koestler Trust Charity founded by Arthur Koestler (1905-1983), a Hungarian born writer and engineer, who attended the University of Vienna, Austria, then worked as a journalist and foreign correspondent in the Middle-East, Berlin and Paris. He joined the Communist party and became a left-wing activist for six years in the face of growing support for Facism in Europe (1932-38); was imprisoned by the Nazis in France (1940); but escaped to England. He wrote *Scum of the Earth* (1940) re his experiences of being held by the Nazis: in English, his adopted language, and *Darkness at Noon* (1941) a fictional account of Stalin's purges drawing on his time as a *prisoner* under sentence of death during the Spanish Civil War after being captured by General Franco's troops. He wrote further novels and works across a broad range of political, scientific and literary subjects, focusing especially on *psychology*. A member of the Voluntary Euthanasia Society, he committed *suicide* along with his wife. His life is commemorated by the UK's first parapsychology chair at Edinburgh University (1984); the **Koestler Trust**, an annual **Koestler Exhibition** and **Koestler Awards**. The trust exhibits and sell artworks (of various kinds) by offenders, detainees and high security patients. It aims 'to help offenders to lead more positive lives by motivating them to participate in the arts' and to demonstrate 'the power of arts activity' in the CJS. For further details see koestlertrust.org.uk

Kray twins The UK's most prominent *gangsters* based in the East End of London from the late-1950s, where they vied for control of the London *Underworld* (below) against the (Charles) Richardson gang from South of the River Thames. Twin brothers **Reggie Kray** and **Ronnie Kray** were each given *life imprisonment* for the *murder* (after *torture*) of Jack 'The Hat' McVitie at the Blind Beggar public house, Whitechapel (1966); following the then longest trial in UK history (at six weeks). The victim had allegedly called Ronnie 'a big fat poof' (homosexual). They were feted locally, almost cult-like, for their *Robin Hood*-style largesse (below) and celebrity lifestyle; but were *dangerous offenders,* both psychopaths. Nonetheless, it is impossible to erase them from *popular culture* (below) or English CJS history. In modern times,

serious allegations have arisen that 'until they went too far' they had long been protected from the consequences of their systemic *violence* or racketeering by Establishment figures ensnared by *blackmail*, *corruption*, *fear* or *threats*. Both died in prison (Ronnie 1995; Reggie 2000) (see *deaths in custody above*). See *Crimes of the Krays Omnibus* (2002), Morton J and Dickson J, Little Brown and for contextual data thekrays.co.uk

Ku Klux Klan (KKK) The most notorious *vigilante* movement of modern times; a secret society of the Southern States of the USA founded by farmers and businessmen, predominantly white Americans (or 'Rednecks') after the American Civil War; to control the recently freed negro population (see generally *race/racism*). The KKK held Kangaroo courts and meted out punishments, including lynchings (including **lynch-law**, i.e. *summary justice* by *hanging* (above) (attributed to among other 'Lynches', James Lynch Fitzstephen, a warden of Galway, Ireland in the early 1500s). The KKK was often active at night, when members wore white cloaks, conical hoods and brandished fire to instil *fear* and *hate*. Various KKK members have since the 1980s stood trial for *'cold crimes'* and been given long terms of *imprisonment*. The KKK still holds ceremonial marches and.

label/labelling Terms used to signify (various) theories of *criminology* which *argue* that given words can cause those to whom they are applied to be adversely *stereotyped* (below), also causing them, e.g. to have that same self-image/'act up to type', etc.

Lady Chatterley's Lover A novel by D H Lawrence (1885-1930) that when first published in the UK by Penguin Books in 1960 led to the most famous trial under *obscenity* laws and one of the biggest turning points in UK criminal justice history and re *freedom* of expression. The case, in which Penguin secured an *acquittal*, centred on graphic (if nowadays 'tame') depictions of sexual matters and use of four-letter words, especially the F-word. Lawrence refused to give way to what he termed 'censor-morons' (as he had re his first novel, *The White Peacock* (1911)); and Penguin, having first printed and warehoused several hundred thousand copies, sent 12 of these to the Director of Public Prosecutions (DPP) (see nowadays

Crown Prosecution Service) challenging him to lay a charge. At the six-day trial at The *Old Bailey* (below), the *defence* called 35 *witnesses*, including bishops and literary icons. The trial is often remembered for a single, misjudged question to the jury (see *juror/jury*) by prosecuting counsel, Mervyn Griffith-Jones QC: 'Is this a book you would want your wife or servants to read?' Within a year it had become a global best-seller at two million copies, outstripping the Bible. Prosecutions against other publishers were also brought in several foreign *jurisdictions*, as far apart as the USA and Japan and with varying outcomes.

Lawrence, Stephen Young black man killed by white youths in Eltham, South London (1993). The inadequacy of the police *response* led to the landmark **Stephen Lawrence Inquiry**, chaired by Sir William Macpherson of Cluny (1998). His **Macpherson Report** criticised the *Metropolitan Police Service* (MPS); accusing it of 'institutional racism'; leading to similar conclusions across the CJS, especially re HM *Prison Service* (HMPS) and the *Crown Prosecution Service* (CPS): see archive.official-documents.co.uk The events transformed public and official attitudes and the character of the debate re the treatment of black and minority ethnic (BME) people. It led to a change in the *double jeopardy* laws (of no avail re the Lawrence case itself). Stephen's parents (Doreen and Neville) continued to fight for *justice*; their private *prosecution* (after the CPS declined) having foundered. They were instrumental in establishing the **Stephen Lawrence Charitable Trust** and **Stephen Lawrence Centre**: see stephenlawrence.org. uk For other aspects of these seminal events, including the coroner's verdict of 'unlawful killing', taunting by the suspects and inquiry by the *Independent Police Complaints Commission* (IPCC) see news.bbc.co.uk/hi/english/static/stephen_lawrence/timeline

Lee, John An example of 'poetic *justice*', possibly. In 1885, Lee (aka John Babba-combe Lee) was reprieved after the gallows trap at Exeter Prison, Devon, malfunctioned during three consecutive attempts by executioner James Berry; what was seen, in effect, as an 'Act of God'. Lee (aged 19), a footman, was convicted of the *murder* of his employer, Emma Keyes. Although the gallows worked each time it was tested (including in-between the three attempts) it consistently remained shut when Lee was standing on the trap with the noose around his neck. The *Home Secretary* commuted Lee's sentence to *penal servitude* for life. He was released after 23 years, married in Devon (1909), then deserted his family and left (it is believed) for America, Canada or Australia. Theories abound: from divine *intervention* to the boards swelling in inclement weather so as to be pliable when stepped on. There have been similar rare instances around the world.

Levellers Radicals and republicans within the 'followers' of Oliver Cromwell (1599-1658); whose aims included a new *constitution*, regular elections, universal male suffrage based on population not ownership of property, *equality*, abolition of rank, *freedom* of *religion* and an end to *corruption* in public life; who were suppressed – especially after **John Lilburne** published pamphlets seeking to establish soldiers' rights. They became a political party (1645); had a newspaper, *The Moderate* (see, generally, *media/press*) and organized petitions. In 1646, representatives from the New Model Army took part with Levellers in **'The Putney Debates'** (i.e. at Putney, South London); leading to calls for a *mutiny*. In 1649, Lilburne, John Widman, Richard Overton and William Walwyn were charged with 'advocating Communism' and sent to the Tower of London. The jury decided against convicting Lilburne and the others were *discharged*; Cromwell agreeing to some demands (but not to extend the franchise). Lilburne's persistence saw him again *imprisoned*; when 10,000 people signed a petition for his *release*, which was refused. In 1655 Edward Sexby, Richard Overton and others formed a *conspiracy* to overthrow Cromwell. When discovered, they all became fugitives in The Netherlands. In 1657, Sexby published 'Killing No Murder', seeking to justify Cromwell's assassination, but was imprisoned before the plan could proceed.

Liberty The National Council for Civil Liberties (NCCL) founded in 1934 as a cross party-political, non-party membership organization 'at the heart of the movement for fundamental *rights* and *freedoms*'. It promotes *values* of human dignity, equal treatment (see *equality*) and fairness (see *fair/fairness*) as the cornerstones of a democratic society (see *democracy*). Its key mission is 'to protect *civil liberties* and promote human rights for everyone'. See liberty-human-rights.org.uk

Longford, Lord Francis Aungier Pakenham ('Frank' to all and sundry) (1905 -2001), Labour peer, zealot, prisoners' rights campaigner (and great-grandson of Sir Robert *Peel*, below) mocked for championing unpopular causes such as the *release* of Myra Hindley (see *Moors Murders* below); an anti-pornography crusader (1970s) (and hence aka **Lord Porn**). He was *Minister of State* at the *Home Office* (1945-1963), having converted to socialism in the 1930s (influenced by events in Europe and, e.g. *Cable Street* above). He became leader of the House of Lords; and helped prepare the *reform* agenda that included abolition of *capital punishment* (above). His books include *Punishment and the Punished* (1991), Chapmans (idiosyncratically he would move his works to the fore of displays in the bookshops he visited). See *The Outcast's Outcast: A Biography of Lord Longford* (2004), Stanford P, Sutton.

Luddites A 'secret society' involved in machine-wrecking *raids* and riots from the Midlands and further north (1811–16); starting in Nottinghamshire (with attacks on 'wide frame stocking machines'), spreading to Lancashire, Cheshire, Derbyshire, Leicestershire, and Yorkshire in protest at falling wages and unemployment due to the Industrial Revolution. There were over 1,000 attacks in the first year, mostly at night. Many **Luddites** (a term still used for those who oppose progress) were sentenced to *capital punishment* (above) or *transportation* (below). Their 'organizer' **General Ned Ludd** (sometimes 'King Ludd') may have been a fiction. Author and publisher William Cobbett faced *incitement* for lending support.

magic bullet Experienced practitioners and *criminologists* tend to reject suggestions that there is any single (or ready) solution to crime, rather than a range of approaches which may be *effective* once they are all in place, such as tackling *social exclusion*, regeneration of *communities*, better *education*, crime prevention and *equality* of opportunity. Similar imagery includes **silver bullet**, **golden arrow**, **gilt-edged guaranteee**.

Magna Carta The Great Charter was issued in 1215 by King John; and its final version by his son Henry III in 1225. Magna Carta was not, as is often supposed, some medieval Bill of Rights, but an attempt to prevent civil war after leading barons tried to limit royal powers. Thereafter, opponents of the *Crown* periodically seized upon sections of the charter in defence of their 'rights'. Key clauses still form part of English law, the best known being: 'No free man shall be seized or imprisoned, or stripped of his rights or possessions ... except by the lawful judgement of his peers' and 'To no one will we sell, to no one deny or *delay* right or *justice*'. Magna Carta came to be seen as encapsulating *liberty*. In 1641 it was used in the struggle between Parliament and King Charles I (beheaded 1649). Following the American War of Independence, its clauses were used to draw up the *Fifth Amendment* (above) and Sixth Amendment to the American Constitution. The continuing symbolism was evident when the Universal Declaration of Human Rights was presented to the United Nations (UN) in 1948 as 'a Magna Carta for the future'; whilst many people see a direct line between it and modern-day *human rights*.

marginal People on the margins of society have always been of interest to *criminologists*, partly because they tend to be 'different' and thus attract *suspicion* or distrust, even though their motives and actions may be legitimate. Thus, historically, foreigners, strangers or people with unusual or challenging views or ways of life have always been a *target* for *law enforcement*. For a survey, see *The Medieval Mind* (1997), Le Goff, J, European History Society, *Chapter 10,* 'Marginal Man'.

Maxwell, (Sir) Alexander Chair of the Prison Commission during the 1930s and Permanent Under Secretary of State at the Home Office (1938-1948); who worked with **Sir Samuel Hoare** and **Sir Alexander Paterson** to bring forward the Criminal Justice Bill 1938, and with Chuter Ede to enact the Criminal Justice Act 1948 (based on the earlier Bill). The Act abolished judicial corporal punishment and reconstructed the framework for custodial sentencing. He was later a member of the Royal Commission on Capital Punishment (1949) and chair of a departmental committee on prison after-care.

Maxwell, (Sir) Ian Robert (formerly Jan Ludvik Hoch) (1923-1991) Multi-millionaire *media/press* baron; decorated for bravery in the Second World War, who then worked for the Foreign Office and became a Labour Member of Parliament (MP) in Buckinghamshire (1964-1970). Sometime owner of Pergamon Press, Macmillan, the *Daily Mirror* (acquiring Mirror Group Newspapers (MGN) in 1984), the *Daily News* (New York), British Printing Corporation (later Maxwell Communications Corporation) and Oxford United Football Club, he died in strange circumstances after 'falling overboard' from his private yacht, the Lady Ghislaine, in the Atlantic off Tenerife. Theories range from *murder* by Israel's secret service to *suicide*. His empire (aspects of which had been under *investigation* by the Department of Trade and Industry (DTI) re *allegations* of *dishonesty*) was near to collapse; with large sums missing from pension funds, raided to fund ventures. His sons/fellow directors, Ian and Robin stood trial and secured *acquittals* re complicity; a chief strand of their *defence* being Maxwell's dominating personality. In 2006, it emerged under the *Freedom of Information Act 2000* that Maxwell was also under investigation for *war crimes*; re the shooting of the defiant mayor of a French town in 1945.

M'Naughten Rules Legal rules re the *defence* of **insanity** formulated at the request of the House of Lords re the case of Daniel M'Naughten (1834) (10 C & F 200) who had attempted to assassinate Prime Minister, Robert Peel (see *Peel, Robert* below); an informal *codification* at Common Law; after that House invited a panel of judges to issue *guidelines*. The rules still apply, centrally stating (paraphrased) that: **(1)** everyone is presumed sane unless the contrary is proved (see *presumption*); i.e. unless **(2)** the accused was suffering from such a defect in reasoning caused by a disease of the mind that at the time of the offence (or trial: re un*fitness* to plead: see also *plea*) he or she was functionally unaware that his or her actions were legally wrong; and that **(3)** whether a particular condition is such a disease is a legal not a medical question; and **(4)** the burden of proof re insanity lies with the accused (see *evidence*). A (jury) **verdict of insanity** (usually) leads to *detention* for an indeterminate period in a special hospital. See *mental impairment*.

Moors murders A series of *murders* of children close to Greater Manchester in 1993-4 when their bodies were buried on Saddleworth Moor; that shocked the UK and made the offenders (who might nowadays have been termed 'predatory *paedophiles*') synonymous with *evil* (above). Brady (still in a special hospital) and Hindley, who died in prison (2003), killed Lesley Ann Downey aged 10, John Kilbride, 12, Keith Bennett, 12, and Pauline Reade, 16, all sexually assaulted and tortured; Lesley's last moments being recorded on tape. Both appear to have acted jointly in a way that they would not have done if on their own. Police identified one grave from a snapshot of a picnic by the pair. Despite continued searches and help by Hindley (permanently vilified and whose continual *imprisonment* became a *symbol* of *law and order* commitment for a succession of *Home Secretaries*) who was befriended by Lord *Longford* (above), Keith Bennett's body was never found. See, e.g. *Beyond Belief: The Moors Murderers. The Story of Ian Brady and Myra Hindley* (1968), Williams, E, Pan.

moral aspects Crime and (im)morality have no necessary correlation, law being of a different order, even though the House of Lords recognised a *Common Law* offence of **conspiracy to corrupt public morals** in what became known as the 'Ladies Directory case', in which details of services offered by prostitutes were published (*Shaw v Director of Public Prosecutions* (1961) (1962) Appeal Cases 220; [1961] 2 All England Reports 466. Similarly, there is some overlap re the offences of **living off immoral earnings** which targets pimps and brothel keepers in particular and **soliciting for an immoral purpose** (see *street offences* below). **Moral ambiguity** is a term often applied to a mis-match between, e.g. *values*, integrity or beliefs and actual events, *policy* or *strategy*, or where, e.g. ends are used to justify the means of achieving them. Certain aspects of *law enforcement* can be said to involve such ambiguity, such as public interest immunity (PII) (see *informer*) or the *national interest*. The term **moral danger** may be used to describe a *risk* that, e.g. *children* or *vulnerable people* could fall prey to such influences, which parents etc. are under duty to prevent or risk *civil* proceedings to remove their children from them. Similarly, **moral dilemma** where someone is faced with a choice re which there is no safe moral solution. **Moral duty** is sometimes contrasted with *legal* duty, e.g. there may be a moral duty to assist the police but no legal duty to do so (special situations such as *terrorism/terrorists* or *suspicious activity reports* (SARS) apart). A **moral panic** is one generated by questionable considerations, methods or 'over-sensitisation', as where *government, law enforcement agencies*, a *campaign* group or the *media/press* 'whips up a storm' re a given kind of offending, so as to create disproportionate *fear* (sometimes where the offence itself has **moral overtones**). A leading work of *criminology* in this field is *Folk Devils and Moral Panics* (2002) (3rd edn.), Cohen, S, Routledge, a study of 'deviant groups'. For classic treatments of the law/morality divide, see *The Enforcement of Morals* (reprinted 1987), Devlin P, Oxford University Press; and *Law, Liberty and Morality* (annotated edn. reprinted 2002), Hart HLA, Stanford University Press. Morality is often associated with aspects of **decency**; see generally *value/values*; and offences such as **outraging public decency** by a deliberate act which is lewd, obscene or disgusting: consult specialist works on *criminal law.*

Mountbatten Report A report by Lord Louis Mounbatten (1900-1979), former First Sea Lord and later Chief of the Defence Staff (but with no CJS credentials as such: compare *Beeching Report* above) into prison security, in *response* to recent escapes including that of the spy George Blake from Wormwood Scrubs (1966). Completed in two months, the report led to the introduction of dispersal prisons (see *prison*) and other *security* changes. In 1979, Mountbatten was *murdered* by an Irish Republican Army (IRA) bomb whilst out sailing at Classiebawn Castle, County Sligo, Ireland.

Nacro Formerly the **National Association for the Care and Resettlement of Offenders,** having since adopted this acronym; a major and leading crime reduction charity specialising in '[making] society safer by finding practical solutions to reducing crime'; that since 1966 has 'worked to give ex-*offenders*, *disadvantaged* people and deprived communities the help they need to build a better future'. It has over 200 projects in diverse locations across England and Wales; whilst 60,000 people benefit directly each year from its work (many more from the influence it brings to bear on national, regional and local agencies/services and the debate on crime and punishment. It issues various publications, including a journal *Safer Society*. See nacro.org.uk For Scotland see the similarly formulated Sacro: sacro.otg.uk

naming and shaming (N&S) A concept with primitive appeal and traceable to Anglo-Saxon times at least; the notion that offenders may mend their ways (or at least be identified to other potential *victims*) if their names are made public; and they themselves feel shame, possibly leading to remorse and *'going straight'*. In modern times, the *media/press* and some police forces have been to the fore in naming and shaming people, including by the publication of names, sometimes addresses and even photographs in local newspapers or on the internet; often re 'run-of-the-mill' offenders but also *paedophiles* in particular. Such practices represent a double-edged sword; risking the negative effects, e.g. of *labelling* (above); *mistakes* and *social exclusion* (*Main Entries*) and re certain offenders, *vigilantes*. Shaming (as opposed to N&S and viewed from a more positive perspective) is often integral to *restorative justice.*

Napo Membership and representative organization for *probation officers* and other staff working for the National Probation Service. Napo celebrated its centenary in 2007. It is a trade union, professional association and *campaign* body which undertakes a range of activities, including training, representations to government and the publication of *Probation Journal* and *Napo News*. Formerly known as the National Association of Probation Officers. See napo.org.uk. There is also an Association of Black Probation Officers (ABPO) which works with staff of African, African-Caribbean and Asian origin to oppose the effects of racism (see *race/racism*).

National Association for Youth Justice (NAYJ) Membership organization established in 1994 by a merger of the National Intermediate Treatment Federation (NITFed) and Association for Youth Justice. Members of the NAYJ work in relation to the *youth courts* and the *Crown Court*, with links to *youth offending teams* (YOTS) and other *youth workers*, educationalists and child specialists. From the late-1990s, the NAYJ undertook a review of its philosophy and policy vis-à-vis the *Youth Justice System*, leading to 'Working with Children: The Philosophical Base' (NAYJ) which offered a set of *values* and beliefs 'which should underpin *legislation, policy* and *practice*'. A manifesto built on this to ensure compliance with *human rights* and children's rights. NAYJ publishes *Youth Justice: An International Journal*. See nayj.org.uk

net widening Bringing a greater number of people into contact with the CJS as suspects, offenders, prisoners, etc. whether via *criminalisation* (above), more active law enforcement or a wider range of *punishments*. Certain commentators argue that the more powers the courts or CJS agencies/services have, the more likely they will be to make full use of them and at a more punitive level; the greater the range of sentences, the more they will be 'tested out'. Net-widening is also connected to the vested interest that some members of the CJS or *private sector* in particular may have in upping the numbers of people 'processed' by its mechanisms; all of which has an escalatory effect.

Newgate Prison Former and historic gaol built in 1188 (rebuilt after being damaged in the Gordon Riots of 1780). In the first half of the 19th century, Newgate was London's main prison and at times place of execution after the gallows were moved there from *Tyburn* (below) (1783). Stories of prisoners appeared in the **Newgate Calendar** a popular publication, originally a monthly bulletin produced by the keeper (or 'ordinary') of the gaol to generate extra income. The title was then applied more generally to other publications, records and memoirs. Many editions have appeared in print or on the internet: see, e.g. britac.ac.uk Hence, also, **Newgate knockers**, gaoler's waxed moustaches.

nipping offending in the bud Simplistic notion heard in many a debate on crime and punishment (particularly re *juveniles*); the analogy being that early *intervention* is the way to cut down on offending. Opponents argue this is counter-productive, *criminalising,* and may cause offending to escalate.

normalisation Description attached to various (sometimes competing) theories of *criminology*, psychology, etc; connoting one or more of the following: (1) a process via which an activity, behaviour, etc. is made to seem ordinary, everyday or 'normal', which may involve offending, but where, e.g. 'everybody does it'; so that victims and others are less inclined to complain or make a *report* (and may 'join in'), e.g. re *sexual offences, drug* use (hence the euphemism 'recreational *drug*') or the *black economy* (above); (2) in, a more positive sense, behaviour once criminal, dubious, against social mores which enters the mainstream as *acceptable behaviour*, due, e.g. to *decriminalisation* or changed social mores, as with homosexuality; lawful *abor-*

tion; (3) where, as a matter of political necessity, policy or strategy there is a return to normal, as e.g. after the fall of Communism in the Eastern Bloc or events in Northern Ireland after the Good Friday Agreement (see The *Troubles* below). The term has also been used (4) to describe a backdrop to situations in which personal responsibility diminishes.

Notting Hill An area of west-London (now 'highly desirable') that was the focus of riots in the 1950s and 1960s; best known for its annual **Notting Hill Carnival** which was for many years a tinder box for *violence, public order* problems and racial tensions (see *race/racism*). Like other such events it is now part of the mainstream and issues of *law enforcement* are only a marginal consideration.

Old Bailey The Crown Court for the London area (aka **Central Criminal Court**). A historic venue re famous trials and notorious offenders. Records of many such proceedings are now available at oldbaileyonline.org

Old Bill One of the many slang terms for police officer (along with **bluebottle, flatfoot,** *gate* (above), **pig, plod, rozzer,** etc.); the origins of 'Old Bill' are debated. Competing theories range from the constables of William IV (King Billy) to the use of a police moustache for a cartoon character, Old Bill. For various explanations, see metpolice.uk

payback Operation Payback started as a *Metropolitan Police Service* (MPS) initiative to *target* offenders through seizing their finances. It builds on the *Proceeds of Crime Act 2002* (POCA) to ensure that 'crime does not pay'. It is now a nationwide term for *asset* recovery and anti-*money laundering* activities. It co-ordinates the use of financial *intelligence* with powers under the POCA. The word 'payback' was also adopted by **Community Payback**, an umbrella name for schemes to provide opportunities for local people to 'have their say' on how offenders should make amends, including in conjunction with unpaid work (as a requirement of a *community sentence*) and/or in some places Safer Neighbourhoods programmes, e.g. removing graffiti, 'street clean-ups', ground clearance, recycling, enhancing public parks etc: see generally communitypayback.co.uk But note criticism by *probation officers* and others that a parallel and long-opposed scheme for the shaming of offenders (see generally *naming* *and shaming* above) via a requirement that they wear high-visibility (often orange) vests (or 'bibs') would be counter-productive and maybe lead to vigilante attacks (2009). **Paying back money or value** has a long history re criminal justice, from Anglo Saxon times (see *wergild* below) to modern day *compensation*, restitution or reparation (see, e.g. sentence/sentencing/'ancillary order'). It was key to the development of community service (a forerunner of requirements of un-paid work): see *Paying Back: Twenty Years of Community Service* (1993), Waterside Press.

Peasants Revolt Seminal event in English *legal* and social history that still resonates re protest, etc; the first time the 'lower orders' rose up against oppression, *corruption* and *taxation*, including re *violence* and *sexual offences* against women to determine whether they were virgins and thus exempt from taxes; and an example of *political* deception. Events began at Fobbing, Essex in 1381 when tax collectors were ejected (hence 'fobbing off') and at Brentwood, where a mob beheaded a tax collector and *murdered* soldiers; such events spreading across south-east England. Some protesters petitioned Richard II (then aged 14); but more and more *citizen*s took up arms and set up camps on the edge of London. Urged on by the poor, they attacked political *targets* until Richard met the petitioners and acceded to their demands. Later, he met others at Smithfield, 'captivated them' and made key concessions. Rebel leader, **Wat Tyler**, offended the *Crown* by his informality and was killed by the Lord Mayor of London. Again, Richard placated the crowd, led them to Cricklewood and conferred a mass pardon; but when the heat had gone out of the situation he changed his mind, set up a *judicial* inquiry and told *commissioners* to use 'all expeditious and sensible means' to deal with the ringleaders - most of whom suffered *capital punishment* (above).

Penal Affairs Consortium An amalgam of leading organizations concerned with penal matters that among other things makes representations to government. See nacro.org.uk

Peterloo Massacre Events at St Peter's Fields, Manchester (1819) during a 'monster meeting' of 50,000 people to hear **Henry Hunt** (aka **'Orator Hunt'**) and *campaign* for an extension of the franchise ('one man, one vote': see generally *democracy*), annual Parlia-

ments, etc. that was policed by the *military*. Events were orderly until a magistrate tried to *arrest* Hunt. A woman was killed and the yeomanry needed to be rescued by the cavalry, leaving eleven people dead and 400 people maimed. Along with other mass protests or riots at places such as **St. Peter's Fields** (involving blanketeers who trekked to London with sleeping blankets over their shoulders) and the **Spa Fields** riot, such events reinforced demands for *civil* policing and led to the New Police (1829). They also triggered the *Six Acts* (below).

Phillips Commission The Royal Commission on Criminal Procedure which reported in 1981 (Cmnd. 8092, 1981), as a result of which among other things new police powers were set out in the *Police and Criminal Evidence Act 1984* and *Public Order Act 1986*. The Commission suggested various tests when assessing police powers or the granting of further powers; during what were less *law and order* and *security* driven times.

Pierrepoint, Albert (1905-1992) Public hangman (1932-1956) (see generally *hanging*) from Clayton, West Yorkshire and landlord of The Poor Struggler Inn who carried out some 450 executions in the UK (maybe over 600 worldwide including in Ireland, parts of Europe, Cyprus and for the USA *military* at Shepton Mallet Prison, Somerset). They included those of con-man Neville Heath, William Joyce (see *treason*, below), acid bath murderer John George Haigh, Nuremberg war criminals, a one-time singing partner (they had appeared together as Tish and Tosh); Derek *Bentley;* Timothy *Evans* (and also later John Reginald Christie) and Ruth *Ellis* (all noted above). From a family dynasty of executioners, his 'skill and art' allowed him to reduce to seven seconds the time between entering the condemned person's prison cell and releasing the trap. Unlike some of his ilk (William Calcraft (1800-1879) is an oft-quoted example), he never bungled an execution. He became a *symbol* of protest re the abolition of *capital punishment* (above); and resigned after a dispute with the Home Office concerning 'cancellation fees'. He later rejected 'the utility, purpose and efficacy' of his work: 'All the [people] I have faced in that final moment convince me [that] I have not prevented a single *murder*. Executions [are] an antiquated relic of a primitive desire for *revenge*': *Executioner*

Pierrepoint: The Amazing Autobiography of the World's Most Famous Executioner (1974), Pierrepoint A, Eric Dobby Publications. In 2006, a feature film, 'Pierrepoint' with Timothy Spall in the title role premiered at the Glasgow Film Festival.

pillory A punishment of former times: a wooden frame that could restrain an offender by the neck and wrists; that was in use from Anglo-Saxon times (at least) until its abolition in 1837; essentially as a form of public display, including for shaming the offender (compare *naming and shaming* above); but the severity of which was largely determined by onlookers. Hence, e.g. the author Daniel Defoe (twice sentenced to the pillory for dissent-related offences) was pelted with flowers not brickbats. The last man to stand in the pillory was Peter James Bossy (1832). The **finger pillory** was a miniature variant whereby the finger(s) of an offender was held by tightening a screw. For further details of these and other primitive *punishments*, see *Punishments of Former Days* (1939) (reprinted 1992), Pettifer E, Waterside Press. 'Being pilloried' survives as a metaphor for, e.g. 'coming under a salvo of criticism'.

Police Memorial Many police officers have been killed in the line of duty, events that tend to *trigger* a huge police *response* to bring the offender to justice. Too numerous to list here, they include PC Sydney George Miles shot by Christopher Craig (1952: see *Bentley, Derek* above); Yvonne Fletcher (outside the Libyan Embassy in 1984); Keith Blakelock (see *Broadwater Farm* above); and Sharon Beshenivsky (Bradford, West Yorkshire, 2005). See also the case mentioned under *weapon*. Some such offenders are notorious, none more so than Harry Roberts, still serving *life imprisonment* and challenging refusals of *parole* re the murder of three police officers in Shepherds Bush, West London in 1966. Hence the **Police Memorial Trust** to commemorate all officers who died thus; formed in 1984 by film producer Michael Winner, who, deeply moved by the death of Yvonne Fletcher, wrote to *The Times* (21 April, 1984), suggesting that a memorial 'would ... indicate that not everyone ... takes seeming pleasure in attacking the police in the execution of their difficult duties'. It triggered donations from the public and a **National Police Memorial** opened at the junction of The Mall and Horse Guards in 2005. Between 1984 and 2008, 36 **local memorials** were opened: see policememorial.org.uk

policespeak All working cultures have their own micro-language in which words, usages, nuances, emphases and abbreviations have particular resonance. One example is 'policespeak'. Examples are: **Altaris:** a computerised control and crime logging system; **CS:** *crime scene* (and hence **CSI** = crime scene investigation) or cs gas or spray used to incapacitate violent suspects or prisoners; **CTU:** central ticket unit; **ETA:** earliest or estimated time of arrival, i.e. at a *crime scene* in *response* to a 999 or other call (sometimes **EAT** = earliest or estimated arrival time); **FSU:** firearms or force support unit; **'the golden hour':** that immediately following an offence when *evidence* is still fresh); **'house to house'**, i.e. inquiries; **HO/RT 1:** Home Office Road Traffic Form No.1 as issued to motorists when stopped for certain *road traffic* offences); **LO:** liaison officer (and hence, e.g. **FLO** = family liaison officer; **LAGLO** = lesbians and gays liaison officer; **VLO** = victim liaison officer); **'misper':** a missing person; **OIC:** officer in charge/commanding; **OCU:** operational command unit; **PMS:** police management system; **'no-crime':** one, e.g. committed outside a given police force area or as to which there is no verifiable information, or one already recorded or reported in error; **PIC:** personal injury collision); **POLSA:** police search adviser; **PPU:** police *protection* unit; **PVC/PVI:** police vehicle collision/incident (but note that **PVC** is also used for 'prison visit check'); **RPET:** road policing enquiry team; **RTI:** road traffic incident; **RVP:** rendezvous point; **SOCO:** scenes of crime officer; **'tradecraft':** police skills; 'twocking': see *TWS* in *Acronyms and Abbreviations*; **VODS:** vehicle online descriptive search. Similarly, **'police rules'** may be driven by pragmatic economy of language, e.g. **'one crime per victim'** (for recording purposes); **'principal crime'** (only the most serious to be recorded); **'finished incident'** (over and done with before it is counted).

police State One in which the Government controls the police and determines, e.g. *arrest*, *trial* (if there is a trial at all), *punishment* or dispensability of individuals. The *judiciary* is non-existent or under orders and *independence* of decision-making unknown across the CJS, thus breaching what, in a liberal *democracy* are fundamental or *human rights*.

Of many examples, among the better known police States were the German Nazi regime of the early 1930s-1945, Communist Russia (especially under Lenin and Stalin) and China (under Mao Tse Tung). Modern suggestions of an emergent police State in the UK are of a different order and appear to signify a gradual erosion of *civil liberties*; which is important to people who believe that this is how advanced police States evolve.

political aspects *Justice* (including *criminal justice*) has traditionally been viewed as 'above politics'; albeit any cursory examination of CJS matters discloses a *radical heritage* (below) with **political issues** often to the fore. This includes the history of policing itself and the struggle for judicial supremacy vis-à-vis the *Crown*. Many CJS developments have caused controversy re official or judicial powers, actions, reasoning etc; the further back in time the greater the traces of direct *State* or *Crown* intervention in processes or outcomes. Nowadays the *Rule of Law*, *separation of powers* and *human rights* are just some of the mechanisms which keep the direct impact of politics at bay; at least so that they do not touch on decision-making in individual cases. Only subject to *safeguards* do **political exhortations** affect, e.g. *judicial policy* (but see further in that entry). In a modern context, the **politicisation of criminal justice** can be traced to the 1970s but is usually associated with the actions of government from 1993 onwards, talking tough (see *tough/toughness* below) and claiming that 'prison works' (see *'what works'* below). The *Bulger* case (above) is often seen as a turning point; as are in more recent times *July 7* and *September 11* (above and below).

Pollard, Vicky Fictional character from a BBC TV series, 'Little Britain' (2003 onwards), whose persona has become synonymous with *anti-social behaviour* (ASB) and the *stereotyping* (below) of defiant young *women;* to the extent that the name entered the language of the courts when a number of defendants were categorised as **real-life Vicky Pollards**. Hence also a *Guardian* editorial summing-up Vicky Pollard as: 'an *out-of-control* . . . [and] inarticulate, abusive and feckless teenage single mother ... In [treating the character as more than a parody and] attempting to hijack that image for its own ends, media Britain [see *media/press*] is creating something more dangerous: a *stereotype* [below] that dissolves the difference between fiction and reality' (12 May 2005).

popular culture Popular culture can be described as resulting from a general or mass understanding of events, issues and ways of doing things as driven, e.g. by the *media/press* (the tabloid press in particular), common understandings, received wisdom, dramatisations, works of fiction or entertainment and word of mouth; a consequence being that it may not represent reality; and it may render potentially sound criminal justice approaches 'counter intuitive'. A survey in 2003, e.g. revealed 26% of broadsheets readers thought crime had 'shot up'; compared to 43% of tabloid readers. Popular culture may be based on *stereotyping* (below) and *labelling* above; the placing of matters in 'pigeonholes' as opposed to *evidence-based research*. Re the CJS, a *citizen's* perception of prisons and *imprisonment* is as likely to be informed by the TV series 'Porridge' (see next item) or feature films such as 'The Shawshank Redemption' (USA, 1994) as it is by the kind of populist reporting that is designed to hook in readers and maintain circulation. Such 'information' may be replicated in **popular genres** such as crime fiction (which is central to 'trade publishing'). An effect, it can be argued, is that *democracy* functions via pressures on politicians stemming from virtual or received understanding rather than accurate or *expert* data. For one treatment, see *Images of Incarceration: Representations of Prison in Film and Television Drama* (2004), Wilson D, Waterside Press. It may also draw on iconic images, as per the *Great Train Robbery* or *Kray Twins,* be associated with *demonisation* (all three above) or owe more to legend than fact. For some further information and a broad range of links to work in this emergent field, see crimeculture.com

porridge Popular and underworld slang for *prison* or *imprisonment*, as in **doing porridge**, i.e. serving time in prison: from the bland, repetitive prison diet of former times when porridge might mean a mixture of anything, however inedible, that could be ground up to make such a meal (and similarly with what was called 'gruel': a watery stew). Hence, **Porridge**, BBC TV's longest running situation comedy (1970-2000), which featured *habitual offender* Norman Stanley Fletcher (played by actor Ronnie

Barker); as conceived for a one-off TV play, 'Prisoner and Escort' (1973).

Poulson, John (1910-1993) Defendant in a seminal case that led to a reappraisal of *standards* in public life; an example of the *normalisation* (above) of criminal conduct. Poulson, a self-made, failed prize-winning, (unqualified) architect-cum-property developer from Pontefract, South Yorkshire grew a one-man practice into one of the biggest in Europe (1960s), via *corruption* of councillors, planners, civil servants, etc. 'The biggest scandal in UK public life' led to his *imprisonment* for five years (aged 59) re activities in 23 towns and cities involving 300 beneficiaries. He was convicted at Leeds *Crown Court* after making a 'partial *admission*' of improper gifts totalling £30,000. The *trial judge*, Mr Justice Waller described him as 'incalculably *evil* [above]... to offer corrupt gifts strikes at the very foundations of our system ...', the Prevention of Corruption Act 1906 *presumption* being that gifts to public officers are corruptly given. Still in *denial*, Poulson stated in *The Price* (1981), Poulson J, Michael Joseph: '[I was] more sinned against than sinning ... a victim and *scapegoat*' (below); claiming sweeteners were routine in public life. Prestigious projects included magistrates' courts and police stations. At his (*civil*) bankruptcy it was said that he 'distributed largesse like Henry VIII'. Certain influential figures were ensnared, including T Dan Smith (leader of Newcastle City Council: given *imprisonment*), George Pottinger (civil servant: likewise); and Reginald Maudling (1917-1979) (*Home Secretary*, a business associate: who resigned from the Cabinet). Compare, *Maxwell, Robert; Bottomley, Horatio.*

Prison Reform Trust (PRT) A leading *reform* group, which holds, e.g. that prison should be reserved for those whose offending is so *serious* that they cannot serve their sentence in the *community*. PRT's central tenets include that: prisoners and their families should be treated with humanity and *respect* and have access to clear *information*, the opportunity to represent themselves and have their views taken into account; that *HM Prison Service* should provide constructive regimes; and that the public, Parliament and those responsible for 'incarcerating offenders' should be fully informed about the state and *effectiveness* of the CJS. For details and PRT publications, see prison-reform-trust.org.uk

prison slang A coded language similar to *Underworld* or 'lowlife' slang. Examples include: **babbler**: 'babbling brook' is rhyming slang for 'crook'; on the **block**: segregated from other prisoners; **care bear** social worker; **carpet**: a sentence of three months, just long enough to weave one; **Dear John letter** (or just '**a Dear John**'): one bringing bad news, especially about the end of a relationship; **Dr Who** (aka '**a screw**': a *prison officer*; **fishtank**: the prison visits room where everything takes place in a state of high visibility; **Gabriel**: an honest person (after the Angel Gabriel); **gate fever**: a condition associated with approaching *release* (and see also generally *gate* above); **flying pastie**: excrement wrapped in paper and thrown from a cell window; **ghosted**: transferred to another prison in the shadow of the night; **knockback** (or **KB**): refusal of *parole* or some other application; **meatwagon**: the prison van; **muppet juice**: tranquillisers, especially as issued by prison *healthcare* authorities; **nevis**: a sentence of seven years, i.e. distorted backslang; **Noah's Ark**: a nark, grass, etc; **noddyshop**: prison workshop, i.e. where tasks could be discharged by a wooden puppet; **nonce**: sex offender; '**on the ones, twos, threes**': on prison landing one, two, three; **playtime**: association period; **red letter**: one smuggled into or out of prison; **rover**: a prison officer on 'roving' patrol; **saint**: incorruptible police officer or prison officer; **shipped out**: moved out; **shit and a shave**: a short sentence: aka 'a breeze'; **sky pilot**: chaplain, as per *military* use; **spanners**: cell keys; **taxing**: bullying, extortion, as if by way of an Underworld 'tax'; **units**: usually those on a prison phonecard (HMPS issues its own); **wax up**: conceal in the anus; **whiteshirt**: senior prison officer; **wombling**: picking up litter, after a BBC TV children's programme 'The Wombles'; **working out**: working outside the prison on day release (as opposed physical training in a gym); **zoo** (aka **menagerie**): a wing/unit for *sex offenders or* misfits. For extensive lists, see *Prison Patter: A Dictionary of Prison Slang* (1996), Devlin A, Waterside Press; *Gangster Speak: A Dictionary of Criminal and Sexual Slang* (2006), Morton J, Virgin Books.

prison writing a genre of writing centring on prisons and imprisonment for its content; meaning by prisoners or people with experience of life inside a prison; including manuscripts, letters, *campaign* manifestos and pure artistic endeavour in terms of articles, novels or poetry. It ranges from the work of **Oscar Wilde** (see also *Reading Gaol* and *Wilde, Oscar,* below), **John Bunyan** and **Daniel Defoe** (all once prisoners) to **gangster memoirs**, to those of other notorious offenders, to 'going straight'-type works (see *Main Entries*) to the **prison diaries** of such authors as Jeffrey Archer (a disgraced Parliamentarian but successful writer of best-selling fiction). For an extensive account see 'Prison Writing' at WatersidePress.co.uk

Punishments of former days Many people appear to have a fascination with *murder* and heinous crime, as shown by many dedicated publications and their place in *popular culture* (above). This can be traced via the 'penny dreadfuls' of the 1700s and broadsheets printed re a public execution (see generally capital *punishment* above) (the speculative nature of the enterprise being discernible from the fact that some reported *hangings* were overtaken reprieves). Early punishments and the often barbaric methods involved are described in works such as *Punishments of Former Days* (1992), Pettifer E, Waterside Press and *Tortures of the Tower of London* (1986), Abbott S, David & Charles. For artefacts, see *Murders of the Black Museum* (1982), Honeycombe G, Hutchinson.

radical heritage Britain's radical heritage of protest and progress encompasses activities/events such as the *Levellers* and *Peterloo Massacre* (above) as well as other landmarks of dissent or insurrection. These were identified in a series of articles published in the *Guardian* in 2007 at a time when it could be argued that historic rights to protest, demonstrate and of *freedom* of speech were in danger of being curtailed to deal with the threat of and from *terrorism/terrorists*.

Rainer Crime Concern (RCC) Modern day incarnation of the **Rainer Foundation** as established by **Frederick Rainer** a printer. RCC works with some 34,000 young people in over 150 communities across the UK to reduce crime, *anti-social behaviour* and *fear of crime* in *disadvantaged* or deprived neighbourhoods: 'By harnessing energies at the grass roots, we're able to see real change in communities. Sometimes this is typified by a young person's personal triumph and achievement, at other times the whole *community* has benefited'. The origins of the

Probation Service (see *probation* in *Main Entries*) lie within Rainer. That service began as an advisory and befriending facility in the late-19th century, leading to formal recognition of its utility, duties and responsibilities in the Probation of Offenders Act 1907 when probation officers were given a duty to 'advise, assist and befriend' offenders; that continued in one form or another until modern times; roots which lie in philanthropic (often Quaker-based) initiatives. For a fine historical account, see *Introduction to the Probation Service* (2001) (2nd. edn.) Whitfield D, Waterside Press.

RAPt a charity to *help and support* people with a *drug* and/or *alcohol* dependency. It provides services to some 13,000 people per year; including as a leading provider of intensive drug *rehabilitation* programmes in prisons and in the *community*, where it delivers pioneering *treatment* and aftercare for (ex-)offenders and other people referred to it (see generally *referral*); including via a 12 step abstinence-based programme: 'With the right help, people ... can move away from substance-dependent and criminal lifestyles, and lead positive and fulfilling lives'. See further *Drug Treatment in Prison: An Evaluation of the RAPt Treatment Programme* (2000), Martin C and Player E (eds.), Waterside Press and for further information rapt.org.uk

Ratcliff Highway murders A spate of killings by highwaymen, essentially *robbery*, in Shadwell, London 1811 (following the Napoleonic Wars); leading to the creation of a 'foot patrol militia' and *moral* panic (above). An example of how developments in criminal justice are often triggered by *high profile* events and the sometimes disproportionate levels of *fear* that these can create.

Reading Gaol Prison in Berkshire, now a young offender institution and remand centre (YOI&RC), immortalised in the penultimate work of *Oscar Wilde* (below), *The Ballad of Reading Gaol,* which tells of the execution of Trooper Charles Thomas Wooldridge during Wilde's imprisonment there in 1887 (see generally *capital punishment*). A must for any student of the CJS, many lines from the poem have become iconic reference points for penal reformers. It can be accessed at WatersidePress.co.uk For an account and explanation of the poem see

Pit of Shame: The Real Ballad of Reading Gaol (2007), Stokes, A, Waterside Press.

reassurance A word that occurs repeatedly re CJS matters and whose central tenets concern the **reassurance of the general public** so that it can have *confidence* in the CJS and its mechanisms. Hence also, in particular, **reassurance to victims** of crime and ideas such as **reassurance policing**, originally e.g. by high visibility police patrols (or 'bobbies on the beat) but nowadays in more subtle ways (as where there is a clear indication that the police are responding to a particular type of crime or concern, including via the *media/press* 'to get the message across' that offenders will be pursued/offending will not be tolerated (compare also **zero-tolerance** below)). Note also the **National Reassurance Policing Programme** under which such policing is described as 'a model of neighbourhood policing which seeks to improve public *confidence* ... It involves local communities in identifying priority crime and disorder issues .... which they then tackle together with the police and other public services and partners'. See further at crimereduction. homeoffice.gov.uk/policing Similarly *citizens* turn to government for broad reassurance as to their *safety* and/or *protection*. For a useful overall commentary, see *Crime, State and Citizen: A Field Full of Folk* (2006) (2nd edn.), Faulkner D, Waterside Press.

rebalancing Criminal justice often concerns **matters of balance**, as where *weight* (below) is given to factors affecting a decision; or generally in terms of *equality* and even-handedness. From time-to-time, CJS outcomes are perceived to be **out of balance**, e.g. as between *offenders*, *victims* and the *community* and **in need of rebalancing**. This is a recurring motif which was also, e.g. one purpose behind the *Criminal Justice Act 2003* as described in the White Paper, *Justice For All* (2002)(Cm 5563). Analogous recurring motifs (some people might say clichés) include 'bringing offenders (or more offenders) to justice' and 'closing the *justice gap*'.

Red Barn The 'Murder in the Red Barn' (1827) is one of the most famous *murders* historically, due largely to its being dramatised for the stage (where it can sometimes be seen to this day). It also inspired broadsheets, melodramas and ballads. William Corder, a farmer from Polstead, Suffolk, made Maria Marten (22) pregnant (she already had three illegitimate children). She was keen to marry, Corder not. One night, they went to a red barn where he promised to elope with her to Ipswich. She was not seen again and Corder vanished. Her mother dreamt that Maria's body was in the barn, where it was found. Corder was traced to London. His *defence* was that they had quarrelled and she had committed *suicide*. After his conviction, Corder made a *confession*. He was hanged in 1828 (see generally *hanging* above).

Redemption The cancelling-out of sins via compensatory good deeds, reparation, remorse, etc; which has strong connections with *desistance* and *'going straight'*. Whilst not a *purpose* of *punishment* and traceable more to religious belief systems (see generally *religious aspects*) (when piety and forgiveness may also feature) than secular thoughts, the idea is a recurring motif. Fyodor Dostoyevsky (1821-1881) the author of *Crime and Punishment* (1866) (who spent four years in prison) used redemption as the central theme of that classic work.

'Reducing Crime: Changing Lives' A Home Office Publication of 2004, 'Reducing Crime: Changing Lives: The Government's Plans for Transforming the Management of Offenders' set out its plans to transform the management of offenders. This was chiefly a *response* to the *Carter Report* of 2003 above. It proposed a *strategy* 'to improve the *effectiveness* [of the CJS as] a once in a generation opportunity to reduce crime by transforming prison and probation services, and those working in *partnership* with them': see homeoffice.gov. uk/documents/reducing-crime-changing-lives

relational justice (or Relational Justice) A way of thinking about *justice* as developed by the **Relationships Foundation**, Cambridge, focusing on inter-actions between people (including CJS practitioners) and repairing *harm*, rather than 'antiseptic' processes or rules which serve to undermine more human elements. See *Relational Justice: Repairing the Breach* (2nd. edn 2003), Burnside J and Baker N, Waterside Press (and compare *restorative justice* in *Main Entries*).

retribution Retribution, sometimes described as vengeance, revenge or reprisal is a quasi-biblical concept that informed thinking on sentencing historically and reappears from time-to-time, including re the more punitive aspects of modern sentencing law: see generally *punishment*. It 'looks backwards' to the offence, and the need to express condemnation (see *moral aspects* above) on behalf of society, to assert the *Rule of Law*, and give a sense of satisfaction or vindication, including to *victims* of crime. It contrasts with contrary developments such as *restorative justice*.

revolving door metaphor for the *response* to imprisonment of some *habitual offenders*, who pass in and out of prison as if via the revolving door of a store or hotel; as also used re other forms of institutional care (especially re *mental impairment*), or other recurring scenarios such as those involving 'problem families' or aspects of *social exclusion*.

Robin Hood English outlaw and a central legend whose exploits have entered the English psyche and *popular culture* (above). He is chiefly associated with Nottingham, Sherwood Forest and/or the Barnsdale area of South Yorkshire ('no fox having only one hole'). The 'Sloane Manuscripts' of the British Library (1160) refer to a **Robyn of Lockesley**; other *records to* Robert Hood of Wakefield, Yorkshire (1290); and an early literary reference occurs in William Langland's *The Vision of Piers Ploughman* (1377). Whether he was a real person, an amalgam of traits generally admired, a relic of Pagan or other ancient belief systems, a fictional character, or a mix of these remains the subject of debate. He is usually depicted as a man of principle and deprived of his proper inheritance; who for *reasons of politics*, poetic or rough *justice*, and general sympathy is allowed leeway, especially re class-based offences such as poaching and even *robbery* of the well-to-do. The backdrop includes 'honour amongst thieves' and chivalry, especially re women, children, the aged and *vulnerable people* (even enemies). A scourge of authority, he is nonetheless a symbol of courtesy, *decency*, fair-mindedness (see *fair/fairness*), engaged in noble causes (but see *bent copper*/'noble cause corruption' above). Hence the notion, central to the story, that it is in certain circumstances morally justifiable to 'rob the rich to help the poor': see, generally, *morals* (above) and *robbery* (in *Main Entries*). Hence also **latter-day Robin Hood** re someone whose offending bears comparable

traits (see, e.g. *Kray twins* above; or as with some forms of internet *piracy* or *hacking*). Hence also, to **tell a Robin Hood** means to tell an understandable or white lie.

section (1) Offences, procedures, rules etc. are frequently referred to simply by the section number of the *Act of Parliament* in which the relevant provision appears, e.g. a **section 20**: the offence of malicious wounding: see *assault*; **section nine statement** (or just a **section nine**): see *witness statement*. Note also **being sectioned**, i.e. taken to hospital due to *mental impairment*: see that entry. Compare use of the word *rule* (see generally that entry) as with **Rule 45**: see *prison*. (2) The term may also be used for a unit, team or part of a department.

Scotland Yard The (original) headquarters of the Investigative Branch of London's Metropolitan Police Service (MPS), off The Embankment, north of the River Thames, Westminster. Hence the MPS present headquarters a stone's throw away at **New Scotland Yard**, Broadway, London, SW1H 0BG.

September 11 (2001) (aka **9/11**) Date of the *suicide bombing* of the Twin Towers of the (symbolic) World Trade Center, Manhattan, New York, USA using two hijacked passenger-airliners, killing over 3,400 people and a third 'strike' killing 125 people at The Pentagon, the headquarters of the USA Department of Defense, in Virginia; presumed to be by al-Qaeda; but also a subject of *conspiracy theories*. A seismic event in world history that has had a key influence on *security* matters, especially re *terrorism/terrorists*; the trigger for a *tough* (see below) new approach to *law enforcement* and public *safety* in particular; leading also to a global search for Osama Bin Laden (leader of al-Qaeda); and a factor re the Iraq War. Notoriously, the USA opened the **Guantanamo Bay Detention Centre** (off Cuba) where people categorised as 'enemy combatants' could be denied *constitutional* rights including *due process* and independent *legal representation* (see generally *Rule of Law*); and used **rendition flights** to convey suspects to *jurisdictions* beyond the reach of *human rights* or similar *protections*. Both these developments and other suspect practices were stopped (and their illegality or at least extreme questionableness thus confirmed) almost as soon as Barrack Obama was sworn in as the 44th President of the USA in 2009. See also *July 7* (above).

Shaftesbury (Earl of Shaftesbury) An example of changes of fortune: (**1**) Anthony Ashley Cooper (AAC), First Earl (1621-83) was a politician and supporter of the Restoration of the monarchy. He became *Lord Chancellor* (1672) and organizer of Whig opposition to the accession of James II. He was accused of *treason* (below) but freed under the Habeus Corpus Act 1679 (see *habeus corpus* above) and fled to Holland; (**2**) the Seventh Earl (also AAC) (1801-85) initiated the 'Ten Hours Act' 1847 to protect women and *children* in mines and factories; and was also associated with *campaigns* for free education for the poor; (**3**) the Eleventh Earl (AAC) (1938-2004) was the victim of *murder* on the French Riviera. A flamboyant playboy, he disappeared from the Noga Hilton Hotel, Cannes. His body was found in a gully near Theoule-sur-Mere using mobile phone tracking *technology*. His wife and her brother were convicted (in France) of his murder; and (**4**) the last mentioned events were followed by the sudden death of the Twelfth Earl (2005); leaving the unlucky Thirteenth Earl to embark on disputes with HM *Revenue & Customs* re 'double death duties' concerning property accumulated since the days of the First Earl.

Shipman, Harold The UK's most *prolific* and possibly baffling *serial killer* (although the former distinction has been claimed for Reading baby farmer, Amelia Dyer: see *baby farm* above). Shipman was convicted of 12 *murders* committed whilst a sole general medical practitioner (GP) (and suspected of 235 more) mainly at his practice in Ashton-under-Lyne, Cheshire, where he administered lethal doses of *drugs*. His *motive* was never discerned. He committed *suicide* in Wakefield Prison in 2004 (see *deaths in custody* above); a report by the *Prisons and Probation Ombudsman* concluding that this was not predictable or preventable. Another notorious murder case involving a doctor is that of **John Bodkin Adams** (1899-1983) who in 1957 was charged with the murder of wealthy elderly widow, Edith Alice Morrell, who left him a Rolls Royce motor car in her will following regular prescriptions of hard *drugs*. He secured an *acquittal* after declining to give *evidence* (see *silence*/'right to silence'); pleaded guilty to lesser charges and received

fines. Information later emerged to suggest he may have killed up to 25 patients who had also made wills in his favour. For an account, see *Easing the Passing: The Trial of Dr John Bodkin Adams* (1985), Devlin P (later Lord Devlin the *Law Lord*), Bodley Head.

Sidney Street In the Siege of Sidney Street, East London (1911) radicals (variously described as activists, anarchists or terrorists: see *terrorism/terrorist*) with automatic rifles held out against the police and *military* for several days; events attended by *Home Secretary*, Winston Churchill. They became the subject of a feature film 'The Siege of Sidney Street' (1960) (directed by Robert Baker and Monty Berman) and a novel, *A Death Out of Season* (1974), Litvinoff E, Sphere.

signal Sending out a signal (or message) is often trumpeted as a purpose of, e.g. a *prosecution* or *sentence* and has obvious connections with notions of *deterrence*; as where Government passes 'tough' or uncompromising legislation (see also *tough/toughness* below), or the courts start to impose *heavy* sentences (above) for a given offence. A signal offence is one indicative of something deeper and more disturbing: as where a *community* begins to commit *public order offence*s; or a *sex offender* to commit a particular kind of crime (i.e. such that this should be sending out a message to the authorities re a need for action). Traffic signals (static, mechanical or electronic) must be obeyed by road users failing which offences are committed under *road traffic* law. Note also mixed signals which give out conflicting messages, at a simplistic level, as with *Robin Hood* (above), re *robbery* of the rich to help the poor. Similarly where a *communication* is contradicted by related events or actions (including 'Do as I say, not as I do'), or another message from the same source gives out an opposite message. It is sometimes said, e.g. that Governments give out mixed messages re *alcohol* (profiting from taxes; decrying consumption); or when *Ministers-of-State* or officials are 'economical with the truth'.

Six Acts *Acts of Parliament* passed late in 1819 at a time when **Lord Sidmouth** was (a notably repressive) *Home Secretary*; designed to suppress dissent and uprising. The Acts were strongly opposed by the Whigs as an interference with fundamental *rights* and *liberties*. They were: a Training Prevention

Act which rendered anyone reporting for training, drilling, etc. liable to *arrest* and *transportation* for seven years; a Seizure of Arms Act allowing magistrates to *search* people/property; a Seditious Meetings Prevention Act to control public meetings of more than 50 people which needed the consent of a sheriff/magistrate; a Misdemeanours Act to *fast-track* lesser cases (see generally *felony and misdemeanour*: above); a Blasphemous and Seditious Libels Act creating harsh *punishments* (including *banishment*) re such publications; and a Newspaper and Stamp Duties Act aimed at the *taxation* of expressions of radical opinion.

Smith and Hogan Leading textbook on *criminal law* as written originally by Professor J C Smith and Professor Brian Hogan. See 12th edn. (2008), Ormerod D (ed.), Oxford University Press.

stereotype/stereotyping Categorising someone by reference to a preconceived example of their supposed type; by reference to features unlikely to be all-embracing or universally applicable; such that the stereotype may be misleading, prejudicial, or offensive to those being described, e.g. 'black youths all carry knives' (see generally *weapon*). Hence stereotyping is nowadays actively avoided by CJS practitioners; whereas historically it may have been common practice. But it can still occur, re which there have been complaints. See, e.g. *hoodie* (above).

Stiffkey (The Vicar of Stiffkey) One of the most bizarre true life CJS tales is that of Harold Davidson, Vicar of Stiffkey (aka **The Prostitutes' Padre**), an eccentric who in the 1930s, after being sent to prison/defrocked re *sexual offences* against young girls in 'rituals to erase demons', joined a circus and was eaten by a lion. In 2008, John Penny, then 'priest in charge' at Stiffkey claimed that it was high time for Davidson's posthumous *rehabilitation* ('Time to Forgive the Stiffkey One', the *Guardian*, 24 November 2008).

Stockholm bank syndrome (or just Stockholm syndrome) The idea (not unchallenged) that victims, especially hostages, may warm to their captors or perpetrators of *abuse* over time, as against the police or authorities trying to 'save' them; a theory now associated with various scenarios including *terrorism/terrorists, controlling behaviour* and *domestic*

violence. Based on events at a five day siege-cum-attempted *robbery* at Kreditbanken, Norrmalmstorg, Stockholm, Sweden (1973). A psychological (but not medically recognised) diagnosis credited to Nils Bejerot, a *psychiatrist* who assisted at the time.

Stockwell shooting Seminal event in the annals of UK policing, the ramifications of which are still unravelling: the shooting dead at **Stockwell Underground Station**, south London of a Brazilian man by armed police officers. **John Charles de Menezes** (aged 27) was killed under a shoot-to-kill policy (part of Operation Kratos) re *suicide* bombing in *mistake* for a terrorist (see, generally, *terrorism/terrorist*) in 2005; two weeks after *July 7* (above); one day after four unsuccessful *attempts* to detonate further such bombs across the London transport system. Security services were on full alert during: 'the biggest operation of its kind ever mounted in the UK': per Sir Ian Blair, then Commissioner of Police for the *Metropolitan Police Service* (MPS). The events occurred in front of rush hour passengers when police chased de Menezes into the station, down escalators, boarded a train and fired bullets into his head and body. The shooting led to an inquest finding that there was no 'unlawful killing' (2008); albeit that there had earlier been a successful prosecution of the MPS for *health and safety* offences; and a critical *report* by the *Independent Police Complaints Commission* (IPCC) to which the drawing of such *weapons* is referred as a matter of course.

Stone's Justices' Manual (aka **'Stone'**) Leading work on proceedings in magistrates' courts which first appeared in 1842 and is now published annually by Butterworths.

Strangeways Riot Rioting by inmates at **Strangeways Prison**, Manchester (1990) when some 1,000 prisoners ran amok and certain of their number went on a spree of *violence* in which three prisoners were killed. It began during a service in the prison chapel, attended by 300 inmates, following which prisoners gained access to the roof and broke into the main prison. Those on the roof tore off slates and pelted prison officers, police and the *emergency services* below them, set fire to buildings and wrecked cells. The events, which gave rise to the expression 'England's Bastille' (after the storming of that

Paris prison during the *French Revolution* above) led to the *Woolf Report,* below.

Street A word used in various CJS contexts, e.g. **on the street**: to symbolise the front line where many CJS practitioners, especially police officers, work; **Street Crime Initiative (SCI)**: as introduced by government to counter the kind of offences which tend to be committed on the street (later superseded by a *Respect Agenda* and modern initiatives re *drugs* and *weapons*); **street bail**: see *bail;* **street level**: again a reference to events occurring 'on the street'; and **street offences**: the umbrella term for offences committed by prostitutes, where soliciting for an immoral purpose under the **Street Offences Act 1959** (as amended) demonstrates that (barring changes) prostitution is not an offence in itself, nor advertising or buying sexual services, even if **kerb-crawling** by men by cruising alongside the pavement in cars is. For specific locations see, e.g. **Bow Street**; **Cable Street**; **Sidney Street** (all above).

Support After Murder and Manslaughter (SAMM) A non-political, non-religious organization and network of *help and support* groups, contacts and volunteers to help the families of victims of homicide and 'make society more aware of the devastating effects of [such] crimes', which it does, e.g. by giving talks to interested organizations and agencies/services and taking part in *media/press* events. See further samm.org.uk

symbol/symbolism Symbols play a significant role in CJS matters, ranging from the blindfold worn (see *blind/blindness*) and scales carried (see *balance/balancing*) by Justicia (atop The *Old Bailey* above) to the police *uniform* (below). See also, e.g. references to symbols/symbolism in *Magna Carta; Hindley Myra; Pierrepoint, Albert; September 11; Tolpuddle Martyrs* (all in *Touchstones*). Symbols act as a reminder of fundamental principles or the existence of power and authority; and are in some instances direct, shorthand references to key developments (as with *Birmingham Six; Lawrence, Stephen; Strangeways;* and *Peterloo Massacre*: all above).

Taser-gun (or just 'Taser': a brand name) A variety of stun gun used by police officers (who are not, in the UK, routinely armed with *guns*) to incapacitate people deemed to be *dangerous*; as rolled out nationwide to UK police forces from 2004 onwards; with 8,000 further Tasers and related training announced in 2008. Hence the invented verb **to Tase**. The **M26 Taser** used in the UK originates in the USA; as a form of 'less lethal force'. It fires twin needle-tipped darts (aka barbs) using compressed nitrogen, up to six metres. These deliver rapid 50,000 volt pulses (static electric shocks) via wires connected to the Taser; but at a power of just 26 watts. A comparable effect can be achieved by pressing the gun against the body of the *target*. Either causes temporary muscle cramps; without further affecting someone in normal health. It can penetrate several millimetres of clothing. When a Taser is drawn this is reported to the *Independent Police Complaints Commission* (IPCC).

'three strikes (and you're out)' An allusion to the USA rule of baseball whereby the batter is given out if he or she fails to strike the ball during three consecutive attempts. Hence a metaphor in the USA for a rule of *imprisonment* on a third conviction for given offences (thus in reality meaning 'three strikes and you're in'); and what is termed the **three strikes law**. In England and Wales there is a similar **two strikes law** re certain mainly *serious* offences, confusingly still referred to in *popular culture* (above) as three strikes rather than two. In the last Queen's Speech of 2008 an intention was announced to pass a **one strike law** re temporary withdrawal of *welfare* benefits following a false claim and possibly without waiting for a conviction (see generally *fraud/*'benefit fraud').

Tolpuddle Martyrs Six agricultural labourers from Tolpuddle, Dorset who in 1834 were sentenced to *transportation* (below) to Botany Bay, Australia, for seven years for joining a trade union (or **'unlawful combination'**). The events which are a *symbol* of draconian *punishment* as a *response* to the assertion of *rights* and *freedoms* are now celebrated by a **Tolpuddle Martyrs Day** and parade every July attended by trade unionists from around the world, a **Tolpuddle Martyrs Museum** and a **Botany Bay Inn**.

transportation A *punishment* from the early-18th century until it was abolished in 1857; but which (remarkably) continued in practice until the late-1860s. It involved taking offenders by sea as slaves (in effect), from Britain (which then included Ireland) to British colonies abroad such as the West Indies, America (until its independence from Britain in 1776) and later Australia and Tasmania. Before the days of regular forms of *imprisonment*, transportation served as an *alternative* to *capital punishment* or the *hulks* (the last two above); sometimes re minor offences. From the 1780s, offenders were taken to **Botany Bay**, Australia (around 165,000 prisoners) and Tasmania (then **Van Diemen's Land**): both still used as metaphors for harsh treatment. Terms of seven years (as per the *Tolpuddle martyrs* above), 14 years or **transportation for life** were commonplace. No arrangements existed to repatriate people after their sentence; many settled abroad, prospering or sometimes leading a twilight existence (the notion of the 'Wild, Colonial Boy' of popular song remains strong: Jack Duggan left Ireland for Australia in the 1800s 'robbing the rich to feed the poor' in the style of *Robin Hood* above). Many died: viz surgeons' logs and those of the penal colonies. It is said some opted for execution. Prisoners (sometimes psychopaths) were used to dispense corporal *punishment* and keep *discipline*. Compare *banishment* (above) and *social exclusion* (see *Main Entries*).

Treason An offence which has a long association with *abuse* of power and manipulation of the *criminal law*; treason itself being a somewhat malleable concept, especially historically and notably so during the time of Henry VIII (hence 'Henry VIII clause' for any widely drawn criminalising *legislation*). In 1352 the **Statute of Treasons** conferred wide and flexible powers of *punishment* for treason; and it was not until 1696 that the **Treason Trials Act** allowed *legal representation* to prisoners charged with this offence. An historic example with *political aspects* is the trial of Thomas Hardy, secretary to the London Corresponding Society, for High Treason in 1794 by 'publishing' his dissent. Notable treason trials include those of James Joyce (Lord Haw Haw: who broadcast Nazi propaganda during the Second World War), Roger *Casement* and of those involved in the *Easter Rising* (see above for the last two).

Troubles, The A label used to describe events in Ireland/Northern Ireland, used in two distinct contexts, i.e. re: **(1)** the long-standing and intractable differences between Britain and Ireland as a whole dating from

the 1600s until 1935 and the creation of the Republic of Ireland; or **(2)** those in the period from the late-1960s until the Good Friday Agreement of 1994 (and power sharing in Northern Ireland from 2009); in which atrocities, disorder, disturbances, mayhem, riots, *terrorism/terrorists* and *security* measures became a feature of everyday life in Northern Ireland; spilling out at times onto the UK mainland. This latter period involved policing without the general consent of the *community* (or 'divided *communities*': on both secular and religious grounds), the use of the *military* to maintain law and order, **direct rule** from Westminster, *emergency* powers, special courts (aka **Diplock Courts**) with no jury (see generally *juror/jury*), *punishment* beatings, reprisals and informal *summary justice/social control* via para-military groups and splinter groups on both sides. For an absorbing account of how a fragile peace was ultimately sustained, see *Great Hatred, Little Room: Making Peace in Northern Ireland* (2008), Powell J, Bodley Head in which the achievements of the Labour government (and Governments before) are recorded. Two iconic events remain unresolved: **Bloody Sunday**, events in Londonderry, in 1972 when members of the Parachute Regiment shot dead 14 people during a demonstration by the *Civil Rights Movement* that had gone ahead despite being 'banned' by the authorities; leading to the Saville Inquiry (still to report and re which there have been accusations and counter-accusations re, e.g. the covering-up of a shoot to kill policy (contrast *Stockwell Shooting* above) and manipulation by the *intelligence services*). There are at least three other 'Bloody Sundays', in 1877 (London); 1916 (Dublin); and 1921 in various places across Northern Ireland; and the **Omagh Bombing** (the biggest single atrocity on 15 August 1998 when a 225 kilogram (500lb) car bomb exploded in the centre of Omagh, County Tyrone, killing 29 people and injuring 300. In 2002, Colm Murphy was sentenced to *imprisonment* for 14 years by a Special Court in Dublin for *conspiracy* to cause explosions. In 2003, Michael McKevitt, leader of the Real IRA received 20 years for directing terrorism. In 2005, following a fresh investigation by the incoming Police Service of Northern Ireland (PSNI) (which took over from a beleaguered Royal Ulster Constabulary (RUC) in 2002) it was announced that Sean Gerard Hoey, from Jonesborough, South Armagh was to be charged with *murder* following a review of the *forensic evidence* by a multinational team of scientists from Canada, the USA and Switzerland; a case later *discontinued*. According to *reports* and *allegations*, the attack was the work of the Real IRA; the Irish National Liberation Army (INLA) being involved in the *theft* of the car and the Continuity IRA building the device. In 2004, Gerry Adams, president of Sinn Féin (the '*political*' wing' of the IRA) said that, whilst he 'regretted' matters, he could not issue an apology. In 2009, it transpired that the former head of the police *investigation* claimed that it was 'effectively sabotaged by the *intelligence* services'. That same year saw a resurgence of splinter group killings to the general opprobrium of *communities* across religious or other divides.

tough/toughness Words which features regularly within the criminal justice lexicon, e.g. in expressions such as being '**tough on crime**' (the Tory Government mantra of the 1990s, re-invented by New Labour as '**tough on crime, tough on the causes of crime**' for its 1997 election manifesto). Similarly '**out-toughing**' to describe confrontations with people of a less physical or a more liberal persuasion; or '**tough guy**', **tough nut**' (or just a '**tough**': see also, e.g. *heavy* above). Note also **tough love**, the idea that it is sometimes necessary to be firm and resolute out of concern for an offender, especially vis-à-vis parents and their children (and as originally piloted by a number of juvenile offender institutions in the USA).

Turpin, Richard (Dick Turpin) (1706-1739) Perhaps the best-known English highwayman, born in Thaxstead, Essex, who became a legend following a marathon ride, as a fugitive, from London to York on his mare, Black Bess, in less than 24 hours; his reputation masking a sordid criminal career. A butcher from Whitechapel, London (and a 'loose and disorderly' apprentice), he took to cattle rustling, *theft*, *robbery* and *smuggling*. By 1735, the *Crown* had put a price of £50 on his head (£100 by 1737); leading to narrow escapes. He worked with 'Captain' Tom King; but after one hold-up the victim circulated handbills describing both. King was *arrested* whilst Turpin fired towards the constables, killing King by mistake, but not before he implicated Turpin, who fled to Yorkshire, settling as a John Palmer and making 'sorties' into Lincolnshire. Caught,

convicted and his *plea* for *transportation* having failed, 'with undaunted courage [he] looked about him and, after speaking a few words to the topsman, threw himself off the ladder and expired in about five minutes'.

Tyburn The main site of the gallows in London from the 12th century until 1784; close to what is now Marble Arch at the junction of Edgware Road/Bayswater Road. Originally, *hanging* (above) was from the branch of a tree (hence **Tyburn Tree**), later a wooden beam and later still a triangle of inter-connected beams allowing simultaneous executions. Events at Tyburn were often accompanied by ceremony, ritual (including a procession from prison: such as *Newgate Prison* above), **gallows speeches**, **gallows humour** (an expression that still resonates re jokes at someone else's downfall), ballads, broadsheets (see *media/press*), fairs, ribaldry (see also *Dickens, Charles* above), and lack of decency or similar *values*. The greatest number of executions at one time was 23 men and a woman (1649); the last Tyburn execution that of John Austin (*robbery*) (1783). Hence allusions to '**the poisoned tree**', i.e. any gallows (with its 'adder bitten root': per *Wilde, Oscar,* below).

Underworld A quasi-mythical place, typically categorised as inhabited by career criminals, *drug*-dealers, gangsters (see *gang*), professional criminals, traffickers (see *traffick/trafficking*) and those involved in *organized crime*, the sex industry, prostitution (see *street offences* above), *money laundering*, *protection* rackets, maintaining territory by *fear*, intimidation, *violence*, etc. A parallel universe, with its own informal *rules*, *codes*, culture and language (overlapping with *prison slang* above). Although not geographically-based, it is often associated with parts of Soho, the East End of London and areas of major cities such as Glasgow, Manchester, Birmingham, Nottingham and Newcastle.

uniform Many CJS practitioners wear a **uniform in the strict sense**: standard issue clothing that can be recognised immediately by *citizens*: such as police officers (other than plainclothes officers), *prison officers* (as opposed to *prison governors*), UK Border Agency staff (since 2007) and *private sector* employees such as *prisoner escorts*; whilst other practitioners wear **special attire**, 'costume' or 'garb' as per *judges* and *barristers* (both of whom wear wigs and gowns in the *Crown Court* and most *higher courts*: a matter of continuing debate, the practice having been abandoned in many *civil* courts). Solicitors may wear gowns but not wigs and neither of these in the *magistrates' courts* where there is a convention of sober dress; as there is in some other CJS contexts when solemnity is required. Great store is placed in the **police uniform** in particular; the wearing of which is as much a *symbol* as it is a *legal* prerequisite to the exercise of power and authority.

Unlock (or sometimes UNLOCK): The National Association of Reformed Offenders) a unique organization founded in 1999 by a small group of ex-offenders, each of whom had successfully rebuilt their life after serving prison sentences. They claimed no accolade, but rightly experience of the great difficulties faced by those coming out of prison; having had first-hand experience of the many problems faced; especially by those genuinely intent on 'going straight' and 'in a society which always finds it hard to forgive and forget'. For information, see unlock.org.uk

up-tariffing A phenomenon whereby the wider the range of sentencing choices that a court has, the more likely it is to gravitate upwards in the sentencing framework; due to experimentation, uncertainty or lack of restraint. Hence and because of this there will be less room for manoeuvre if an offender is later charged with a further offence as he or she will already be well up the sentence ladder. Compare *net widening* (above).

Victorian aspects A significant number of modern-day offences stem from or have their roots in the Victorian era, such as those under the Vagrancy Act 1824 and *Offences Against the Person Act 1861* (see also *assault*); as do various (still) leading cases (see also *precedent*) and certain *criminal procedures* and rules of the Common Law; albeit that the era from the late-1990s in particular has been one of widescale *reform* and up-dating. Many court and prison buildings date from Victorian times (causing some commentators to say that CJS matters were for years stuck in the same timewarp). Similarly, attitudes to *crime* and *punishment* generally. **Victorian prisons** serve as a monument to outmoded ways: typical features including arches and archways, castellations, crenellations, limestone floors, turrets, high vaulted ceilings, a

chapel (often the size of a substantial church building), iron walkways, spiral staircases and perhaps '**Victorian Gothic**' features such as arrow slits for windows or mullioned windows (mostly now refurbished). Yet the Victorian era was also one of *campaigns* and *reform,* encompassing the origins of various key *voluntary sector* bodies. There were at least eight assassination attempts on **Queen Victoria** of which the Jubilee Plot (1887) is perhaps most often cited. She once declined a chain mail parasol designed by husband, Prince Albert; and rejected claims that, by moving to Osborne House, Isle of Wight (1861), she would be at-risk of abduction by Fenians. Suggestions that she sought to influence her *Ministers of State* and *judges* persist; one such involving the case of *Dudley and Stevens* (above). The era is rich in **Victorian slang** and colloquial terms, many of which survive, e.g. jemmy, lag, peterman (for a safe-blower: some originally using saltpetre).

villain The history of crime and *punishment* demonstrates the existence of people who can be described as villains, or **real villains**, to be *feared* even by their associates; yet there may be a high level of tolerance within certain (especially small or tight knit) communities so long as they know that one of their own number is 'a villain' or potentially so; a phenomenon described in *Marginal Man, etc.* noted under *marginal* above. See also *rogues, villains and eccentrics* above.

Walter Mitty Fictional character, originally from, 'The Fictional Life of Walter Mitty' (1939), a short story by of the American author James Thurber (1894-1961). Hence '**Walter Mitty character**' and '**Walter Mitty syndrome**' re people who live in fantasy worlds or have delusions; usually according to the *Oxford English Dictionary* re 'a life much more exciting and glamorous than their own'. Such terms are frequently used in the courts, e.g. by *advocates* and psychologists (see generally *psychiatry/psychology*) re offenders who acted foolishly, whose offences, often based on *deception,* were misguided but may have primarily sought to enliven a dull existence; as a form of *mitigation.* In 2003, a spokesman for Prime Minister Tony Blair, apologised for referring to David Kelly (who committed *suicide* during *investigations* into the leaking of official secrets re the Iraq *War*) as such a character, i.e. re information passed to a representative of the *media/press.*

Ward, Stephen (d.1963) Central character in one of the most questionable legal events in UK history, i.e. his trial which arose out of the Profumo Affair (1963). Ward committed *suicide* in prison during the trial at The *Old Bailey* for living off immoral earnings (see *deaths in custody* and *moral aspects* above), i.e. for acting as a 'pimp' to high society; and appears to have been a scapegoat (see generally *scapegoat/scapegoating* above). Earlier, John Profumo MP (1915-2006), Minister for War, had lied to Prime Minister, Harold Macmillan and the House of Commons when denying impropriety with Christine Keeler (aged 19) a dancer, model or call girl. She was a protégé of Ward. Over and above her relationship with Profumo, she was a recent lover of a senior Russian Naval attaché, Yevgeny Ivanov; also 'an acquaintance' of Ward: who may have been a spy or simply a *Walter Mitty character* (above) so far as his claims of involvement in espionage were concerned. This entire scenario was the trigger for allegations of a breach of *national security* and various *conspiracy theories*. Ward, to be certain, had infiltrated the Establishment as an osteopath; and the reverberations ultimately unseated the Tory Government. One *response* in cross-examination (see *evidence*) by Mandy Rice-Davies, Keeler's friend, has passed into legend. When told that Lord (Bill) Astor had denied having an affair with her, she replied, 'Well he would; wouldn't he?'; now a stock illustration in the armoury of every *legal representative*. Outside London, the focus of activities was Cliveden, a stately home near Marlow, Buckinghamshire, now owned by the National Trust but then by Lord (Bill) Astor (who allowed Ward to use a weekend cottage there). Along with others on the periphery of events, Astor escaped prosecution re associated matters; but was shunned by the Establishment. In his report of a *judicial* inquiry (1964), Lord Denning described Ward as 'one of the most *evil* [above] men I have encountered', but the reasons remain undisclosed. In *An Affair of State: The Profumo Affair and the Framing of Stephen Ward* (1987), Knightley P and Kennedy C, London: Jonathan Cape Ltd, allegation were made that the police were intructed 'from on high' to find matters which 'might fit' a *prosecution*, rather than to begin an *investigation* into a known offence.

watch A word which links vigilance to notions of public or communal *safety* and public *protection*; touching at once on the origins of the CJS, many of which are bound up with ideas of **'mounting a watch'** or lookout, especially at night or times of increased *risk* (as per a practice of **watch and ward**) and modern-day schemes such as **Neighbourhood Watch** (see *Main Entries*) and *surveillance*. Hence the term **'watchman'** which has changed its meaning over time: originally a *community* lookout but now usually a *private sector* security guard re a specific undertaking. The word 'watch' has also been adopted by various organizations whose own **watchword** is vigilance.

weight A word that occurs repeatedly re CJS matters along with the idea of **weighing** matters, e.g. **weighing evidence.** When making a decision, a court or practitioner will give weight to competing factors, priorities, claims, etc. in order to arrive at a balanced decision (see also *balancing* above). Even if facts, *information, intelligence*, etc. exist, they may have **insufficient weight** to support a particular choice or outcome.

Wergild (aka **Wergeld** or **'wote'**): the 'man price' or 'blood price', i.e. *value* to be paid in Anglo-Saxon times as a form of *compensation* if *murder* (or other killings) occurred; initially as an *alternative* to the blood feud. This was the responsibility of the entire *community*; members of different social classes having different 'worth', by which they were sometimes referred to more generally. For lesser injuries, botgeld was used in a similar way. For such developments generally, see *A History of Criminal Justice in England and Wales* (2009), Hostettler J, Waterside Press.

'what works' (or **'what works?'**) Expression/question encapsulating the notion that the CJS should rely on methods/approaches/outcomes that are shown by *evidence*-based *research* to have a predictable outcome, i.e. nowadays meaning in terms of *crime prevention/crime reduction* or possibly other key CJS aims. A 'what works' Home Office initiative is described at crimereduction.homeoffice.gov.uk What works has been linked to the delivery of services to a consistent standard and which are *effective* for all groups of victims and offenders; but has other subtleties of meaning and became a part of the mantra of the New Labour government in 1997 (when it was adopted by managers in many public services); together with an insistence on procedures for *monitoring* and *evaluation.* What works has long been associated with the realisation that some sentences work, others not so well. But contrast the pessimistic, **nothing works**; and the over-certainty of **prison works** (which was prevalent from 1993 onwards more as an exercise in blind *political* tactics than on the basis of evidence). Variants include **what works for women, children, sex offenders** or re **parenting**. In a criminological context, what works is associated with Robert Martinson who in 1974 published an essay: 'What Works? Questions and Answers About Prison Reform'; and since with various *experts*.

whipping Public whippings (aka 'floggings') were a common *punishment* for vagrants (and their families), as local communities endeavoured to drive homeless people (see generally *home*) back to their own parish as vagrants; and subsequently for a range of offences. Henry VIII's **Whipping Act** stipulated that they and beggars should be tied naked to a cart-tail and whipped out of the locality. Mainly from the 16th to 18th centuries, most towns and villages had **'whipping posts'**; wooden frames in prominent public places which as well as being used for whippings served as *symbols* (above) of *law and order*. Notoriously, Titus Oates, the *informer* and rumour monger was, in James II's reign, publicly flogged until unconscious, over two days. The **cat-of-nine-tails** was a nine-tailed whip, knotted at its ends, used mainly in the navy, but also in some prisons. The whipping of *women* for vagrancy was abolished in 1791; all whippings of women in 1920 by when it had become redundant. Public whippings ceased from 1817 onwards; and whipping was abolished for all purposes in 1948. It continues in certain part of the world.

white collar crime Crime committed by office workers or their superiors, by people who formerly wore white shirts (and suits and ties) at their desks or when seeing clients (which fewer and fewer people wear). The scale of white collar crime is said to be vast, but by virtue of its hidden nature and the fact that much of it never reaches the stage of *detection* or *investigation* (see also *report*/'reported crime') its true scale goes unassessed (compare *black economy* above: of which it can in some respects be considered a part). There is also a degree of *normalisation* (above). It involves, e.g.

(unlawfully) taking things home from the office or the unauthorised use of resources, etc, backhanders and sweeteners (see also *corruption*). Sometimes it is not prosecuted due to equivocal attitudes by employers and businesses who do not wish to be tainted, or a failure to equate it with crime proper, including due to safeguarding reputations. Hence also **blue collar crime** to signify that committed in an industrial context, e.g. by taking home machine parts. The existence of such offences (or similar 'condoned behaviour' that in other contexts might be actively deemed to be 'criminal' or be relied on re processes of *criminalisation*), creates difficulties with regard to any single or 'tidy' theory of *criminology.*, especially re those of the *broken windows* variety (above).

wider criminal justice family Beyond the formal CJS lies what is sometimes styled 'the wider criminal justice family'. It includes people and agencies/services involved in CJS-related tasks, such as *Victim Support*, the *Witness Service, Nacro*, the *Howard League for Penal Reform, Prison Reform Trust* and *Unlock* (all in *Touchstones*); and others less visible, such as people who befriend offenders, act as mentors, engage in crime prevention/crime reduction or are members of *Independent Monitoring Boards* (IMBs). Hence also more specific usages such as **wider police family**.

Wild, Jonathan (1682-1725) According to the *Newgate Calendar* (above), 'History cannot furnish an instance of such complicated villainy as is shown in the character of Jonathan Wild'; an early example of a career criminal and inspiration for the fictional *The Life of Mr. Jonathan Wild: The Great* by Sir Henry Fielding (see, *Fielding, Sir Henry,* above). Born in Wolverhampton, Wild moved to London as a valet and honed his knowledge of lowlife during four years in Wood Street Debtors' Prison. He then opened a brothel (in partnership with pickpocket Mary Milner), established a detective agency, became a fence (see, now, *handler/ handling*) trading back property to *victims* at a premium from a 'Lost Property Office' at The *Old Bailey* (above). He bought a sloop to export stolen goods; manipulated thieves, highwaymen, footpads and *witnesses* (bought to swear to anything). As self-appointed **Thieftaker General** he claimed 57 executions. In 1718, under new *legislation,* he was arrested for 'selling back' stolen lace and following a *suicide* attempt was hanged at *Tyburn* (above) before a large crowd.

Wilde, Oscar (Oscar Fingal O'Flahertie Wills Wilde) (1854-1900) Irish socialite and writer of prose, plays, poetry etc; a flamboyant relic of minor Irish aristocracy, feted for his incisive wit and as a leading light in the Aesthetic Movement ('Art for art's sake'). His relationship with the younger Lord Alfred Douglas led to Wilde bringing an action for criminal libel (now defunct) against Douglas' father, the Marquess of Queensbury (1894), for calling Wilde 'a sodomite' (homosexual); a tactic that rebounded by way of criminal proceedings against Wilde due to matters disclosed in the libel trial, which Wilde lost. Ignoring advice from friends, he declined to become a fugitive, was arrested, convicted and given two years' *imprisonment*, served in Pentonville Prison and *Reading Gaol* (above). On his release, Wilde lived in self-imposed exile in France where sexual tolerance prevailed, and where he died and is buried. 'The love that dare not speak its name' (Wilde), is no longer an offence; the law having accepted that homosexuality in private between consenting adults should not be unlawful; leading to *protection* from sexual *discrimination*, *hate crime* based on *sexual orientation* and to such *motives* being an aggravating factor (see generally *aggravate/aggravation*).

witch The pursuit of witches and banning of **witchcraft** has a long and unsavoury history in the UK and Europe, including on the biblical pretext 'Though shalt not suffer a witch to live' (nor 'a sorceress') (Exodus 22:18); appeals to primal instincts being capable of generating *fear,* especially re base superstitions. Countless texts link devils, demons, heresy, witchcraft and official or religious purges, including *Demonologie* (1604), a treatise by King James I. In a modern context, **witch hunt** still connotes *demonisation* (above), *hate*, *abuse* lack of fairness (see *fair/fairness*) or *objectivity,* etc. Mathew Hopkins from Manningtree, Essex was a self-appointed **Witchfinder General** (1645-1647) and central figure re such persecution, whose zeal led to 200 executions of women in East Anglia (often by burning at the stake: see generally *capital punishment* above). His short-lived regime accounted for hundreds more deaths across the southern counties. His first 'success' was re Elizabeth Clarke, a one-legged widow, who made

a *confession* to 'keeping familiars' (1645). Ultimately, a reaction set in, with allegations of exploitation and *abuse* of power. Legend has it that Hopkins was himself made to endure the practice of **'swimming a witch'** (to see whether demons would cause him to float) before his own execution. His Scottish counterpart of that era was John Kincaid.

Woolf Report (1) The 1991 report by Lord Justice (later Lord Chief Justice) Woolf and His Honour Judge Stephen Tumim, *Report of an Inquiry into the Prison Disturbances of April 1990* (Cm.1465), including the *Strangeways Riot* (above). It concluded that the Strangeways disturbance began as a limited protest after the majority of prisoners shared a belief that conditions there were 'unacceptable' and 'inhumane'; and that HM Prison Service had failed to conform to three basic rules affecting *security*, *control* and *justice*. A summary and information concerning the later impact of this key report is available from prisonreformtrust.org.uk **(2)** Later **'Woolf Reports'**, i.e. by Lord Woolf, e.g. into *access to* [civil] *justice* (1996); and *BAE Systems* (above) (2007).

Woolmington v Director of Public Prosecutions Seminal case in the annals of criminal law, *Woolmington v. DPP* [1935] Appeal Cases 462 in which Lord Sankey reasserted the duty of the prosecutor to prove the accused person's guilt: 'Throughout the web of the English criminal law one golden thread is always to be seen - that is the duty of the prosecution to prove the prisoner's guilt . . . If, at the end of and on the whole of the case, there is a reasonable doubt, created by the evidence given by ... the prosecution or the prisoner . . . the prosecution has not made out the case and the prisoner is entitled to an *acquittal* . . . No matter what the *charge* or where the *trial* [this principle] is part of the Common Law of England and no attempt to whittle it down can be entertained'.

Wootton, Dame Barbara (1897-1988). Penal reformer (see *reform*), *criminologist* and magistrate who was made a life peer (1958). Barbara Wootton was professor of Social Studies, University of London (1948); a member of the Advisory Council on the Penal System (ACPS); and chair of the ACPS report on 'Non-Custodial and Semi Custodial Penalties' (1970) (see, generally, *custody*); that introduced two experiments of a pioneering nature, *community service* and *probation* 'day centres'. Her publications include *Social Science and Social Pathology* (1959), Wooton B et al, George Allen & Unwin and *Crime and Penal Policy: Reflections on Fifty Years Experience* (1978), Wootton B, Allen & Unwin. She is credited with two celebrated observations: 'If men behaved like *women*, then the courts would be idle and the prisons, empty'; and (re her experience of 30 years in the then juvenile court at Chelsea, west-London, 'Juvenile court magistrates should never forget that ... they are always dealing with other people's *children*'.

Yorkshire Ripper Peter Sutcliffe (aka Peter Coonan) a long-distance lorry driver from Bingley, West Yorkshire who murdered 12 women (possibly more) in the 1970s claiming that voices drove him to do so. He is still detained in a special hospital (see *Main Entries* under *mental impairment*) despite his claim of schizophrenia having been rejected at his *Old Bailey* trial (above). West Yorkshire Police failed to identify him despite several opportunities and one report which noted that he should be a prime suspect, which went astray; due in part to chaotic record-keeping (see now *Holmes* above). The *investigation* was deflected by hoax messages from 'Jack', gaoled re that almost forgotten *'cold case'* after an unsolicited *confession* 30 years on. Sutcliffe changed his name to Peter Coonan some years ago. In 2009, following a news report that he might no longer be a *danger*, Prime Minister Gordon Brown declared that he could not envisage circumstances in which Sutcliffe would be released or moved to less secure prison accommodation.

zero tolerance (ZT) A law enforcement *strategy* that relies on virtually automatic *arrest, charge, prosecution*, etc., pro-active, vigorous (and possibly aggressive) policing backed by a resolve on the part of courts to deal firmly with offenders; including re *low-level offences* and *anti-social behaviour* (ASB); thus indicating that *serious offences* will be tolerated even less. ZT eliminates or reduces *discretion*. It seeks to reassure *citizens* via *deterrence* and by instilling *respect* (see *reassurance* above). Opponents argue that it merely stifles disrespect, failing to create that deeper form of respect which is a prerequisite to changing attitudes; and that it leads to *displacement* of crime. It began in

the New York Police Department (NYPD), USA under Commissioner William Bratton (early 1990s). In the UK, it is often linked to Cleveland Constabulary (late-1990s), in particular, initiatives by Superintendent Ray Mallon (later directly elected mayor of Hartlepool). ZT may *target* offences of a given type, or ASB; sometimes due to CPS *strategies*, e.g. re *domestic violence* or *hate crime*. Trends in ZT have been towards *community*-based crime prevention/crime reduction.

Zito Trust A *charity* concentrating on *mental impairment* (see *Main Entries*) which seeks to highlight related issues; established in 1994, following the report of an independent inquiry into the care and treatment of **Christopher Clunis**, who killed Jonathan Zito, while suffering from schizophrenia. The trust describes Clunis as 'among the one in one hundred people in the UK who will at some time ... suffer from schizophrenia ... the most chronic and disabling of the major mental illnesses'. It is funded by the UK pharmaceutical company, Eli Lilly and Co. For further information, see zitotrust.co.uk

---

What to do for an encore?

The Geese Theatre is one of many arts-based concerns working in the criminal justice sphere to help change people's lives for the better. Other leading CJS-linked theatre groups include **Clean Break** (cleanbreak.org.uk) and **Escape Artists** (escapeartists.co.uk).

The **Geese Theatre** functions as a cooperative, working in *prisons, young offender institutions, probation areas* and other CJS settings; using 'masks' to signify attitudes, etc. and provoke audience participation; also performing playlets on topics such as *anger* or *domestic violence*. See geese.co.uk

Timeline of key dates and events

The following selection is intended to give the reader a sense of the long heritage of and backdrop to matters of crime and punishment in England and Wales. Italicised references are to *Main Entries* (purple section) except when stated otherwise. I am grateful to **John Hostettler**, **Peter Villiers** and **David J Cornwell** whose books on criminal justice history, policing and restorative justice are gold mines of chronological and absorbing information. They can be previewed at WatersidePress.co.uk

560	England's first written laws
946	Edmund I killed during a *robbery* in Gloucestershire
978	Edward II (aka 'Edward the Martyr') *murdered* at Corfe Castle, Dorset
1066	Norman Conquest; the first stirring of the *Common Law* and the *jury*
1108	*Tyburn* first used as a place of execution: see *Touchstones*
1160	Keepers of the Peace appointed
1164-66	Assize of Clarendon commands sheriffs to assist each one another in the pursuit of known felons; and sows the early seeds of modern-day trial by *jury*
1190	First substantial treatise on the law: *Tractabus de legibus consuetudinibus regeni Angliae*: 'On the Laws and Customs of the Realm' (aka 'Glanvill' after the warrior statesman and Chief Justiciar to Henry II, in recognition of his key contribution)
1195	Richard I (1189-1199) appoints knights to swear men over 15 to keep the peace on behalf of the *Crown*, the origins of the Conservators of the Peace (later *magistrates*)
1197	First Fleet Prison built in London
1215	*Magna Carta* (see *Touchstones*) creates an enduring foundation for *rights* and *liberties*
1230	Origins of the *legal profession*
1275	Statute of Westminster I formalises the hue and cry and leads to 'pressing to death'
1285	Statute of Westminster II introduces severe *punishments* (burning to death for *arson*, hanging for *rape*). Statute of Winchester orders sheriffs to punish lax *law enforcement*.
1352	Statute of Treasons confers wide and malleable powers of *punishment*
1361	Justices of the Peace Act consolidates the magistracy; *Peasants Revolt*: see *Touchstones*
1400	The criminal law comprises eleven Common Law offences, almost all attracting *capital punishment* (see *Touchstones*), plus 30 statutory felonies (other *serious* crimes) and 30 or so misdemeanours (less serious): a rapid growth since the 12th century.
1406	Each parish has to erect a wooden stocks and a *pillory*: see *Touchstones*
1540	Star Chamber evolves as an early version of the modern-day *Privy Council*
1550s	*Bail* and *committal* statutes, including the **1555** 'Marian Committal Statute' which requires JPs to conduct speedy pre-trial examinations of defendants following arrests. An era of corruption. Magistrates first dubbed *basket justices* (see *Touchstones*).
1553	First known Bridewells: town and city gaols that presage police cells and local prisons
1572	Stricter *punishments* for *begging* (and for constables who fail to arrest them)
1601	Guy Fawkes and other Catholics foiled in their *attempt* to kill James I in Parliament
1615	*Transportation* begins as an alternative to *capital punishment*: see *Touchstones* for both

1628	Sir Edward Coke champions the *Common Law* as against that of the *Crown* or Church. His 'Institutes' set out basic *rights*. They are suppressed until after his death.
1649	Execution of Charles I, i.e. 'regicide'. England a republic subject to *military* justice, a network of *informers* but also relative tolerance: see, e.g. *Levellers* in *Touchstones*.
1650	Expansion of early prisons, originally, as now, egged on by the *private sector*
1660	Restoration of the monarchy; paid watchmen, aka 'bellmen' or 'Charleys' (after Charles II). Magistrates must read the Riot Act before calling in the militia.
1670	Chief Justice Vaughan states that the *verdict* of a jury is sacrosant
1689	Glorious Revolution and Bill of Rights: Parliament free from the *Crown* (as progressively are the *judges*). Freer elections. *Freedom* of speech in Parliament. *Fairness* in assembling a *jury*. Excessive *bail*, *fines* and cruel and unusual *punishments* outlawed.
1696	Treason Trials Act allows *legal representation* for prisoners facing such charges
1700	Rewards for thief-takers. A judge's certificate (aka a *Tyburn* Ticket: see *Touchstones*) allows favourable treatment of what are now *informers*, leading to tickets being traded, *counterfeiting and forgery*. Black Acts extend *capital punishment* (see *Touchstones*).
1701	Act of Settlement establishes an early but fragile form of *judicial independence*
1723	Waltham Black Act takes 'hanging offences' to over 200: England's Bloody Code, see *capital punishment* in *Touchstones*. London dubbed 'the City of the Gallows'.
1725	Execution of the first 'head' of *organized crime*, Jonathan *Wild*: see *Touchstones*
1730	An Act for the Better Regulation of Juries is passed after MPs hear of 'evil practices used in corrupting jurors [and of widespread] *abuse*': see generally now *juror/jury*
1730s	Second-hand (aka hearsay *evidence*), gradually being excluded in criminal trials
1739	*Bow Street* 'Police Court' established: see *Touchstones*
1749	*Bow Street Runners* started by Sir Henry *Fielding*: see *Touchstones*
1760	John Wilkes convicted of criminal libel; *Gordon Riots*: see *Touchstones*.
1764	The Italian jurist Cesare Beccaria (1738-94) publishes *Dei Delitti e delle Pene* ('Of Crimes and Punishments') in protest at 'the inhumanity of the criminal law'
1774	Gaol Act after John *Howard* (1726-1729)(see *Touchstones*) tours Britain's prisons
1775 on	Floating vessels known a 'hulks' used as places of *imprisonment* on the River Thames and at places such as Chatham, Gosport, Plymouth, Portsmouth and Sheerness
1777	*The State of the Prisons, etc.* is published by John *Howard*: see *Touchstones*
1779	The first prison of a new era opens following John Howard's recommendations (above) at Bodmin, Cornwall. Penitentiary Act establishes two prisons for London.
1780	The *Old Bailey* and *Newgate Prison* are destroyed in the *Gordon Riots*: see *Touchstones*
1786	Attempted assassination of George III. Police assume 'royal *protection*' duties.
1787	Convict settlement opened at Botany Bay, Australia: see *Touchstones/'transportation'*
1789	*French Revolution* (see *Touchstones*) leads to repression across England and Ireland
1791	Barrister William Garrow establishes the *presumption of innocence* (in the trial of George Dingler at The Old Bailey on a charge of *murder*). Jeremy Bentham suggests the panoptican: a prison overseen from a single vantage point. It was never built: but 'radial prisons' with wings projecting outwards like the 'spokes' of a wheel were.
1792	Fox's Libel Act gives juries control over what is defamatory (then a criminal matter)

1794	*Habeus corpus* (see *Touchstones*) suspended (as at many later times of emergency). Thomas Hardy of the London Corresponding Society, tried for High Treason ('corresponding').
1797	Coke's Institutes (see 1628) are freed from their shackles and published in full
1800	Imprisonment of both offenders and the 'dispossessed'. Dirty prisons. Gaol fever.
1810	Sir Samuel Romilly notes that there is 'no other country in which so many and great a variety of human actions are punishable with loss of life': see *capital punishment*. *Luddite* riots add a new word to the English language: see *Touchstones*.
1811	*Ratcliff Highway* murders of travellers lead to para-military Foot Patrols: see *Touchstones*
1812	A Parliamentary Select Committee report leads to increased police powers. Magistrates get supervisory powers re the police and an era of 'police courts' begins.
1814	'Peacekeeping' measures in Ireland in *response* to Fenian activities
1815	Society for Investigating the Causes of the Alarming Increase of Juvenile Delinquency in the Metropolis formed. Corn Law riots.
1815	Elizabeth Fry founds 'schools' for children imprisoned with their parents
1816	Millbank Penitentiary built close to where the Tate Gallery now stands
1817	Spa Fields riot leads to calls for better policing. Public whipping of women abolished. Elizabeth Fry helps to form an Association for the Improvement of Female Prisoners.
1819	Peterloo Massacre (Manchester) fuels concern about police methods: see *Touchstones*
1820	Arthur Thistlewood and ten associates are executed for the Cato Street conspiracy in which they try to kill the Prime Minister and his entire cabinet
1822	Robert Peel becomes *Home Secretary*. Head constables, prosecutors and a police Horse Patrol initiated. Police wear 'blue lobster' uniforms, i.e. with red waistcoats.
1823	Gaol Act allows magistrates to regulate *prisons* and prescribes for an improved diet for prisoners: the origins of outside involvement, prison visitors and inspections.
1825	*Archbold's Criminal Pleading and Practice* first published
1826	Wholesale *reform* of the police
1827	Criminal Law Act ends remaining traces of *benefit of clergy*: see *Touchstones*
1829	*Metropolitan Police Service* (MPS) formed as 'The New Police'
1830	England in the throes of extreme *violence*. Various radical groups are thwarted.
1833	Criminal Law Commissioners appointed under William IV: eminent lawyers and reformers they set about *codification* of the criminal law leading to eight reports, two million words but little progress. Other reforms occur throughout the century.
1835	Doctrine of 'temporary insanity' overruled in *R. v. Carroll*
1836	Prisoners Counsel Act allows *legal representation*. A Royal Commission looks at 'the best means of establishing an efficient constabulary'.
1837	Vagrancy Act targets rogues, vagabonds and the 'idle and disorderly'. Lord John Russell's legislation abolishes *capital punishment* for all but 16 offences: see *Touchstones*
1838	Horse Patrol removed from the jurisdiction of the chief magistrate
1839	*Bow Street Runners* disbanded (see *Touchstones*). Newport Rising by *Chartists* (see *Touchstones*) urging civil/democratic rights is met with a huge physical *response*.
1842	Pentonville Prison, north London, opens. Thomas Carlyle writes of 'palaces for felons' (an early precursor to 'holiday camps'). *Stone's Justices' Manual* first published;
1843	M'Naughten Rules: see *Touchstones* and *mental impairment* (in *Main* Entries)

1847	Select Committee inquires into *juveniles* and *transportation*. Iron crank introduced (which prisoners turn by hand as futile in-cell 'labour'). Juvenile Offenders Act gives *magistrates* power to sentence children aged 14 or under to *whipping* (see *Touchstones*).
1848	Summary Jurisdiction Act (aka Jervis's Act after *Attorney General* Sir John Jervis) greatly enlarges the powers and duties of local *magistrates*
1849	After attending the public executions of Maria and Frederick Manning, Charles *Dickens* campaigns for *capital punishment* 'behind prison walls': see *Touchstones* for both
1850	Juvenile Offenders Act
1855	Criminal Justice Act paves the way for an expansion of the work of *magistrates* in the 19th and 20th centuries. They eventually deal with over 95 per cent of criminal cases.
1861	Larceny Act (see now *Theft Act 1968*). Offences Against the Person Act (see *assault*).
1862	Whipping of Offenders Act restricts *punishment* to 12 strokes for *juveniles*
1863	Security From Violence Act is passed (against the Government's will), providing for severe flogging and penal servitude for *garroting* (see *Touchstones*) or other *violence*
1864	Royal Commission on Capital Punishment: see generally *capital punishment*
1865	Criminal Law (Amendment) Act under which Oscar *Wilde* (see *Touchstones*) is later imprisoned for sodomy. Prison Act enables 'hard bed, hard board and hard fare'.
1868	Last public executions: of Michael Barrett and others for the Clerkenwell Explosion
1880	London Police Court Mission introduces a welfare element in dealing with offenders and presages the Probation Service: see *Rainer Crime Concern* in *Touchstones*
1881	Military flogging is abolished
1884	Celebrated case of *Dudley and Stephens* touches a popular nerve: see *Touchstones*
1887	10,000 unemployed Irish people attend a meeting on what becomes the first of several 'Bloody Sundays' spanning Anglo-Irish history: see The *Troubles* in *Touchstones*
1895	Herbert Gladstone's report on *prisons* published, recommending abolition of the prison treadmill, less solitary confinement and a better diet for prisoners; backed by the belief that as many offenders as possible should be kept out of prison altogether. Recidivism (see *reoffending*) it declares, is 'a growing stain on our civilisation'.
1898	Criminal *Evidence* Act enables accused people to give evidence in their own *defence*. Prison Act abolishes the treadmill and crank, reduces flogging, shortens hard labour and introduces (as per today) purposeful activity in prisons, *prisoner* categories and early *release* for good behaviour. A short run of Oscar Wilde's *The Ballad of Reading Gaol* is printed by a speculative 'under-the-counter' pornographer: see *Touchstones*.
1901	Tolling of the prison bell at the time of an execution ceases
1904	Early *road traffic* laws in the wake of 'arrogant behaviour' by motorists
1907	*Court of Appeal* established. *Probation* of Offenders Act creates the Probation Service and allows courts to 'suspend' a sentence if the offender is placed under supervision
1908	*Children* Act (aka 'Childrens Charter') deals with *child protection*; forbids the *imprisonment* of children; and establishes *juvenile* courts. Older juveniles can only be sent to prison if a court issues an 'unruly certificate'. Capital punishment (see *Touchstones*) is restricted to those aged 16 and over. *Local authorities* get power to keep poor children out of the workhouse and protect them from *abuse* (the genesis of *social services*). Children are barred from dangerous trades and buying tobacco or *alcohol*. Prevention of Crime Act introduces *borstals*: see *Touchstones*.
1910	Winston Churchill Home Secretary. Alexander Paterson Prison Commissioner
1915	Indictments Act revises the arrangements for cases at Assizes and Quarter Sessions

1916	Larceny Act (precursor of the *Theft* Act 1968); *Easter Rising*: see *Touchstones*.
1920	*Magistrates' Association* formed
1922	Infanticide Act halts trials for *murder* of women who kill their very young children
1927	Departmental Committee on Young Offenders (1925-1927) reports
1933	Landmark Children and Young Persons Act 1933 establishes the 'welfare principle' which applies to children in all courts for whatever reason and still exists today
1935	House of Lords ruling in *Woolmington v. DPP* entrenches the Common Law principles concerning the burden and high standard of proof in criminal cases: see *evidence*
1936	*Public Order Act* follows disturbances such as those in *Cable Street*: see *Touchstones*
1938	Further Infanticide Act (see 1922). Cadogan Committee on corporal punishment (the birch and cat-o'-nine-tails were still in use with a maximum of 36 strokes) analyses *reoffending* by people flogged. It is greater than after other sentences.
1945	Post-war Labour Government. An era of *reform, welfare* and *rehabilitation*
1946	William Joyce (aka Lord Haw Haw) executed for treason despite legal niceties
1948	European Convention On Human Rights (ECHR): see *human rights*. Criminal Justice Act creates *detention centres* for *juvenile* offenders, makes the *probation* order an alternative sentence, creates preventive detention (a longer sentence for *repeat offenders*) and ends *whipping* (see *Touchstones*) (except re *assaults* on prison officers or prison mutiny).
1950	Execution of Timothy Evans: see *Touchstones*. *Prison(er) population* reaches 20,000
1952	Magistrates' Courts Act and Prison Act: foundations for the present-day arrangements
1953	Execution of Derek *Bentley* and likelihood serial killer John Christie committed the 'Timothy *Evans* murders' causes disquiet: see *Touchstones*. Gower Report on Capital Punishment.
1955	Execution of Ruth *Ellis*, the last woman to be hanged in the UK: see *Touchstones*
1956	Sexual Offences Act causes homosexuals to inhabit a twilight world
1957	Homicide Act introduces capital and non-capital offences of *murder* and a defence of diminished responsibility: see *mental impairment*. Magistrates' Courts Act frees up the courts by introducing written pleas of guilty for minor offences. Wolfenden Report and Street Offences Act confront the public face of prostitution.
1959	A 45 per cent rise in reported crime since 1949 and three times the amount of *violence* leads to police pay increases in the face of a 14 per cent shortfall in officers
1960	Indecency With Children Act. Royal Commission on the Police. Ingleby Report on 'Children and Young Persons in Custody'. *Prison(er) population* reaches 25,000.
1961	Criminal Justice Act. *Detention centre* powers and regimes for *juveniles* and *young offenders* modified. Streatfield Report on the Business of the Criminal Courts.
1963	Children and Young Persons Act. Home Office publishes *The Adult Offender*. *Great Train Robbery*: see *Touchstones*. England in the throes of the 'permissive society'.
1964	Police Act. *Prison Rules* establish a disciplinary *code* and place *prison governors* in charge of *prison/*'discipline'. Challoner police *corruption* case: see *bent copper* in *Touchstones*. Peter Anthony *Allen* and Gwynne Owen Evans are the last people to be executed in Britain: see *Touchstones*. Home Office publishes *The Sentence of the Court*.
1965	*Capital punishment* is suspended (see *Touchstones*). Ronald Biggs escapes from a prison sentence of 30 years, flees the UK and remains 'beyond the law' until 2001.
1967	Criminal Justice Act creates the *Parole Board*; abolishes corrective training and preventive detention; and creates 'extended sentences' to *protect* the public. Sexual Offences Act. Road Safety Act introduces the breathalyser and offence of excess alcohol (see *road traffic*). Spy George Blake escapes from a 40 year sentence of *imprisonment*.

1968	*Theft Act* 'codifies' theft and related offences. *Mountbatten Report* on Prison Escapes and Security leads to dispersal prisons for high security offenders: see *Touchstones*.
1969	*Capital punishment* abolished except in war-time (potentially). Prisons now intended to be for 'humane containment'. Parkhurst Prison riot one of many across the UK.
1970	*Prison(er) population* reaches 35,000
1971	*Beeching Report* (see *Touchstones*) leads to the abolition of Assizes and Quarter Sessions and the creation of the *Crown Court*. *Criminal Damage Act* 'codifies' such offences.
1972	*Criminal Justice Act* introduces community service (the genesis of the present re-quirement of 'unpaid work') and 'deferment' of sentence (see *sentence/sentencing*).
1973	Powers of Criminal Courts Act. Prison unrest grows
1974	Community service begins (at first as an *alternative* to custody). It later becomes the community punishment order and, in 2003, a requirement of 'unpaid work' within a generic *community sentence*. Juries Act: see *juror/jury*. 'Nothing Works' published: see *'what works'* in *Touchstones*. *Rehabilitation of Offenders Act* creates 'spent' convictions.
1976	Andrew von Hirsch publishes *Doing Justice*. The *justice model* supersedes the *reha-bilitative ideal*. *Bail Act* 'codifies' the general right to bail. Hull *Prison* riot
1977	Criminal Law Act increases the powers of the *juvenile* court (later the *youth court*) and introduces 'partly suspended' sentences of *imprisonment* (later abandoned).
1978	May Report on *Prisons*. A further *Theft Act* adds new offences of dishonesty.
1979	Wormwood Scrubs prison riot
1980	Magistrates' Courts Act. 'Too Many Prisoners' (All Party Penal Affairs Group report).
1981	*Brixton Riots* (see *Touchstones*). *Contempt of Court Act*. Criminal *Attempts* Act. For-gery and Counterfeiting Act (see *counterfeiting*, etc). Prisoners serving fixed terms can obtain their *release* on licence under the supervision of a *probation officer* after serving not less than a third of their sentence or 12 months, whichever is the longer.
1982	*Criminal Justice Act* abolishes *borstal* (see *Touchstones*), modifies *detention centre* orders and introduces youth custody. First Juvenile Justice Units (JJUs), the forerun-ners of *youth offending teams* (YOTs) become influential in developing 'initiatives'.
1984	*Police and Criminal Evidence Act* (PACE) and PACE codes. *Parole* criteria tightened for sentences over five years for *violence* and *drug*-related offences. Brighton Bomb-ing (see *Prime Minister*). Miners Strike: 'the enemy within'.
1985	*Crown Prosecution Service* (CPS) formed. Sexual Offences Act.
1986	*Public Order Act*. Widespread prison riots and *unrest*.
1987	Hennessy Report on prison disturbances. Anti-*fraud* legislation.
1988	Home Office publishes *Punishment, Custody and the Community*. Carlisle Report con-cludes *parole* should be retained but modified. *Criminal Justice Act* gives the *Attorney General* power to challenge an 'unduly lenient sentence'. Criminal Justice *Compensa-tion* Board created. An era of *private sector* CJS functions starts with remand *prisons*.
1989	'Grisley' Risley Prison severely damaged by a prison riot
1990	Home Office issues *Crime, Justice and Protecting the Public* as a prelude to *reform*. Courts and Legal Services Act. Poll tax riots and civil disobedience lead to the aboli-tion of a perceptively unfair measure. *Victims Charter*. *Prison(er) population* 45,000.
1991	Criminal Procedure (Insanity, etc.) Act (see generally *mental impairment*). *Criminal Jus-tice Act* introduces the first statutory *sentencing framework*, based on *just deserts* (*Touch-stones*) and proportionality. First CJS anti-*discrimination* laws. *Woolf Report* (*Touchstones*).

1992 Sexual *Offences* Amendment Act formalises a recent Common Law rule that a man can be guilty of raping his wife. First National Standards (see *standards*) for *probation* work.

1993 Stephen *Lawrence* is *murdered* in Eltham, South-London (see *Touchstones*). Criminal Justice Act abolishes key parts of the 1991 Act (including a directly means-related system of 'unit fines'). The era of 'prison works' begins (see '*what works*' and *political aspects* in *Touchstones*). Home Office issues the consultation paper, 'Police Reform: A Police Service for the 21st Century'; *Probation* Services Act. Sexual Offences Act.

1994 Criminal Justice and *Public Order* Act. *Drug* Trafficking Act. Police and Magistrates' Courts Act. Whitemoor *Prison escape* of IRA prisoners.

1995 *Proceeds of Crime Act*. Criminal *Appeal* Act. Criminal Injuries *Compensation* Act. Escape of high security prisoners from Parkhurst Prison, Isle of Wight, leads to the departure of the Director General of HM *Prison Service* and the *prison governor*.

1996 Offensive *Weapons* Act. Prevention of *Terrorism* Act. *Public Order* (Amendment) Act. Sexual Offences Act. Home Office publishes *Protecting the Public*.

1997 Home Office publishes *No More Excuses: A New Approach to Tackling Youth Crime*. Crime (Sentences) Act introduces a '*three strikes*' law re certain repeat offences (see *Touchstones*). New Labour in power with a *reform* agenda. Sex Offenders Act. Justices of the Peace Act. Law Commission report on *evidence* in criminal proceedings.

1998 Crime and Disorder Act introduces the *Youth Justice Board* (YJB), *youth offending teams* (YOTS), statutory purposes of sentencing for juveniles and the first *anti-social behaviour orders* (ASBOs). Human Rights Act 1998: see *human rights*.

1999 *Access to Justice Act*. Youth Justice and Criminal Evidence Act.

2000 Criminal Justice and Court Services *Act* creates the National *Probation* Service and renames *community sentences* in terms of *punishment* and/or *rehabilitation*. Sexual Offences (Amendment) Act. Powers of Criminal Courts (Sentencing) Act. *Terrorism Act 2000* is the first of a number in coming years. An era of enhanced public *protection*: expansion of *databases*, increasing reliance on *technology*, *identification* procedures, *surveillance* and *border* controls. Greater reliance on *evidence*-led policing, *targeting* of offenders and the *proceeds of crime*. Prison(er) *population* reaches 65,000.

2001 Criminal Defence Service (Advice and Assistance) Act. Criminal Justice and Police Act. *Halliday Report* and *Auld Report* (see *Touchstones* for both). Home Office publishes a series of White Papers, including 'Criminal Justice: Way Forward'. *September 11* (USA) (see *Touchstones*) heightened public *fears* and leads to increasing *safeguards*.

2002 *Child Exploitation and Online Protection Agency* established. White Paper, 'Justice For All'. Police Reform Act gives the *Home Secretary* stronger default powers re police forces and creates an Independent Police Complaints Commission (IPCC).

2003 Carter Report (see *Touchstones*) proposes a National Offender Management Service NOMS)(see *offender management*). Coulsfield Report into *alternatives* to custody. *Criminal Justice Act 2003* revises the *sentencing framework*; creates statutory purposes of *sentencing* for *adults*; introduces new sentences, including the *indeterminate sentence for public protection* (ISSP) and a new-style 'generic' *community sentence* (together with others not yet in force); and creates a *Sentencing Guidelines Council*.

2004 Home Office publishes a series of consultation papers, including on crime, crime reduction, *organized crime* and 'building communities'

2005 Serious Organized Crime and Police Act (SOCPA) creates the *Serious Organized Crime Agency* (SOCA). London bombings of *July 7* and *Stockwell shooting*: see *Touchstones*. Home Office publishes 'Rebuilding Lives: Supporting Victims of Crime'. *Constitutional Reform* Act moves key *judicial* responsibilities to the *Lord Chief Justice*.

2006 Criminal *Defence* Service *Act*. Police and Justice Act. Violent Crime Reduction Act (see, generally, *violence*). Road Safety Act introduces new *road traffic* offences (increasing maximum penalties for many such offences) and graduated *fixed penalties*. Racial and religious hatred *legislation*. Home Office launches new and enhanced public *protection* strategy placing increased reliance on *science* and *technology*.

2007 *Bow Street Magistrates' Cour*t closes (see *Touchstones*). Capital punishment removed altogether from the *Statute Book*. Legal Services Act. Mental Health Act (see generally *mental impairment*). Ministry of Justice (MOJ) created. Lord Chancellor becomes the *Justice Secretary* and Lord Chancellor'. Home Office reformed. Department for Children Schools and Families (DCSF) assumes de facto responsibility for juveniles. *Offender Management Act*. *Serious Crime Act* creates the serious crime prevention order (see *anti-social behaviour* (ASB)/'gangster ASBO') and revises *incitement*, etc. Second *Carter Report* (see *Touchstones*). Britain dubbed a 'surveillance society'.

2008 MOJ issues 'HM Courts Service Framework'. UK *Border Agency* launched. Criminal Justice and Immigration Act revises sentences for *juveniles* and contains measures re the police, *offender management, criminal law, public order,* international *fine enforcement, immigration* status when there is 'criminality' and powers of automatic *deportation. Metropolitan Police Service* commissioner, Sir Ian Blair, 'forced' from office. House of Lords causes Government to abandon *terrorism*-related plans for up to 42 days *detention* without charge. Children and Young Persons Act. Criminal Evidence (Witness Anonymity) Act. *Prison(er) population* tops 80,000.

2009 Borders, Citizenship and Immigration Bill seeks to amend the law on *immigration, asylum* and *citizenship* and introduce *child protection* measures. Proposals for wide ranging *interception of communication* powers. Convention On Modern *Liberty* launched in London and across the UK amidst claims of a continuing erosion of *civil liberties. Justice Secretary* Jack Straw MP denies that Britain is becoming a police state, claims that *citizens'* rights are better protected today, and that there never was a 'Golden Age' of liberty. Home Office announces plans to allow open searching on the internet by postcode to discover 'who the criminals are in the neighbourhood'.

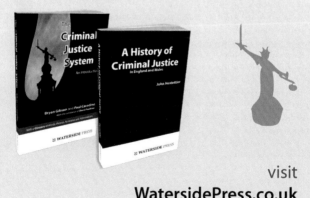

For criminal justice

visit
WatersidePress.co.uk